D1604002

THE WORLD OF SICILIAN WINE

FRONTISPIECE.

Map of Sicily by Robert Morden and William Berry from 1680. Reproduced in *L'Isola A Tre Punte: Maps of Sicily from the La Gumina Collection (XVI-XIX Century)*, edited by Enrico Iachello (Catania: La Gumina/Sanfilippo Editore, 1999), 151.

THE WORLD
OF SICILIAN WINE

Bill Nesto, MW, and Frances Di Savino

UNIVERSITY OF CALIFORNIA PRESS

Berkeley   Los Angeles   London

The publisher gratefully acknowledges the generous support of the General Endowment Fund of the University of California Press Foundation.

University of California Press, one of the most distinguished university presses in the United States, enriches lives around the world by advancing scholarship in the humanities, social sciences, and natural sciences. Its activities are supported by the UC Press Foundation and by philanthropic contributions from individuals and institutions. For more information, visit www.ucpress.edu.

University of California Press
Berkeley and Los Angeles, California

University of California Press, Ltd.
London, England

Library of Congress Cataloging-in-Publication Data

Nesto, Bill, 1951–
    The world of Sicilian wine / Bill Nesto and Frances Di Savino.
        p.   cm.
    Includes bibliographical references and index.
    ISBN 978-0-520-26618-6 (cloth : alk. paper)
    1. Wine and wine making—Italy—Sicily.   2. Wine and wine making—Italy—Sicily—History.   3. Sicily (Italy)   I. Di Savino, Frances, 1960–
II. Title.
    TP559.I8N47   2013
    663′.2009458—dc23

                                                    2012026490

Manufactured in the United States of America

22   21   20   19   18   17   16   15   14   13
10   9   8   7   6   5   4   3   2   1

The paper used in this publication meets the minimum requirements of ANSI/NISO z39.48-1992 (R 2002) (*Permanence of Paper*).

To our fathers and mothers,
R. William and Antoinette Nesto
&
Sabino and Geraldine Di Savino,
we dedicate this work,
our labor of love

Almost a year . . . a year in Sicily . . .
a year that coursed so quickly . . .
And what I now inscribe is but a trace,
a vestige of the visions shared when we
were wanderers in Sicily: for me,
you made each pilgrim path a joyous journey.

Ovid, *Ex ponto* 2.10 ("My Eyes," translation
by Allen Mandelbaum in *Ovid in Sicily*)

CONTENTS

MAPS

ACKNOWLEDGMENTS

We acknowledge and thank all of the Sicilians who have helped us in our research and travels. We are grateful to the Istituto Regionale Vini e Oli di Sicilia (IRVOS) and its director general, Dr. Dario Cartabellotta. The Region of Sicily's dedicated team of enologists, agronomists, and other experts working in the field from Marsala to Mount Etna provided us with valuable insights and information. We also express our appreciation to Blake Edgar, Dore Brown, and Kate Marshall of University of California Press and to our copy editor Juliana Froggatt for their wise guidance and professionalism. To our mothers, Anne Sirugo Nesto and Geri Saporito Di Savino, and our cherished family and friends, we shall forever be grateful for your love and encouragement. Finally, we acknowledge and express our profound respect for the countless Sicilians—past, present, and future—who have tended their vines and sacrificed so very much for their magnificent land. It has been an honor to tell their story.

Grazii da nostri cori pri sempri.

Frances Di Savino, my wife, and I explored the island of Sicily for two weeks in June of 2008. I was there to research an article about Sicilian wine. Fran was with me because we do almost everything together, and we both love Italy. I say *almost* everything since the hand that writes this preface is my own. But she is at my side. This is our introduction to our book.

We were astounded by the enthusiasm of the Sicilians we met. Visits to vineyards and wineries and sips of wine inevitably began with, ended with, and were blended into visits to historical sites and breathtaking panoramas and tastes of the vibrant flavors of produce and cuisine. We came back to Boston knowing that there was a compelling story to tell, a book to be written, and many returns to Sicily in the near future.

The book was also in our genes. Fran and I are both 100 percent southern Italian by ancestry. I am 50 percent Sicilian. My ancestors on my mother's side came to New York from Ragusa. Fran's ancestry comes from elsewhere down the boot. She feels Sicilian, though. We played with the possibility that her Saporito ancestors came to Campania by way of Sicily. In fact, Saporitos have thrived on the island since the thirteenth century.

Fran's avid interest in Latin and Greek in high school led her to make her first pilgrimage to Italy with her schoolmates and her Latin teacher. She returned to Florence to study Medieval and Renaissance history and art. Of course, she became fluent in Italian. She speaks Italian so well that Italians ask her where she comes from in Italy.

After being a fine arts painter, I became interested in food and then wine and eventually became a sommelier, wine journalist, and Master of Wine. I gravitated to Italian

wine because I felt more at home in Italy than in France, my other favorite wine destination. After my many visits, I speak Italian too. Though Italians understand me, they
ask me where I come from in the United States.

Seeing our task in front of us, we made our plan. Fran took on the challenge of
revealing the historical and cultural dimensions of Sicilian wine. She would write the
first chapter to introduce readers to the history of Sicilian wine, set within the context
of Sicilian culture through the mid-eighteenth century. As the wine expert, I would
describe and analyze the Sicilian wine industry from the late eighteenth century to the
present day. Hence, in the text, the *I* associated with tasting notes always refers to me.
Furthermore, the opinions expressed about wine regions, wine producers, and their
wines are mine and mine alone.

Woven throughout the book are three vignettes. We profiled three Sicilian winegrowers who through their work show their own love for Sicily. In their wines, we can taste
and enjoy the genuine flavors of Sicily. I wrote the first two vignettes. Fran wrote the
final one, set on Etna, and the afterword, finishing our journey as we had begun.

It has been a joyous journey.

Bill Nesto, MW

Whatever I shall have reported to you, I submit for you to correct or to adorn with the
roses of your knowledge, so that like a vine cultivated and watered with the care of your
knowledge, it may, yielding the most copious fruit, be rendered worthy of greater praise
and gratitude. (Geoffrey Malaterra, *The Deeds of Count Roger of Calabria and Sicily and of
His Brother Duke Robert Guiscard*, 44)

The monk Geoffrey Malaterra came as a foreigner to Catania at the end of the eleventh
century. He was born north of the Alps and resettled in Sicily as part of the Norman
conquest of Sicily ending in 1090. In a prefatory letter to *The Deeds of Count Roger*,
Geoffrey appeals to the nobler instincts of his future readers and critics. We humbly
do the same.

Bill Nesto, MW, and Frances Di Savino

1

THE ORIGINS OF SICILIAN WINE
AND CULTURE

The culture of wine in Sicily is both ancient and modern. There is evidence of vine training and wine production from the earliest settlements of the Phoenicians on Sicily's west coast and the Greeks on Sicily's east coast from the eighth century B.C. In the long parade of foreign powers and people who have invaded and settled Sicily, it was the Greeks who brought an established culture of wine to this island. For the Greek settlers from mainland Greece and its islands, Sicily was the fertile and wild frontier on the western edge of their Mediterranean world. The gods and heroes of Greek mythology also ventured to Sicily. Upon sailing to Sicily, the protagonist-hero of Homer's *Odyssey*, Odysseus, together with his crew of men, approached the mighty Mount Etna and the untamed land of the Cyclops with more than a little trepidation. The Cyclops are the giant one-eyed creatures who in ancient mythology dwelled on Mount Etna (and who were reputed to eat wayward explorers). Homer gives us the following account of this forbidding race:

> At last our ships approached the Cyclops' coast.
> That race is arrogant: they have no laws;
> and trusting in the never-dying gods,
> their hands plant nothing and they ply no plows.
> The Cyclops do not need to sow their seeds;
> for them all things, untouched, spring up: from wheat
> to barley and to vines that yield fine wine.

1

The rain Zeus sends attends to all their crops.
Nor do they meet in council, those Cyclops,
nor hand down laws; they live on mountaintops,
in deep caves; each one rules his wife and children,
and every family ignores its neighbors.[1]

From these twelve lines, probably written around the time of the earliest Greek settlements in eastern Sicily, Homer tells us much about the image and reputation of Sicily among his fellow Greeks since Odysseus's mythical time during the Mycenaean Age, between the twelfth and thirteenth centuries B.C. He describes the island as a lawless but wildly fertile place. The natives are beasts who lack any farming skills or tools. The Sicilians, according to Homer, lack culture (i.e., the essential skills to cultivate soil). And yet the wheat, the barley, and the "vines that yield fine wine" thrive all the same. We also learn that the indigenous people are an insular patriarchal tribe who ignore even their own neighbors. Homer then adds that such creatures are neither explorers nor artisans but inhabit a generous land which a little industry could make an island of plenty.

The Cyclops have no ships with crimson bows,
no shipwrights who might fashion sturdy hulls
that answer to the call, that sail across
to other peoples' towns that men might want
to visit. And such artisans might well
have built a proper place for men to settle.
In fact, the land's not poor; it could yield fruit
in season; soft, well-watered meadows lie
along the gray sea's shores; unfailing vines
could flourish; it has level land for plowing,
and every season would provide fat harvests
because the undersoil is black indeed.[2]

What is so striking about this description is how little the outsider's image of Sicily and Sicilians has changed in the intervening 2,700 years. Many of the cultural shortcomings and natural qualities that Homer chronicles are writ large throughout much of Sicily's history, for reasons that this chapter will explore. That may make Homer as much an epic prophet as an epic poet. The history and culture of Sicily, however, are far richer and more complex than any literary representation of them. Sicily has been defined and dominated by outsiders since its earliest time. Odysseus and his fellow Greeks were among the first. They would be followed in turn by Romans, Vandals, Goths, Byzantines, Muslims, Normans, Germans, French, Spanish, Austrians, and Northern Italians. Sicily's fertile land, sun-filled climate, and strategic position in the Mediterranean made the island enticing plunder for the pillaging forces of these various outside powers. And yet the Sicilians themselves have played a central role in their land's history of glory, subjugation, violence, and unrealized promise. In the thirteenth-century world map known as the *Ebstorf Mappamundi* (which was the largest on record prior to its destruction by Allied bombing over Hanover, Germany, in World War II), the island of Sicily was portrayed as a plump heart-shaped apple or pomegranate smack in the center of the area between Europe, North Africa, and the Middle East. Sebastian Münster's sixteenth-century book of world geography, known as the *Cosmographia*, depicts Sicily as the cross-bejeweled orb (the symbol of Christian temporal power) in the right hand of the "Queen Europe" map. But by the end of the twentieth century, Sicily would sadly have no place in the popular cultural landscape beyond Corleone, the Mafia town made famous by *The Godfather*. For the modern wine lover, however, the search for Sicilian *terroir* demands an understanding of place beyond the conventional historical and cultural narratives.

GREEK ROOTS AND SHOOTS

Before the Greeks and the Phoenicians reached the shores of Sicily, there were at least two groups of "indigenous" peoples, the Sicans on the western side and the Sicels on the eastern side. The Sicans are thought to have come from the Iberian Peninsula and the Sicels from Calabria (the toe of Italy). There were also settlements in northwestern Sicily near modern-day Erice, Segesta, and Contessa Entellina of a people called the Elymians, believed to have migrated from ancient Troy (in modern-day Turkey). While documented archaeological evidence does not substantiate that these early settlers trained vines or made wine, there is botanical evidence of wild grapes during this prehistoric period. There is also speculation that the Mycenaean Greeks, who had an established culture of wine by the thirteenth century B.C., introduced wine and other luxury products to Sicily well before the earliest Greek colonies settled there in the eighth century B.C.[3]

In an oft-quoted passage in the same book of the *Odyssey* that introduces us to the Cyclops, Homer offers a critique of the quality of Sicilian wine in comparison with the strong, full-bodied Maronean wine from the southern Balkan region (known as Thrace in his time) that Odysseus carried on board his ship. After Odysseus offers a taste of his wine to the Cyclops named Polyphemus, the native beast declares:

> Surely the earth, giver of grain, provides
> the Cyclops with fine wine, and rain from Zeus
> does swell our clustered vines. But this is better—
> a wine as fragrant as ambrosia and nectar.[4]

According to Homer, a natural Sicilian wine made from wild grapes was no match for Greece's finest wines. To the modern reader, this might sound like the chauvinism of a connoisseur of Old World wines assessing the wines of the New World. However, it is well established that the Greek colonists brought their cultivated knowledge of vine training and winemaking to southern Italy and Sicily beginning with their earliest settlements. It is also believed that the Greeks brought distinct vine varieties from the Aegean to Sicily. Homer describes the vineyard of Odysseus's father, King Laertes, on the Greek island of Ithaca as having "some fifty rows of vines, each bearing different grapes—so many kinds—that ripened, each in turn and in its time."[5] As a testament to the influence of the Greek settlers on Italian viticulture, the ancient Greeks referred to southern Italy and Sicily as Oenotria ("The Land of Trained Vines").[6] In the wooded hills above the town of Sambuca in southwestern Sicily, a young winegrower by the name of Davide Di Prima brought us to a clearing in a forest on a high plateau to see a stone *pigiatoia* ("outdoor winepress") from the fifth century B.C. These ruins are believed to be a place where a Sican settlement crushed and vinified grapes. While the age of this site does not predate Phoenician or Greek settlement on the island, it does point to an indigenous culture of wine that coexisted with such settlements.

Greek settlers in Sicily brought other vital elements of their wine culture to their new home. Archaeologists have discovered that the earliest Greek settlers traded ceramic wine wares with the Sicel native population in the coastal areas of eastern Sicily, including amphorae, large bowls, and other wine-drinking vessels. Archaeologists discovered a small pouring vessel from the fifth century B.C. called an *askos* near the central Sicilian town of Enna. It is inscribed with the word *vino,* among the earliest documented uses of this word prior to its introduction into the Latin language. One object that has not been identified in Sicel archaeological sites is the krater, or mixing bowl, which Greeks used to mix their wine with water in varying proportions depending on the occasion. This leaves open the question of whether the Sicels (like the Cyclops) drank their wine undiluted. Regardless, the evidence of this trading pattern demonstrates an immediate interest by the local Sicels in the consumption and culture of wine. Anthropologists call this process acculturation. This acculturation would have necessarily involved other elements of the Greek wine culture, such as the ritual of the symposium (which literally means "drinking together" in Greek). The Greek symposium was an extended after-dinner wine-drinking celebration (men only) that often involved the recitation of poetry, the playing of music, dancing, and other earthly pleasures. Archaeologists theorize that wealthier Sicels adopted certain elements of the symposium into their own cultural traditions. With the eventual intermarriage of the Greek colonists and the native Sicels, the assimilated Greek Sicilians added a new activity to their wine parties: the drinking game of *kottabos.* Kottabos was played toward the end of the party, when celebrants had emptied their cups and spirits ran high. The aim of the game was for each player to fling the remaining wine drops and sediment in his cup toward a suspended disc or other target to bring it crashing to the ground. The game became associated with Sicily, and its popularity spread to Greece as a fashionable staple of the Athenian symposium.

Beginning in the sixth century B.C., Greek Sicilian poets, playwrights, and philosophers were honored in the classical Greek world. The stature of such cultural figures in Greece suggests that literary exchanges were an integral part of the Greek Sicilian symposium. The Greek word *symposium* also refers to a category of literature regarding food and wine. Epicharmus, the Sicilian playwright and philosopher from the late sixth and early fifth centuries B.C. (who was also a student of Pythagoras), is considered the father of the Greek comic play. The Greek word for comedy derives from *comus,* "wine lees," and literally translates as "lees song." In ancient Greece, drunken, rowdy processions in honor of the Greek god of wine, Dionysos, accompanied the harvest festivals. Epicharmus was the first playwright to introduce the drunkard as a stock comic character. The remaining fragments of his plays are also replete with references to the culinary delights of his fellow Greek Sicilians in the city of Syracuse.[7] Epicharmus preached moderation and perhaps was using the vehicle of comedy to caution his fellow Greek Sicilians on the pitfalls of excess wine and food consumption. One of the many moral maxims attributed to him exhorts: "Be sober in thought! Be slow in belief! These are the sinews of wisdom."[8]

The Sicilian-born poet Theocritus, who is credited with creating the genre of bucolic poetry in the third century B.C., celebrated the beauty of the Sicilian countryside and the joy of country life. In one of his idylls, Polyphemus (the milk-guzzling Cyclops of Homer's *Odyssey*) is a fellow Sicilian countryman who sings a love poem about the natural glory of Mount Etna, including the "sweet-fruited vine."[9] From Theocritus we learn that Greek Sicilians even savored aged wine. In the idyll called "The Harvest Home" the poet refers to a four-year-old vintage opened for a harvest feast.

> Darted golden bees; all things smelt richly of Summer,
> Richly of Autumn; pears and apples in bountiful plenty
> Rolled at our feet and sides, and down on the meadow around us
> Plum-trees bent their trailing boughs thick-laden with damsons.
> Then from the wine-jar's mouth was a four-year-old seal loosened.[10]

Sicily by this time was widely regarded as the gastronomic epicenter of the classical Mediterranean world. Sicilian chefs were renowned in ancient Greece as the Ferran Adriàs and Thomas Kellers of their day. Sicilian raw ingredients, including cheese and tuna, were also prized as luxuries on the Greek table. Archestratus, a Greek Sicilian of the fourth century B.C., wrote a detailed poem titled "Gastronomy," "Art of Cooking," or "Life of Luxury" depending on the translation. In it, he describes and ranks the food and wine of the entire Mediterranean basin. Like Theocritus, he confirms that "gray-haired" wine is for special occasions.[11] Like our modern wine journalists, he also assesses the relative merits of wines from various places. In one passage, the author compares the wines from the Greek island of Lesbos with the Bibline wine from Phoenicia, concluding that the Bibline wine is more aromatic than the Lesbian wine but inferior on the palate. Archestratus boasts that unlike other writers of his day, who just "like to praise what they have in their own land," he is able to critique wines from everywhere.[12]

In chronicling the distinctions among various wines and foods throughout the Mediterranean, the poetic works of Archestratus and the Greek Sicilian Philoxenus provide ample evidence that Sicilians by the fifth century B.C. understood and appreciated the concept of place and its impact on flavor and quality. What was essential to this understanding and appreciation was the flow of people and goods between the Greek settlements in Sicily and the Greek mother cities (metropolises). Sicilian athletes regularly went to Greece to compete in the Olympics, and Sicilian cooks traveled through Greece as celebrity chefs on tour. In this same period the Greek city now known as Agrigento, on the southern coast of Sicily, built its magnificent temples with the wealth derived in no small measure from the exporting of wine and olive oil to North Africa. In time, merchants from other Sicilian city-states also entered the export wine trade and began to compete successfully with Greek wine merchants throughout the Mediterranean and as far north as Gaul in modern-day France. In the third century B.C. the ruling tyrant of Syracuse, Hiero II, commissioned the construction of a massive "garden ship" named *The Syracusan*. The top deck was carpeted with flower beds and an arbor of ivy and vines. Capable of carrying more than three thousand tons of crops and other cargo, the ship was renowned for both its opulence and its tonnage. Like Agrigento, the celebrated city-state Syracuse built its wealth on the production and export of abundant grain, olives, and wine. Hiero II himself controlled vast agricultural holdings and even wrote a handbook on agronomy. Both the poets and the merchants of the classical Greek world recognized the quality of Sicilian wine and food. The era of Sicily as a wine-producing and wine-exporting region had arrived.

ROMAN BREAD AND WINE

By the beginning of the second century B.C., Sicily was firmly under the control of Rome and would be relegated to serving as the granary of the Roman Empire for almost six hundred years. The fertility of Sicily, which had made it the land of plenty for Greek settlers and their vines beginning in the eighth century B.C., also made it the bread basket for the Romans and the succeeding foreign powers that came to control and exploit the island. In the mythology of ancient Rome, Ceres, the goddess of agriculture and grain, made her home in Sicily and as the creator of the art of husbandry was considered the first giver of laws to mankind. Unlike the cultivation of wine grapes and olives, which required intensive skill-based farming and harvesting, the growing of grain was more efficiently accomplished on large expanses of land. These vast farms, known as latifundia, were managed by wealthy absentee landowners (both Roman and Sicilian) and worked by local or imported unskilled slave or peasant labor. Following the end of the Roman era many of these latifundia were in the hands of the Catholic Church and increasingly a growing class of landed "nobility." During Roman rule the absentee landowner, as would be the case with ecclesiastical and noble landowners in subsequent epochs, would lease out significant holdings of land to an intermediate "tenant-in-chief," who in turn would wield enormous control over the peasant tenant farmers who worked the land. This pattern would ultimately become the foundation for the feudal economy that suffocated Sicily into the nineteenth century.

The extent of Sicily's wine production and wine exports during the period of Roman rule is not precisely known. However, there is historical evidence that several Sicilian wines were known and prized on the Roman table. Amphorae have been discovered in the ruins of Pompeii (itself a celebrated wine zone in ancient Rome) bearing the inscription "Mesopotamium," the Latin name of a wine from the southeast coast of Sicily. In his treatise from the late first century B.C. and early first century A.D., the Greek geographer Strabo states that the district around Messina "abounds in wine" called Mamertinian, which "vies with the best produced in Italy."[13] Strabo also gives us a description of the volcanic terroir of Mount Etna that could come right out of a modern wine book: "However, after the burning ashes have occasioned a temporary damage, they fertilize the country for future seasons, and render the soil good for the vine and very strong for other produce, the neighboring districts not being equally adapted to the produce of wine."[14]

The Latin agricultural treatises of the Roman writers Pliny (*Natural History*) and Columella (*On Agriculture*) of the first century A.D. and the Greek literary work known as *The Learned Banqueters* by Athenaeus of Egypt in the second century A.D. include several specific references to the esteemed wines and foods of Sicily. Columella also praises the written contributions of learned Sicilians to the science of husbandry.[15] Pliny cites the Hybla region of Sicily as producing some of the finest-quality honey, being that it is "obtained from the calyx of the best flowers" and ferments in its first few days "like new wine."[16]

The notable Sicilian wines that Pliny, Columella, and Athenaeus catalogue include the esteemed Mamertine wine from near Messina that was named Potitian after its original grower and was an early example of "'*château*-labelling' of a good growth."[17] In reference to the Eugenia vine variety, which was transported from Sicily to the Alban Hills southeast of Rome (the equivalent of a Roman grand cru), Pliny wrote that "with its name denoting high quality" it was "imported from the hills of Taormina to be grown only in the territory of Alba, as if transplanted elsewhere it at once degenerates: for in fact some vines have so strong an affection for certain localities that they leave all their reputation behind there and cannot be transplanted elsewhere in their full vigour."[18] Pliny's statement provides ample proof that the idea of terroir is indeed ancient.

Two other Roman vine varieties believed to be of Sicilian origin were Murgentina and Aminnia. Murgentina was exported from Sicily to the region of Mount Vesuvius and was the principal variety in a wine aptly called Pompeiana or Vesuvinum. Aminnia, on the other hand, was part of a group of vine varieties identified with both the Italian mainland and Sicily and was the only varietal wine classified among the most permissibly expensive by edict of the Roman emperor Diocletian at the end of the third century A.D.[19] The migration of vine varieties and viticultural knowledge from Sicily to Rome evolved out of the original migration of Greek viticulture to Sicily beginning with the earliest Greek settlements in the eighth century B.C.

The founding legend of Rome is based on the story of a mythical hero, Aeneas, who spends formative time in Sicily on his epic voyage from Troy to central Italy. The Roman poet Virgil, writing in the first century B.C., recounts the adventures of Aeneas in the epic Latin poem the *Aeneid*. Like the *Odyssey*, the *Aeneid* takes place after the legendary conquest of Troy by the Mycenaean Greeks, believed to be sometime between 1300 and 1100 B.C. Aeneas, the last surviving prince of Troy following its defeat by the Greeks, is compelled to reach the shores of Italy in order to fulfill a divine prophecy that he will found Rome. On their voyage to the Italian mainland, he and his countrymen travel by ship around the Sicilian coast and land in northwestern Sicily. King Acestes, who is also of Trojan lineage and who founded the Elymian cities of Eryx, Segesta, and Entella, gives Aeneas a gift of Sicilian wine before Aeneas sets sail for Italy. After Aeneas and his men have shipwrecked on the shores of Carthage and the men have all but given up any hope of ever reaching their longed-for new home in Italy, Aeneas

> . . . shares
> the wine that had been stowed by kind Acestes
> in casks along the shores of Sicily:
> the wine that, like a hero, the Sicilian
> had given to the Trojans when they left.[20]

Aeneas "soothes [the] melancholy hearts" of his men with the wine gifted by the heroic Sicilian king.[21] Unlike in the *Odyssey*, where it is the Greek hero who offers ambrosial wine to the brutish Sicilian Cyclops, in the *Aeneid* it is the gracious Sicilian king who gives the precious gift of wine and solace to the Trojan hero. Virgil, who was writing seven centuries after Homer, would have been well aware of the influence of Greek culture and viticulture in Sicily. The founding legend of Rome, however, envisioned a Sicily whose culture was built by its mythological ancestors, the last surviving Trojan kings and princes, not by the Greeks. In reality, Sicily—apart from tourist attractions like Mount Etna and the ancient ruins of Syracuse and Agrigento—did not have a high profile in the official annals of the Roman era. Its utility was based principally on the quality and reliability of its production of summer wheat, a commodity. In purely mythological terms, however, Sicily and Sicilian wine played a seminal role in the epic narrative of Roman history as told in Virgil's *Aeneid*.

After the fall of the Roman Empire, first Vandals and then Goths, two different Germanic tribes, overran Sicily. Beginning in the sixth century A.D. the emperors from Constantinople (modern-day Istanbul), the capital city of the Eastern Christian Empire, took control of Sicily. Then, in the first quarter of the ninth century, a sizable army of Arabs, Berbers from North Africa, and Spanish Muslims began to invade Sicily. As for previous conquerors, Sicily's strategic position in the Mediterranean and its lush fertility were powerful draws for the Muslim invaders. It would take approximately seventy-five years for the Muslims (referred to by medieval chroniclers as Saracens) to complete their conquest of the island and to supplant Sicily's Greek culture with a Muslim one (except in the northeastern part of the island known as Val Demone, which remained predominantly Greek).

The period of Muslim control lasted almost two hundred years (878–1061) and ushered in a golden age for Sicilian agriculture. Based on the system of Islamic fiscal administration in the Muslim strongholds of Libya and Tunisia, the Muslims in Sicily imposed a fixed-rate annual land tax (called the *qānūn* or *kharāj*) that landowners had to pay regardless of their crop yield.[22] This incentivized the productive use of cultivatable land. (By contrast, with certain limited exceptions, the baronial class in Sicily following the decline of the Normans would jealously resist any taxation based on their agricultural landholdings until the middle of the nineteenth century, even when their foreign sovereigns urged them to undertake such tax reform.) The Muslim rulers used a portion of the revenue from land taxes to make land grants of small farms to soldiers, creating a broad base of free landholders. The Muslim laws of inheritance led to the further fragmentation of farms among families over generations, thus providing an additional incentive for the efficient and intensive cultivation of land by the heirs of ever-smaller parcels. These smaller landholdings, while not supplanting the latifundia established in the Roman era, were concentrated in hamlets around the island (particularly around the cities) and provided peasant farmers with the opportunity to own and work their own land. The Muslims also provided exemptions from the land tax to certain classes of disadvantaged landowners—such as widows and the blind—as well as young married couples and immigrants for a period of time, as a direct incentive to "establish their new household and their new lands."[23]

With an advanced knowledge of irrigation and intensive farming, the Muslims created a polyculture of small farms, orchards, and gardens principally in the western and southeastern areas of the island. They cultivated a variety of new food plants and other crops in Sicily, including hard durum wheat. Beginning in the Muslim era, the market gardens of Palermo brimmed with lemons, bitter oranges, melons, apples, pomegranates, pears, peaches, grapes, quinces, mulberries, eggplant, saffron, date palms, dried figs, sugarcane, apricots, bananas, mangoes, sesame seeds, pistachios, hazelnuts, and almonds.

During this period, however, there was less emphasis on the cultivation of wine grapes than during the Greek and even Roman eras. Still, although Muslim law prohibits the drinking of wine in public, it is unlikely that the cultivation of wine grapes and the production of wine ceased in Sicily (any more than it did in Prohibition-era United States). The Muslim Sicilian poetry of the twelfth century is replete with references to wine and the pleasures of wine drinking. While such poetry is consistent with a Muslim genre that uses the image of wine metaphorically, it also reveals an intimate familiarity with an established wine culture in Sicily. In one of his odes recalling the idyllic pleasure of his youth in Sicily prior to the Norman conquest, the Muslim poet Ibn Hamdis describes in familiar detail the qualifications of a wine expert:

> A youth who has studied wine until he knows
> the prime of the wines, and their vintage
> He counts for any kind of wine you wish
> its age, and he knows the wine merchant[24]

In the lines of another Arabic poem, written by an anonymous poet believed to be an emir in Palermo during the period of Muslim rule, the imagery of the garden paradise is intricately woven with the recollections of a self-avowed wine lover who savors "a well-matured wine, more exquisite than youth itself."[25]

Notwithstanding the nostalgic image of Sicily as a garden paradise in Muslim Sicilian poetry, internal strife among the various Muslim factions controlling the island ultimately created ripe conditions for its conquest by the Normans in the second half of the eleventh century. The first Norman ruler, Count Roger, came from northwest France and was of Viking lineage. The unique legacy of the Norman line of kings, beginning with Count Roger's son, King Roger II, was the degree to which these foreign rulers established centralized authority in Sicily and incorporated a professional class of Greek and Muslim Sicilians into their administrative, military, and court regimes. For the first and only time, an all-powerful and resident sovereign ruled the island, directly enforcing the rule of law, the payment of taxes, and the administration of justice—for baron, landowner, and peasant alike. The early Norman rulers even established almost complete control over ecclesiastical matters.

During the initial period of their rule, the Norman kings maintained the Muslim pattern of existing small farms while carving out the majority of the island as bigger landholdings for themselves and a tight group of fellow mercenaries-cum-barons. Many of the land grants that the early Norman rulers made to the new barons did not, however, convey rights of inheritance. In addition, because the Norman rulers employed a professional army and navy (using Muslim troops and expertise), they were not as dependent as their feudal counterparts in northern Europe on their baronage. As a result, the new Sicilian baronial class was politically weak. The Norman kings set and steered the economic, political, military, judicial, and cultural course of Sicily from their palace courts in Palermo. The court of Roger II and his successors was a dazzling synthesis of Latin, Greek, and Muslim traditions and influences. As under Muslim rule, Sicilian agriculture and commerce thrived under the efficient governance of the Norman kings. Small farmers continued the intensive cultivation of fruit trees and vines along with grain. *The Book of Roger*, written in the twelfth century by King Roger II's Muslim court geographer, al-Idrisi, describes Sicily as a garden paradise where exquisite fruit and other cultivated crops abound. It also celebrates the presence of perennial water and identifies grapevines as being well adapted to certain locations, such as Caronia on Sicily's north coast and Paternò on Mount Etna.

The wealth of the Norman kingdom of Sicily under Roger II was astounding. By one account, his revenue from the city of Palermo was greater than that of the first Norman king of England, William the Conqueror, from the entire country of England. Another account tells of the retinue of ships sailing from Sicily with King Roger II's mother, Adelaide, on her way to become the queen of Jerusalem, laden with "wheat, wine, oil, salted meats, arms, horses and, not least, an infinite amount of money."[26] Under Norman rule Palermo was esteemed as one of the great cities of the civilized world, along with Cordoba, Cairo, and Baghdad. Shipwrecked on the eastern coast of Sicily on his return from Mecca, a Muslim scholar named Ibn Jubayr chronicled his travels across the island on his way home to the royal court of Granada. He had left Spain on a pilgrimage to Mecca as penitence for having been pressured into drinking a cup of wine. His chronicles alternate condemnation of the ruling Norman infidels with praise for the richness of Sicily and its rulers. On the final leg of his voyage to the port of Trapani on Sicily's western coast to board a ship bound for Spain, Ibn Jubayr recounted how the fertility of the Sicilian soil, both tilled and sown, was unlike any he had seen before and surpassed even the choiceness of Cordoba's countryside.[27] As further testament to the prosperous and vibrant culture of Norman Sicily, a Norman chronicler writing under the name Hugo Falcandus described Palermo as a luxuriant garden under the last king of pure Norman origin, William II.[28] While his language is consistent with the rhetorical flourishes of a public eulogy for a royal patron, the image and detail cannot be ignored for what they reveal about Sicily's agricultural wealth under Norman rule.

In addition to its creation of magnificent palaces, churches, and parks, the period of Norman rule was exceptional for its protection of Sicily's islandwide natural resources: water, plains, woodland, and marshes. The Norman rulers also assumed responsibility for maintaining the kingdom's roads. The continued vibrancy of Sicilian agriculture during the Norman era must have been served well by the safeguarding of the public's interest in these vital resources. The common good was served not just by the Norman kings and their feudal nobles but by the *boni homines* ("good men") of the local countryside, who honored their civic responsibilities to defend public property (*res publica*).

Alas, there was trouble in paradise. By the middle of the twelfth century a growing and restive baronial class was pushing for greater political power and autonomy. Unlike the city-states of Tuscany and northern Italy, Sicily's Palermo, Messina, and Catania had no independent urban merchant class to balance the power of the landowning baronage. The synthesis of Latin, Greek, and Muslim cultures in the courts and palaces of the Norman rulers also never reflected a true integration among the cultures throughout the island. The building tensions between Christians and Muslims ultimately erupted in open violent conflict. Muslims escaped to the interior of the island or were exiled to other parts of the Mediterranean. The loss of Muslim farmers and culture fundamentally eroded the splendid quality and diversity of Sicilian agriculture. Upon the death of the last Norman Sicilian king, William II, the chronicler Hugo Falcandus grasped what was at stake for Sicily and prophetically asked what his fellow Sicilians were prepared to sacrifice to maintain their freedom and prosperity: "What plan do you believe the Sicilians will pursue? Will they believe that they must name a king and fight against the barbarians with united forces? Or rather with diffidence and a hatred of unaccustomed labor make them slaves of circumstance: Will they prefer to accept the yoke of a prodigiously difficult slavery, rather than defend their reputation and their dignity and the liberty of their land?"[29]

This would tragically remain Sicily's unanswered challenge. The Norman kings were succeeded by a line of German (Swabian) kings, who inherited the mantle of Norman rule through Henry VI's marriage to Constance, the daughter of King Roger II. Although the succession of these German kings, culminating with King Frederick II in the first half of the thirteenth century, would in many ways extend the prosperity enjoyed by Sicily under their Norman predecessors, Sicily following their reign would never again be an independent or self-sufficient state. It would once again, as under Roman rule, become a granary of continental European empires. In the end, both distant kings and local barons would exploit Sicily's cherished fertility.

WINE-DARK AGES

The last king in the Swabian line died in the middle of the thirteenth century, and during the next five centuries Sicily became an increasingly impoverished and backward corner of western Europe. The island was treated as geopolitical chattel by the French, Spanish, Piedmontese, Austrians, and Bourbons before becoming unified with the Italian mainland in the middle of the nineteenth century. Instead of a heart-shaped apple or pomegranate, Sicily would have been more accurately depicted in a map during this period as a soccer ball kicked around by the power players of continental Europe. The easy historical narrative dwells on this external reality and hardship. And while Sicily's prolonged subjugation to foreign powers undoubtedly was a root cause of its people's poverty and ignorance, this was not the only cause. As the Norman kingdom disintegrated, the noble class in Sicily grew in size and wealth. Beginning with the first waves of Norman and German mercenaries who ventured to Sicily to fight for and support their new sovereigns and who were awarded with land grants and noble titles, the island's baronage consisted largely of the second (and third and fourth) sons of continental Europe, who came to Sicily to make their fortunes and buy their stripes. This was neither an indigenous upper class nor a noble class with shared values and a common purpose. In contrast with the Florentine Republic (a Tuscan city-state dating from the early twelfth century), which began to emerge from the Middle Ages by the end of the thirteenth century, Sicily declined into its own "dark ages" at that time. The Renaissance never flowered in Sicily. And while vines were widely planted and wine was continuously made for local (and even foreign) consumption by Sicilians during the following centuries, the science, art, and business of viticulture and vinification languished in Sicily. If a true culture of wine represents the most cultivated expression of agriculture, then it can be fairly stated that the five centuries following the fall of the last Swabian kings were Sicily's "wine-dark ages" in terms of its agricultural evolution.[30]

With certain notable exceptions, the Sicilian barons fought to preserve their rights and privileges as feudal lords over their ever-expanding lands, including the powers of taxation and justice, without honoring their historical duties of military service or protection of the public good on behalf of their sovereign. The Sicilian baronage succeeded in preserving the benefits while burying the responsibilities of feudalism. This was a perverted form of feudalism, with deep roots and a rotten core. The foreign sovereigns of Sicily, for their part, were prepared to give the Sicilian barons almost complete local control over their feudal lands in exchange for their subservience. Owning property in Palermo exempted nobles from the taxation of their latifundia in the countryside. Although the Sicilian nobles controlled only one of the three houses in the Parliament based in Palermo, they almost fully controlled the apportionment and collection of taxes to be paid to their foreign rulers. Rather than assuming the payment of taxes based on their vast landholdings, the nobles pushed taxation down to the level of the peasants who worked their lands. Beginning in the sixteenth century, a regressive tax called the *macinato* was implemented, taxing the milling of grain by tenant farmers. The large landowning barons compelled their tenant farmers to pay multiple additional taxes—for the protection of the baron's property on which they toiled, the right to press olives and grapes in the baron's press, the right to hunt on the baron's land, the right to use the baron's poultry yard, and even the right to attend Mass in the baron's private church. As late as the end of the eighteenth century, some baronial landowners compelled their tenant farmers to pay such taxes by forcing them to grind their grain at the barons' mills and to crush their olives and grapes in the barons' presses.[31] A baron exercising his ancient rights as a feudal lord could even impose a marriage tax as a condition of granting permission for his tenant farmers' daughters to marry. In effect, these *lati-fondisti* created a private system of taxation to squeeze (in Italian, *sfruttare*) as much as possible from their tenant farmers.

Sicily's polyculture from the Muslim and Norman eras devolved over the succeeding centuries largely into a monoculture of grain: hard durum wheat. Barons extended their power and prestige by acquiring greater tracts of lands. They used the revenue from their holdings not to improve the quality of agriculture on their lands but rather to acquire more lands and to establish new town settlements under their sole legal, fiscal, and judicial jurisdiction. Such wealth also funded the opulent urban lifestyles to which this noble class had become deeply attached. The nobles commonly became absentee landlords who shunned the active management of their lands and in many cases were ignorant of the boundaries of these lands.

In stark contrast with the Norman era, when there was a strong central authority based in Palermo and the unwavering rule of law islandwide, in the five centuries from the end of the thirteenth century until the end of the eighteenth century, there was not one set of laws or one ruler to enforce them in Sicily. The island had one set of laws and courts for clergymen and different legal systems and forums for nobles, merchants, and peasants. The debts and taxes of nobles remained unpaid at the same time that the same nobles hired brigands and gangs to enforce (with the emphasis on *force*) the subjugation of their sharecropper tenants to the "law" of their lands. As the nobles expanded their landholdings, they hired former field workers and local strongmen to aggressively manage their lands in a form of tenancy called *gabella*. The gabella usually involved a three-to-six-year lease on the whole estate and required the manager, known as the *gabelloto*, to pay his rent up front. The gabelloti in turn became the tyrannical enforcers of their overlords' lands, collecting rents and taxes and meting out "justice" to the peasant sharecroppers. The sharecroppers were subject to short-term leases, which gave them no security of tenure on the land and thus no incentive to invest in capital- or labor-intensive arboriculture such as vines or olive, nut, or fruit trees. Short-term leases also resulted in severe overcropping and the destruction of precious woodland to create more pasturage and farmland. The sharecropper farmers (and itinerant day laborers) had only the most primitive tools and often had to travel hours each day to work the land. In the end, the short-term interests of the nobles and their gabelloti led to severe long-term problems of soil erosion, landslides, and the disappearance of rivers and streams. The export market for Sicily's durable hard wheat was also dwindling, given its high costs of production and the emergence of ships that could more quickly transport northern Europe's less-durable summer wheat to market.

Given the difficulty of collecting taxes from the nobles, Sicily's foreign rulers resorted to other revenue-raising measures. They sold all manner of noble titles and privileges. In the seventeenth century alone, the Spanish king granted 102 new princedoms in Sicily.[32] The competition in the baronial class for social rank and prestige was astounding, even by the standards of the foreign sovereigns and their emissaries.[33] The Sicilian nobles, by and large, were not educated or even literate. They poured their agricultural revenue into ornate palaces and grandiose lifestyles in Palermo, Messina, and Catania. Many spent themselves into poverty and became borrowers from their gabelloti underlords. The gabelloti, as the new so-called *buon signori* ("good men") or *galantuomini* ("honorable men") of the countryside, then aspired to noble titles and palaces themselves. Unlike the *boni homines* of the Norman era, they—and their noble bosses—were unconcerned with the res publica. In marked contrast with the power of the urban mercantile class in the Tuscan and northern Italian city-states, Sicily's cities had no robust intellectual, merchant, or artisan class to check the power of the bulging noble class. These urban classes were dependent on the nobles and largely servile to their unilateral interests, not the public good. By one account, there was not one bridge built or fixed in all of Sicily for a two-hundred-year period.[34] With the island's deep valleys and steep mountains, the lack of a proper road system further alienated the country peasantry from the urban landed nobility. The divisions within and among the classes of society (and Sicily's principal cities) ran deep. The conditions for lawlessness and violence were ripe as barons, gabelloti, merchants, and peasants all took the law into their own hands. There are historical accounts of noble families hiring armed bandits to settle scores against rival noble families in broad daylight in Palermo.[35] Other accounts provide evidence that even justice was for sale, with nobles being able to buy their way out of criminal convictions and jail sentences.[36] These criminal elements would grow and harden with time, and it can hardly be doubted that the seeds of the Mafia took root in this climate of lawlessness and injustice.

For one brief, shining period during the seventeenth century, there was a form of landholding that had the potential to create the conditions for an agricultural renaissance in Sicily. It was called the *enfiteusi* ("emphyteusis") and involved long-term leases (sometimes as long as twenty years) whereby the tenant farmer rented small parcels of land for his home and his farming. He also had the legal right to prepay the balance of the long-term lease and effectively buy this land. The word *enfiteusi* derives from a Greek verb that means "to plant and to graft." In other words, this form of long-term tenancy gave the peasant farmer the opportunity to plant his crop, harvest it, and then select which plants to graft to improve his crop. This form of farming is precisely the kind that fosters the careful cultivation of grapevines and olive and fruit trees, with crop rotation and selection for quality improvement. This was the method of farming that in northern Italy and France permitted the selection of vine varieties and other crops for quality over centuries. The use of the enfiteusi was concentrated near Menfi in the Val di Mazara, Vittoria in the Val di Noto, and Mount Etna in the Val Demone. Nobles who acquired licenses from the ruling Spanish viceroys in Palermo created hundreds of new town settlements throughout the island built on this form of land tenancy in the 1600s. Sadly, this experiment in land reform did not survive into the eighteenth century beyond specific locales. Barons were desperate to revert to shorter-term tenancies that gave them greater protection against inflation. The degeneration of Sicilian agriculture throughout most of the island was ensured.

It is no coincidence, however, that in two of the areas where the enfiteusi leaseholds were most firmly rooted, Mount Etna and Vittoria, grapevines were systematically planted and wine production thrived through the end of the nineteenth century. Beginning in the late sixteenth century, the bishop of Catania, in his capacity as the count of Mascali, granted long-term leases in tracts of land on the fertile plain between the Ionian coast and the eastern slopes of Etna to bourgeois families in exchange for their payment of the tithe based on the land's annual production. These families, in turn, subleased parcels of their land to long-term tenant farmers, who transformed Mascali from an uncultivated forest into the flourishing wine zone that it became by the eighteenth century. By the middle of the nineteenth century, Mascali had more land under vines than any other area of Sicily and was a vibrant center for wine production and export to England, Naples, and Malta. Mascali's success as a wine-producing area created the conditions for the freer flow of capital and a nascent middle class to take hold. In the growing towns of Giarre and Riposto, wine merchants, barrel makers, shipbuilders, artisans, shopkeepers, lawyers, and other professionals all played vital roles in strengthening the agricultural and maritime economy of Mascali during this epoch.

From the beginning of the eighteenth century through the first half of the nineteenth century, three succeeding foreign powers, the Piedmontese, the Austrians, and the Bourbons, recognized the need for fundamental, islandwide reform in Sicily. They had concluded that with its fertility and other natural resources, there was no objective reason for Sicily to be destitute. The island exported raw materials such as silk, cotton, sugarcane, and sulfur as commodities to overseas commercial industries, only to buy back the finished goods at a premium. Four principal reforms were required. First, the rule of law would have to be restored and enforced if Sicily ever hoped to develop the conditions for entrepreneurship and commerce. Second, land reform would be required to improve the agricultural economy in Sicily. Third, Sicily would need a public infrastructure of roads and bridges to facilitate the movement of people and goods. Fourth, the hundreds of different weights and measures used across the island would need to be made uniform. In response to the various reforms proposed by these successive foreign rulers, the Sicilian baronage actively resisted and ultimately defeated any changes that would diminish its own wealth or stature.

The Sicilian nobles were extravagant consumers of foreign luxuries such as clothing and wine. With limited exceptions, they had the affectations and pretenses of northern European nobility without the commensurate education or culture. They imported French chefs, called *monzù,* for their kitchens and French wine for their cellars. Rather than improve domestic sugarcane production by allowing the imposition of an import tax on refined sugar, the Sicilian nobles refused any such reform that would raise the price of their most precious imported commodity. In 1839 Sicily spent twenty-five times more on sugar than coal.[37] The Sicilian nobles jealously vied for social status based on the outward demonstration of wealth, not its production. A continuous cycle of social engagements—weddings, baptisms, promenades, balls, theatergoing, gambling, religious festivals, funeral ceremonies—consumed the competitive zeal and precious capital of the Sicilian nobility. As a class, they demonstrated little attachment to the people or fruit of their lands, just the lavish trappings bought (and more frequently borrowed) with its revenue.

With the exception of select Sicilian nobles and clergymen who vigorously improved their lands and advanced the science of agriculture in Sicily, the larger story is of a noble class that abandoned its responsibilities to the land. At a time when the ruling classes of England, France, and Germany were embracing revolutionary improvements to the sciences of agronomy and botany and increasing their agricultural output dramatically, the landed nobility of Sicily were robbing Sicily and its true farmers of their agricultural patrimony.

In his iconic novel *The Leopard*, Giuseppe di Lampedusa (himself the last prince of an old line impoverished noble family on the verge of extinction in the late 1950s) provides a nostalgic look at the fading baronial class on the eve of Sicily's unification with mainland Italy in 1860. The protagonist is the prince of Salina, Don Fabrizio. He is the Leopard of the novel's name, an archetype of the noble class that had ruled Sicily since the fall of the Norman/Swabian kings. He dabbles in astronomy and neglects the productive use of his vast lands. In the center of the book, the Leopard is offered the opportunity to become a senator and represent Sicily in the national parliament of the newly unified Italy. In declining this honor, he declares that nothing in Sicily will ever change and that its history is doomed to repeat itself. In his flowery soliloquy, he states that "in Sicily it doesn't matter whether things are done well or done badly; the sin which we Sicilians never forgive is simply that of 'doing' at all."[38] This is Sicilian fatalism in its purest form. The Leopard's words are often quoted, even by modern-day Sicilians, as prophetic. But they are not. The Leopard of Lampedusa's book is not the sympathetic Burt Lancaster figure of Luchino Visconti's film. He is no prophet. He is the ghost of Sicily past, a man of great privilege who, in keeping with his decadent class, has squandered the opportunity to do something fruitful with his life.

When the reader first meets the prince of Salina in chapter 1, it is in the formal garden of his Palermo palace. "It was a garden for the blind: a constant offense to the eyes, a pleasure strong if somewhat crude to the nose. The Paul Neyron roses, whose cuttings he had himself bought in Paris, had degenerated; first stimulated and then enfeebled by the strong if languid pull of Sicilian earth, burned by apocalyptic Julys, they had changed into things like flesh-colored cabbages, obscene and distilling a dense, almost indecent, scent which no French horticulturist would have dared hope for."[39] Lampedusa's vivid description of the rotting garden is the perfect metaphor for what the garden paradise of Muslim and Norman Sicily had become in the intervening centuries. When the prince of Salina visits his country estate in the second chapter, he wanders through the garden gazing at the nude statuary and lost in his aimless musings. It is his young and vital nephew, Tancredi, who calls to him to take notice of a grafted peach tree that has yielded beautiful fruit.

"Uncle, come and look at the foreign peaches. They've turned out fine." . . . The graft with German cuttings, made two years ago, had succeeded perfectly; there was not much fruit, a dozen or so, on the two grafted trees, but it was big, velvety, luscious-looking. . . .

"They seem quite ripe. A pity there are too few for tonight. But we'll get them picked tomorrow and see what they're like."

"There! That's how I like you, Uncle; like this, in the part of *agricola pius*—appreciating in anticipation the fruits of your own labors."[40]

The "foreign peaches" are an exquisite symbol of Sicily's promise as a garden paradise governed by dutiful farmers (singular: *agricola pius*) who appreciate the fruits of their labor. In direct contrast with the prince's oft-quoted speech about the irredeemable Sicily, this small scene and Tancredi's simple words reveal what could have been a true path for Sicily's redemption. Unlike the French roses in the prince's Palermo garden, which had been left to wither in the blistering heat, the foreign peaches in his country garden are the product of the gardener's careful selection and a symbol of practical agriculture (as embraced by the foreigners of northern Europe, such as the English, the French, and the Germans). The prince seems disappointed by the small yield, but Tancredi intelligently appreciates the fruit's quality. At the end of this scene, the prince glimpses Tancredi's servant bringing a "tasselled box containing a dozen yellow peaches with pink cheeks" as a gift for the local beauty—who also happens to be the daughter of the mayor, a local strongman and the biggest new landowner in town.[41] Even if only in symbolic terms (in place of the prosaic dozen roses), Tancredi surely sought to convey an enlightened noble's appreciation of his land and its promise with this offering.

One Sicilian noble who was guilty of the "sin of doing" was Prince Biscari, the antithesis of the fictional prince of Salina. In the eighteenth century, Prince Biscari, Ignazio Paternò Castello of Catania, personally funded the construction of an aqueduct to reach his rice fields, excavated the ruins of a Greek theater, created one of the most respected private museums to showcase Sicilian antiquities and natural history, imported foreign artisans to bolster the local production of linen and rum, and largely fed the entire city of Catania for a month. His palace and museum in Catania were must-sees on most grand tours in the eighteenth and nineteenth centuries. Prince Biscari surely was more deserving than the prince of Salina of the moniker the Leopard.

During Sicily's wine-dark ages there were other real-life Sicilians—nobles, clergymen, farm managers, peasants, and other *boni homines*—who contributed magnificently to their land and its culture. Antonino Venuto, a farmer (*agricoltore*) from Noto in southeastern Sicily, authored the first agricultural treatise in Sicily to focus exclusively on the cultivation of fruit trees and vines, *De Agricultura Opusculum*. This work, first published in 1516, has individual chapters for twenty-five types of fruit trees (including orange, mulberry, cherry, carob, fig, pomegranate, almond, pear, and apple) and an eight-chapter "treatise about vines and the soil they like," describing how to plant, prune, and propagate grapevines.[42] Another distinguished Sicilian from the sixteenth century was a Dominican friar named Tomaso Fazello. Fazello discovered ancient Greek ruins in Agrigento, Palazzolo Acreide, and Selinunte and wrote a multivolume history of Sicily from its earliest age. The work is a thousand-page tome called *De Rebus Siculis* and was published in 1558. Fazello's first volume begins by extolling Sicily's rich fertility. He describes fruit trees and grapevines planted in the mountains, where the richness of the soil, the sweetness of the water, and the freshness of the air made them as fruitful in winter as in summer. While chronicling Sicily's place in ancient history, Fazello makes reference to the area of Entella, modern-day Contessa Entellina, as celebrated since Roman days for its wines. King Acestes's gift of treasured wine to Aeneas comes to mind. Fazello states that by his time, Entella had been all planted to grain and thus was ruined for wine.[43] This observation echoes the historical record that many small farms in western Sicily formerly planted with vines and olives were consolidated as part of latifundia planted almost exclusively with grain during this period. Regardless of this historical reality, Fazello claimed, whether from provincial or justified pride, that the Sicilian wines of his day were celebrated because they were as fine as any in Italy. He described them as sweet, soft, and good for the stomach because they were capable of long aging without the need for reinforcement with alcohol spirits.[44] As evidence for Fazello's praise of Sicilian wine, a century before, King Alfonso, the Aragonese ruler of Sicily, commanded his Sicilian officials to send the wines of Trapani, Corleone, Aci, and Taormina to his court in Naples to prove they served him well. The wines he ordered from Trapani and Aci included "some newly pressed, some two to three years old and some 'of the oldest you can find.' "[45]

What is known about vine varieties and wine production in seventeenth-century Sicily comes directly from the written works of two other distinguished Sicilian clergymen, Francisco Cupani and Paolo Boccone. Cupani was a Franciscan botanist in charge of a botanical garden outside Palermo. He is the author of a book titled *Hortus Catholicus* ("Catholic Garden"), which was published in 1696 and formally classified Sicilian plant and vine varieties. Boccone was a Cistercian monk from a noble family who, prior to his entry into the Cistercian order, had been a professor of botany at the University of Padua and the official botanist for the grand duke of Tuscany. He wrote more than a dozen respected works on botany, including a classification of Sicilian flora.

At the end of the eighteenth century, a Sicilian clergyman named Abbot Paolo Balsamo became the first professor of agricultural science and political economy at the Royal Academy in Palermo. Balsamo had spent three years studying advanced agricultural methods and rural economics in England and France. He returned to Sicily armed with the conviction that his island home was capable of achieving agricultural excellence, asserting that if Sicily were "cultivated with the same attention and care with which England, for example, is cultivated, it would certainly produce at least four times more than it does at present."[46] In a published journal reporting on the state of agriculture in Sicily in 1808, Balsamo exhorted Sicily's landowners and farmers to dedicate themselves to "every sort of useful cultivation" based upon a "real love of the soil."[47] He describes a former feudal property that had been divided by order of the Bourbon king among many small tenant farmers. Prior to this division, the land "was wild and desert, and nearly a third of it barren and uncultivated, and from that time it has so changed in appearance and become so rich in farm houses, trees and shrubs of various sorts, that it may now be called one continued village, and one of the most delightful retreats. . . [, and] of the plantations that of the vine is beyond comparison the chief."[48] From this experience, Balsamo concluded that "the culture of the vine is superior in effective value to that of corn," provided that the soil is adapted to it, the land is not too expensive, and the wine finds a ready market at a reasonable price.[49]

A Sicilian baron named Filippo Nicosia was one of Sicily's truly noble farmers. In 1735 this baron of Sangiaime published a manual on arboriculture that distilled decades of his personal observations and field experience. The book, called *Il Podere Fruttifero e Dilettevole* ("The Fruitful and Delightful Farm"), paid homage to the glories of the fruit orchard and the cultivation of grapevines (probably not a book in the Leopard's library). As a young man, Baron Nicosia had inherited his country estate in the center of Sicily (near Enna), and instead of taking up residence in Catania, where his noble family had its origins, he went to live on and improve his farmland. He was among the first Sicilians, following Venuto, Cupani, and Boccone, to treat the science of agriculture in a serious written work. He understood that agriculture was the foundation of Sicily's wealth, and he dedicated himself to its betterment. Baron Nicosia represented the ancient Greco-Roman ideal of the *agricola pius*, who appreciated the fruits of his own labors. In tending his trees and vines with his own hands, he could never have been mistaken by any latter-day Odysseus as part of that arrogant race of Cyclops who planted nothing and plied no plows. While the Age of Enlightenment largely bypassed Sicily, there were Sicilians of both noble and humble birth who advanced their island's culture and carried the torch for Sicily during these wine-dark centuries.

2

THE LOST OPPORTUNITY
1775 to 1950

In 1774 a Florentine named Domenico Sestini came to Sicily to study the island's indigenous vine varieties, wine regions, and wines. A little less than forty years later he delivered a series of lectures titled "Recollections of Sicilian Wines" (*Memorie sui vini siciliani*) to the prestigious Florentine society of agronomists and scientists known as the Georgofili Academy. Sestini had gone to Catania at the age of twenty-four as the guest of Ignazio Paternò. In addition to studying the written works of the historian Tomaso Fazello and the botanists Francisco Cupani and Paolo Boccone in Paternò's vast library, Sestini spent three years traveling the island and studying its soil, climate, viticulture, and vinification methods. Unfortunately, the treatise that is thought to be the culmination of his study is no longer in existence. In his first lecture, Sestini declared that Sicilian wines had been prized since antiquity for their "exquisiteness and richness" and that he would report on seven subregions: Mascali (Etna), Vittoria, Syracuse/Augusta, Castelvetrano, Milazzo, Messina, and Catania.[1] By the end of the third lecture he had covered only two, Mascali and Vittoria. Sestini began his third lecture, about the wines of Vittoria, with a rebuke to his Tuscan audience: any "Turk," he told them, would be interested in what he had to say, even if these Florentines were not![2] Originally, Sestini had intended to give at least seven lectures to the academy, but the evident disrespect for Sicilian wine among his audience persuaded him that his observations would be better kept to himself.

While the late eighteenth century saw the growth of its wine industry, Sicily at that time still had not overcome many of its historic socioeconomic challenges. In the early 1700s Sicily barely had its own merchant fleet—only about twenty of its ships were capable of reaching even Genoa. From the late eighteenth to the early part of the nineteenth century, the British fleet's need for wine supplies allowed Sicily to sell enormous quantities of wine without need of its own merchant fleet. When Admiral Horatio Nelson left Sicily for the Nile in 1798 to fight an expeditionary force of Napoleon Bonaparte, he took more than forty thousand gallons of Sicilian wine.[3] The Sicilian wine industry was dependent on the British fleet and on foreign merchants and their ships until the early nineteenth century.

Giovanni Attilio Arnolfini, an economist from Lucca, in a 1768 visit to Sicily identified the principal areas of both its production and its export of wine as Castelvetrano, Marsala, Castellammare del Golfo, Alcamo, Vittoria, Mascali, Milazzo, and Syracuse.[4] More specifically, he noted that the white wines of Castelvetrano were shipped to Genoa and Gibraltar, the red wines of Vittoria were sent to Livorno, and wines from the Modica area and Augusta in southeast Sicily and the wines from Mascali, north of Catania, went to Malta.[5]

While Sestini praised Sicily as being capable of producing fine and stable wines, it lacked an indigenous wine culture that valued both careful viticulture and enology. In 1786, Pietro Lanza—an ancestor of the Tasca d'Almerita family, the owners of Regaleali and other wine brands—published his prescription for the deficiencies of Sicilian agriculture, "An Account of the Decline of Sicilian Agriculture and the Way to Remedy It" (*Memoria sulla decadenza dell'agricoltura siciliana e il modo di rimediarvi*). He recognized that the bounty of Sicilian harvests had attracted the attention of foreign merchants but that indiscriminate harvesting practices, including rough handling of the grapes, and a lack of cleanliness in the winemaking process compromised wine quality.

BRITISH INFLUENCE

Entrepreneurship landed on Sicily's west coast in the late eighteenth century. In 1770 John Woodhouse, an Englishman, arrived at the port of Marsala looking to increase the exports of sodium carbonate, widely used in the production of glass and soap. Well before Woodhouse arrived in Sicily, British merchants had played a pivotal role in the development of the fortified wines Sherry and Madeira. Fortification (the addition of spirits) ensured stability during transport by ship.

After tasting the local wine, Woodhouse realized that he could make a less expensive version of Madeira for British consumers. He perceived the potential of the local grapes. They were inexpensive. Labor was both plentiful and inexpensive. Other British entrepreneurs, such as Benjamin Ingham and John Hopps, followed in his wake. They saw the market opportunity to sell popular wine styles made in Sicily at a time when some of Britain's other supplier countries, such as France, were subject to an embargo during the naval blockade against Napoleon. They brought with them something even rarer in Sicily than capital: the spirit of enterprise, the understanding of commerce, the knowledge of markets, and the ethos of industry and collaboration. They also brought a market-driven standard of consistency to Sicilian winemaking. They fronted money so Sicilian farmers could expand their vineyards and improve the quality of their grapes. They hired and otherwise supported innumerable Sicilians by investing in the farming, the production, and the transport of Marsala wine. They also invested in the infrastructure of the town of Marsala. Woodhouse built the first of a series of jetties that improved the harbor of Marsala for shipping and transport. The British entrepreneurs also rented and built structures to house their businesses and improved roads to facilitate the transport of goods in and out of the town of Marsala.

By 1805, Thomas Jefferson had procured a pipe (a barrel that holds four hundred liters [106 gallons]) of Woodhouse's Marsala wine for his Monticello wine cellar through the office of the U.S. secretary of the navy. In a thank-you letter to a representative of the navy, Jefferson wrote, "I received the hogshead of Marsala wine you were so kind as to send me. Altho' not yet fined (which operation I always leave to time), I perceive it is an excellent wine, and well worthy of being laid in stocks to acquire age."[6] Ingham, who followed Woodhouse in 1806, wrote a handbook that prescribed improvements in viticultural and enological practices for Sicilian winegrowers. In the early nineteenth century, he was already shipping Marsala wine to local agents in Boston, New York, Philadelphia, Baltimore, and New Orleans.

From 1806 to 1815, Britain stationed its army on Sicily to defend the Bourbon kingdom against a possible invasion by Napoleon and to block the French from controlling the central Mediterranean. This strengthened the Sicilian political clout of the British Marsala merchants, who had also lent money to the Bourbon king. Their influence was so great that when the town of Marsala asked the Bourbon government if it could levy an exportation tax on the producers of Marsala, the government refused.

Beginning in the period of their occupation of Sicily and then rule of the nearby island of Malta, the British also helped to fuel demand for the inexpensive table wines (*vini da pasto*) from the ports of Riposto, Messina, and Milazzo in northeastern Sicily. Their navy, under Nelson's command, recognized the stability of Sicilian wine on long sea voyages. During the Napoleonic wars, the British navy became a flagship customer for both Marsala and the red table wines from eastern Sicily. As a colony of the British Empire, Malta served as a shipping depot for larger British merchant ships plying the Mediterranean Sea and the Atlantic Ocean. By 1824 it was the principal export destination for ships originating from Riposto, about twenty-five kilometers (fifteen miles) northeast of Catania, that carried much of the wines and other products of eastern Sicily. By 1850, Riposto exported almost as much wine annually as did Marsala.

SICILIAN ENTREPRENEURIALISM TAKES ROOT

The British merchants, with their values and innovations, served as models for Sicilians to emulate. The first half of the nineteenth century saw a great expansion of the Sicilian wine industry. For example, by 1824 more than 90 percent of the cargo ships departing for Malta from Riposto were built by local shipbuilders and owned by merchants and investors from eastern Sicily. In addition to the table wines and other produce of Mascali, the ships of Riposto transported chestnut wine barrels and vats made from wood harvested on the slopes of Mount Etna. A traveler's guide published in Sicily in 1859 identified the island's most highly regarded wine-producing areas: Milazzo, Bagheria (just east of Palermo), Partinico, Alcamo, Castellammare, Castelvetrano, Vittoria, Syracuse, Mascali, "terre forti" (the low southern slopes of Etna where strong, full-bodied wines were made), Savoca (between Taormina and Messina, south of the Faro area, which had been famous for wine since the turn of the nineteenth century), and, of course, Marsala.[7] Before then, the only wine producers to become famous had come from Marsala and made fortified wine. There was, however, one exception.

In 1824, Giuseppe Alliata, the duke of Salaparuta, near Palermo, began bottling estate wines at his Villa Valguarnera at Bagheria. At first he bottled them for family use and to share his winemaking triumphs with his guests. The wines, a dry white, a dry red, and a sweet wine, were considered French in style because of their delicate taste. They were later named Corvo, after the *contrada* ("neighborhood") where the grapes originated. The wines of Duca di Salaparuta would be Sicily's beacons of quality for the next 150 years.

In 1832, Vincenzo Florio became a Marsala producer and merchant. He was born in Calabria in 1799. The Florio family was entrepreneurial and had business interests in the town of Marsala. As a young man, Florio had traveled for six years throughout the Italian mainland, to France, and to Britain, gaining a broad understanding of the world of business. Several years after his return, he set up the Florio Marsala business. Within a few decades, Florio's business activities had vastly expanded in diverse commercial sectors, and he even joined with a business competitor, Benjamin Ingham, to form a shipping company. Meanwhile, to supply the expanding Marsala trade, vineyards had spread beyond Marsala to Mazara del Vallo, Partinico, and Balestrate. By 1854, Florio's annual Marsala production almost equaled that of Woodhouse. Florio became Sicily's model entrepreneur and industrialist. And at the time of his death, in 1868, his Italian assets were worth one-third more than those of Ingham, the most successful of the British merchants in Marsala.

On May 11, 1860, Giuseppe Garibaldi, leading a thousand volunteers called redshirts, embarked from Genoa in two ships and landed in Marsala. His goal was to unite Italy into a single nation. Sicilians, many of them poor peasants from the countryside, flocked to his army to liberate their island from Bourbon rule. After three months of battles, his army controlled Sicily. Garibaldi then pressed on to mainland Italy, but during a return visit to Marsala in 1862, he toured the cellars of Florio. Meanwhile, the British Marsala merchants were finding the newly liberated Sicily less hospitable to their commercial interests. Once liberation was won, many of Garibaldi's Sicilian volunteers, armed and without battles to fight, terrorized the countryside. They became mercenaries for wealthy landowners. It was increasingly difficult to conduct business in a climate where theft was rampant, contracts were not enforced, and protection money was part of the cost of doing business. The new Italian government imposed higher taxes on spirits, an important ingredient in Marsala production. As a result, Marsala producers had to increase their prices, which contributed to a contraction of the market.

As the influence of the British entrepreneurs waned, more Sicilians entered the Marsala trade. In the decade after unification, Sicilians established five new houses— Diego Rallo & Figli, Nicola Spanò & C., Giacomo Mineo & Figli, C. & F. F.lli. Martinez, and D'Alì & Bordonaro. By 1880, in the province of Trapani, the focus of Marsala production, there were about eighteen. By 1895 there were about forty. Many of the Sicilians who entered the Marsala industry were merchants with little or no connection to the world of agriculture, a circumstance that ultimately undermined Marsala's potential as a producer of quality wine in the century to follow. Faced with the challenges of the phylloxera infestation that arrived in 1893, taxation not only on buying spirits but also on making wine, and a worsening market in the United States due to the increasing anti-alcohol sentiment there, many merchants gutted the quality of Marsala at the expense of their industry's long-term health.

THE IMPACT OF PHYLLOXERA

The phylloxera louse had been identified in the south of France as early as 1866. Its spread across France devastated vineyards and left French merchants without enough wine to supply their clients. For the next twenty years, French merchants increasingly came to Sicily looking for inexpensive, deeply colored, alcoholic, tannic cutting wine (*vino da taglio*), which they could bring back to France, mix with lighter and less-rich northern wines, and then clarify, stabilize, and sell using false indications of origin. Sicilian growers and merchants seized the opportunity to supply the French merchants. During the 1870s the Sicilian cutting wine industry flourished. To satisfy the demand, Sicilian winegrowers planted more vines. In 1874, there were 211,454 hectares (522,514 acres) of vineyards in Sicily. In 1880 that rose to 321,718 hectares (794,982 acres). This was the historic high point for vineyard surface in Sicily. As of 2010, the island had 115,686 hectares (285,866 acres) of vineyards, 36 percent of what was planted in 1880. In 1880 Sicilian wine production reached 8,043,000 hectoliters (212,473,582 gallons).

But the boom went bust. By 1892, Sicilian vineyard acreage and wine production had both sharply decreased, to 213,237 hectares (526,918 acres) and 4,246,000 hectoliters (112,167,453 gallons) respectively. To restore their vineyards, French farmers had been replanting with vines grafted onto American rootstocks. The volume of wine produced by the French harvest had rebounded by 1885. In 1888, the Italo-France Treaty of Commerce of 1881, which had lowered barriers to trade between the two countries, expired. Not only had the French vineyards been restored, but the political relationship between Italy and France had soured, due to Italy's increasingly close ties with Germany, which remained a rival to France after having humiliated it during the Franco-Prussian war. Protectionist measures such as tariffs took the place of the treaty, and French merchants left Sicily—without having made significant contributions to its wine industry, unlike the British. A British consular report of 1888 describes the crisis at the port of Palermo: "There was also a great falling-off in French ships, due to the enormous increase in tonnage dues on French vessels imposed during 1887. Only 13 vessels, of 17,925 tons, arrived, against 108 of 130,773 tons in 1886."[8] The British consular report of 1889 describes the consequences in Sicily: "The failure to renew the treaty of commerce between Italy and France has had most disastrous effects upon the wine trade, and prices have fallen greatly . . . to 50%, nearly."[9]

As of 1887, the Catania wine trade, which exported mostly from the port of Riposto, felt the greatest impact from the loss of French trade. In response, Riposto merchants looked for British and U.S. buyers. While the dark, coarse vino da taglio wines might have suited the needs of French merchants, they did not suit British and American merchants, who required finished dry wines with a lower alcohol content. The British vice-consul at the time described the Sicilian export wines as "green," "shipped . . . in badly coopered casks of chestnut," and as a result not likely to be sold abroad.[10] The British understood that "defective final preparation" was the reason that Sicilian producers were not finding export markets for their red wines, given that "the French for many years have been enabled to introduce them into the world's markets after due manipulation at Cette and Bordeaux."[11]

The absence of French traders, however, was not Sicily's only challenge. Phylloxera invaded the island in 1880 at Riesi. By 1885, provinces throughout Sicily were reporting infestations. Given the poor demand for Sicilian wine, it made no sense to replant the devastated vineyards, particularly the ones on slopes that were more difficult and more costly to work. Though the economic forecast for its wine industry was not good, the Italian government supported Sicily's efforts to halt the progress of the infestation and to provide phylloxera-resistant rootstocks developed in Sicily, at first free of charge and later at growers' cost. Sicily's success in combating its phylloxera infestation was founded on its historic strength: agriculture. By 1889 the British vice-consul was also reporting improvements in Sicilian vinification practices. Some producers were beginning to show "a greater care and cleanliness, and their wine has been of a better quality."[12] Perhaps the loss of the French market had forced some Sicilian producers to improve their wine. At the same time, among a small group of wealthy entrepreneurs and nobility, an interest in making fine wine developed.

PROTO–MODERN QUALITY WINES EMERGE

In the wake of the collapse of the French bulk wine market, a small but significant quality wine industry developed in Sicily during the last quarter of the nineteenth century and the first decade of the twentieth. The British consul William Stigand's report of 1889 to the British Parliament noted, "The most enterprising of Sicilian wine growers having already taken part in the exhibitions of Italian wines at Rome, Bologna, and other Italian towns with considerable success, and also gained distinction by medals and diplomas at the Italian Exhibition in London, at length determined to hold exhibitions of their own."[13] There seemed to be a strong spark in 1889, when the first Grand Sicilian Fair and Enological Exposition was held in Palermo and the Circolo Enofilio Siciliano ("Circle of Sicilian Oenophiles") met for the first time, also at Palermo.

Edoardo Alliata, the duke of Salaparuta, had taken over the production of Corvo on the death of his father, Giuseppe, in 1844. Under his direction, Corvo went from the low-volume production of a family estate to a high-volume commercial product. During several visits to France and Tuscany, Alliata realized that he had to modernize the way Corvo was made. He constructed the first wine production facility at Casteldaccia, near the Corvo contrada. He sought the advice of his brother Fabrizio, who lived in Paris, and of Louis Oudart, the French enologist of Camillo Benso, Count of Cavour, a Piedmont politician who in 1861 became the first prime minister of Italy. Alliata hired the French technician Giovanni Lagarde and bought new French presses, whose design made Corvo white wine delicate and fresh tasting. It was a great contrast to the amber-tinted, high-alcohol, coarse-textured white wines typical of Sicily. After the unification of Italy in 1860, fifty thousand bottles of Corvo, half of the annual production, were sold in Sicily and the other half on the Italian mainland. By 1876, Corvo white and red were being exported to America and northern Europe. Some bottles even reached Australia. The wines won numerous awards at competitions and fairs around the world, medaling in Paris in 1878, Melbourne in 1881, and Bordeaux in 1882. Corvo white, according to the British consul Stigand, was held in higher esteem than the red. He likened it to a "white Burgundy, though heavier in the palate than Chablis." The red Corvo was "pure" and "like a strong Burgundy" "but does not keep very well."[14] Stigand also compared Corvo sweet wine to Sauternes. In 1889, Alliata became the first president of the Circolo Enofilio Siciliano.

Some forty-eight kilometers (thirty miles) southeast of Palermo at Montemaggiore, Prince Baucina planted vine cuttings from the famous Rheingau wine town of Johannisberg in the vineyards on his property, La Contessa. These faced northeast, north, and northwest at 550 meters (1,804 feet) above sea level on the slopes of a mountain. The exposition and high elevation guaranteed temperatures that, though warmer than those of the Rheingau, would have been suitable for these vine varieties (which should have included Riesling, although there is no specific mention of it). According to Stigand, La Contessa's clayey soil resembled that of Johannisberg.[15] The king of Italy had the emperor of Germany sample La Contessa's wine, though there are no records of his comments. Baucina fermented his wine in cask rather than in vat and let it mature in cask for three and a half years, with many rackings. It was reputed to be light and delicate. He sold his wine in fluted bottles in twelve-bottle cases from stores in Palermo, Rome, and Naples.

For about twenty years bracketing the turn of the twentieth century, the Tasca family bottled a wine named after their villa, Camastra, at the southwest edge of the Conca d'Oro, the semicircular plain that encompasses Palermo. The white Camastra was principally a Catarratto and Inzolia blend. Perricone, Nerello Mascalese, and Nero d'Avola dominated the red Camastra. These wines won awards such as a Medal of Honor at the Syracuse Exposition of 1871 and were sold in Europe and America.

About fifteen miles west of Palermo, Duc d'Aumale produced a wine called Zucco. He was a Frenchman, Henri d'Orleans, who came to Sicily in 1853 and acquired the six thousand hectare (14,826 acre) Lo Zucco estate four miles south of the village of Terrasini. He brought cuttings from Spain, the Rheingau, and Bordeaux, planted native varieties such as Perricone and Catarratto, and employed French technicians, including a viticulturist and an enologist. He began planting vineyards in 1860. As of 1889 he had reached about two hundred hectares (about five hundred acres) and was employing some five hundred to six hundred workers. He made at least two white wines, one called Moscato Zucco or Lo Zucco, which was very aromatic and sweet, with 15 to 18 percent alcohol, and Lo Zucco Secco, made with the Catarratto grape variety and much like a Marsala: dry and amber colored, with 16 to 17 percent alcohol. He also made red wines, but these were less highly esteemed. The British consul Stigand said the sweet white Zucco was more similar to Sauternes than to Sherry or Marsala.[16] It was in such demand in France that it was not available in Palermo. In 2011 a Palermo wine company, Cusumano, released a Moscato dello Zucco inspired by d'Aumale's sweet white. Cusumano's first vintage of this wine was the 2007. Though Cusumano uses Moscato Bianco, as the Moscato dello Zucco brand registered by the Istituto Regionale della Vite e del Vino (IRVV) requires, the historical Moscato Zucco used raisined Moscato Giallo.[17]

Stigand also reported on the wine Tornamira, produced by Cavaliere Melchiorre Striglia, who was originally from Piedmont. About five miles southwest of Zucco, at the village of Tornamira near the large town of Partinico, Striglia set up an estate of seventy hectares (173 acres). His vineyard, planted in the mid-1870s, was at six hundred meters (1,969 feet) above sea level on a slope facing northwest. Stigand describes red Tornamira as similar to a "clean, full-bodied Burgundy."[18]

Near Zucco and Tornamira is an ancient Moorish castle, Castel Calattubo. It is deserted, sits atop a cliff, and is visible from highway A29, which connects Palermo to Marsala. Principe don Pietro Papé di Valdina named his wine after this castle. His vineyards of some thirty hectares (seventy-four acres) were on slopes overlooking the Bay of Castellammare. The white Castel Calattubo contained 14 to 15 percent alcohol. Stigand described it as "one of the finest of Sicilian white wines," even more delicate than Corvo white.[19] It was made from Catarratto and kept two years in barrel and one in bottle. It won gold medals at several international exhibitions, including the one that the Palermo Chamber of Commerce awarded at that city's first Grand Sicilian Fair and Enological Exposition. In 1898 Castel Calattubo was served at a court reception in Rome for King Umberto I of Italy, along with a Gattinara from Piedmont and Champagne.

Near Mezzojuso about twenty miles southwest of Palermo, at an altitude of 550 meters (1,804 feet), Marchese Policastello made both red and white wines called Castel di Mezzoiuso. At the Grand Sicilian Fair and Enological Exposition at Palermo in 1889, one of these won a silver medal. Stigand describes the white Mezzoiuso as "something similar in flavour to a Chablis, with a slight dash of Sauterne; the red wine could not be distinguished from a good Bordeaux."[20]

The British consular reports of this epoch catalog several more noteworthy Sicilian wine producers. Cavaliere Salvatore Salvia at Casteldaccia made a white wine called Vino Navurra from Inzolia and a red wine from the Perricone variety. He exported his wines to France, Germany, and the north of Italy. Pietro Mirto Seggio of Monreale made a wine named Renda after its contrada of origin. He fitted out his cellar with three state-of-the-art Mabille presses from France. In 1889 the Italian government awarded several enologists in the province of Palermo for the modernity and cleanliness of their wine-making facilities. Seggio and his technician, Signore Saluto, both won silver medals. Edoardo Alliata's winery and Giovanni Lagarde both won bronze.

At Mazara del Vallo, south of Marsala, Vito Favara Verderame, a British vice-consul, established a large winery, Fratelli Favara e Figli, which made a wine called Irene. Stigand reported that it tasted much like white Zucco.[21] Fratelli Favara also made Sicilian "Champagne." At the Grand Sicilian Fair and Enological Exposition at Palermo in 1889, the company won honorary medals for Irene and its "Champagne."[22]

For the Etna area circa 1889, the British vice-consul Robert O. Franck singled out Baron Antonio Spitaleri as the most important winegrower. He had facilities and 150 hectares (371 acres) of vineyards between Adrano and Biancavilla on the southwest slopes. With grapes coming from elevations of between eight and twelve hundred meters (2,625 and 3,937 feet), he made a range of wines, including a Pinot Nero–based Sicilian "Champagne," a Sicilian "Cognac," and an Etna Rosso. He exported to both America and India. In 1888 he made seven thousand export shipments of his wine, some in cask and some by the case.[23] At the Grand Sicilian Fair and Enological Exposition at Palermo in 1889, Spitaleri won silver medals for his Etna Rosso and his "Champagne."

On the western flank of Etna, Alexander Nelson Hood, a distant heir of Admiral Horatio Nelson, made great investments in wine production at a farm in the Gurrida contrada near his family estate, Castello Maniace. Ferdinand III, the Bourbon king of Naples, had granted the castle and its grounds (along with the title "the first Duke of Bronte") to Admiral Nelson in 1799 for his service protecting Sicily against the advances of Napoleon. Hood inherited the estate in 1868. During the 1870s, he tested the suitability of various foreign varieties to the soil and climate of his ninety-seven hectares (240 acres) of vineyards. He brought vines from the island of Madeira, from Bordeaux and Roussillon in France, and from Spain, particularly the area of Granada.[24] He finally settled on Grenache Noir. He had the assistance of two French technicians. Before vinification, the grapes were destemmed and damaged berries culled. The "winepressers" wore moccasins of gutta percha, a natural latex with properties similar to those of rubber, while they gently trod the grapes. Asepsis was maintained. The wine then matured in cask for seven years. Hood's winery had a capacity of 180,000 bottles, similar to that of a Bordeaux château. Stigand describes Hood's white wine as "of a light, amber colour, dry, of pleasant bouquet, of a good aroma, with full natural body . . . , esteemed beneficial for invalids; lighter than Marsala, with something of a flavour between Madeira and Sauterne. It has a clear, *primesautier* [lively] taste, and it is said to keep any length of time and improve in bottle."[25] Hood also made a red wine, labeled *Claret,* the name the English gave to the red wines of Bordeaux.[26]

The Mannino dei Plachi family of Catania also produced Etna wines, which they sent to the World's Fair at Vienna in 1873, an exposition in Philadelphia in 1876, the 1880 International Competition in Melbourne, and the World's Fair at Paris in 1900. One of the other early foreign wine producers in Sicily, Moritz Lamberger, a.k.a. the Flying Dutchman, set up a winery on Etna in 1900. Capitalizing on the phylloxera infestation of the vineyards in Austria-Hungary, he helped to open up this market for Sicilian wine. In the early twentieth century, the two most famous Etna producers were Carlo Tuccari of Castiglione di Sicilia, who made a wine named Solicchiata after a nearby village, and Biondi & Lanzafame of Trecastagni, which in 1913 and 1914 won top awards in several national exhibitions at Paris and Lyons in France.

At the Italian Exhibition in London in 1888, the fine wines of Sicily were as well represented as those of any other region of Italy. More sophisticated perspectives, both from abroad and in Sicily, had stimulated the growth of an indigenous quality wine industry that was connected to and even recognized by the world. On Edoardo Alliata's death, in 1898, his nineteen-year-old grandson Enrico took over the management of the Corvo estate. Just two years earlier he had worked as an errand boy and cellar hand at a Sauternes wine estate in Bordeaux. Applying techniques that he had learned there, he created Corvo's Prima Goccia ("First Drop," or, in the language of winemaking, "Free Run"), a wine even more delicate than the regular Corvo. It won the Grand Prix Bassermann at Rome in 1903. But two years later the Palermo Chamber of Commerce severely criticized the wine, judging its delicacy and low alcohol to be evidence of weakness. This disparaging assessment signaled the beginning of the end for Sicily's unusual period of quality wine production. The traditional Sicilian standard that white wines be amber-tinted, alcoholic, slightly sweet and viscous, and with little aroma was reasserting itself. Despite this critical chastisement, the Corvo of Duca di Salaparuta lasted beyond World War I. All the other fine wine producers of the late nineteenth century disappeared. What a tragedy for Sicilian wine!

More tragic for Sicily in this period was the plight of its peasant farmers and small winegrowers, who suffered the impact of the phylloxera infestation and the lingering stranglehold of feudalistic agrarian contracts and taxes. At the beginning of 1894 the government of Prime Minister Francesco Crispi (a Sicilian by birth and a liberal in name) summarily crushed the fast-growing social and political movement that had banded urban artisans, sulfur mine workers, and rural peasants together under the banner Fasci Siciliani dei Lavoratori ("Sicilian Workers' League") to protest and strike against the island's abusive land, labor, and tax practices. In the wake of the Fasci suppression, Crispi unexpectedly introduced legislation in July 1894 that proposed fundamental agrarian and tax reform. After his government fell in 1896, the new government of Prime Minister Antonio di Rudinì (a Sicilian aristocrat and wealthy landowner who beginning in 1897 personally oversaw the construction and operation of his own massive, state-of-the-art winemaking facility in Pachino in the southeastern corner of Sicily) wrestled with the aftermath of the Fasci repression and these questions of reform.

In a two-part article in the scientific and literary journal *Nuova Antologia* ("New Anthology"), the British-born journalist Jessie White Mario wrote about the state of Sicilian viticulture and the great cause of long-overdue land reform.[27] She argued that in order for Sicily to realize its promise as an important wine-exporting region of Italy, the government would have to do much more than simply replant vineyards devastated by phylloxera. Above all, according to Mario, it had a political and moral duty to save Sicily's agricultural economy by supporting productive land use and the intensive cultivation required for grapevines, olives, and fruit trees. She argued in favor of the legislation proposed by Prime Minister Crispi to Parliament in 1894 that would have forced the largest landowners (*latifondisti*) to enter into long-term leases (*enfiteusi*) with local tenant farmers for medium parcels, ranging from twelve to fifty acres. It also would have provided tenant farmers with fair credit terms and tax breaks. However, Parliament left for its summer break before taking up debate on this legislation, which it ignored on its return. When he came to power in 1896, Prime Minister di Rudinì did not betray his aristocratic class or large landowning constituents. He could have championed the cause of land reform, but he did not. It would be another half century before significant land reform was implemented in Sicily.

THE TWENTIETH CENTURY (1900–1950): THE EMBERS DIE OUT

From 1901 to 1913 Sicily lost more than 30 percent of its agricultural work force to mass emigration to the United States, Argentina, Australia, and other distant countries. Both vineyard acreage and total wine production steadily diminished in the first decade of the twentieth century. When phylloxera infested the vineyards of Salemi and Marsala in 1898, the Marsala industry did what the French wine industry had done twenty-five years earlier. Marsala traders went to the international bulk wine market for substitutes for the local wine. During the first decade of the twentieth century, they imported bulk wines from Apulia, Sardinia, and Tunisia and made concoctions that were supposed to resemble local base wines. As a result, the quality of Marsala was compromised and its image began to suffer. At the same time, a wave of consolidation blurred the identities of Marsala's most famous houses. In 1904 the Florio Marsala company joined with eight other Marsala producers to form a larger company, named, two years later, the Società Vinicola Florio. By 1924 the Cinzano company controlled it. As of 1929 this larger company had purchased the Marsala houses of Woodhouse and Ingham-Whitaker. Though Cinzano successfully restructured and improved product quality and sales, there was a proliferation of small companies making low-cost, low-quality Marsala. The loss of its great names signaled the end of Marsala's golden century.

At the beginning of the twentieth century, foreign wine merchants sought out table wines more than vini da taglio. With little interest from French or British buyers, Sicilian wine producers turned to other markets, particularly northern Italy, Austria-Hungary, Germany, Switzerland, the United States, and Argentina. Success in the Austro-Hungarian, German, and Swiss markets was in part determined by the same phenomenon that had stimulated France's interest in Sicilian wine: the spread of phylloxera, which arrived in these countries later than in France but earlier than in Sicily. As these countries restored their vineyards, Sicilians had more difficultly entering their markets. Sicilian producers wanting to export now also had the healthy French wine industry and the recovering Spanish wine industry to contend with. And they faced more problems. In 1904 the Austro-Hungarian Empire closed its borders to Italian goods because of a deteriorating political relationship between the two countries. France and Spain were strong competitors for the German and Swiss markets. World War I destroyed the German market. Beginning in 1919, Prohibition in the United States eliminated what had been another promising market. By 1920, vineyard acreage island-wide had declined to its lowest point since the mid-nineteenth century. The Italian government of 1920 to 1924 imposed heavy taxation on wine. During this period, taxes accounted for 43 percent of the cost of a hectoliter (twenty-six gallons) of Etna wine.

Between the two World Wars, Sicily's vineyard acreage increased. Italy's entry into World War II on the side of the Germans in 1940 interrupted Sicily's commerce until British and U.S. forces liberated the island in 1943. The volume of Sicilian wine production was 6,900,000 hectoliters (182,278,716 gallons) in 1938. In 1949 this had dropped to 3,790,000 hectoliters (100,121,208 gallons). After World War II there was also another mass emigration of agricultural manpower, this time to northern Italy, which offered jobs in heavy industry.

By 1950 the Sicilian wine industry had lost almost everything it had achieved during the nineteenth century. The Marsala trade opened the nineteenth century with the potential to increase in size and reputation, which it had largely fulfilled by 1900. But fifty years later Marsala had tied itself too closely to sweet concoctions designed for sale to bakers and the processed food industry. Moreover, from 1950 to 2000, consumer tastes gradually moved away from oxidized, fortified wines. The large-scale vino da taglio business returned briefly during the 1950s and halfway through the 1960s, until consumer demand for inexpensive, fresher, lower-alcohol table wines diminished its market. Sicily should have learned from its experience during the nineteenth century that vino da taglio confers nothing on the producer or the producing country.

Sicily's fine wine efforts of the late nineteenth century, like many of its native vines, have largely been erased from memory. In many European cultures (and particularly in Sicily), aristocrats did not want to be perceived as dirtying their hands doing business, let alone the lowliest of all businesses, agriculture. Stigand observed that proprietors were reluctant to share information about their winemaking activities because they wanted to be perceived as "exclusively occupied with the cares of polite life."[28] He chastised Marchese Policastello for making "no efforts" to put his wine, Mezzoiuso, in the market. Stigand's words still ring true today: "The great thing lacking among Sicilians for putting their products into the market is the spirit of association. If they have little confidence in the foreigner, they really have next to none among themselves; and, when invited to unite for a common purpose, suspect that the invitation is made to get some advantage prejudicial to their individual interests."[29] Instead of establishing their own identity, they have let foreigners determine it for them. When business was not good, Sicilians blamed outsiders for taking advantage of their natural resources and labor. They characteristically ignored the impact of their own behavior and actions when faced with declining prosperity.

Edoardo Alliata, however, was cut from different cloth. According to Stigand, he had "a deep interest in the general extension of the wine trade in Sicily, and has expressed his desire to enter into communication with any persons, foreign or native, who might be willing to join in operations for a common good—the introduction of pure Sicilian ordinary wines into England."[30] The spirit that Alliata demonstrated would revisit Sicilian winegrowers in the last decade of the twentieth century, giving them another chance to take the reins of their own destiny.

3

THE MODERN SICILIAN WINE INDUSTRY

EUROPEAN UNION POLICIES
OF THE 1950S THROUGH THE EARLY 1980S

The 1957 Treaty of Rome ensured that goods could move freely across the borders of European Union member states.[1] Following this, the Stresa Conference of 1958 outlined agricultural policy for members of the EU, which supported the principle that they would act as a bloc to solve problems associated with the agroeconomic difficulties of individual members. The conference guaranteed farmers in the EU that prices for their products would not fall below a predetermined level common to all member states. These prices would ensure farmers a secure livelihood. The system was essentially one of price supports.

Before the creation of the EU, the wine industries of France and Italy, the two leading wine-producing nations of the world, were remarkably insulated from each other. The policies of the Stresa Conference were the first steps in breaking down that insulation. Because both France and Italy had, at that time, high levels of per capita wine consumption and access to the northern European markets that desired their wine exports, EU bureaucrats did not foresee that there would be mercantile conflict between these two wine production giants.

There was an expansion of vineyard planting in Italy during the Fascist period between the two World Wars. After 1950, vineyard acreage declined slightly until expansion began again in 1957. This decline was due to the extirpation or abandonment of old, diseased, and difficult-to-work vineyards and to the dwindling agricultural labor force.

Vineyard acreage reached its postwar high in 1959, when 236,000 hectares (583,169 acres) produced 6,270,000 hectoliters (165,635,877 gallons) of wine.

Until the 1960s, the principal wine production of Sicily was dedicated to either high-alcohol white wines for Marsala production or high-alcohol red wines for export. These concentrated wines could only be produced with low yields and *alberello* (literally "little tree") training, a labor-intensive method of inducing low-lying vines to produce a small crop per plant. Before the 1960s, yields were low, on average less than fifty quintals per hectare (4,461 pounds per acre). In western Sicily most of the wine produced was white, in eastern Sicily, red. Much of the high-alcohol red wine was bulk wine that was shipped to northern and central Italy, where it was blended into local wine that needed color or alcohol.

During the late 1950s, French merchants purchased large volumes of cheap wine from other sources, notably Tunisia and Algeria, which were both still colonies of France. French wine technology, the most advanced in the world, helped develop their wine industries. Tunisia's independence in 1956 resulted in the deterioration of its wine industry. Its role as a supplier of bulk wine to France diminished. After Algeria's independence in 1962, its bulk wine exports to France also dwindled. Still, treaty obligations forced France to buy seven million hectoliters (184,920,437 gallons) of Algerian wine until 1970.

In 1968 the EU for the first time removed internal customs duties. This allowed for a free flow of products across member borders. Uniform customs duties on imports from nonmember states protected EU members equally. These policies made the EU a trading bloc. In the following year the EU began to standardize wine regulations. It approved member state laws that regulated the quality but not the quantity of wine produced. Yield regulations—part of the geographically based certifications *appellation d'origine contrôlée* (AOC) in France and *denominazione di origine controllata* (DOC) in Italy—associated with the quality wine categories made it highly unlikely that the quantity of quality wine would become a problem. France, however, expressed concern about the quantity of largely unregulated bulk wine, principally what was produced in Italy. Italian wine producers wanted to exploit two EU member markets, France and West Germany. Italian politicians successfully stifled the passage of EU regulations that would have limited Italian wine production. The most the EU could do was set up a system to monitor the quantities of wine produced by member states. Concern over oversupply remained. EU members discussed emergency policies such as the storage or distillation of surplus bulk wine as a means of controlling supply and demand, which would assure a bulk wine price that would protect the livelihoods of EU grape farmers and wine producers.

Domestic consumption trends within France and Italy aggravated the balance of wine trade between the two. Annual domestic wine consumption in France had registered an overall downward trend since at least 1960. In Italy, annual domestic consumption rose until 1969, when it began a downward trend that culminated in a steep decline from

1974 to 1978. These downward trends continued throughout the rest of the twentieth century. They set the stage for an enormous overproduction of wine after 1970 in Italy, particularly Sicily. Not only were the prices of Italian bulk wines generally lower than those of French bulk wines, but the Italian wine industry grew in leaps and bounds because it believed that there was unlimited potential in both overseas and domestic markets. The diminishing supply of Algerian and Tunisian bulk wine and the EU agreements that opened up trade among EU members induced French wine merchants to look for cheaper bulk wine than could be purchased in France. They found it in Sicily and Apulia.

A series of large harvests in the early 1970s in France and Italy began to create an oversupply of bulk wine in the EU market. French bulk wine producers, largely from the Languedoc area on the Mediterranean coast, had a difficult time selling their wine. They became infuriated when they saw Italian wine, purchased by French merchants, arriving in their country. In 1974, French wine producers began a series of provocative actions aimed at calling national attention to their problem.[2] They blocked the unloading of tanker ships at the Mediterranean port of Sète (named Cette until 1928), where most of the Sicilian bulk wine arrived. The "War of Sète" that these incidents kicked off lasted until 1980. Such demonstrations stirred the sympathy of French citizens. French politicians, under pressure to act, imposed import taxes on Italian wine. These taxes, however, violated the EU agreements guaranteeing free trade among member states. In 1976 the taxes were rescinded. By the end of the decade, of a total Sicilian production of about ten million hectoliters (264,172,052 gallons), five million (132,086,026) were exported. Eighty percent of Sicily's wine exports went to France, a pattern that resembled the one of one hundred years before; the remaining portion went mainly to Russia.

After Sicily reached its postwar vineyard acreage high in 1959, the modernization of viticulture began to have a profound influence on its wine industry. By 1984, vineyard acreage had dipped significantly, to 186,300 hectares (460,357 acres), about 80 percent of the 1959 figure. However, during the same period wine production rose from 6,270,000 hectoliters (165,635,877 gallons) in 1959 to its postwar high of 10,893,000 hectoliters (287,762,617 gallons) in 1984, an increase of almost 75 percent. Increases in grape yields per acre caused this remarkable about-face. The combined effects of higher yields per vine—due to modern agribusiness practices and technologies (irrigation, increased use of fertilizers, higher-yielding training systems, higher-yielding cultivars, and increased mechanization), in many cases advocated and financially supported by the EU—and diminishing per capita wine consumption in the wine-producing countries of Europe were creating a runaway crisis of overproduction. Yields increased twofold during the 1960s, from about thirty-four to seventy quintals per hectare (18,522 to 38,134 pounds per acre). From 1970 to 1979, yields almost doubled again, from 65 to 107 (the historic high point) quintals per hectare (35,410 to 58,291 pounds per acre). At EU meetings, the

French government continued to lobby for controls on the quantity of wine produced by member states.

The three principal methods that EU bureaucrats devised to limit wine production were vine-pull schemes, bans on vineyard expansion, and forced distillation of excess wine. Vine-pull schemes, which paid farmers for each hectare of vines they uprooted, were one of the first solutions suggested for taking vineyards out of production. As early as 1953, the French government had considered its own vine-pull scheme. In 1976 the EU authorized payments to growers to permanently uproot vineyards. It also capped vineyard expansion. Unfortunately, the rapid growth in yields more than offset the reduction of acreage under vine.

Distillation was a more complicated solution. It was considered a solution of last resort because its effects were short term and because it occurred at the end of the production process, not the beginning. Subsidizing the distillation of such excess wine essentially meant that EU monies would pay for not only the growing of grapes, with all its costs, but also the making, storage, and distillation of the wine, plus various transport costs. Though EU countries as of 1969 had agreed that forced distillation could be used to deplete stocks of unsalable bulk table wine, it was only in 1979 that guidelines for the practice were first discussed. Bounteous harvests in 1979 and 1980 further aggravated overproduction problems in both France and Italy. The distillation solution was complex, and discussions continued until 1982, when the EU approved policies of voluntary and forced distillation. It set different percentages of "guide prices" for bulk table wine depending on whether wine producers distilled it of their own accord or under EU coercion. The EU used the following scheme (much simplified here, of course): The producers involved arranged to have their excess wine distilled at a distillery. The distiller paid the guide price to the wine producer. The EU then bought the distilled wine from the distiller. The EU paid for storage of the ethyl alcohol produced by distillation until it could be sold on the bulk industrial alcohol market. Guide prices for each season were based on the market prices for the previous one. It was a byzantine scheme.

The reforms of 1982 proved insufficient to control overproduction, however. EU bureaucrats had not foreseen that they would inadvertently give birth to an industry dedicated to making wine that would be distilled for the sole intention of collecting EU subsidies. By providing technological guidance and matching grants, the EU had helped make viticulture and vinification processes more efficient. Mechanization in vineyards and wineries, often subsidized by EU programs, lowered production costs. These factors not only contributed to the huge oversupply of wine but also made it possible for wine producers to profit substantially even when they sold their wine to the EU for distillation. The industrial production of wine with the express intent of selling it for distillation became both pervasive and perverse in Sicily, reaching its high point from 1986 to 1988, when nearly five million hectoliters (132,086,026 gallons) of wine were distilled each year, the same annual amount that had been exported for sale almost a decade earlier.

COOPERATIVE WINERIES

The wine-producing facilities in Sicily that became the principal protagonists in the making-wine-for-distillation industry were the cooperative wineries. In Italy, a cooperative winery is usually called a *cantina cooperativa* or a *cantina sociale*. Cooperatives seem, at least in theory, to be constructive and durable enterprises. Governmental or political bodies provide organizational support to farmers to help them set up cooperative wineries. Participating farmers become part-owners based on an initial contribution of investment capital and the subsequent dedication of all or nearly all of their grape harvests to the cooperative. The cooperative thus has fixed sources of grapes. The winery uses its income to cover its operating expenses and capital costs or to pay farmers higher prices for their grapes. As a result, its taxable profits are usually small. Moreover, cooperatives typically receive tax breaks because they are perceived as providing social benefits to their members. Italian cooperatives are often recipients of subsidies from the EU, the Italian state, and the regional governments (such as that of Sicily). Because cooperatives can deliver large numbers of votes to politicians and their affiliated parties, many become political protectorates. Using their connections, cooperatives tend to have significant leverage in getting regulatory issues decided in their favor.

The cooperative movement arose out of socialist sentiments that were popular in the late nineteenth and early twentieth centuries. The cooperative movement in Sicily got off to a bumpy start. The cantina sociale Il Lavoro formed at the end of the nineteenth century but dissolved several years later. The first successful one in Sicily and one of the first in Italy was Cantina Sociale Marsalese, which was created in 1914. This dissolved in 1930 over a scandal regarding the illegal distillation of its wine stocks. Using the same facilities, in that same year, another cooperative formed: Cantina Sociale UVAM (Unione Viticoltori Agro Marsalese). It was unusual in that it was started solely with the capital of its farmer-partners. For twenty-five years it was the only cooperative in Sicily. At the end of the 1950s, only 6 percent of the Sicilian grapes made into wine were processed by Sicilian cooperatives, and nearly all of that by Cantina Sociale UVAM. While the growth of the cooperative movement had been slow in Sicily during the first half of the twentieth century, on the mainland of Italy it was much more successful. As of 1956, there were 169 cooperatives throughout Italy.

The fragmentation of large Italian landholdings into small ones helped set the stage for the rapid growth of cooperative wineries in Sicily. From 1950 to 1962, land redistribution reforms cut sizable chunks off large landholdings (latifundia) for this purpose. For example, Regaleali, Tasca d'Almerita's vineyard and winery site in central Sicily, was downsized from twelve to five hundred hectares (2,965 to 1,236 acres). The appropriated land was redistributed to landless farmers, many of whom took control of land on the farms where they had previously worked as sharecroppers. The Italian government also set up the Fund for the South (Cassa per il Mezzogiorno), which operated from 1950 to 1984. This was a development fund that supported land redistribution and farm and village construction projects; agricultural infrastructure projects such as the creations of dams, dikes, and reservoirs, largely for irrigation works; and the introduction of new agricultural techniques and equipment. The resulting increase in landholdings of smaller dimensions, combined with financial and technical support from the Fund for the South and subsequently from EU programs, stimulated the creation and expansion of cooperative wineries. In Sicily the coincidence of an oversupply of grapes, the rapid proliferation of cooperatives that could process these grapes into wine, and the cooperatives' low costs of operation, which reduced their bulk wine prices below those of their competitors, made feasible the Sicilian export boom of the 1970s and the "wine lake" distillation saga of the 1980s.

The cooperative movement bettered the lives of innumerable poor farmers. Before the existence of cooperative wineries, growers had been at the mercy of merchants' agents. These agents often ruthlessly took advantage of a buyers' market for grapes. An agent, for example, would typically agree to buy a farmer's grapes at the harvest, then intentionally arrive late, after the harvest, when the grapes were on the verge of becoming unsalable. He knew that at this point the farmer would be desperate enough to sell at well below the agreed-upon price. Before the 1970s, small grape farmers made a precarious living in an inhospitable business environment.

The downturn in the mid-1960s of the Marsala industry, by far the largest purchaser of bulk wine in Sicily, left farmers in the island's west, where most of the grapes for Marsala were grown, in a desperate situation. Cooperatives allowed them to organize, to work in an organization that understood their interests, and to take the first step toward self-determination. The vast storage capacities of the cooperatives also let them concentrate large volumes of wine in one location, helping them to benefit all the more from the opening of the French market in the 1970s. The merchants' agents who preyed on small farmers gradually disappeared. So did their employers, many of them small companies making Marsala. Large merchant concerns, some on mainland Italy and some in France, took their place, sending representatives to Sicily, usually to cooperatives, to purchase and arrange for the transport of large volumes of bulk wine.

Though the fragmentation of land ownership was one of the conditions that favored the creation of cooperative wineries, it also remains one of their innate weaknesses. Fragmented ownership obstructs the realization of the economies of scale possible in large agricultural operations, particularly those that involve mechanization. At cooperatives, 90 percent of the viticultural work is manual labor. The cost of the grapes is higher (by about 50 percent) than it would be if the cooperative could take advantage of economies of scale. Fragmentation also leads to disparities of grape quality among cooperative members. Farmer members by nature resist changes that markets ask for, demand, or necessitate. A lack of collaborative behavior stymies development. Extrafamilial collaboration is challenging for many Sicilians. They have historically preferred to work alone or within a family structure. In a cooperative, the farmer-owners meet regularly and elect an executive committee and/or president from their ranks. Typically the committee or president then selects a managing director, who hires a technical and marketing team, and fills all the other positions necessary to run a winery. Unfortunately, with the exception of the technical team, these positions customarily have been handed out as favors to influential farmers, politicians, and friends and relatives of the executive board. The selection process typically takes little account of training, experience, or talent.

Sicilian cooperatives largely sell grape juice (must) and wine in bulk. The must is mechanically concentrated into a syrupy sweetener called concentrated rectified must. In 2006 this accounted for 25 percent of the Sicilian wine grape harvest. EU subsidies supported the production of the must as a means of venting excess juice and wine. Italian wine law requires wine producers to use concentrated rectified must as the means of enriching grape juice to achieve higher alcohol levels in the finished wine. Cooperatives unload must and wine quickly at low margins rather than bottling, branding, and selling their wines to specific markets. Even if cooperatives wanted to take advantage of the profits associated with selling wine in bottle, the characteristic incompetence of their untrained marketing teams would doom such initiatives to failure. Even so, loans for cooperative development and creation have often been secured based on business plans that feature increased profits from bottling and merchandising. The weaknesses of the marketing team become a problem only a decade after a cooperative's founding, when stocks of bottled wine remain unsold, loans have dried up, and debts have devoured income. Cooperatives thus typically have enabled farmers to take the first step toward self-determination, but not the second or the third.

After cooperative wineries, particularly in western Sicily, facilitated the export bulk wine boom of the 1970s, they transferred their energy toward obtaining distillation subsidies. Their near-monopoly of the Sicilian bulk wine industry and their close ties with political structures were advantageous. Cooperative creation and expansion intensified during the 1970s and early 1980s. By 1970 there were seventy-three cooperatives vinifying 37 percent of Sicily's grapes. By 1980 there were 197 cooperatives, which processed 51 percent of all Sicilian wine grapes. As of 1987, 191 cooperatives produced 78 percent of the volume of Sicilian wine, but 97 percent of what they sold was bulk wine.

EU POLICIES FROM THE MID-1980S THROUGH THE 2000S: THE DECLINE OF COOPERATIVES

Distillation schemes kept the cooperatives busy throughout the 1980s. Sicilian politicians did their best to preserve distillation subsidies. By the mid-1980s, it became evident that distillation policies had neither remedied overproduction nor helped Sicily to restructure its wine industry in a positive direction. In 1984 the EU reduced subsidies for the production of must concentrate, which has a number of uses, including the enrichment of Italian wines. Until the early 1980s, Italian wine law allowed producers to add as much as 15 percent of other wine products to DOC wines. When this loophole was closed, the Sicilian bulk wine industry lost an important source of income.

Before the twentieth-century advent of European wine law, the wine industry and its commentators recognized the existence of unethical blending. But even after wine laws made some of that blending illegal, unethical, if not illicit, blending continued. It was well known that Sicilian bulk wine was still being added to all sorts of wines, both in Italy and abroad. The Sicilian wine industry profited from this business. In 1986, a seemingly unrelated incident had a profound effect on this illegal market. Producers in northwest Italy added methanol to wine, killing or blinding thirty-four people. Regulatory authorities immediately put all shipments of wine under close scrutiny. This disrupted the underground flow of illegal Sicilian bulk wine into mainland Italy, France, and other countries.

In 1987 the EU faced the entry of yet another huge overproducer, Spain, into its economic community. This new source of bulk wine not only was a major competitor to Italy in the EU trading bloc but also compelled EU bureaucrats to more carefully monitor and enforce the criteria for distillation subsidies that the reforms of 1982 had established. Still, the interventions were insufficient to stabilize the market. An aggressive EU vine-pull program went into effect in 1988. Vine acreage in Sicily dropped from 202,000 hectares (499,153 acres) in 1987 to 144,152 hectares (356,207 acres) in 1995. Additional subsidies supported the changeover to recommended industries such as vegetable and fruit farming. The result can be seen in the fields of polyethylene tubular tents (greenhouses, or *serre*, the plural of *serra*) that line the southeastern coastline of Sicily.

Reforms since 1999 have sought to eliminate EU market intervention, not always successfully. Crisis distillation went into force as of 2000. Instead of following a complex tiered system of forced and optional distillation measures decreed by Brussels, regions of the EU were left to regulate their own oversupply problems. When they could not and oversupply reached crisis levels, certain regions asked their state governments to seek financial support from the EU to pay for crisis distillation. The EU in 2006 balked at continuing this program, concerned that its distillation strategies were not effective in reducing overproduction. It singled out France and Italy for making excess demands on the fund and approved distillation of lower quantities of wine and at lower prices than the two countries wanted. For the 2009–10 crisis distillation campaign, Sicily requested and received more of this assistance than any other region of Italy. The tally for Sicily was 174,054 hectoliters (4,598,020 gallons) designated for crisis distillation. Apulia was second in distillation requests, with 120,749 hectoliters (3,189,851 gallons).

Italy has continued to make requests for crisis regulation. As of 2010, farmers could apply to receive EU funds for the premature removal of grapes, an action called *vendemmia verde* ("green harvest"). This is considered an anticrisis tactic because its implementation anticipates rather than responds to a wine oversupply. It targets farmers for financial assistance more precisely than coerced distillation, which spreads the money to wine producers, distillers, and support industries. Vendemmia verde subsidies alone, however, cannot cure the fundamental problem, which is too many vineyards producing grapes that do not have a market. In addition to vendemmia verde, the EU has continued to offer assistance for grubbing up vines.

During the 1990s, with wine distillation subsidies waning, many cooperatives began to fold or combine with others to form larger entities. The idea was that economies of scale could help improve efficiency. By 2008 there were about eighty Sicilian cooperative wineries, producing about 80 percent of Sicilian wine. However, New World countries, such as Australia and Argentina, with more advanced technologies and greater economies of scale, particularly at the viticultural level, threatened to outcompete Sicily in making wine at all price points, including for the bulk market. Though this domination has not occurred, the bulk market has continued to deteriorate as consumer demand for low-cost wine has waned. Cooperatives in particular have not been able to transition from making low-cost bulk wine to higher-cost bottled wine. Without capable direction, the cooperative system seems doomed to failure.

In an effort to prevent the demise of smaller cooperatives, in 2010 the regional government of Sicily proposed awards of up to five hundred thousand euro for new consolidations of existing cooperatives. One beneficiary of this program was a large consolidation that was born in 2008 when two cooperatives united under an umbrella company, Cantine Siciliane Riunite. As of 2012, its member cooperatives numbered ten, with a total 13,375 hectares (33,050 acres) of vineyards. The managing team commercializes, promotes, and bottles the wines of the members. At Vinitaly 2012 the cooperative presented its first wine, Sicilì, a white made by blending lots of Catarratto wines of member cooperatives.

THE SETTESOLI EXCEPTION

There is one exceptional cooperative: Settesoli. Settesoli took initial steps toward bottling quality wine in the mid-1970s. As of 2010, 58 percent of its wine production was sold in bottle—that is, thirteen million bottles annually. The Settesoli cooperative is in Menfi, a city on the southwest coast of Sicily, and played a seminal role in the renovation of Sicily's quality wine sector, characterized by privately owned companies. It was formed in 1958. Typically, small, relatively poor farmers are the founding members of cooperatives. Settesoli's farmer-founders came from the upper, middle, and lower classes, and its socioeconomic mix remains unusually diverse. Today the combined six thousand hectares (14,826 acres) of Settesoli's twenty-three hundred cooperative farmers account for 5 percent of Sicilian vineyards, making the company the largest in Sicily to grow its own grapes and vinify and commercialize its own wines. Its wines have a reputation for value for money and are well distributed in domestic and export markets. Beyond the diversity of its founding members, another underlying reason for the success of Settesoli could be its location. During the 1600s, Menfi was one of several areas in Sicily where farmers were allowed to lease property as a step toward ownership, in the arrangement called *enfiteusi*. In most areas of Sicily, landless farmers worked for only a percentage of their crop. The empowerment associated with working toward land ownership and hence toward self-determination may be embedded in the psyche of Menfi's citizens. Today it is one of the cleanest and best-organized towns in Sicily. Citizens speak well of their town and its key economic engine, the Settesoli cooperative.

Most Sicilians and foreign specialists attribute a large part of Settesoli's success to its remarkable former president, Diego Planeta. He became president of Settesoli in 1973 and resigned in May 2012. Forward-thinking and dynamic, he skillfully managed the company's business and internal politics, relationship with the region of Sicily, and position in world markets. Early in his career, Planeta believed that world consumers would take note of Settesoli and Sicilian wines only if those they first encountered were similar in style and name to wines already present in their own markets. In 1985 he advocated the experimental planting of internationally recognized yet nonnative varieties such as Cabernet Sauvignon, Chardonnay, Merlot, and Syrah. He linked these plant-ings and those of native varieties with the innovative research of the Istituto Regionale della Vite e del Vino ("Regional Institute of Vine and Wine"; see below). As the trial results came in, Settesoli paid its farmers to plant those varieties that performed the best and were likely to result in wines that the market would appreciate. In 1989 Planeta lured the Piedmontese enologist Carlo Corino away from his job as the technical director of Montrose Wine in Australia to become Settesoli's chief enologist. Corino had grown up in and was trained at the School of Enology in Alba, the town closely associated with the wines Barolo and Barbaresco. His professional background, a blend of Old World and New, was ideal to help project Settesoli into the modern wine world. From 1989 to 1994 he introduced many of the technologies that he had seen in Australia to Settesoli. His focus was on preserving the freshness and flavor of harvested grapes in the final wine.

PROTAGONISTS OF THE QUALITY WINE INDUSTRY FROM 1950 TO 1990

Before the 1950s there were few producers of quality wine in Sicily. Although it had many producers of Marsala, a fortified wine that became world famous in the nineteenth century, Sicily had only two surviving producers of quality still wine: Duca di Salaparuta, known for its brand Corvo, and Tasca d'Almerita, known for its brand Regaleali. Duca di Salaparuta has the longest history, dating back to 1824. Succeeding the founder, Giuseppe Alliata, and his son Edoardo was Edoardo's grandson Enrico, who success-fully guided Corvo through the difficult first half of the twentieth century. Enrico had worked in a Bordeaux winery and returned to further refine Corvo Bianco and expand the range of wines produced. Duca di Salaparuta showed that Sicilian wine, previously known as alcoholic and coarse, could be stylish and elegant yet modest in alcoholic degree. In 1961 Enrico's daughter Topazia sold the winery and brand to the region of Sicily. ESPI (Ente Siciliano per la Promozione Industriale), a department for industrial promotion, managed the winery for the government. Remarkably, under public owner-ship the company expanded and maintained high standards. During the 1970s, Corvo White and Corvo Red became the first Sicilian wines to gain wide popularity in the United States, though the label mentioned only Italy, not Sicily, as the site of origin. Corvo's U.S. importer, Paterno, played an important role in its success. By the 1980s, Duca di Salaparuta was producing eight million bottles of wine per year, a staggering number for a Sicilian wine producer. From 1974 to 1997 its Piedmontese winemaker, Franco Giacosa, traveled throughout Sicily, selecting the best sources of fruit. He helped perfect the estate's top red wine, Duca Enrico. This 100 percent Nero d'Avola wine, first issued with the 1984 vintage, established the potential of this vine variety.

By 1880 the Tasca d'Almerita family was bottling wine under the name of their palazzo, Villa Camastra, which had extensive vineyards in the plain surrounding Palermo. Though production was more limited than at Duca di Salaparuta, the wine won awards and acclaim. Production stopped after the turn of the twentieth century. The family also owned an enormous farm, Tenuta di Regaleali, at Vallelunga in the north-central highlands of Sicily. Though there were vineyards there, the modern era of Regaleali wines began in 1957, when Giuseppe Tasca and his wife, Franca Camma-rata, took over management of Regaleali. During the 1960s they emphasized in-bottle over bulk production and developed their estate's principal wines, Regaleali Bianco and Regaleali Rosso. During the 1970s they introduced modern vine training and trellising to the farm, expanded viticultural activities, and refitted the winery. In 1970 Riserva del Conte, renamed Rosso del Conte in 1979, became a standard-bearer for quality Sicilian red wine. This wine was labeled as being produced by Regaleali initially, then as pro-duced by Tasca d'Almerita, to disassociate it from the less-expensive Regaleali brand. Lucio Tasca, Giuseppe's son, had begun working alongside his father as early as 1961. He moved the estate into the current of world wineries that vinified French vine varieties. With difficulty, he convinced his father to allow him to experiment with one half acre. In 1985, Lucio planted Cabernet Sauvignon, Chardonnay, Pinot Noir, and Sauvignon Blanc. The Chardonnay and Cabernet Sauvignon gave great results and the Pinot Noir good ones. The Sauvignon Blanc was similar to the estate's preexisting Sauvignon Tasca, an old biotype identified by Tasca in the 1950s. The estate's first experimental Cabernet Sauvignon was the 1988 vintage. Its first commercial vintage of Chardonnay was the 1989. Both wines were released to the market in 1990. Pinot Noir was used in a blend with Chardonnay to make a sparkling wine that debuted in 1990 as a wine that the Tasca family shared with friends. The company purchased its first French *barriques* in 1988. The Tasca bottlings of Chardonnay and Cabernet Sauvignon were positively reviewed and brought attention to the estate. They were the first internationally recognized ver-sions of these varietal wines in Sicily.

During the nineteenth century, a small number of wealthy Sicilian wine producers sought enological help directly from France. During the twentieth century, enologists from Piedmont were the most influential. In that region of Italy, careers in viticulture and vinification are considered worthy and respectable, much more so than in Sicily. The caliber of Piedmontese wine professionals has been very high. Moreover, the region's wine merchants have been deeply involved in the transport, transformation, bottling, and sale of Sicilian wine throughout the nineteenth and twentieth centuries. In the 1960s Sicily was transitioning from supplying the world with roughly made *vino da taglio* to, during the 1970s and 1980s, making stable, good-value table wines. A key person who brought the requisite vinification technology to Sicily during this era was the Piedmont enologist Ezio Rivella. He was one of Italy's first enological consultants. In 1963 he formed a wine consultancy company, Enoconsult. In that year, he visited Sicily to investigate its wine industry and develop clients. He consulted for Settesoli in 1965 and 1966. Tasca d'Almerita also wanted to hire him in 1966. Explaining that he was too busy to care for the company personally, he assigned an associate at Enoconsult, Lorenzo "Renzo" Peira, to be responsible for the technical oversight of Tasca's wine production. Rivella's company consulted for Duca di Salaparuta from the mid-1960s to 1974 and from 1991 to 1997. It also assisted Donnafugata, which emerged as an important Sicilian wine producer during the late 1980s, for a couple of years after its inception in 1983.

While Duca di Salaparuta and Tasca d'Almerita largely built the foundation on which the modern quality wine industry rests, other estates also played important roles. At Milo on the east face of Etna, the Nicolosi family had set high standards of viticulture and vinification since the eighteenth century. On a small scale, in 1948 Carmelo Nicolosi Asmundo bottled Etna Rosso. In 1971, Rapitalà, at Alessandro di Camporeale near Palermo, began the production of quality wine. Three years earlier the Frenchman Hugues Bernard had married Gigi Guarrasi, who owned the estate. Bernard moved to Rapitalà and brought his French sensibilities about wine with him. During the 1980s, he added French varieties to the native ones already planted there. The first vintage of Tentua Rapitalà to be bottled was the 1976. The next step in the ascent toward the modern quality wine industry was Donnafugata. Giacomo Rallo foresaw both the problems that the Marsala industry would face in the ensuing years and the eventual opening of the quality wine sector. In 1983 he left the Marsala house Diego Rallo & Figli, which his family owned, and, with his wife, Gabriella Anca Rallo, established the wine estate and brand Donnafugata. Their wines, many of which are named after characters and places in the literary works of Giuseppe Tomasi di Lampedusa, the author of *The Leopard*, sparked the public's imagination. Meanwhile, in 1980 three friends studying at the University of Palermo, Giambattista ("Titta") Cilia, Giusto Occhipinti, and Cirino Strano, fused their surname initials to create *COS*, the name of their winery in Vittoria in Sicily's southeast. Though Strano left the partnership in its early days, his *S* has stuck. Eager to discover the wine world beyond Sicily, Cilia and Occhipinti traveled to Tuscany and France. In 1983 they bought used French *barriques* from the Piedmont producer Angelo Gaja. In the late 1980s they purchased new French ones.

During the 1980s, Sicily's leading light in the drive for quality was a race car driver turned winemaker. Marco De Bartoli took over one of his family's estates, Vecchio

Samperi, in 1978. He believed that Marsala wine had lost its historic quality and its ability to compete in the quality wine sector. He purchased barrels of different fine old Marsalas, then masterfully blended and bottled them. His Vecchio Samperi, created in 1980, caused a stir in the Marsala community. It was not fortified, which, by law, all wines that bear the name Marsala must be. As a result, De Bartoli was not allowed to put the appellation Marsala on the label. His wines and boundless enthusiasm and pride found advocates among journalists, though his Marsala was never a market success. Beginning with its first vintage in 1984, De Bartoli's Passito di Pantelleria Bukkuram brought attention to the sweet wines of the island of Pantelleria. He made a style that respected tradition but was less oxidized and fruitier than extant versions. The wine became a sensation. Unlike those of Vecchio Samperi, sales of Bukkuram were brisk. While most Sicilians winemakers in search of quality adopted international, particularly French, vine varieties and techniques and made wines stylistically similar to French ones, De Bartoli celebrated the raw materials of Sicily.

THE DIEGO PLANETA ERA AT THE IRVV

In 1985, Diego Planeta assumed a role that put him at the center of the Sicilian style and quality revolution of the 1990s. He became president of the Istituto Regionale della Vite e del Vino (IRVV, "Regional Institute of Vine and Wine"). The mission of the IRVV, a state-owned company founded in the early 1950s by the region of Sicily, is to help the Sicilian wine industry improve viticulture, wine production, and marketing techniques. The IRVV is charged with conducting research and making it available to all Sicilian grape farmers and wine producers. The timing of Planeta's presidency was crucial. In the early and mid-1980s the Sicilian wine industry was drowning in a sea of low-quality wine without any solution in sight.

The selection of Planeta was revolutionary. Putting an entrepreneur and the president of a winery in this position gave the IRVV the opportunity to move in a dynamic direction. Through his work at Settesoli, Planeta had an intimate understanding of cooperative associations and the political dynamics of the EU, Italian, and regional controls and subsidies. He understood both the bulk and the quality wine markets. The results of the IRVV research were made available to sectors of the Sicilian wine industry.

During the 1960s and 1970s the IRVV put in place the initial scaffolding to support research focused on assessing new technologies, which it made available to vine growers and wine producers. Bruno Pastena, a professor of viticulture at the University of Palermo, in Sicily's west, and Carlo Nicolosi Asmundo, a professor of enology at the University of Catania, in the east, were focal points of this research and its related scientific dialogue. Then, in the 1970s, Nicola Trapani began his long research and teaching career at the Technical Agrarian Institute in Marsala. He, Pastena, and Asmundo became the teachers of the key generation of winegrowers and enologists who would renovate the Sicilian wine industry.

At the beginning of the 1980s, there were stirrings that set the stage for the revolutionary perspectives and great achievements of Planeta's IRVV presidency. In those years, the IRVV agronomist Vincenzo Melia, with the help and guidance of Pastena, set up a program that placed experimental vineyards throughout Sicily starting in 1984. These vineyards tested not only viticultural techniques but also the potential of Sicily's native varieties and those varieties in the process of a rapid international diffusion, such as Cabernet Sauvignon, Merlot, and Chardonnay, mostly selected and perfected in France. The early results were so exciting that they gave impetus to larger strides.

The year after Planeta became the president of the IRVV, he set up a collaborative program between it and the Istituto Agrario di San Michele all'Adige (IASMA), Italy's foremost viticultural and enological research institute. Attilio Scienza, a professor at the University of Milan and a leading expert in the selection of clones and vine varieties, was then the IASMA's general director. The University of Palermo and Marsala's Istituto Tecnico Agrario ("Technical Agrarian Institute") were also actively involved in the research. The Menfi area became the focus of their viticultural experimentation, particularly the vineyards owned by members of the Settesoli cooperative. The IRVV and the IASMA studied the performance of fifty varieties, both native and international, which were grafted onto diverse rootstocks and farmed using diverse training systems.

In 1990 the IRVV rented a small space at the Spadafora winery at Virzi for research microvinifications. Soon 250 were under way. Grapes culled from the experimental vineyards were brought to Virzi, where technicians of the IRVV and the IASMA studied their vinification and the resulting wines. According to Scienza, the most interesting varieties from these studies were Fiano, Chenin Blanc, Chardonnay, Cabernet Sauvignon, Merlot, and Syrah. Blends of these wines and native varieties were studied to determine the best partnerships. When the initial results were in, the IRVV invited groups of thirty Sicilian wine producers at a time to taste the experimental wines and to discuss them with IRVV technicians. To fill the first thirty seats, the IRVV sent out 150 invitations. According to Planeta, only about ten producers accepted, and only three attended, representing Tasca d'Almerita, Settesoli, and the new Planeta winery. Soon, however, interest in what the IRVV was doing spread. Wine producers who did not want to be left out of the excitement started their own experimental vineyards, which they linked to the IRVV's work. Sicily's most important winery of the 1980s, Duca di Salaparuta, did not participate. In general, the IRVV was more active in western than eastern Sicily.

Planeta believed that he had to open the eyes of Sicilians to what was going on beyond Sicily. He knew that if quality wine was to be developed, Sicily would have to compete on the world stage. He sent members of an IRVV committee that was composed of mayors, winery owners, heads of cooperatives, and so forth with several IRVV employees to the Trento province of northern Italy to visit the IASMA. Faculty members and researchers exposed them to the latest viticultural and enological technologies. Planeta also organized a group of young Sicilian enologists to be trained as the vanguard for the island's new quality wine industry. He directed them to spend the first year of their program observing the innovation that was taking place all over the world and then in the second year to implement that innovation in Sicily. In the early 1990s the IRVV organized educational excursions for Sicilian enologists to visit the wine industries in France, California, Australia, and South Africa. During the same period, it organized the first Sicilian delegations to Vinexpo in Bordeaux. These initiatives helped to expose Sicilian wine producers to the wine world.

Under Planeta's direction, the IRVV invited the participation of some of the most highly regarded wine experts in Italy. Besides seeking the assistance and advice of Scienza, it engaged Giacomo Tachis, the former chief enologist at Marchesi Antinori and a consulting enologist for many well-known Italian producers. For marketing, Planeta sought the assistance of Giampaolo Fabris, a professor at the University of San Raffaele and a specialist in the sociology of consumers, best known for his promotional campaigns for Barilla and the creation of its Mulino Bianco brand. Fabris kept the IRVV and the Sicilian wine industry informed of market trends. He also developed mechanisms such as conferences that communicated the improvements in Sicilian wine to the trade and consumers.

THE IMPACT OF GIACOMO TACHIS

Giacomo Tachis, as the most celebrated enologist in Italy, the architect of Tignanello and Sassicaia and other legendary wines, was the idol of young Sicilian enologists, wine professionals, the wine press, and connoisseurs of Italian wine. Though the Marchesi Antinori company had been the principal driving force behind the rise of Tuscan wine during the 1970s, 1980s, and 1990s, Tachis was the technical architect of the style of wines for which Marchesi Antinori became known.

Without Tachis, Italy's entry into the post–World War II international wine market would have been delayed. Of Greek ancestry, born and educated in Piedmont, he had a profound respect for French wine. In the early 1950s be began a lifelong correspondence with Emile Peynaud, a professor at the University of Bordeaux and a consultant to some of the most important Bordeaux châteaux. Peynaud, as a teacher and a friend, passed on to Tachis his perspectives and methods. In the 1960s and 1970s, Peynaud was the pivot point for changes in Bordeaux enology. His influence did much to alter Bordeaux's red wine flavor profile. He advocated harvesting at higher than customary levels of ripeness, complete control of malolactic fermentation, maceration customized to grape skin conditions, and maturation that effectively used oxygenation, all of which helped to protect and preserve ripe fruit character of the wine while making its palate supple yet dense and pleasantly tactile. From Peynaud's perspective, vegetal smells, excessive sourness (high acidity), bitterness, thinness (low alcohol), and coarse-textured astringency were to be avoided in red wines. Tachis translated the Peynaud model into the enological context of Italy.

Tachis saw his job consulting for the IRVV as an exciting challenge. Both he and Planeta felt that for Sicily to be taken seriously as a quality producer on the world stage, great red wines with a distinctly Sicilian taste would have to be developed. During the early 1990s, about 80 percent of the vineyards in Sicily were planted with white grapes. Given Sicily's history of bulk wine and little else, Tachis had a relatively blank slate to work with.

Tachis was familiar with the climatic parameters of Sicily. Its ample sunlight and heat and lack of summer and harvest rain were similar to the climate of the Tuscan coast, where he had done much of his pioneering work on the Super Tuscan wine Sassicaia. In Sicily, grape skins and seeds become so physiologically mature that anthocyanins, the dominant pigment compounds in most grape skins, are easily extractable. Traditionally, Sicilian red wine maceration periods were brief, usually one to three days. A lack of temperature control and hygiene had made long macerations unsafe. Tachis preferred higher than normal pHs in red wines so that the expression of sourness did not cover or confuse that of astringency. He knew that the developed tannins of Sicilian red wines would need less maturation time in new barrel and less aging in bottle. With the wine having less contact with new oak, oak smells would mask fruit smells less. Wines could be released earlier than would be the case in northern Italy.

When considering Tachis, we have to remember that his inspiration was the red wine of Bordeaux. He was, comparatively speaking, less familiar with Burgundy varieties and Burgundian wine technology. In Tuscany he had often recommended that Sangiovese wines include some Bordeaux varieties, particularly Merlot and Cabernet Sauvignon, to add color and texture. Similarly, because of his great familiarity with Bordeaux wine technology, he also prescribed Bordeaux techniques when making Sangiovese wine. For example, he generally advocated pump-over and closed fermentation vats, typical to Bordeaux, over punch-down and open fermentation vats, typical to Burgundy. Tachis was an important influence who pushed traditional Tuscan wine flavor in a Bordelais direction, which was more likely to be appreciated by international wine critics and non-Italian consumers.

Like his master Peynaud, Tachis had more expertise in dry red than dry white wine production. Bordeaux wine producers had not put great effort into producing top-quality dry white wines until the mid-1980s, when they adopted Burgundian barrel fermentation techniques, particularly in the Pessac-Léognan appellation. While the world model for top-quality red wine has been Bordeaux, the world model for top-quality dry white wine has been Burgundian barrel-fermented Chardonnay. Though Tachis consulted for estates, such as Querciabella in Tuscany, that made excellent barrel-fermented Chardonnays, he was not recognized as a white wine specialist. Nor was he known for his expertise in rosé, sparkling, or fortified wine production.

However, he took a special interest in and had great appreciation for what are commonly called dessert wines. In this case, *dessert wines* refers to a category that contains dry as well as sweet wines and those that are often consumed by themselves or as an aperitif with a small plate of cheese, fruit, and nuts. These wine types had a long history of production in the Mediterranean area. Tachis studied these wine types from historical and cultural perspectives. He wrote a book about Vin Santo, a traditional wine typical to Italy, particularly Tuscany. Vin Santo wines can range from dry to sweet. Like many Mediterranean dessert wines, they are made by fermenting dried or semidried grapes. Though Tachis has a profound understanding of and appreciation for historic techniques and styles of dessert wines, when consulting for clients he would recommend moving their wines toward a profile that he thought modern markets would better appreciate. This profile emphasized golden-yellow over amber coloration, fresh fruit over nutty aromas and the piercing pungency of volatile acidity, and levels of acidity that supported sweetness and gave length to the finish. He favored carefully monitoring and controlling the desiccation of grapes. He advised producers to avoid conditions in which the coincidence of direct sunlight and intense heat limits enzymatic activity in the grape skins and increases oxidation. Such enzymatic activity releases exotic flavors from the skins. He also recommended fermentation and maturation practices that reduced oxidation and the loss of fruit. He encouraged producers to have an open mind regarding the use of selected yeasts. He advised low-temperature fermentation and maturation in cool environments where oxygen contact was controlled.

It was with these predilections that Tachis assessed the microvinifications at Virzi in 1992 and subsequent years. He identified Nero d'Avola as the variety that expressed Sicilianness for red wines. The focus of its use was in southeast Sicily. As he had in Tuscany, Tachis prescribed additions of Merlot, Cabernet Sauvignon, and Syrah to supply more depth of color and more structure, principally astringency. He believed that Nero d'Avola would be less successful in the market as a monovarietal wine. Tachis did not see much potential for Nerello Mascalese, the principal variety in the Etna area. For him, its color was too pale, its palate too sour, and its texture too harshly astringent. On the other hand, he was fond of Frappato, a variety historic to the Vittoria area. He liked its fresh fruitiness and acidity. Tachis gave rave reviews to several samples of Pinot Noir grown at Castiglione di Sicilia in the Etna area. He put forward the possibility that Etna Pinot Noir could one day rival red Burgundy.

Though Duca di Salaparuta's Duca Enricos of the late 1980s and early 1990s had quietly demonstrated that Nero d'Avola could be successful as a principal variety and even as a monovarietal wine, Tachis's advocacy convinced Sicilian winemakers that Nero d'Avola was *the* Sicilian quality red grape. Inspired by his advice, farmers and wine producers planted it nearly everywhere. They planted it in locations both good for the variety and bad. Because journalists were awarding high marks to dark, thick, ripe, and alcoholic wines, producers across Sicily making Nero d'Avola wine did what they could to sculpt their wines accordingly. The preferences of journalists reinforced, if not exaggerated, Tachis's prescriptions. In many cases, the additions of Cabernet Sauvignon, Merlot, Syrah, and other varieties covered the character of Nero d'Avola to the extent that it was lost.

With respect to white wines, Tachis thought well of a blend of Inzolia and Catarratto. Inzolia gave some spice in the nose and had some fatness in the mouth. Catarratto had little to add in the nose and was thin in the mouth but supplied acidity. Tachis believed Grillo had enough body to stand on its own as a monovarietal wine. It could support some barrel maturation and/or aging. He worked with the Piedmontese enologist Carlo Casavecchia at Duca di Salaparuta in the late 1990s and early 2000s on a barrel-fermented Grillo called Kados. For Tachis, 100 percent Carricante from Etna did not have enough aroma. He recommended adding 10 to 15 percent of Traminer or another aromatic variety. He showed an interest in Moscato, in particular Moscato Bianco in southeast Sicily and Zibibbo (Muscat Alexandria) on Pantelleria. As he had done elsewhere in Italy regarding dessert wines, he suggested techniques that would result in cleaner and fresher styles without moving the tastes too far from tradition. He noted that Chardonnay performed well in many locales in Sicily and gave Sicilian winemakers directions on how to barrel-ferment and mature it. In 1993 he entered a Sicilian Chardonnay produced at Virzi in an international competition in Burgundy. It won third prize.

Tachis earned the respect of most Sicilians not only because he was a star enologist but because he showed great respect for Sicily's history and culture. When the young Sicilian enologist Vincenzo Bambina at Donnafugata asked for his advice, Tachis replied, "To really understand wine, you must be culturally mature." Tachis believed that the wines of the Mediterranean islands made up a special class that had to be understood on their own terms. He was also an effective communicator. At many conferences he led tutored tastings of Sicilian wines to show their uniqueness to the wine world. His message was that the great natural resource Sicily had was the sun. The sunlight was in the flavor of the wines. He has always been a humble man who never sought credit for what he achieved and always generously bestowed credit on those who worked with enthusiasm, spirit, and professionalism.

Tachis finished his work consulting for the IRVV in 2003. For more than a decade he had given direction to Sicily's wine evolution at a time when it was ripe to grow. Andrea Franchetti, the owner of the Passopisciaro winery on Etna, once told me that Sicilians are passionate and creative by nature but quarrel constantly among themselves. They need outsiders to arbitrate and to provide a framework for moving forward. Tachis has been the Sicilian wine industry's most important outsider. He helped to organize and channel Sicilian energy and creativity. Yet at the same time, Sicilian wine producers have to see beyond Tachis's instruction. He directed them to use their raw materials so that the resulting wines would appeal to the global market's palate. This was necessary for Sicilian wine to be accepted as something beyond *vino da taglio* and low-cost *vino da pasto*. Outside cosmetic winemaking, Nero d'Avola and Nerello Mascalese, Sicily's two premier vine varieties, have very different appearance and flavor profiles than red Bordeaux or Napa Valley Bordeaux blends. Now that Sicilian wine producers have demonstrated their ability to make international-style wines, the next step is to transform the island's raw materials into something more faithful to the uniqueness of the Sicilian climate, soil, and gene pool. The challenge for Sicilian wine producers is to successfully market these true Sicilian wines to the world.

THE DE BARTOLI YEARS AT THE IRVV

Diego Planeta's term as president of the IRVV ended in 1992. In the following year, Marco De Bartoli became president. De Bartoli put more emphasis on the development of indigenous varieties and native wine styles. He advocated setting a maximum yield of one hundred quintals per hectare (8,919 pounds per acre) for all Sicilian wine as a means of controlling quantity and improving quality. He envisioned that much of Sicily's bulk wine could someday graduate to being sold by the bottle as DOC wine. He advocated promotional activities that would help producers get their wines to market and that would improve the image of Sicilian wines. He criticized the region of Sicily for reducing its financial support of IRVV research activities. Nonetheless, the vinification research center at Virzi continued its operation and Tachis remained a consultant throughout the 1990s.

De Bartoli, however, was not as skilled as Planeta in managing interpersonal and political relationships. In a conference held on the island of Pantelleria in August of 1995, rather than directing debates, be became embroiled in them, in particular arguing with local producers over the extent to which the drying of Zibibbo grapes could diverge from the traditional sun-drying. A producer on the island himself, De Bartoli had his own practices to defend or advocate: a month later he was charged with the illegal adulteration of wines. His winery south of Marsala, including its entire inventory, was sequestered. In 1997 he finished his term as president of the IRVV, but the court action continued and his business nearly collapsed. In June 2000 he was absolved of all charges. To this day, the why and the who behind the accusations remain a mystery. It was emotionally difficult for De Bartoli to put this incident behind him. Planeta's presidency of the IRVV is well recognized. There is very little written about De Bartoli's presidency. People who were close to the controversy surrounding him either claim ignorance of the circumstances and people involved or do not want to tell what they know or suspect.

FAMILY WINERIES OF THE 1990S

From about 1995 to 2005, the stage was set for the rapid evolution of private Sicilian companies that offered quality bottled wine to the international market. Many Sicilians owned vineyards and consigned their production to cooperatives or merchants. The success of the Sicilian wine industry encouraged the sons and daughters of these Sicilians to start companies, vinify and bottle their own grapes, and commercialize the wine. These companies emerged with a family management model. They took their positions among a smaller number of wineries that were established during or before the 1980s. Examples of these are Alessandro di Camporeale, Barbera, Fondo Antico, Rizzuto-Guccione, Morgante, Valle dell'Acate, Di Prima, and Giuseppe Russo. All grew at different rates and in different ways during the heady boom days of the late 1990s and early 2000s.

Firriato and Cusumano, established in the mid-1980s and mid-1960s respectively, are examples of large family companies that grew rapidly during the 1990s by relying on skillfully branded products. They buy in grapes as needed to expand their brands. Spadafora and Feudo Montoni, which evolved out of family estates, use only estate grapes, and their proprietors remain physically involved in all aspects of wine production and sale. Because family-owned-and-managed wineries tend to engage in longer-term planning than partnerships and publicly owned companies, their presence improves the stability and long-term growth of the Sicilian wine industry. With respect to wine companies, Sicilians rarely engage in business partnerships exemplified by COS and Feotto dello Jato. During this rapid growth period of the Sicilian quality wine industry, three family wineries emerged as the cornerstones: Planeta, Tasca d'Almerita, and Donnafugata.

PLANETA: SICILIAN METEOR

Diego Planeta's entrepreneurial genius, combined with the experience he had gained as the president of Settesoli and the president of the IRVV, put him in the perfect position to create a private winery that represented the interests and engaged the talents of his family. His connections to Settesoli helped to make him aware of the latest technologies and business strategies. His presidency of the IRVV put him at the helm of an organization that had funded advanced but fundamental research in the fields of viticulture, enology, and marketing.

A half-hour drive from Settesoli, his family owned a fortified *baglio* ("farmhouse") in a contrada called Ulmo. It had been a summer home where the family managed the harvesting of its wheat. In 1985, Planeta, with Scienza as his viticultural consultant, had vineyards planted there. Initially their grapes were conferred to Settesoli. The new plantings incorporated the most up-to-date viticultural technology available for producing high-quality-wine grapes. The Planeta vineyards thus became the research center for the future Planeta winery. Along with native varieties such as Nero d'Avola and Grecanico, Planeta had French varieties planted there.

The enologist Carlo Corino, on his arrival in Sicily in 1989, began working simultaneously for Planeta and Settesoli. In 1991 Planeta sent his nephew Alessio to work at the COS winery to prepare him to manage the family winery. In 1994 Alessio returned to the Planeta family winery project. The Planetas built a winery at Ulmo in 1995. Diego's daughter, Francesca, then joined her cousin Alessio. While Alessio learned about vinification under the wing of Corino, Francesca focused on marketing and public relations. Alessio's brother Santi joined the team at a later date, taking over the direction of Planeta in the Italian market. Six cousins now work at the winery in different capacities. Alessio, as winemaker and production director, appears to be the leader among them. But although Diego is not involved in day-to-day matters, his word is the final one.

Planeta's first release, in 1995, was a 1994 barrel-fermented Chardonnay that immediately grabbed the attention of the media. The winery also became known for its Merlot. The Planeta winery quickly became the best expression of the innovation and internationalization that characterized the Sicilian premium wine industry in the late 1990s and early 2000s. Its rapid success, though deliberately and quietly planned for a decade, encouraged other Sicilian producers to believe that they could sell mid-to-high-priced international-style wines to the world market.

TASCA D'ALMERITA: SICILIAN CLASSICISM

From the 1960s, Tasca d'Almerita built itself up slowly and deliberately from a large, well-managed agrarian base. The agrarian skills and instincts of the presiding Tasca d'Almerita family members—Giuseppe at first, then his son Lucio during the 1980s and 1990s—combined with the marketing genius of the winery's sole marketing and sales agent, Ignazio Miceli (who opened global markets for the wines from Regaleali during the thirty-four-year period from 1963 to 1997), ensured that the world took notice of Tasca d'Almerita. The oldest son of Lucio, Giuseppe, an agronomist by training, entered the business in 1988, accompanying Miceli on his visits to the United States. Giuseppe's brother, Alberto, joined him alongside Lucio: in 2005, while Lucio remained president, Alberto became Tasca d'Almerita's CEO and Giuseppe its vice-president. Though Corvo was the first Sicilian wine brand to enter the U.S. market, Regaleali was the first to put Sicily on a label, proudly. The synergy between the Tasca family, Miceli, and the Palermo-born Leonardo LoCascio, the founder of the U.S. importer Winebow, helped shine a positive light on the image of Sicily and its wines.

DONNAFUGATA: SICILIAN STYLE

Donnafugata would not exist but for the entrepreneurial genius of Giacomo Rallo, whose business intuition was apparent when he made the difficult decision to leave his family's traditional Marsala business in order to embrace the new market for quality wine. In a subtler way, the same statement could be made about his able partner and wife, Gabriella Anca Rallo. She was the force behind early viticultural renovations at her family's Contessa Entellina estate. This farm is the source of most of Donnafugata's grapes. Soon after Tachis's arrival in Sicily as a consultant to the IRVV, the Rallos hired him to consult directly for Donnafugata, which he did until 2000. Like the Tascas and the Planetas, the Rallos carefully groomed their family members to take key roles at Donnafugata. Daughter Josè and son Antonio joined the business in 1990. While Antonio is in charge of production, Josè focuses on marketing and public relations. Donnafugata buys in about 40 percent of its grape needs, a larger share than either Tasca or Planeta buys in. Its brands by image and flavor are less linked to specific terroirs. Donnafugata front labels rarely mention the identities of grape varieties. While its wines are technically excellent, the company has the edge on its friendly rivals Tasca d'Almerita and Planeta in its creative, style-driven marketing, which expresses a confident, fanciful, and jubilant Sicilianness.

"INVADERS" FROM THE NORTH

In the late 1990s three wine investors from northern Italy arrived in Sicily and gave momentum to a wave of investment from the boot of Italy. Most significant was the arrival of Gianni Zonin. The family-run Zonin winery has more acreage of vineyards than any other family-run winery in Italy. It bought a large estate, Feudo Principi di Butera, in the province of Caltanissetta in 1997. Also in that year, Paolo Marzotto from Vicenza in the Veneto bought Baglio di Pianetto in the hills south of Palermo. A year later he invested in a sizable vineyard in the Noto area in southeast Sicily. In 2003, when his state-of-the-art winery at Baglio di Pianetto became operational, he stepped down as the chair of his family's Santa Margherita winery group in the Veneto. In 1998, Vito Catania, a successful businessman from Milan but Sicilian by ancestry, came to the Vittoria area to start the Gulfi winery.

Italian wine producers were becoming aware of Sicily's potential. It could produce ready-to-drink red wines in styles that would appeal to wine critics and the public. Furthermore, these wines could be made at a low enough cost and great enough volume to compete with the onslaught of New World wines on the world market. The feeling in the air was invest or be left behind. In 1999, Gruppo Italiano Vini (GIV), the largest wine company in Italy, entered into a joint venture with the de la Gatinais family of Rapitalà. The Gruppo Cooperativo Mezzacorona, a large cooperative from Trento, created the wine estate Feudo Arancio in 2001 by buying extensive vineyards and building a winery in Sambuca di Sicilia near Menfi. In 2002 the sparkling wine specialist Fratelli Gancia from Piedmont gave birth to the Capocroce brand after buying land and planting vineyards at Borgata Castellazzo in the township of Trapani. Two Tuscan producers with high-quality profiles made smaller targeted investments. Antonio Moretti, an entrepreneur and the owner of the Tuscan estate La Tenuta Sette Ponti, bought vineyards and started the Maccari winery in 2000 in the Noto area. Closer to the city of Noto, in 2003 Filippo Mazzei of Fonterutoli in Tuscany purchased a baglio in the contrada of Zisola, giving that name to the new wine estate. After 2000, most of the new investment interest moved to the Etna area and was on a much smaller scale. Andrea Franchetti from Rome began the Passopisciaro winery on Etna in 2000. The Florentine Marco de Grazia founded Tenuta delle Terre Nere in 2003. Roberto Silva and Silvia Maestrelli from Milan and Federico Curtaz from Valle d'Aosta created Fessina in 2007. Beyond these investments in the Etna area, there have been few from outside Sicily since the early 2000s.

VARIETAL CHOICES OF THE 1990S

During the late 1980s and the 1990s, interest in red wines grew, and there was a marked increase in the number available on the international market. A prestige category developed. Wines in this category competed on the world stage of public opinion. Usually that stage was the pages of magazines printed in Italy, the United Kingdom, Germany, the United States, and other countries with sizable wine markets. Such international publications favorably reviewed red wines that smelled of toasted new oak and were deep in color, alcoholic, and soft textured. Following Tachis's prescriptions, Sicilian winemakers produced red varietal wines using well-known international varieties or blends of Nero d'Avola with those varieties.

No Sicilian red variety besides Nero d'Avola has risen to international market acceptance. Though Nerello Mascalese–dominant red wines are gaining attention, the reputation of the variety remains in the shadow of Etna and its appellation. Syrah is plentiful in Sicily, but it has not been associated with Sicilian wine. The images of Cabernet Sauvignon and Merlot were stronger in the late 1990s and early 2000s. Now the popularity of these two varieties is on the wane. Frappato is gaining recognition, but too little is planted for it to become popular on the international market.

No one indigenous white variety became the calling card for Sicily. Inzolia, Catarratto, Grillo, Grecanico, and Chardonnay varietal wines and blends vied in the marketplace. Sicilian producers planted Chardonnay nearly everywhere on the island from 1985 to 2000. With the exception of only the hottest of climates, where the skins were subject to burning, Chardonnay made wines that combined richness on the mouth with moderate acidity. At the prestige level, barrel-fermented Chardonnay became the means by which Sicilian producers distinguished themselves on the Italian and international stages. By 2005 the focus on Chardonnay, particularly barrel-fermented Chardonnay, had begun to wane as tastes moved to other varieties and unoaked wine. Sweet wines, such as Moscato di Pantelleria and Malvasia di Lipari, a category in which Sicily had historically excelled, remain niche products.

THE RISE OF SICILIA IGT

An Italian wine law passed in 1992, Law 164, among its many provisions created the IGT (*indicazione geografica tipica*) category of wines. Higher legal yield limits and the possibility of sourcing grapes or wines from large areas enabled wines labeled *IGT* to cost less than those labeled *DOC*. IGT wines could be vintage dated and display a variety name as long as that variety was allowed by IGT regulations and constituted at least 85 percent of the blend. A Sicily-wide IGT, Sicilia IGT, was created in 1995. By the end of the 1990s, Sicilia IGT wines, many featuring Nero d'Avola, increasingly dominated the sold-by-the-bottle market. As of 2008 more than 25 percent of all Sicilian wine, bulk and otherwise, was bottled at the IGT level, and Sicilia IGT was and remains by far the largest category of Sicilian bottled wine. In fact, in most instances, Sicilian producers who could register and label their wines as DOC prefer to use the Sicilia IGT category instead because it gives them more flexibility in all aspects of production. Existing regulations allow the bottling of Sicilia IGT wines on the mainland of Italy. Northern Italian merchants have become the principal bottlers of Sicilian wine, much to the irritation of Sicilian producers.

SICILIA DOC

As of October 2011, Italy's national commission that assesses proposals for legal wine designations (under the auspices of the Ministry of Agricultural and Forestry Affairs) has approved a new islandwide Sicilia DOC. Large Sicilian wineries have championed this development. They assert that the rock-bottom prices and low quality of Sicilia IGT wines, particularly those bottled on the mainland, are degrading the image of Sicilian wine. Only 20 percent of Sicilian wine production is bottled on Sicily. A lot of wine leaving the island in bulk ends up being bottled and sold by mainland bottlers under the Sicilia IGT designation. No one seems to know exactly how much. Sicilians suspect that mainland bottlers not only use illegal blending to construct their Sicilia IGT wines but also illegally blend Sicilian wine into their other Italian appellation wines. The fact that mainland producers are making money by selling Sicilian wine awakens the mistrust of Sicilians, who feel that over the millennia outsiders have misused the island's natural resources and agricultural products.

The stricter DOC regulations of the new law place greater quality and identity controls over a portion of the wine that has been bottled as Sicilia IGT. It is also expected that this DOC will better position Sicily to consolidate EU, national, and regional funding behind the new appellation. As originally proposed by the established Sicilian wineries, besides Sicilian producers who met the qualifications, only those mainland bottlers of Sicilian bulk wine who had sold it as IGT wine for three years prior to the enactment of the DOC rules would be allowed to use the Sicilia DOC label, provided that they adhered to the new, stricter regulations. But something funny happened on the way to the forum! The final version of the Sicilia DOC *disciplinare* ("regulation") approved in Rome conspicuously does not prohibit or restrict off-island bottling of Sicilia DOC wines. In addition, the Italian government accepted a Sicilian proposal for a new islandwide IGT called Terre Siciliane that replaces the former Sicilia IGT.

Sicily would have been better served by a new DOC that strictly required all such wines to be bottled in Sicily. Off-island bottlers should only have been allowed the possibility of using the new Terre Siciliane IGT. In this way, producers who were bottling

Sicilia IGT wine under specific brand names could have continued using those brand names but under the new IGT. This would not have damaged the image of such brands in the eyes of consumers. In addition, Sicilian cooperatives would have continued to have a ready market for their bulk wines. Even prior to the adoption of the final Sicilia DOC discipline, many producers making DOC wines within Sicily were opposed to it because they did not want to share the acronym *DOC* and its associated prestige with large wineries, whether in Sicily or on the mainland. The implementation of the new DOC and IGT designations will apply to wines of the 2012 harvest. Consumers likely will not see *Sicilia DOC* or *Terre Siciliane IGT* on labels until after April 2013.

ETNA ERUPTS!

The massive volcano, its unusual climates and soils, and the elegant, refined Etna Rosso wines have given Sicily its most convincing tastes of terroir. Etna wines veer away from international stereotypes. They are unique. But comparisons of Etna red wines to Burgundy or Barolo and Etna white wines to Alsace help us to understand their character.

Before 2000, the wines of Etna, save for those of exceptional producers such as Barone di Villagrande, have largely been discounted because of their low quality. As of 1988, Giuseppe Benanti, a businessman from Catania, resolved to make a fine wine from the grapes of his family's vineyards on the slopes of Etna. He focused on indigenous varieties, particularly Nerello Mascalese for the red wines and Carricante for the whites. His Carricante-dominated Pietramarina captured the attention of the Italian wine scene. Salvo Foti, whose grandfather had vineyards on the slopes of Etna, was Benanti's pioneering enologist until the close of 2011. Foti brought with him a love of the mountain and a respect for the Etna culture of family production. He also wrote about the history of Etna, helping to provide a foundation for the explosion of interest in it that was to come.

But as has been so often the case in Sicily, it was two non-Sicilians, Marc de Grazia and Andrea Franchetti, who brought the wines of Etna to the attention of the world. American by birth, Tuscan by origin and current habitation, the longtime wine agent de Grazia had a knowledge of the wines of the world and the world wine market. He pollinated the concept that Etna could be understood in terms of Burgundy. The red "Burgundy" of Sicily, however, did not feature the grape that Tachis had felt would make great wine from Etna, Pinot Noir. It featured the native Nerello Mascalese. Curious about the potential of Etna since the early 1990s, de Grazia had visited the area often and made some prototype vinifications before releasing his first commercial vintage, the 2002 Tenuta delle Terre Nere Guardiola, named for the contrada of origin on the north side of Etna. In 2004 he moved into his own facility. Franchetti, from Rome, also had a U.S. connection. As well as being born there, he had spent time in the United States in the 1980s developing a wine distribution company, which he eventually sold before returning to Italy. He set up his own wine estate, Trinoro, in Tuscany during the 1990s.

For many years he had visited eastern Sicily on holiday. In 2000 he bought vineyards in the village of Passopisciaro on the north side of Etna. *Passopisciaro* became the name of the winery he built there. He first made wine in 2000 from grapes he purchased from farmers on the mountain. Franchetti, a frequent visitor to Bordeaux, initially overlooked the potential of Nerello Mascalese, believing that his favorite variety, Petit Verdot—in his own words, "a prince of a grape"—outclassed it. After making several vintages of Nerello Mascalese side by side with Petit Verdot, he realized that although his Petit Verdot–based *Franchetti* was a thick, tactile wine in the image of Bordeaux, his Nerello showed uncommon elegance, finesse, and Sicilianness. In 2008 Franchetti created, organized, and financed an event at his estate called Le Contrade dell'Etna. He invited all Etna producers, as well as journalists from Italy and abroad. Le Contrade dell'Etna has showcased the wines of nearly all Etna producers every year since.

De Grazia and Franchetti were essential in getting the message of Etna out to the world, but Frank Cornelissen, a former wine trader from Belgium, has also helped ignite interest. Since 2000, when he first visited Etna, he has tantalized both locals and wine cognoscenti with his boldly intuitive artisanal wines. His first vintage was the 2001.

BACK TO SICILY: INDIGENOUS VARIETIES

The success of Etna wines has helped convince the Sicilian wine community that it should focus more on indigenous varieties. Demands from journalists and the trade for indigenous varietal wines are also driving this change. Through regional and state-owned cloning companies such as the Vivaio Governativo di Viti Americane "F. Paulsen," experimental wineries at Milazzo and Noto, and the Istituto di Patologia Vegetale at the University of Catania, Sicily has been a pioneer in developing hybrids of *Vitis vinifera* and American vine species that are viable rootstocks for phylloxera-infested soils.

Historically, Sicily has not conducted much research in developing the gene pool of its indigenous vines. In 2003, however, under the auspices of the region of Sicily's Department of Agriculture and Forestry, the then-director Dario Cartabellotta assembled a group of agronomists and enologists to study a wide assortment of biotypes of both well-known and largely ignored autochthonous varieties under the project name Development of Autochthonous Sicilian Varieties (Valorizzazione dei Vitigni Autoctoni Siciliani). He developed a collaboration between the University of Milan and the University of Palermo and selected Attilio Scienza, Rosario Di Lorenzo, and Marina Barba to head the research team. Cartabellotta also spearheaded the funding of a state-of the-art research facility in Marsala (Centro per l'innovazione della filiera vitivinicola "E. Del Giudice") to serve as the program's center. After developing a comprehensive profile of individual vine varieties and their different biotypes, including assessing their growing habits and microvinifications, the research team will select the most useful ones for eventual distribution to nurseries and grape farmers. (Nurseries will propagate and make available to the wine industry budwood from clones of such native vines, grafted onto appropriate rootstocks.) With hundreds of presumptive varieties or biotypes, about fifty recently discovered individual vines with unusual characteristics, and several thousand individual vines under observation at hundreds of locations, this study could move Sicily forward to improve and recover what it can of its patrimony of native vines before unique historic varieties and biotypes are lost.

ASSOVINI: A DYNAMIC QUALITY WINE LOBBY OF THE NEW MILLENNIUM

Assovini, founded in 1998, is a dynamic marketing and lobbying organization of about sixty-five highly visible Sicilian wineries. It pressed politicians to push forward the Sicilia DOC. In 2010 it applied for and won EU matching funds for seven projects that promote Sicilian wines in overseas markets (Switzerland, Canada, Japan, the United States, Russia, China, and Brazil). It organizes promotional events for its members, such as "Sicilia en Primeur," which draws journalists to Sicily from around the world to taste the wines of the most recent vintage and those already in commerce. Of the original nine founders, only Tasca d'Almerita, Settesoli, and Donnafugata remain. Giacomo Rallo was Assovini's first president, in 1998. He was followed by Lucio Tasca d'Almerita and then Diego Planeta, who served from 2008 to 2011. In 2011 Antonio Rallo, a son of Giacomo Rallo, became the new president. The naming of Antonio Rallo, in his forties, symbolizes the generational change occurring in Sicily and, perhaps more importantly, the continuing powerful role of his family, along with the Tascas and the Planetas.

FORWARD TO THE PAST

From 1995 to 2010, several high-profile Sicilian producers expanded their interests by buying vineyards in historic wine zones. The wines they then created highlighted those zones, their histories, and the associated indigenous grapes. The two principal protagonists were Planeta and Tasca d'Almerita. Planeta has a policy of vinifying and bottling in each area where it owns vineyards. In 1997 it moved beyond its birthplace in Sambuca di Sicilia near Menfi and developed vineyards and a winery on land that it already owned in Vittoria. It now makes a best-selling Cerasuolo di Vittoria. A year later Planeta purchased vineyards in Noto, then built a winery there, where it makes two historic wines, a Nero d'Avola (Santa Cecilia) and a Moscato di Noto. In 2010 it released a 2009 Carricante white wine from vineyards on Etna that it had purchased and planted several years before. Moreover, it has secured a long-term lease on a site just outside the city of Milazzo on the northeast coast, where it plans to bring new life to the ancient Roman cru of Mamertino. Mamertino is a DOC, but the existing producers do not have the dynamism or capital to develop the appellation. Planeta plans to build wineries both on Etna and in Milazzo.

Tasca d'Almerita is the other winery reaching into historic sites, from its base at Regaleali in Vallelunga in the center of Sicily. It bought five hectares (twelve acres) of vineyards on the island of Salina in the Aeolian Islands, where it makes a sweet white wine, Capofaro. Though not labeled a Malvasia delle Lipari DOC, this is very similar in style to one. Tasca d'Almerita plans to build a winery on Salina. The company has also purchased vineyards on Etna to make Tascante, an Etna Rosso DOC. It vinifies the grapes from Sallier de la Tour, an estate in Camporeale, and markets the resulting wines. It also has an agreement to buy grapes grown on the island of Mozia, near Marsala. Mozia was once a major seaport of the Phoenicians. Tasca d'Almerita's Mozia wine features the island's Grillo grapes.

Other wineries that have made similar expansions into historic areas during this period are Firriato, Duca di Salaparuta, Gulfi, and Benanti. Donnafugata launched its Pantelleria project in 1989 and built a winery on the island in 2002.

THE MODERN IRVV

Senator Calogero Mannino, an ex–agricultural minister and a Christian Democrat, had recommended both Diego Planeta and Marco De Bartoli as president of the IRVV. In 1997 Leonardo Agueci took De Bartoli's place as president and Elio Marzullo assumed the role of director. They provided continuity and stable leadership until 2003. From 2003 to 2006, political upheavals left the IRVV without a president or a director general. In that vacuum, an administrator simply kept the agency in operation. In 2009 Dario Cartabellotta became the director, working under Agueci, who had returned as president. In November 2011, the Istituto Regionale Vini e Oli di Sicilia (IRVOS) was created to take the place of the IRVV and to promote Sicilian olive oil. Cartabellotta is its director general. IRVOS has continued the IRVV's research, principally on viticultural and vinification techniques. It sets up conferences promoting the Sicilian wine industry and manages the Sicily Pavilion at Vinitaly in Verona, the Italian wine trade's largest annual fair. It has also taken on a task previously performed by chambers of commerce, conducting checks to ensure that farmers and wine producers are following appellation laws. This involves inspecting vineyards and wineries, sometimes unannounced, and analytically and sensorially examining wines.

Since the dissolution of the Christian Democratic Party in 1994, waves of new parties, each bearing their own squad of politicians, have entered and left the national and Sicilian regional government within the span of a year or two. In this political climate, appointees such as Cartabellotta must be politically agile in order to survive. He has adroitly moved between Sicily's Department of Agriculture and Forestry, the IRVV, and now IRVOS. With eloquence, enthusiasm, and boyish charm, he displays knowledge of Sicily's complex history, culture, and wine industry. Sicilians rarely rally around one of their own. But Sicilian wine producers and technicians rally around Cartabellotta. Will he spark another great era, like the one that Diego Planeta brought to the Sicilian wine industry of the early 1990s?

THE MARKET SITUATION CIRCA 2010

The producers who attend Vinitaly want to show their wines to Italian and foreign buyers so they can maintain old business relationships and make new ones. Having a booth there is synonymous with being a player, though some smaller fairs that focus on specifics markets, such as the ones for organic wines, also attract a number of serious producers. There are many costs beyond those of having a booth, such as travel and lodging. Attendance at Vinitaly is expensive and therefore a useful indicator of the health of the Italian wine industry. Twenty-four Sicilian producers participated in the 1986 Vinitaly. By 1991 their number had swelled to fifty-three; by 2001, 102; and by 2009, 232. In 2010, for the first time, the number of Sicilian producers at Vinitaly dropped, to 180. Vinitaly 2011 had 168 Sicilian producers. At the 2012 fair, IRVOS listed 199 Sicilian exhibitors. Despite this improvement on paper over 2011, one end of the pavilion had some vacant areas.

The years 2009, 2010, 2011, and 2012 were difficult for the Sicilian wine industry. The word *crisis* peppered the conversations of many producers. From 1996 to 2000 the market was growing so rapidly that producers had little problem finding buyers for their wines. Then the increasing number of producers and their brands began to make the prospects for many new market entrants more difficult. Growth continued but slowed after the U.S. market plunged in March 2000 and after September 11, 2001. New York City restaurants are important showcases for Italian wines. The World Trade Center devastation had a chilling effect on restaurant dining in the city. Moreover, it led many Americans to immediately curtail overseas air travel. Soon after the attacks, the value of the euro increased, particularly against the U.S. dollar, making Italian wines more expensive to many countries outside the EU.

The Sicilian wine industry, however, continued to grow, but at a slower rate than before 2000. It was the banking crisis of September 2008 that made it regress. Consumer demand for high-cost Sicilian wines decreased. Overseas importers intensified their search for value and identified Sicilian producers' ex-cellar prices as targets for hard-nosed haggling. Many reduced the number of producers they carried. From 1995 to 2008, many Sicilian wine producers secured loans from banks. The later that loans were secured during this period, the more difficult it was to make timely repayments. Start-ups that included new vineyard plantings were most at risk. In such cases, it usually takes at least seven years before income can be realized. Italian banks suddenly tightened their lending policies after September 2008 and, in an attempt to have more cash on hand, sought to restrict the credit that they had extended to wine producers or foreclose on related collateral. Sicilian wine producers' principal response was to curtail investments. They also lowered prices, made less wine, stopped investing in their vineyards and wineries, and cut down on staffing. Importers of Sicilian wines also had financial problems. Many delayed payments to Sicilian suppliers or simply never paid. Some went out of business. Fortunately, the growing Asian and other developing markets for Italian wine are offsetting the sagging Western markets.

The present quality wine market crisis should be seen in the context of a structural problem that cannot be fixed easily. Small landholders grow the grapes that make up 80 percent of the volume of Sicilian wine. Most sell their harvests to cooperative wineries. The other 20 percent mainly comes from a small number of large, privately owned Sicilian wine companies that each produce more than one million bottles annually. There are few midsize or small companies. Unfortunately, a few large, private companies seem to have benefited the most from the Sicilian quality wine revolution of the 1990s. The Italian economy has been weakening, and total Italian wine consumption has been decreasing gradually. Large Sicilian producers who were able to establish dependable relationships with importers in growing export markets are in the best position to profit.

In the first decade of the new millennium, the importance of marketing began to overwhelm individual opportunity. While the midsection of the Sicilian wine industry has not developed, the bottom segment may be heading toward what looks like a cliff. What can be done with the excess Sicilian bulk wine produced annually, nearly all of which moves through the cooperative system? European taxpayers in the past have paid to destroy such excess wine production by distillation, extirpation, and *vendemmia verde*. Such strategies have put tens of thousands of farmers, as well as thousands of workers in connected industries, on life-support systems. There have been some encouraging signs that Sicily is moving forward to address these structural challenges. First, Sicily's total vineyard surface area has declined by 29,653 hectares (73,274 acres) or 21 percent in the ten-year period from 2001 to 2011. Second, for the 2012 vintage Sicily did not request a vendemmia verde contribution from the EU.

Will the Sicilian wine industry downsize enough before the road paved with subsidies comes to an end? EU policies that have kept these vineyards in existence are increasingly diminishing. For instance, the crisis distillation scheme is scheduled to be phased out at the end of the 2012–13 season. Will thousands of grape farmers and workers at cooperative wineries adjust quickly enough? Or will they all be swept away, leaving families without incomes or work, fields of untended vines and weeds, and ruined, vacated wineries? My greatest fear is that Sicilians' collective Achilles's heel—their reluctance to collaborate and coordinate—will reassert its power and allow this bountiful land to fall into the hands of a few, perhaps even investors from outside. And Sicily's cycling domination of a few over the many will continue. May Sicilians protect their patrimony and make their own future!

4

PERPETUAL WINE

About ten years ago, Giacomo Ansaldi bought and restored the nineteenth-century Baglio dei Florio, on a rocky plain that overlooks the vineyards of the contradas Birgi and Spagnola, the Stagnone saltworks and nature reserve, the island of Mozia, the Egadi Islands, Erice, and Marsala. *Baglio* is an Italian word for a rectangular building enclosing a central courtyard. The Florio family had built this structure amid their vineyards to house equipment, employees, and, during the height of the harvest, the family itself. To avoid trademark infringement with today's Florio Marsala wine company, also no longer owned by the namesake family, Ansaldi renamed the building Baglio Donna Franca, after Franca Florio, the vivacious and stylish wife of Ignazio Florio III. Today Donna Franca comprises both a hotel-restaurant and Ansaldi's boutique winery, La Divina.

On our visit to La Divina, we tasted wines out of barrel with Giacomo in the basement cellar. We faced a lineup of eight large oak barrels supporting a layer of seven on top. An impish smile spread over Giacomo's face. He tossed me a piece of chalk. "Taste them and write your notes on the barrels. You are the master. I'll be back in fifteen minutes."

He climbed the spiral staircase that ascended into the winery. A door opened. Voices and the clang of metal against metal flowed down like water into the cool, still air of the cellar. This being early September, the harvest was in progress. The tanks in the winery were filled with "boiling" musts, turbulent, bubbling grape juice at the most active point in fermentation. There was much for Giacomo to do. He closed the door behind him with a decisive thud. Silence. We were alone in his nursery of perpetual wines.

Vino perpetuo means "perpetual wine." It is perpetual because its high alcohol content, 16 to 18 percent, makes it stable and because whatever is consumed is replenished with younger wine. Hence it goes on forever. Just as cheese is a way of preserving milk, vino perpetuo is a method of preserving wine. Its existence as a wine type probably goes back further than historical records can take us.

Small farmer families near the western coastline of Sicily still maintain vino perpetuo *a casa* ("at home"). Its flavor is unique, serendipitous, and essentially familiar because it results from where and how it is kept. The decisions of generations of individual family members become embedded in the wine. Overmature Grillo grapes are the preferred *materia prima* because this native variety is the most likely to yield wine with the presence and body to endure extended aging. When harvested late, Grillo grapes have higher sugar levels than other Marsala grapes. The result is higher alcohol in the wine.

Though each vino perpetuo is unique, their exposure to oxygen through barrel staves and bungholes causes reactions that lead to similarities in color, smell, and taste. Each is amber in color and powerfully nutty and airplane-gluey (the latter from ethyl acetate) in smell. Sicily's dry climate causes water to evaporate faster than alcohol. As a result, the wine's alcohol percentage rises above 16 percent, which adds a fiery, "hot" taste. Grillo grape skins and pulp contain unusually high potassium levels. Normally potassium means a wine is less acidic in taste, but most of Grillo's acidity remains fixed. The resulting potassium salts may account for a subliminal perception of salt. Mediterranean Sea spray landing on the grapes—which are not washed before vinification—enhances that salinity.

Earlier in the day, Giacomo had brought us to the shoreline several miles north of the port of Marsala. "*Qui nasce il perpetuo*" ("Here is born the perpetual wine"), he proclaimed as he braked his silver Mercedes wagon. He pointed over his left shoulder at the other side of the road, where there was a sprawling vineyard with low green-leafed vine bushes scattered higgledy-piggledy in black soil. Giacomo next pointed to our right. "Over there is the Stagnone Lagoon and the island of Mozia." Alongside the lagoon were mounds of shining white crystals covered by red roofing tiles. "That is sea salt, the best in Sicily." Then there was the lagoon. Lines of rocks crisscrossed it, creating a checkerboard of muted shades of blue, green, and violet. He explained that the sun and the wind caused the water to evaporate rapidly in the shallow square pools, concentrating the seawater until a salt residue was all that was left. Workers collected the salt, piled it on the mounds, and protected it from wind and rain with the roofing tiles. Windmills punctuated the scene, their bony sails pinwheeling in the steady breeze. In the Marsala area, winds blow three hundred days a year. The mills grind the salt before it is sold. Across the lagoon was Mozia, a low-lying island of green with a few buildings visible. Beyond that was the Mediterranean Sea.

Giacomo pointed to the island. "The Phoenicians, then the Carthaginians had an important trading settlement there from 700 to 400 B.C. The whole island is covered with ruins of buildings. In a museum on the island, you can see clay jars that must have once contained wine. Vases and cups showing images of grapes and people drinking wine show that they enjoyed wine. More than likely, the inhabitants grew grapes along the coastline, probably in this field right here." He waved his hand at the vineyard on the other side of the road.

Looking up as if he could see something in the sky, he said, "My dream is that my vino perpetuo will be born here. I want to buy this vineyard. The vines, nearly all Grillo, are very old, some nearly one hundred years old. I will make the wine, then barrel it. As it becomes old, I will bottle some and then replace what I draw out with young wine from this same vineyard."

At first glance it was hard to believe the vines were that old, because they looked like small leafy bushes, or *alberelli*. "Look at this one!" He raised a mound of leaves to show us the ankles of a small tree. "*Questo è vecchissimo!*" ("This one is very old!") He then pointed to a low-lying, sprawling vine bush with wide, shiny round leaves. "That is Riparia, an American vine, planted long ago as a base for the Grillo. The top of the plant, the vinifera part, has died. All these vines have American roots. Rootstocks like this one are no longer available through commercial sources like nurseries. These were introduced in the late 1800s. Because of their age, the roots of these vines reach down deep into the soil, deep into the past."

Giacomo yanked a bunch of ripe golden grapes off the *vecchissimo*. He pressed one between his thumb and forefinger, looked at it and smelled it, then showed us. "The skins are thick but disintegrate easily. The grape is ripe. The citrusy, musky smell is intense. The skins are loaded with aromatic precursors." He chewed the brownish grape seeds. He looked up smiling. His eyeballs danced. "*Croccanti!* [They are crunchy!] Like nuts. Perfect!"

"An old man owns this vineyard. After years of my asking him if I could buy his fruit, he has finally said yes. One day I hope to buy this vineyard from him. I can't tell him that, because if he knows I want it, he will raise his price." We zigzagged through the alberelli, making our way back to the car. A sign indicated that an adjacent vineyard was for sale. Giacomo took out his cell phone and dialed the seller's telephone number. He turned his back and lowered his head, spoke into the phone, then snapped it shut. "I left the owner a message telling him that I was inquiring about the vineyard for sale. I can bargain better because I want it less. He will sense this, so he will sell it to me cheap. Once I buy it, I will, by Italian law, have the option to buy the one I really want as soon as it comes up for sale. In Sicily you must be patient and work in ways that are not obvious." We got back in the car and made our way east, inland.

When John Woodhouse first arrived in Marsala, in 1770, he sampled a local wine referred to as vino perpetuo. A wine connoisseur, he noted its similarities to Madeira, a fortified wine prized by the English market. He realized that he could fortify the local wine and make a wine similar to vino perpetuo. He could then sell this in the British market at a competitive price. The Marsala wine industry was born.

"Old maps show that along the coast here north of the port of Marsala was where the vineyards were when Woodhouse first arrived in Marsala," Giacomo told us. As we drove inland, the land gradually rose. Pitted white-gray stones appeared more frequently. About a mile inland, the incline increased. Giacomo pointed out that we were moving from the littoral plain, where the soil was black and rich, up and over a limestone plateau. Vineyard expansion occurred here during the early nineteenth century. I could see that the soil varied from deep red to light brown. Giacomo told us that the red was from iron leached from the limestone by thousands of years of rain. (The rains come during the winter.) We drove along this plateau, which gave us a panorama of the sea. The vegetation was scrawny. Vineyards alternated with spaces littered with chalky rocks of all shapes and sizes. At some points in the journey, it looked like we were on the surface of the moon.

Our guide spoke as he drove: "Woodhouse's success attracted others, first fellow Englishmen in the early 1800s, then, by the mid-1800s, Sicilians." We stopped in front of a stone archway rising up among rocks and weeds. Behind the archway were the ruins of a large stone house. Where the roof should have been there was blue sky. We stood on a rock wall to get a better view. Through one window we could look through another to the shimmering Mediterranean. The smell of burned vegetation filled the air. Farmers were burning brush. The weeds in front of the wall grasped clear plastic bottles and white plastic shopping bags. A mangy dog sauntered like a ghost through the ruins.

"This is one of Woodhouse's baglios," Giacomo announced as we peered in. "Marsala families built these stone houses. Woodhouse and the other large producers set up many baglios in the vicinity of their grape sources, as well as one large one at the port of Marsala. This one is in contrada Mafi. Look how this baglio commands a view of the plain below and the Mediterranean Sea. Most baglios were strategically positioned. Sicily has always been invaded from the sea. Baglios were sentinels as well as places to live and work." Later we found out that as many as twenty-seven people owned a part of this ruin. One might own half a wall, half a stairway, half an arch. In order for this baglio to be restored, all twenty-seven would have to agree to sell. Everyone waits for others to sell first. They believe that they can get a higher price as the buyer becomes more desperate to own the final plots. So nothing happens. Not having this historic property and others like it sensitively restored cuts the nose off Sicily, disfiguring its face. Giacomo, however, feels the magic and the potential of this baglio. "I would love to buy this place. I would love to bring it back to life."

We went back to the car and drove to the northern edge of the limestone plateau, which looks over a vast plain carpeted with patches of vineyards. In the distance loomed Erice, a well-preserved medieval town atop a mountain. Erice Mountain rose like a huge sperm whale out of a green sea. We could see the profiles of the buildings of the town bristling like tiny teeth on the summit. On many days, when the sun pours down on

Trapani, Erice's closest port, just to its east, the town of Erice is veiled in clouds. The province of Trapani has more acres planted to vines than any other province in Italy. It accounts for more than 55 percent of the vineyards planted in Sicily. Just visible to the east were the hills of Salemi, where the higher altitudes and distance from the sea make lower-alcohol wines with less tactile structure. The grapes grown in Salemi are better suited for modern white wine sold by the bottle than for base wines for Marsala. South of Marsala is Mazara del Vallo, where growing conditions are similar to those near Marsala.

Giacomo pointed out, though, that the soil of the plains between us and Erice consisted of heavy clay, better suited to growing cereal than vines. Innumerable local families owned tiny plots. Most owners had other jobs that supported them. They farmed these vineyards to supplement their incomes and to retain their families' historic connection to agriculture.

Giacomo showed us a vineyard his family owns. As a child, he loved working with his father in the family vineyards. This particular plot had an added attraction. A shepherd had bivouacked his sheep within the walls of an eviscerated nineteenth-century baglio just down the road. Every morning he made fresh ricotta. The warm ricotta was young Giacomo's early morning treat.

He walked over to the ruins of that baglio. Another shepherd now presided. Giacomo went up and joked with him in the local Sicilian dialect. He wanted to assure the man that we were not there to make his life difficult. The shepherd was a squatter. We walked past a shed surrounded by a litter of cats and several scruffy dogs. Opposite the shed, an imposing stone arch allowed entry into the courtyard. As was the case with Woodhouse's baglio, there was no sign of a roof. Stones had been pulled from the walls to barricade windows and doorways so as to confine the sheep to the courtyard. Clumps of wool stuck in crevices. An overturned cast-iron bathtub had been their feeding trough. We walked up to a stone well in the center of the courtyard. An apron of rounded stones spread out and was then buried in the sea of black sheep feces that covered the courtyard. I tried to imagine the smell of the fresh, warm ricotta that young Giacomo had savored decades earlier.

"This is a baglio, Baglio Musciuleo, once owned by Ingham," he said. Benjamin Ingham founded his Marsala company in 1812. While Woodhouse modified the local wines, Ingham improved the base wines by systematizing viticulture. In time, his company became larger than that of Woodhouse. A handful of English entrepreneurs, most notably John Hopps and Joseph Gill, also came to Marsala to produce their own Marsala wine. It is ironic but telling that Sicily's most famous historic wine was the invention of foreigners. It is also telling that the first Sicilian producer of Marsala, Vincenzo Florio, was not originally from Sicily but Calabria. For Giacomo, as for Sicily, the age of Woodhouse, Ingham, and Florio was pivotal.

Giacomo's final stop was Baglio Donna Franca. Across the street from Baglio Woodhouse, the Florios had built this much larger baglio. Phalanxes of vines on our right loaded with purple Nero d'Avola grapes marched across brownish white soil. On our left, behind a low rock wall, vines carrying golden-yellow bunches of Grillo paraded across brilliant red soil. In front of us the large dimensions of Baglio Donna Franca signaled the heyday of the Marsala wine industry. The massive high white wall was almost blinding in the sun. Midway along its breadth was an arched entry to a central courtyard. Giacomo looked up and pointed at a squat structure above and to the side of the archway. "That is an old Saracen tower. It dates back to the eleventh century. From that high point the Saracens looked out across the sea, searching for the ships of their enemies."

Giacomo sighed, his mind revisiting the moment a decade ago when he had strolled through the ruins of what came to be called Sceccu d'Oru ("The Golden Ass") after World War I. During the war, the Florio family had set up a clandestine distillation operation in the baglio. This was to avoid the taxes the government set on spirits that Marsala producers had to buy to fortify their wines. *Ass* was the code name for a still in the local language. The spirits that came out of it were as valuable as gold. "You should have seen this place when I bought it. It looked as bad as what we saw at Woodhouse's and Ingham's baglios." We entered the central courtyard. Several large palm trees provided shade. Circling the courtyard were buildings constructed at intervals along the surrounding walls. A larger-than-life artistic rendering of Franca Florio gazed dreamily from an elevated perch. She flaunted a string of pearls that dangled down to her knees. This fashion diva reigned supreme, as if she had never left. Just as the Florios' entrepreneurial bent had irritated Sicilian blue bloods, Franca Florio's interest in fashion, culture, and politics went beyond what was considered ladylike for well-bred Sicilian women of her day.

Giuseppe Garibaldi landed at Marsala in 1860 on his way to his victorious march across Sicily and revisited the city in 1862. During a visit to the Florio headquarters at the port, he sampled a range of Marsala wine. He preferred sweetened Marsala. Marsala experts snickered, for they considered the sweetened wine a lady's drink. For connoisseurs, Marsala Vergine, a blend of top dry wines, mostly Grillo, fortified and matured for years in barrel, is the reference point of essential Marsala wine. It is what Woodhouse first devised after being inspired by the local wine. Eventually, tinted and sweetened styles came to dominate the industry.

Giacomo took us into his winery. Though small, it gleamed with the newest stainless steel tanks, presses, filters, and other equipment. Several workers scurried around, carrying hoses, climbing ladders to the tops of tanks, and wrestling with machines. Giacomo had me taste some of the sweet musts that were in fermentation. An experienced enologist, he knew what to look for. I have trained myself to assess finished wine. The samples tasted like fresh, delicious grape juice. He waved us over to a large conical wooden fermentation vat. A door had been cut into it. He opened it as if he were Ali Baba. "Let's go down and taste my perpetuo." A metal spiral stairway led to an underground cellar.

From Mozia to Woodhouse to Ingham to Donna Franca: this was the path we followed that day in September 2010 that ended with being left alone in Giacomo's nursery of perpetual wines. I went from barrel to barrel, from spigot to spigot, draining amber liquid into a glass, noting its color, smell, and taste, and then, with the piece of chalk that Giacomo had tossed me, scribbling my impressions on the heads of each big barrel. The samples I liked best were the palest, pure tan without even a tint of chocolate brown. They had clean toasted hazelnut and citrus smells and were thick and luscious in the mouth but finished dry with a decisive crisp, clean bitterness, the way a gulp of lager beer ends. I preferred less those samples that were browner, smelled burned or leathery, and were coarse in the mouth. After about fifteen minutes, Giacomo returned. He silently stood in the background waiting for me to finish, all the while reading what I had written. I turned to him. He crossed his arms and cocked his head with his hand supporting his chin. I pointed at two barrels. "I like these two the most." Giacomo smiled and replied, "They are the same wine but in two different barrels, 100 percent Grillo from Mozia from the 1996 vintage, a spectacular vintage. The wines that I will make from that vineyard we visited in Spagnola will be like these wines from Mozia. They will be unctuous and soft like these." I also liked two other samples from Mozia, from the 1998 and 2003 vintages. He called these three *ragazzini*, "young guys." The implication was that they needed twenty years or more to become dons, or mature men.

Two such dons, a 1937 and a 1970 from Petrosino, a township along the coast to the south between Marsala and Mazara del Vallo, were darker, with burned Indian spice and leather smells. They were also drier and more bitter in the mouth. The Marsala trade calls such vintage wines *lieviti* (the plural of *lievito*). They are precious collectibles. Small amounts of various lieviti are pulled and blended into less-special wines. The older wines impart character and wisdom to the younger ones. What is removed from each barrel of lievito may be topped up with wine from the same year, if available, in which case it remains a lievito. Alternately, the winemaker may top up the lievito with a younger wine, sending it in the direction of a vino perpetuo. Giacomo prefers older vini perpetui that are composed of the wines of numerous vintages. He has those in his cellar too.

From 1989 to 1994 he had made the wines from the grapes grown in the old vineyards of Mozia for the Whitaker Foundation, which owns the island. After this period, the foundation decided to uproot the relatively unproductive old Grillo vines trained in *alberello* in order to set up a more productive and systematic modern vineyard. Giacomo Tachis selected budwood from these vines. It was grafted onto modern rootstocks and then replanted. After two or three years the young vines were trained on wires in rows. The key changes were the move away from alberello, the use of different rootstocks, and, most important, the reduced vine age. These changes disturbed Ansaldi. Subsequently the foundation sold its grapes to Tasca d'Almerita, which makes and markets a dry, fruity Grillo white wine called Mozia. Tasca d'Almerita's Mozia wines are universes away from the vintage Mozia Grillos in Ansaldi's nursery.

He now buys the next-best thing to those earlier grapes from Mozia: the grapes from the old Grillo vineyard overlooking Mozia that we had visited at the start of our day. One day their wines will taste like the samples I preferred in his winery, with flavors recalling those of the local wine that existed before the time of Woodhouse, a wine that is truly Sicilian. Through the medium of flavor, Giacomo is traveling back to build a new future for Sicilian wine.

5

THE GEOGRAPHY OF SICILY

Sicily is a triangular island at the toe of the boot-shaped Italy. The largest island in the Mediterranean Sea, it is about one-third of the size of Ireland and roughly the same size as Vermont. Only very detailed maps of the area include the small islands that surround it. It is bounded by the Tyrrhenian Sea to its north, the Ionian Sea to its east, and the Mediterranean Sea to its south and west. Due to its size, insularity, and geographic diversity, Sicily has been called the little continent in the center of the Mediterranean. It is the most populous island in the Mediterranean, home to about five million people. Sicilians live principally along the coastline, where much of the commercial activity and tourism occur. Agriculture is widespread and is Sicily's most important industry.

Sicily has a varied topography. About 15 percent of its surface is flat, 60 percent hilly, and 25 percent mountainous. The average elevation is just over five hundred meters (1,640 feet) above sea level. Of the roughly 116,000 hectares (286,642 acres) of vineyards across the island, approximately 30 percent are in flat areas, 65 percent in hilly areas, and 5 percent in mountainous areas. Flat areas are primarily associated with the narrow band of plains that hug the northern coastline, the wider coastal plain in western Sicily extending from the city of Trapani to that of Sciacca, the plain surrounding the southern coastal city of Gela, and a substantial circular area called the Plain of Catania southwest of that city. An expansive swath of rolling hills and low mountains extends from Castellammare, a port halfway along the northwestern coastline between Palermo and Trapani, southeast to Agrigento and then east to Ragusa. Sicily's rivers are generally small, sluggish, and not navigable. The ones that flow all year are useful for irrigation.

Most of Sicily's mountains are in the north, particularly the northeast. The highest mountain in Sicily (and in all of Italy south of the Alps) is Mount Etna, an active volcano. It rises to 3,350 meters (10,991 feet), changing its height by as much as a few meters following eruptions. The Apennine-Maghrebian chain, an extension of the mountains of northern Tunisia and Algeria, comprises clusters of mountain ranges: the Nebrodi to the north of Etna; running west, the Madonie; then small ranges surrounding Palermo; then outcroppings culminating in San Vito lo Capo, a neck of rugged land at Sicily's extreme northwest; and finally the Egadi Islands, off the coast of the city of Trapani. Pizzo Carbonara, reaching 1,979 meters (6,493 feet), is the highest peak in the Madonic Range and the second-highest peak in Sicily, after Etna. The highest mountain in the Nebrodi Range is Mount Soro, at 1,847 meters (6,060 feet). There are also outcroppings of mountains in west-central Sicily called the Sicani. Rocca Busambra, at 1,613 meters (5,293 feet), is the highest among the peaks scattered throughout this range. In the northeast apex of Sicily are the Peloritani Mountains, an extension of the Calabrian Arc on the other side of the Strait of Messina. The Peloritani's highest peak is Montagna Grande, at 1,374 meters (4,508 feet). In Sicily's southeastern corner are the low-lying Hyblaean Mountains, whose Monte Lauro reaches 986 meters (3,176 feet).

Soils are composed of varying proportions of parent rock eroded in place; material transported by gravity, wind, water, or glacial activity; and organic material deposited in place or similarly transported. Soils cover parent rock. Red granites, schist, and other types of igneous and metamorphic rocks characterize the parent rock of the Peloritani Mountains. The parent rock of Etna is volcanic lava. While the parent rock of the Peloritani is slightly acidic, that of Etna is neutral. All other Sicilian parent rock is basic, containing calcium carbonate. Some soils, such as those at Ficuzza in the hills south of Palermo or at Tindari on the Sicilian coast south of the Aeolian Islands, are acidic, due to above-average precipitation. Uplifted sedimentary rocks, principally sandstones, characterize the higher elevations of the Nebrodi. At lower elevations, shaly clays predominate. In the Madonie, the Sicani, and the mountainous areas extending from Palermo to the Egadi Islands, the rocks are principally sedimentary and feature sandstone and calcareous stones. On the western shore the underlying rock is also sedimentary, composed of broken fragments of minerals, rock, and marine fossils cemented together with calcareous clay. Moving east from the town of Menfi, sand replaces clay as the matrix of this conglomerate rock. Below a line running roughly from Sciacca to the western edge of the Plain of Catania, minerals and mineral salts, the evaporative residue of ancient lagoons, are found in the rocks and soils. The heart of this area is a triangle with apexes at the cities of Sciacca, Enna, and Syracuse. Patches of soil located roughly in this triangle have particularly high levels of mineral salts, mixed with calcareous clay, sand, silt, and organic matter. The southeast corner of Sicily, bounded by the line between the cities of Gela and Catania, has calcareous soil derived from the parent rock, a hard, rugged limestone that frequently protrudes above the soil. Within this area, the Hyblaean Mountains—including an extinct volcano, Mount Lauro, which predates

Etna—are the apex from which strands of volcanic rock extend down to the Ionian and Mediterranean coastal areas.

Until 1900 the provinces of Enna, Agrigento, Caltanissetta, Ragusa, and Siracusa were the world's most important sources of sulfur. Besides its many industrial applications, sulfur has been used for dusting vines to thwart Sicily's most persistent fungus infection, powdery mildew, since the mid-nineteenth century. Gypsum (calcium sulfate dihydrate), a soft sulfate mineral, has also been mined in the provinces of Caltanissetta and Agrigento. Pre-twentieth-century winemakers added it to grapes, must, and wine to enhance their wine's acidity. The same two provinces have substantial deposits of rock salt (sodium chloride). The Salso ("Salty") River runs north to south through the center of this area. In addition, according to Franco Giacosa, one of Sicily's most experienced enologists, there is so much sodium chloride in the soils around Pachino just inland from Cape Passero that he can taste it in the wine.

Generally, the best soils for vines are a mix of particles of different sizes. Clay has the smallest particle size, followed by silt, sand, and stones. Red wine grapes benefit from a substantial amount of clay in the soil because its particle size is ideal for allowing the uptake of nutrients and water by tiny rootlets, though too much of it can suffocate them. This better nutrient delivery helps the grape skins develop polyphenolic compounds, which account for wine color, aroma, and texture. The minerals and micronutrients in sand and stones, even small ones, are inaccessible to vine rootlets. Soils with high compositions of sand and stones and low concentrations of clay tend to be nutrient poor. Water drains too quickly from them for rootlets to absorb. Such soils make paler and more delicate red and white wines. Silt has neither the nutritive-delivery and water-retaining characteristics of clay nor the low-vigor and fast-draining characteristics of sand. A mix of sand and clay with a low proportion of silt is generally optimum for vines. Climate, exposition, soil depth, and vine and rootstock variety determine the best proportions.

As mentioned above, one chemical constituent quite common in Sicilian soil is calcium carbonate. Only in the northeast corner and on some volcanic islands are calcareous soils absent. All of Sicily except for much of this corner was, millions of years ago, under water. Over vast periods of time the skeletons and shells of marine organisms accumulated on the seafloor, decomposing and releasing calcium carbonate, which formed into sedimentary rocks of varying hardness and friability. Eventually calcium carbonate–rich rocks and particles are pushed to the surface or exposed by other means. Calcium carbonate offers the soil few nutrients but enhances its water-holding capacity. Soils with calcium carbonate are white or pastel and reflect light. Thus they are cooler than darker soils. Vines growing in moist, cool, low-nutrient soils such as these tend to produce wines that are paler, more aromatic, higher in acidity, and lower in tannin. Because these are positive characteristics for most white wines, white vine grape varieties benefit from being planted in calcareous soils. With respect to red wines, Nero d'Avola in particular produces fresher, more elegant styles of wine when its vines are grown in calcareous soils. In some areas, rains have progressively leached calcium carbonate from the limestone, leaving an iron oxide residue that tints the topsoil red. This soil is called *terra rossa* and is quite common in the western coastal area and in Vittoria in the southeast.

Volcanic soil is found on Etna, the Hyblaean Mountains, the Aeolian Archipelago, and the island of Pantelleria. Soil particle size ranges from dust to rocks. Sand usually predominates. Rock types include pumice (lightweight volcanic rock), smaller particles of black volcanic rock (lapilli, the plural of *lapillus*), and tuff (hardened volcanic ash). Volcanic soils are rich in micronutrients but poor in the macronutrients nitrogen and phosphate. They are often rich in potassium. When eruptions cause pyroclastic flows, as has been the case on Etna, the deposited volcanic ash is chemically transformed into an intermediate compound, allophane. This amorphous clay mineral transforms ash—much more rapidly than lava—into nutrient-rich soil. Erosion and the action of bacteria, fungi, and larger organisms over hundreds of years help to make many of these soils cultivable, unleashing their high nutrient capacity. Due to their fiery origin, volcanic rocks and soils are usually very porous, allowing vine roots to easily exploit what they have to offer. They are largely inhospitable to phylloxera lice, which prefer oxygen-deficient soils such as clay. Volcanic soils contain a lot of oxygen. It is not uncommon to see vines on their own roots in Sicily's volcanic soils. Like clay soils, volcanic soils have the nutrient capacity to allow for a high degree of physiologic development in the skins of grapes. This maybe one reason why Nerello Mascalese excels on the volcanic soils of Etna and not in most other places.

Another exceptional soil derives from eroded schist. Schist is a foliated metamorphic rock. It can store water between foliations. Vine rootlets enter and split the layers while searching for water. Depending on its degrees of friability, hardness, and composition, schist can quickly decompose into sand, silt, or clay. The resulting soil is in a continuing evolution from rock to smaller particles. While loose sedimentary and volcanic soils are commonplace in Sicily, schistose soils are rare. There are some shaly schists in the Nebrodi. The Peloritani contain a complex mix of calc-schists and paragneiss, an even harder foliated rock, both derived from metamorphic action on sedimentary rocks. There are also some areas of metamorphic rock originally formed from igneous rock. Geologically speaking, the Peloritani is a world apart from the rest of Sicily. It would be a fascinating place to plant vineyards for fine wine. The only producer that I know of in this area is Palari. Its vineyards perch on the edge of these mountains overlooking the Ionian Sea. Palari is one of the best producers of red wine on the island, if not the best.

Though many connoisseurs believe that the impact of minerals from the soil, some of them micronutrients, is perceivable in the flavors of wine, such impact is subtle. Climate, however, has an obvious impact on the growth of vines and hence ultimately the flavor of wine. Vines need heat for photosynthesis to occur. Many locations on Earth between 30° and 50° latitude are suitable. Sicily is on the warmer end of this band, between 36° and 38° latitude. It is surrounded by warm waters and well protected by mountain ranges in France, Spain, and Portugal from strong storms coming off the Atlantic. Sicilian farmers can avoid excessive heat by planting their vineyards at the many high-altitude sites on the island. Sicily has some of the highest vineyards in the world. On Etna I have visited a vineyard at thirteen hundred meters (4,265 feet). At such high elevations, only with good viticulture and favorable weather can vines ripen their grapes. Across Sicily the harvest period spans more than one hundred days, which may be the longest of any region on the planet. Chardonnay, for example, is harvested as early as mid-July at Menfi. On Etna the harvest for the same variety can occur as late as November.

Sicily has a subtropical Mediterranean climate characterized by hot, dry summers and cool, rainy winters. During the winter the temperature rarely drops below freezing. During the summer the average monthly temperature is about 22°C (72°F). However, midday and afternoon temperatures over 38°C (100°F) are not uncommon. The Mediterranean, a large, warm sea, keeps the climate relatively temperate. The mean average February sea temperature at Palermo and Catania is 14°C. This makes frost virtually impossible in their coastal areas. The average August temperatures of the sea at these cities are 26°C and 25°C respectively. The coastal areas of Sicily also benefit from off-shore daytime breezes that lower the ambient temperature. Interior valleys have the highest afternoon temperatures. The warmest areas on average are the Plains of Catania and the flat areas along the western, southern, and southeastern coastlines. Only the center of the island has a continental climate.

Grapes for white wines benefit greatly from cool temperatures and shading, which preserve aromatic precursor compounds in the skins. During fermentation, the enzymatic activity of yeast transforms these compounds, activating their scent potential. One of the reasons why Sauvignon Blanc is not generally successful in Sicily is that the combination of heat and light is too great to preserve its characteristic vegetal smell. Cool temperatures, particularly at harvest time, result in higher levels of wine acidity. Just as high-acid foods like citrus fruits and tomatoes have longer shelf lives than low-acid ones like bananas and melons, so high-acid wines resist oxidation, a principal agent of degradation, better than low-acid ones. The foreign wine merchants of the eighteenth and nineteenth centuries valued Etna wines because the high-elevation vineyards there preserved grape acids, producing wines that were stable for transport. Nero d'Avola varietal wines have been durable ambassadors for Sicilian wine because of their natural high acidity.

The production of fine red wines with deep color and fine-textured but substantial astringent tannins depends on the full ripening of skins that are exposed, but not overexposed, to direct sunlight. In the final weeks of ripening, the right balance of heat and light is essential. If the growing season is too hot, grapes may achieve their optimal sugar levels without their skin ripening. If there is both too much heat and too much light, the skins can burn. If the growing season is too cool, the immature skins give too much bitterness and coarse astringency to the resulting pale red wines, whose fruit aromas are vegetal rather than berry nuanced. Their alcohol is also too low and acidity too high.

Another factor affecting viticulture is the temperature variation between day and night. Cool nighttime temperatures help ripened grapes retain acidity. They are best harvested in the morning, when their pulp and skin temperature are lowest. This can mean a slower and more controlled start to fermentation, particularly important for white wine, whose aroma intensity and complexity high-temperature fermentation destroys. Two principal factors in Sicily determine diurnal temperature range: elevation and distance from the Mediterranean Sea. For example, Tasca d'Almerita's meteorological data for July to August 2009 shows a 12.5°C (22.5°F) diurnal temperature variation for Mozia, a low-lying coastal island just north of Marsala, while for Regaleali, in the center of the island, the variation was 17.1°C (30.8°F). The vineyards of Regaleali are between 400 and 750 meters (1,312 and 2,461 feet) above sea level, avoiding the extreme heat of the inland valleys and the insufficient heat at higher elevations. Its inland location and elevation give it both a low temperature for viticulture (compared to most other vineyard areas in Sicily) and an unusually high diurnal temperature variation. This provides the best growing environment for most white vine varieties, which can, under these conditions, be harvested in the morning at very cool temperatures and then vinified into wines with strong, fresh aromas and high acidity. A higher-elevation site near a large body of water, such as on Etna facing the Ionian Sea, has smaller temperature swings because of the capacity of the water to store heat. The cloud cover more common at higher elevations also reduces diurnal temperature differences at such sites.

At lower elevations in Sicily, a northerly exposure is usually better than a southern one and an eastern exposure is usually better than a western one (particularly for sun-sensitive grape varieties such as Sauvignon Blanc, Pinot Gris, and Pinot Noir). Northerly exposures expose vines less to the dangerous combination of high heat and brilliant sunshine that can scorch leaves and grape skins. And at all elevations except the highest ones, northern exposures in Sicily provide enough warmth and light for ripening. Eastern exposures result in more-efficient photosynthesis. This is mostly because the morning sun warms up the soil earlier, allowing for an earlier onset of photosynthesis. (This early daylight also evaporates moisture that rises from the soil, reducing the risk of mold.) In a western exposure, photosynthesis rates in the morning are lower, because soil is cooler due to indirect light exposure. A secondary factor is the air's concentration of CO_2, which the vine's respiration at night produces and which remains close to the topsoil in the cool morning. The photosynthetic process needs this ambient gas. By the evening and at warmer temperatures, less of it is available to the vines.

In Sicily the selection of exposure must also take wind into account. At high altitudes, winds have no topographic obstructions and can move over local weather patterns. The steam always blows away from the summit of Mount Etna in a southeasterly to easterly direction. This indicates that at about 3,000 meters (9,843 feet) in elevation, the prevailing winds are northwesterly (*maestrale*) to westerly (*ponente*). At lower elevations, however, local weather patterns, topographic features, and air that rises or falls due to ambient temperature conditions greatly affect winds. Local weather patterns can change wind patterns from day to day, if not hour to hour. When winds blow over seas, they pick up humidity. As they hit land and move up to the higher and cooler elevations associated with hills and mountains, the cloud vapor they carry condenses into rain. Winds drop the most rain at the highest elevations. When they move from higher elevations to lower ones, the clouds associated with them largely disappear, leaving drier and sunnier conditions on the hills' and mountains' leeward side. During afternoons of the growing period, warm air rising in the interior draws cool winds off the sea. Because of these winds, it is always cooler at the coastline than several miles inland. At night, cool air descends from higher elevations. Beyond these factors, winds that enter Sicily move like balls careening off the pins in a pinball machine.

The distribution of precipitation in Sicily tells us a lot about the direction of winds. The areas with the highest precipitation are in mountainous areas, particularly along the northeastern and northern coasts. The coastal strip from Catania to Messina is the wettest area in Sicily. This is because the warm wind from the southeast (scirocco) has a great capacity to absorb moisture. Landmasses on either side of the Strait of Messina · channel and intensify the power of the scirocco. Where land is unprotected by mountains and hills, this wind pummels the coastline with hot, humid wind and rain. Along the northern coast, the cooler maestrale bears moisture from the Mediterranean. During the winter, the storms coming off the Atlantic find their way to and rain on the northern coastline of Sicily. Some make it over the Nebrodi and rain on the north-facing slopes of Etna. Along the western coastline, the winds come mostly from the west. These are drier, with low precipitation rates. Along the southern coastline, protected from the maestrale by northern mountains, there is very little rain. Most of the winds that reach it come from the Sahara Desert. Along the southeast coastline there is more precipitation. The scirocco drops its rain there, and on the Hyblaean Mountains. In the interior of the island, winds concentrate in and careen through valleys, hit and deflect off mountains. The pinball analogy fits perfectly here.

Winds come from all directions, and each has its name, derived from thousands of years of sailing on the Mediterranean. By far the wind that Sicilians talk about the most is the scirocco. If mountains protect a location from it, as they do Palermo to the south, the winds there are hot and dry. On a shoreline in an unprotected spot such as Messina, the winds are hot and humid. In the spring, the scirocco can dry out and destroy buds and knock off young green shoots. Before harvest, the high heat and wind can stop the maturation of the fruit and dry the grapes on the vine.

From May to September it rarely rains in Sicily. About three-quarters of the island is semiarid, receiving between three and five hundred millimeters (twelve to twenty inches) of rain per year. Its average annual precipitation is about 610 millimeters (twenty-four inches). Local annual precipitation averages vary. At Zafferana Etnea, facing the Ionian on the eastern slopes of Etna, the annual precipitation is 1,192 millimeters (forty-seven inches). A triangle with apexes at Catania, Messina, and Cefalù encloses Sicily's high-rainfall area. The Plain of Catania, west of the city of Catania, is a dry spot, with an average annual rainfall of 350 millimeters (fourteen inches). Conditions vary west of Cefalù. In the mountains south of Palermo, rainfalls can be more than nine hundred millimeters (thirty-five inches). Low spots in the interior can have averages as low as 450 millimeters (eighteen inches), the same as along the western coast. Along the south-western coastline the average is four hundred millimeters (twelve inches) per year. Gela and the plain surrounding it register 350 millimeters (fourteen inches) per year. Dry conditions extend to Capo Passero at the southeastern corner of Sicily. Contrarily, in the high areas of the Hyblaean Mountains, precipitation rates average 750 millimeters (thirty inches).

Though Sicily has few rivers that can supply water for irrigation, it is blessed with an abundance of underground water reserves. This is particularly true in the northern mountains and the southeast corner of the island. Underground water can be the source for streams. It can be pumped out of the ground for irrigation. It can rise from the subsoil to the topsoil as humidity, providing moisture to rootlets. In the center of the island, where there is the least rainfall, water availability varies according to location. While there is underground water at some volcanic sites, such as Etna, the Hyblaean mountains, and Salina, at others, such as Pantelleria, there are few or no such reserves.

Though too much humidity, particularly in the absence of wind and the presence of shade, encourages fungus growth on vines, ambient humidity is an important source of water for vines growing in semiarid conditions. During the morning and into the day, warming surface temperatures pull humidity from the subsoil into the topsoil and into the vine canopy. This humidity is a source of water to the vine. It also buffers extremes of temperature. During the day, offshore winds can blow humidity onto vineyards. At night, cooler temperatures condense that humidity into dew that coats the vines and the soil. The soil absorbs this moisture and provides it to rootlets. Sea-air dew may account for the taste of salinity in coastal wines, particularly white wines.

Sicily is blessed with a long, warm, dry growing season. Though periods of heat and drought can slow the maturation of grapes, it resumes the normal pace when cool weather returns. Consumers should pay attention to vintages when buying wine made from grapes grown at high elevations, where there is marginal heat available for maturation. The grapes for Etna wines are grown at such places. Weather conditions are crucial during the final ripening period, which occurs at the very end of the growing season, as late as November. Periods of rain and cold can set in and downgrade the quality of the harvest significantly. It is difficult to make generalizations about weather patterns because weather varies all over the island. Sicilian producers look back on the last years of the 1990s and the first years of the 2000s as characterized by unusually dry and hot weather. On the other hand, many consider the middle to the end of the first decade of the twenty-first century to have been cooler and wetter than usual. Like buoys that mark a passage in water, some years mark the passage of seasons for wine growers, such as 2003, which was remarkably hot and dry, and 2009, which was cool and wet. Starting in 2010, however, concern over climate change seems to have abated within the wine community.

In comparison to French winegrowers, who from generation to generation have preserved the understanding of what to plant where, Sicilians are at the beginning of their learning curve of knowing where to plant which varieties. Some areas of Sicily are uncharted territory for the wine producer who wants to uncover new Sicilian flavors. Many areas in Sicily once upon a time knew viticulture but have since lost their vineyards. The experience that created them has evaporated. They need to be rediscovered. Isolated successes hint at what the future could hold. The red wines of the Palari wine estate on the skirts of the Peloritani demonstrate how the eroded metamorphic soils facing east make wine filled with nuance. The wines of Abbazia Santa Anastasia at Cefalù show that northerly exposures on clay soils facing the Tyrrhenian Sea could be a source of fresh yet rich and complex red wines. A winegrower friend dreams of growing Riesling high up in the mountains. Perhaps in that vineyard of dreams he will meet Prince Baucina, who had the same dream and realized it more than a century earlier.

6

VINE VARIETIES

Most consumers learn about emerging wine categories first by vine variety and second by country or region of origin. In a varietal wine, the grapes of one variety predominate: they must be at least 75 percent of the blend in the United States and 85 percent in the European Union. Legal minimums vary among countries and wine categories. Some varieties impart distinct characteristics and become an important factor in determining wine style. Once the legal minimum for varietal labeling has been satisfied, producers may add other varieties into a varietal wine. Varieties are transported around the world until people select, plant, and propagate them. We say that a vine variety is native to a place when it has been living or growing naturally there. The development of a variety depends on recurrent propagation. Successive generations of farmers using an increasingly sophisticated knowledge base to make further selections and propagations of chosen varieties eventually developed the star international varieties such as Chardonnay, Cabernet Sauvignon, Merlot, Syrah, and Riesling.

Wine producers need discerning markets and consumers to motivate them to select vine varieties with the potential to be transformed into quality wine. For example, for many centuries the discerning palates of the English market encouraged the winemakers of Bordeaux to select vine varieties that made more satisfying and stable wines. In cultures without sophisticated internal or foreign markets, varietal selection is principally motivated by yield (the higher the better), ease of cultivation, effective land use, manpower issues (including coordinating the timing of harvests), and maximum utility—for example, whether a grape variety can be eaten, cooked, or transformed into raisins, wine, or brandy. Save for Marsala, a wine conceived by English merchants for the British market in the late eighteenth and early nineteenth centuries, Sicily's wines never had discriminating consumers until mainland connoisseurs recognized them in the 1990s. As a result, the selection process for quality raw material to make quality wine did not happen in Sicily before the 1980s.

Most researchers believe that Greek settlers from the eighth to the beginning of the second century B.C. brought to Sicily most of the varieties that today are considered native. From then until the nineteenth century, there were few introductions of others, with the notable exceptions of Zibibbo (also called Muscat of Alexandria), which was probably introduced through North Africa during the third century B.C., and Malvasia, which Venetian traders perhaps brought from Greece at the end of the sixteenth century A.D. In the nineteenth century Sicily became deeply invested in the international wine trade, and various foreign merchants and sophisticated wine producers encouraged the importation and planting of Grenache, Merlot, Cabernet Sauvignon, and other varieties. They were, however, planted on a very limited scale. Meanwhile, the names and identities of varieties long resident in Sicily remained unknown beyond Sicilian wine merchants, academics, and horticulturalists. Several factors made it difficult for even the wine trade to understand the differences among these varieties. Natives were planted in mixed vineyards. Varieties were harvested and vinified together. Characteristics that might appear after fermentation were buried within wine blends and by maturation flavors. A lack of asepsis in wineries allowed microbial attacks to distort wine character. Almost all Sicilian wine was sold within and beyond Sicily as anonymous bulk wine.

The phylloxera infestation that occurred in the late 1800s and early 1900s led to a gradual replantation of Sicily's vineyards. Substitutions reduced the number of varieties on the island: in many instances, easier-to-grow and higher-yielding varieties took the place of harder-to-grow and lower-yielding ones. Many varieties of the latter type were more suitable for high-quality wine production. They were largely anonymous, the vine farmers' secret weapons used in small doses to improve the color, smell, and structure of the resulting wines. During and after the phylloxera infestation, many of these varieties went out of circulation and were lost. Bruno Fina, who was responsible for managing microvinifications at the Istituto Regionale della Vite e del Vino (IRVV, "Regional Institute of Vine and Wine") from 1991 to 2001, noted the dominance of a few varietal populations in Sicily: "As of 1980, 50 percent of the grapes planted were Catarratto. There was also Inzolia, Grillo, and Trebbiano Toscano. Nero d'Avola was planted largely in Riesi and Pachino. Nerello Mascalese, on the other hand, was planted widely but only achieved good results at Etna."

By the early 1990s the role and importance of varietal identity had become apparent. The IRVV advised the Sicilian wine industry to develop a menu of varieties that would make wines which would appeal to consumers. International consumers were already familiar with international varieties, for the most part selected by the French, such as Chardonnay, Cabernet Sauvignon, Merlot, and Syrah. Diego Planeta, the IRVV's president during this period, and Giacomo Tachis, its consulting enologist, understood that international varieties that produced exceptional wine and adapted well to the Sicilian climate would be the best initial adoptions. Through these varieties, consumers could begin to recognize the word *Sicily* on wine labels and associate it with another word, *quality*. Once Sicilian wine had established a positive quality association, it would be easier to introduce native Sicilian varieties to the market.

The IRVV's extensive work studying the potential of native and foreign varieties provided Sicilian wine producers with the expertise they needed to enter the varietal wine market. In 1984 and 1985 the IRVV began experimental plantings of Chardonnay, Sauvignon Blanc, Cabernet Sauvignon, Merlot, Syrah, and Petit Verdot, which would form the basis of its studies during the 1990s. By 1991 producers were using these grapes to make varietal wines. At the same time, the IRVV also studied how varietal wines could best complement one another in blends.

By 2005 international consumer interest was shifting from international varieties toward native ones. A research facility at Marsala, the Centro Innovazione Filiera Vitivinicola di Marsala ("Center of Innovation in the Field of Viticulture and Vinification of Marsala"), is recovering ancient varieties (*reliquie,* the plural of *reliquia*) from near extinction. If microvinifications of certain varieties reveal potential, the vine wood will be released to commercial nurseries for propagation and sale to winegrowers. These new-old varieties would enhance Sicily's unique vinous identity.

As of 2011, white varieties occupy about 64 percent of the vineyards in Sicily. Largely due to the historic importance of the Marsala industry, most of these vineyards are in the west, particularly in Trapani, Agrigento, and Palermo. For this reason, the listing below begins with white varieties. The order of both red and white varieties reflects the prevalence of their use and my estimation of their importance to the Sicilian wine industry. After discussing each variety, I recommend well-made varietal wines so that readers can taste what the text says. You can find more examples in the wine producer profiles in chapters 11, 12, and 13.

WHITE VARIETIES
CATARRATTO

Francisco Cupani first mentions *Catarrattu vrancu* in his compendium of Sicilian native varieties, *Hortus Catholicus,* published in 1696.[1] Domenico Sestini in his lectures to the Georgofili Academy in 1812 identified vines planted in the Mascali area near Etna as Catarratto and used the plural, *Catarratti,* when describing the varieties used in Vittoria.[2] In the late nineteenth century the Zucco estate of Henri d'Orleans, Duc d'Aumale, near Partinico made a white wine almost exclusively from Catarratto. Egidio Pollacci, a professor of chemistry from Tuscany, described it as "highly prized."[3]

The Italian National Catalogue recognizes Catarratto Comune and Catarratto Lucido as distinct varieties. However, research indicates that although they may have phenotypic differences, genetically they are identical. Catarratto Extralucido is another biotype. As the name indicates, Catarratto Comune is the most common type. There is about four times as much Comune as Lucido and Extralucido. Comune has the highest sugar content and lowest acidity of the three biotypes. This profile makes it well suited to the production of Marsala. Its surface area is now in steep decline, though Giuseppe Tasca of Tasca d'Almerita values it for its "elegance." The grape skins have a dusty look.

In expansion is the more highly prized Lucido. This type has small berries with less bloom coating (*lucido* means "glossy"). It produces wines that are lower in alcohol and higher in acidity than those made with Comune. When Comune and Lucido are planted in the same location, Lucido ripens a week or two later than Comune. Extralucido ripens another one to two weeks later than Lucido. Extralucido, strongly associated with the area around the town of Alcamo, has the lowest sugar and the highest acidity of the various Catarratto biotypes. If the berries are not fully ripe, the wines can be very bitter. It also produces wines with the most aroma. Its berries appear to have no bloom whatsoever.

The Catarratto family of biotypes accounts for 34 percent of all Sicilian wine vineyards, or approximately thirty-eight thousand hectares (93,900 acres). It is second only to the Trebbiano group in surface area of white wine grapes planted throughout Italy. Catarratto, though it can provide high yields, is not as consistent a producer as Trebbiano. Nearly all Catarratto is planted in three provinces: Trapani (which accounts for more than 75 percent), Palermo, and Agrigento. There were increased plantings of Catarratto after the 1930s because it had more consistent production and higher yields than Grillo, which it largely replaced for Marsala production. Until the 1980s, much Catarratto wine was also sold for vermouth production. Before the twentieth century, it was planted in the hills and on the high plains, not along the coastline. Later it was planted there too. Today it predominates in the hilly areas in the interior of Trapani, particularly around the towns of Salemi and Alcamo. It is commonly planted at about 250 meters (820 feet), though plantings exist at more than one thousand meters (3,281 feet), such as at Valledolmo in the province of Palermo.

The wine's color is pale straw yellow with green tints. It smells mildly fruity and has notes of fresh straw. Compared to other white varieties, Catarratto makes wine with moderate alcohol levels and high acidity. The wine has a bitterness that is slight but noticeable, particularly at the back of the palate. This induces winemakers to blend in other varieties with a softer character. Inzolia is Catarratto's traditional blending partner. When Catarratto is grown in the vicinity of the sea, its varietal wines tend to oxidize despite their natural high acidity. Grapes from high elevations in the interior contain even higher acidity. Catarratto is rarely fermented or matured in new-oak barrels.

Recommended producers and their wines (in italics):

Brugnano *Lunario*
Caruso & Minini *Isula*
Castellucci Miano *Miano*
Castellucci Miano *Shiarà*
Porta del Vento
Rapitalà *Casalj*
Viticultori Associati Canicattì *Aquilae*

INZOLIA (INSOLIA)

Inzolia is a very old native variety. Cupani lists it in his 1696 compendium along with *Inzolia impiriali* and *Inzolia di Napuli.*[4] Sestini mentioned *Inzolia vranca.* He asserted that *Inzolia vranca* is the same variety as Tuscany's San Colombano, still eaten in Tuscany and dried for Vin Santo production. He also suggested that Sicilians might have corrupted the name of the variety Irziola, mentioned by Pliny the Elder, to *Inzolia.*[5] Before powdery mildew (oidium) attacked in the mid-nineteenth century, it was the variety most planted throughout the island and the most important grape in the Marsala wine blend. In Tuscany the same variety is called Ansonica. Sometimes Sicilians use this name too. Inzolia wine has a tendency to oxidize, which makes it useful as a base for Marsala. It is used not only for wine production but also as a table grape. By surface area it is now third in Sicily behind Catarratto and Nero d'Avola, occupying about sixty-eight hundred hectares (16,803 acres), or 6 percent of Sicilian vineyards. More than 85 percent of it is planted in the provinces of Trapani and Agrigento. Less than 10 percent is in the province of Palermo. Despite this, producers in Palermo consider Inzolia their premier native white variety. One of the first prestige wines of Sicily was Duca di Salaparuta's Inzolia-dominated Colombo Platino. The first vintage was the 1957. It became 100 percent Inzolia in 1980. The variety came into vogue for several years in the late 1990s, when its richness and spiciness were promoted as similar to those of Sauvignon Blanc. Because the variety is very productive, planting it in low-fertility soils lowers yields and improves quality. Hill sites generally provide the best expositions. Inzolia's thin skin makes it highly susceptible to powdery mildew, an almost ever-present problem given the dry and windy conditions common to most of Sicily. The grapes are large. The sun can easily burn and break their skins. During the mid-1980s, the installation of better presses and refrigeration in many Sicilian wineries helped produce fresher wines. Inzolia wines have a light straw color. Their nose is spicy, slightly floral, but otherwise difficult to describe. Alcohol levels are moderate and acidity tends to be low. According to Carmelo Morgante at Morgante in the Agrigento area, a traditional practice was to add Inzolia to high-acid musts to reduce acidity and thereby encourage malolactic fermentation. Enzo Cambria of Cottanera at Etna confirmed that Inzolia was also added to red grapes before vinification for this purpose. Marc de Grazia noted its presence in some of the oldest vineyards on Etna. Inzolia has played a role in Nero d'Avola and Nerello Mascalese wines similar to that of Marsanne in the Hermitage Rouge blend or Viognier in the Côte Rôtie blend. Historically in the production of white wines, it was blended with Catarratto. Inzolia provided the alcohol, Catarratto the acidity. When Carlo Casavecchia was the general manager of Duca di Salaparuta in the late 1990s and early 2000s, he found the best Inzolia along the shores of Lake Arancio at Sambuca di Sicilia and at Ribera, a town to the southeast of the lake, both in the province of Agrigento. Pierpaolo Messina, the manager of Marabino, described Inzolia as incompatible with the growing conditions at Pachino in Sicily's southeastern corner. The warm climate, high humidity, high-alkaline soils, and negligible day-to-night temperature differences run counter to what the variety needs. Planting at higher altitudes—such as seven hundred meters (2,297 feet), perhaps the highest, for Cusumano's Cubìa—increases wine aromas and acidity.

Recommended producers and their wines:

> Cantine Barbera
> Caruso & Minini *Terre di Giumara*
> Cusumano *Cubìa*
> Donnafugata *Vigna di Gabri*
> Fazio

TREBBIANO TOSCANO

Trebbiano Toscano, native to Tuscany, is the fourth-most-planted variety in Sicily. It is the most-planted white wine grape in Italy. This high-volume producer of low-alcohol, high-acid wine became popular in Sicily during the 1970s. Its thick, tough skin endows it with good disease resistance. As of 2011 there were about fifty-four hundred hectares (13,344 acres), mostly in Trapani, making up about 5 percent of Sicilian vineyards. Other varieties are increasingly replacing this one. Producers rarely use it for quality wine.

GRILLO

Since the start of the 2000s the improving quality of Grillo wines has encouraged both the trade and wine critics alike. Grillo vineyards occupy about six thousand hectares (14,826 acres), about 5.5 percent, of Sicily's vineyard acreage. Most is planted in the province of Trapani. From 2000 to 2012 Grillo spread to other areas in Sicily. Though the variety has been believed to have been brought from Apulia, DNA studies indicate that it is a spontaneous crossing of Zibibbo and Catarratto. Grillo, Catarratto, and Inzolia make up the base wine of Marsala. In the 1870s, Grillo was first described in the Marsala area.

It became widespread thereafter in the vicinity, where the soils are dry and sandy. These conditions help reduce Grillo's high vigor. Notable spots where Grillo has produced excellent wine are the coastal contradas of Birgi and Spagnola just north of Marsala and the Triglia Scaletta contrada in the town of Petrosino between Marsala and Mazara del Vallo. Joseph Whitaker, who took over the Benjamin Ingham Marsala company after Ingham's death in 1861, planted it exclusively on the small island of Mozia, offshore from contrada Birgi. This island became a cru for Grillo. In the late nineteenth century, Grillo was the preferred grape variety for making top-quality Marsala and was planted throughout western Sicily. After the phylloxera infestation, winegrowers in western Sicily largely replanted their vineyards with it. As of 1930 it accounted for 65 percent of the surface of Trapani's vineyards, its highest spread. But erratic fruit set at harvest and the resulting inconsistent yields reduced interest in Grillo. Marco De Bartoli brought attention back to the variety in the 1980s. He recognized its role in producing top-quality Marsala. In 1984 and 1985 he began cold-fermenting Grillo, making what may have been the first modern Grillo varietal wine. He later released it with the name Grappoli del Grillo. By 2000, however, Grillo accounted for only 3 percent of Trapani vineyards. West of Monreale, Salemi, and Castelvetrano, the variety was rare until recently. But new vineyards have been planted, even on Sicily's east coast. The selective propagation of biotypes has largely solved Grillo's problems at flowering. Along the coast, sandy soils suit the variety best. The low-nutrient and dry soil there reduces yield, thereby increasing concentrations of flavor and alcohol. The grapes' thick skins protect them from the sun, wind, and wind-born salt. Late-harvested coastal Grillo wines can be a distinctive gold that turns amber with time. They have a light nose of citrus fruits, apple, and almonds. Wine texture is solid, by virtue of high glycerin content. The taste is slightly astringent and salty in the mouth. These wines' acidity remains average, yet their alcohol levels can reach 18 percent. Alberello-grown, late-harvested coastal Grillo provided the backbone for quality Marsala. Exposed to oxygen, its wine becomes golden amber and develops a nutty smell, ideal for the production of Marsala. If harvested early, however, Grillo can make a light, anonymous wine. Grillo grown at higher altitudes and in cooler soils, such as those near Salemi, produces more aromatic and sourer but lighter-bodied wines. Duca di Salaparuta uses Grillo from its Risignolo farm at three hundred meters (984 feet) to produce Kados, which is partially fermented in small oak barrels. Some producers make a blend of low- and high-elevation Grillo. Bruno Fina, for example, blends Grillo from the sea-level vineyards of Mozia with the 450-meter-high (1,476-feet-high) vineyards of Salemi. When vinified with selected yeasts at cool temperatures in stainless steel tanks, Grillo can make pleasant, lighter-styled wines. Like De Bartoli with his Grappoli del Grillo, Fondo Antico, a Trapani producer, has been quite successful with the variety. Fondo Antico's vineyards range from 50 to 250 meters (164 to 820 feet) above sea level. These altitudes provide a middle ground between the western-coastal and Salemi styles. The winemaker Lorenza Scianna keeps the acidity of these Fondo Antico wines low to let Grillo's saltiness show. If Grillo is protected from oxygen before, during, and after a cool fermentation, it can acquire grapefruit and passion fruit smells not dissimilar to those in Sauvignon Blanc. Baglio del Cristo di Campobello's 2010 Lalùci tasted in the spring of 2011 showed the Sauvignon Blanc side of Grillo. This estate is in the hills between the cities of Agrigento and Gela on Sicily's southern coast, far from Grillo's home in western Sicily. Grillo's style also varies depending on the vine-training method. Alberello results in concentrated and high-alcohol Grillo wine. Grillo grown on vines trained several feet off the ground and supported by wires makes lighter, more-delicate, and more-refreshing wine. *Grillo's* straightforward pronunciation in English and easy spelling should help it become recognized in foreign countries. That it means "cricket" in Italian does not help it in the home market.

Recommended producers and their wines:

Caruso & Minini *Timpune*
Cristo di Campobello *Lalùci*
De Bartoli *Grappoli del Grillo*
Duca di Salaparuta *Kados*
Fazio
Fondo Antico *Grillo Parlante*
Gorghi Tondi *Kheirè*
Rapitalà

CHARDONNAY

By most accounts, Chardonnay was not planted in Sicily before the 1980s. However, Giuseppe Milazzo brought cuttings of it from Franciacorta, Italy, in 1972 and planted them on his estate at Campobello di Licata. Lucio Tasca planted one hundred Chardonnay vines at the Tasca d'Almerita Regaleali estate in 1981 and then, in 1985, an additional five hectares (twelve acres). Several wineries in collaboration with the IRVV planted experimental Chardonnay plots in 1984 and 1985. In the late 1980s, Tasca d'Almerita came out with Sicily's first varietal Chardonnay. The variety was widely planted on the island during the following decade. Beginning with the 1994 vintage, Planeta produced a ripe, rich, extracted style barrel-fermented in new small barrels, which created the archetype for quality Chardonnay. As of 2011, Chardonnay was the most planted international white variety in Sicily, occupying about five thousand hectares (12,355 acres), more than 4 percent, of Sicily's vineyards. The provinces of Trapani, Agrigento, and Palermo account for 98 percent. In Menfi, Chardonnay is harvested as early as mid-July, while at the Passopisciaro winery on the north face of Mt. Etna, at elevations between nine hundred and one thousand meters (2,953 and 3,281 feet), the harvest can occur as late as November. Cusumano's site south of Palermo at Ficuzza, at seven hundred meters (2,297 feet) and with clay-dominant soil, has produced some excellent Chardonnay wines. Chardonnay planted on calcareous clay soils has an even better track record. Nakone, Fessina's Chardonnay from a vineyard site near Segesta at 650 meters (2,133 feet), expresses the structure often associated with this soil type.

Provided that the grapes are not too ripe, Chardonnay provides an excellent base for sparkling wine. Producers commonly blend Chardonnay with native varieties because its subtle and pleasant smells rarely obscure those of the natives and because its characteristic firm, refreshing taste rounds out the excesses and inadequacies of the palates of native white varietal wines. In 1991, heavy rain during a three-day period at the beginning of the Regaleali Chardonnay harvest set off a botrytis infection. Tasca d'Almerita turned this potential disaster into a public relations coup by releasing a sweet botrytis Chardonnay. The wine became a sensation in Italy. This and Planeta's Chardonnay, two extreme wines, helped publicize the variety's presence in Sicily.

Recommended producers and their wines:

Cristo di Campobello *Laudari*
Cusumano *Jalé*
Disisa
Fessina *Nakone*
Masseria del Feudo *Haermosa*
Passopisciaro *Guardiola Bianco*
Planeta
Principi di Butera
Rapitalà *Grand Cru*
Settesoli *MandraRossa*
Tasca d'Almerita

GRECANICO

There are about forty-six hundred hectares (11,367 acres) of Grecanico planted in Sicily, making up more than 4 percent of the island's vineyards. Most is in the provinces of Agrigento and Trapani, in the towns of Menfi, Mazara del Vallo, Marsala, and Castelvetrano. It is here and there in small amounts in vineyards throughout the island. Marc de Grazia mentioned that he has found it in old vineyards on Etna. Though Grecanico's role in the Sicilian wine industry is becoming more important, it has not been in the limelight. It has long been thought that this variety was native to Sicily. The widely held assumption was that the Greeks brought it two thousand years ago. DNA studies have revealed that the Grecanico Dorato of Sicily is genetically identical to the Garganega variety commonly associated with the Soave area of the Veneto.[6] The Planeta family planted Grecanico in its vineyards at Sambuca di Sicilia in 1985. It sold the grapes to Settesoli, which first brought attention to Grecanico. The Planeta winery has since become a champion of the variety. La Segreta Bianco, Planeta's value-priced white wine, is a blend based on Grecanico. Planeta's Alastro is 100 percent Grecanico, from twenty-five-year-old vines planted at its Ulmo outpost in Sambuca di Sicilia. In 2010 Alessio Planeta told me that the 1995 and 1996 Alastro vintages were still in fine shape. Grecanico vines are very productive. Though Grecanico wine lacks aroma, in the mouth it is firm, elegant, and never top-heavy with alcohol, with moderate to high levels of acidity. As a means of lightening and livening up high-alcohol, low-acid white wines, Grecanico could have an important role in Sicily's future. Wines with more than 14.5 percent alcohol, a common outcome in Sicily, have a difficult time completing malolactic fermentation. Blending in Grecanico, thereby lowering the alcohol level of the wine, allows malolactic fermentation to occur more easily and lowers the impact of sharp malic acid by transforming it into the softer lactic acid.

Recommended producers and their wines:

Planeta *Alastro*
Settesoli *Mandra Rossa*

ZIBIBBO

Zibibbo is an ancient variety. Known internationally as Muscat of Alexandria, it is planted in Mediterranean coastal areas. It probably found its way to other countries from Alexandria in Egypt. The Romans, who occupied Pantelleria from 217 B.C., called it Moscato Romano. What accounts for the playful name *Zibibbo*? The Muslims and Berbers controlled Pantelleria for two centuries. They dried the grapes to produce raisins for eating. *Sabib* (or *zabib*) means "dried grape" in Arabic. Another theory has the variety and its name coming to Pantelleria by way of Cape Zibib (which has many different spellings) on the coast of Tunisia. Sestini noted that Cupani refers to *Zibibu*, but he offered another name for what he identified as Zibibbo, *Zubidia*, of which he claimed, "È questa il nostro Zibibbo" ("This is our Zibibbo").[7] There are about eighteen hundred hectares (4,448 acres) of Zibibbo in Sicily, making up 1.5 percent of its vineyards. The greatest concentration of these plantings is on the island of Pantelleria. Zibibbo's large grapes are excellent to eat fresh. Their skins are crunchy due to their thickness. This thickness enables the bunches to dry in the sun without incurring severe skin damage. Bunches tend to mature unevenly. They have to be carefully selected for ripeness at harvest. Early-harvested Zibibbo can be used in the production of aromatic sparkling wine. Zibibbo also makes aromatic, spicy, rich, alcoholic, low-acid, and moderately bitter dry white wine. Marco De Bartoli made his first experimental cold fermentation of Zibibbo in 1988. He followed with the release of the 1989 Pietra Nera, a fresh, aromatic, dry wine. Other Pantelleria producers have released dry varietal Zibibbos. A handful of producers in the Marsala area on the Sicilian mainland do the same. When the grapes are harvested fresh or late and then vinified, Moscato di Pantelleria is born. When semidried or dried grapes are added to the fermenting must, Passito di Pantelleria is the result. These are sweet, viscous wines that smell of dried fruits, flowers, oranges, and spices.

Recommended producers and their wines:

Abraxas Passito di Pantelleria
Dietro L'Isola Passito di Pantelleria
Donnafugata *Ben Ryé* Passito di Pantelleria
Donnafugata *Kabir* Moscato di Pantelleria
Ferrandes Passito di Pantelleria
Gorghi Tondi *Rajàh*
Marco De Bartoli *Pietra Nera*
Murana *Martingana* Moscato di Pantelleria Passito
Murana *Mueggen* Moscato di Pantelleria Passito
Murana *Turbè* Moscato di Pantelleria

VIOGNIER

The IRVV brought this variety to the attention of Sicilian wine producers after experimental plantings and subsequent microvinifications yielded positive results between 1993 and 1995. Viognier needs a warm growing season, which many areas of Sicily can provide. It has one of the earliest harvest periods in Sicily, about a week after Chardonnay. Its skin resists sunburn better than Chardonnay. In 1995 Ignazio Miceli, a marketing wizard who was an early advocate of international varieties, released a varietal Viognier from grapes grown in the Selinunte area of southwest coastal Sicily. In 1998 Paolo Marzotto planted Viognier at 650 meters (2,133 feet) at his Baglio di Pianetto estate south of Palermo. He eventually released a 100 percent Viognier wine, Ginolfo. Viognier has seen a rapid increase in vineyards off a small base, with an 800 percent growth in surface from 2004 to 2010. As of 2011 there were about 1,180 hectares (2,916 acres) of it in Sicily. Trapani, Agrigento, and Palermo account for 98 percent of these plantings. Viognier produces a floral and fruity varietal wine, high in alcohol and with average to low acidity and a slightly bitter finish. Since the early 2000s, wine producers have used Viognier more as a component in blends than as a soloist, blending it into Catarratto, Inzolia, and Grillo wines to add aromatic lift. Viognier even partners well with Zibibbo, with whose exotic smells its aromas harmonize rather than compete. There are about a dozen varietal Viognier wines produced in Sicily.

Recommended producers and their wines:

Baglio di Pianetto *Ginolfo*
Calatrasi *Accademia del Sole*
Maurigi *Le Chiare*

Miceli *Dedicato*
Settesoli *Mandra Rossa*

MOSCATO BIANCO

Another member of the Muscat family, like Zibibbo, is Moscato Bianco, "White Muscat" in English. Cupani's volume refers to what is likely the same grape variety, *Vitis muschatella*, and its Sicilian-dialect equivalent, *Muscateddu vrancu*. He believed this was the same vine variety that Pliny the Elder called Vitis Apiana, whose name suggests its fruit was so aromatic that it attracted bees (*ape* is the Italian for "bee").[8] The variety is widespread throughout Mediterranean basin coastal areas. There are about 250 hectares (618 acres) planted in Sicily, at two locales: near Syracuse, with which it has long been associated and where it (and the famous wine it makes) is known as Moscato di Siracusa, and near the village of Pachino in the township of Noto, where it is called Moscato di Noto. Wines made at both places are in the DOC quality category. Moscato Bianco's grape skin is delicate and burns easily when dried in the sun. Some producers therefore shelter the grapes while drying them. Moscato Bianco grapes are also extremely susceptible to fungus attacks, making ventilation necessary during the drying phase. To emphasize the peach and floral perfumes of Moscato, fermentation is stopped before completion.

Recommended producers and their wines:

Barone Sergio *Kaluri*
Planeta Moscato di Noto
Pupillo *Solacium* Moscato di Siracusa

CARRICANTE

This is the premier white grape of Etna. About 146 hectares (361 acres) are planted in Sicily. It was becoming rare until 2003, when the boom of interest in Etna wines began to inspire more planting. Carricante accounts for 98 percent of the white grapes grown on Etna but only about 10 percent of all white vine varieties in the province of Catania. It is planted sparsely in the provinces of Agrigento, Caltanissetta, and Ragusa. Sestini noted the variety on Etna in the late 1770s, describing it as regularly giving high yields of grapes, which it then had difficulty ripening. In his judgment, it was of mediocre quality for wine production.[9] More than two hundred years later, Tachis agreed with him. The farmers in the township of Viagrande, on Etna's eastern slope, are reputed to have selected the variety centuries ago. According to local legend, they gave Carricante its name, which derives from the Italian *caricare*, meaning "to load up," undoubtedly referring to the variety's customary high yield. It is planted at roughly 950 meters (3,117 feet) on Etna's eastern slopes and 1,050 meters (3,445 feet) on its southern slopes. At lower elevations it was mixed into vineyards of Nerello Mascalese and Nerello Cappuccio, with the likely intent being to lighten the color and body of red wine that these produce, as Trebbiano Toscano and Malvasia Bianca Lunga lighten the impact of red grapes in the traditional Chianti blend. Though it has been prized on the slopes of Etna, its tendency to produce low alcohol levels (11 to 12 percent) never appealed to producers elsewhere on the island. Recently, however, in the search for a great white variety, the spotlight has moved to Carricante. Alessio Planeta likens Etna Carricante to Alsace Riesling. As if to make this correspondence more evident, he has planted Riesling next to his Carricante with the intention of blending some into the Planeta Carricante. Pure Carricante wine has subtle smells that prompt tasters to use the descriptor *minerals*. It is not nearly as aromatic as Riesling. Carricante wines are rich in malic acid, which is common in unripe fruits, and have a low pH, which makes them aggressively tart. According to Frank Cornelissen, a wine producer on Etna, it is the "worst variety" because the wines "end up being all acidity." Well-made examples can keep for at least ten years. Then diesel smells can be detected. Etna Bianco DOC must contain at least 60 percent Carricante, and Etna Bianco Superiore DOC at least 80 percent. Benanti's Noblesse demonstrates that Carricante can be an excellent base wine for classic method (*metodo classico*) sparkling wine.

Recommended producers and their wines:

Barone di Villagrande Etna Bianco Superiore
Barone di Villagrande *Legno di Conzo* Etna Bianco Superiore
Benanti *Bianco di Caselle* Etna Bianco
Benanti *Noblesse* Vino Spumante Brut Metodo Classico
Benanti *Pietramarina* Etna Bianco
Bonaccorsi *ValCerasa* Etna Bianco
Cavaliere *Millemetri* Etna Bianco
Fessina *A' Puddara* Etna Bianco
Gulfi *Carjcanti*
Planeta

MALVASIA DI LIPARI

Many different varieties, from white to black, are referred to as Malvasia, with a suffix attached to distinguish the identity. For example, in Friuli there is a grape variety called Malvasia Istriana. Malvasia di Lipari is a distinct variety grown on the island of Lipari in the Aeolian Islands. It also grows on other islands in the archipelago, particularly Salina, where most is planted. There is one added confusion: while Malvasia di Lipari is the name of the grape variety, Malvasia delle Lipari, meaning "Malvasia of the Lipari Islands," is the name of the wine. *Malvasia* derives from *Monemvasia*, the name of the Greek port of origin of many cuttings of different vine varieties. There are about one hundred hectares (247 acres) of Malvasia vineyards. Though some sources claim this Malvasia dates to the period of Greek colonization, wine producers have told me that the Venetians first brought it during the sixteenth or seventeenth century.[10] Giovacchino Geremia, in an 1839 addendum to his compendium of Etna varieties, lists Malvasia di Lipari.[11] To make Malvasia delle Lipari *passito,* a sweet, spicy, aromatic wine, the grapes are harvested late, dried, and then vinified. The name comes from the past participle of *appassire,* meaning "to wilt" in Italian, shortened to *passito.* Because Malvasia di Lipari is very susceptible to fungus infection, great care has to be taken during the drying process, when this risk is highest.

Recommended producers and their wines:

Barone di Villagrande Malvasia delle Lipari Passito
Fenech Malvasia delle Lipari Passito
Tasca d'Almerita *Capofaro*

SAUVIGNON BLANC

Sauvignon Blanc is an international variety. Tasca d'Almerita has propagated its own biotype, Tasca Sauvignon, which it found in its vineyards in the 1950s. Tasca's enological consultant Carlo Ferrini describes it as an "anomaly" and says "its characteristics are very similar to those of Sauvignon Blanc." It makes up about 20 percent of the white wine Nozze d'Oro. The IRVV planted Sauvignon Blanc on an experimental basis in 1984 and 1985. Altogether there are more than 325 hectares (803 acres) of Sauvignon Blanc planted in Sicily, but it is difficult to grow there. The maturing grape bunches need both cover from the sun and cool temperatures to preserve Sauvignon's vibrant wine aromas. The moment of harvest has a strong impact on the character of the wine. Because of Sicily's sunny, warm conditions, the harvest window is brief. Picking the perfect harvest moment is difficult. Hence Sicilian Sauvignon Blancs lack consistency. They do not have many of the smell characteristics typical of cool-climate Sauvignon Blancs, such as those from New Zealand or coastal Chile. The consulting enologist Vincenzo Bambina makes no apologies for the lack of green character in Alessandro di Camporeale's Il Kaid Sauvignon Blanc, whose grapes grow at 450 meters (1,476 feet) at Camporeale. It has little of the grassy or grapefruity smells of international Sauvignon Blanc. Its aroma is more muted, and it is rounder and less vibrantly sour in the mouth. Bambina has chosen to ferment it in a 70–30 percent mix of acacia and oak. On the other hand, the consulting enologist Giovanni Rizzo has mined Sauvignon's vivid bouquet of passion fruit and grapefruit and crisp mouth from grapes from Maurigi's north-facing Coste all'Ombra vineyard, on sand at six hundred meters (1,969 feet). High elevations in the interior with cool nights and hot days provide the best climate in Sicily for bringing out Sauvignon vegetal fruit. The stainless steel tanks Rizzo uses help showcase this fruit all the more.

Recommended producers and their wines:

Alessandro di Camporeale *Il Kaid*
Maurigi *Coste all'Ombra*

FIANO

This is an ancient Greek variety used in Avellino in Campania and also in Apulia. Planeta was the pioneer developer in Sicily. The company planted it in 1996 and released Sicily's first Fiano varietal wine in 2000. The farmers of Settesoli, another early adopter, grow about 70 percent of Sicily's Fiano. Vineyards in the provinces of Agrigento and Trapani account for about 75 and 20 percent, respectively, of Sicily's 250 hectares (618 acres) of Fiano. It is difficult to grow. It is particularly sensitive to powdery mildew. Yields are low. The grape skins maintain their integrity even when late-harvested, and the resulting wines have exotic dried fruit flavors. Late harvesting also allows the amount of vegetal proteins in the pulp to increase. After pressing, some of these proteins need to be removed by fining and cold sedimentation. When the alcoholic fermentation has finished, the lees have to be carefully managed so as to avoid reduction. The wine is very aromatic, with citrus, apricot, and exotic fruit smells. In the mouth, it has a thick texture. Planeta's Cometa demonstrates that barrel fermentation of Fiano grapes can yield exceptional results.

Recommended producers and their wines:

Fina Vini
Planeta *Cometa*
Settesoli *MandraRossa*

RED VARIETIES
NERO D'AVOLA

Nero d'Avola is the second-most-planted variety in Sicily after Catarratto. There are about 18,300 hectares (45,220 acres) planted, constituting more than 16 percent of Sicily's vineyards. From 2000 to 2008, Nero d'Avola's Sicilian acreage increased by more than 33 percent. Then in 2010 and again in 2011 this decreased slightly, probably due to the economic downturn that began in September 2008. Nero d'Avola is grown all over the island, but until 1990 most was planted in Sicily's southeast. Today the province of Agrigento leads Trapani and Caltanissetta in total vineyard acreage of the variety. Though Siracusa is fourth among provinces planted with it, more than 85 percent of its vineyard acreage is dedicated to Nero d'Avola. The variety also has a privileged position in Caltanissetta, where it occupies more than 63 percent of the vineyard area. Moving from the provincial to the township (*comune*) level, Noto (in Siracusa), which includes the village of Pachino, and Butera (in Caltanissetta) vie for the most surface area dedicated to Nero d'Avola, with more than fifteen hundred hectares (3,707 acres) each.

Sicilians, particularly older ones, frequently call Nero d'Avola *Calabrese,* as does the Italian National Registry of Vine Varieties. Perhaps because this causes confusion with the neighboring region of Calabria, Sicilian wine producers have promoted the variety as Nero d'Avola to the world. There has been speculation that *Calabrese* is an indication of Calabrian origin, but it is widely accepted as an Italianization of the old dialect name Calavrisi (spellings of this word vary slightly), which means "grape from Avola." This meaning is close to that of the variety's "more" Italian name, Nero d'Avola: "black grape from Avola." Most likely, the farmers in the vicinity of the port city of Avola in southeast Sicily selected this biotype many centuries ago. In 1696, Cupani described Calavrisi, noting its "round" fruit.[12] But the variety's fruit is not as round as he said. In an early section of *Recollections of Sicilian Wines,* Sestini says he believes that Cupani's Calavrisi was another variety, "Aleatico," found on the island of Elba and along the southern Tuscan coast. However, the part of the book relating to his experiences in Vittoria lists the plural of *Calabrese, Calabresi,* next to *Frappati,* the plural of *Frappato,* the area's other native red grape.[13] Given that context, there can be little doubt that Sestini was in fact identifying today's Nero d'Avola.

By the middle of the nineteenth century, farmers were aware of two biotypes of the variety, based on the shape of the berry: elliptical or oval. Franco Giacosa, the winemaker who selected Nero d'Avola for Duca di Salaparuta for twenty years and has continued his work at Principi di Butera, believes that the elliptical-berry biotype produces better wines. There are at least two registered clones, AM28 and AM39, though in the field there are many different biotypes.

Though Nero d'Avola can have problems at flowering, its tolerance of fungus disease is good. Its bunches are looser than those of Frappato but tight enough to prevent spray treatments from reaching inside. The vines grow radially, requiring more handiwork than those with upright growth. The variety's high vigor has to be controlled through vine-nutrition and canopy management. If free of flowering problems, yields are regular and generous.

Nero d'Avola wine has a distinct violet or ruby hue, particularly at the meniscus. Its color can vary from quite dark to medium intensity. Training in alberello, harvesting riper grapes, and macerating vigorously produce darker wine. In fact, the Pachino *vini da taglio*—dark, high-alcohol blending wines produced for northern European and Italian wine merchants from the 1880s to the 1980s—were called *rossissimi* ("most red" or "very deep red") and Nero Pachino ("Black Pachino"). The color, however, is fugitive unless the wine matures in either barriques, to allow oxygen contact to fix the pigments, or stainless steel tanks, where micro-oxygenation can have the same effect. The wine typically has vivid blackberry smells. In the mouth, it has moderate to high alcohol, but its most outstanding characteristic is the high acidity that balances the otherwise soft texture. Alberello training increases the likelihood that the wines will be not only darker but also more alcoholic and less acidic. In warmer climates and at later ripening levels, prune smells and spice can dominate Nero d'Avola, as is the case with many red varieties.

Before the twentieth century, Nero d'Avola was grown in mixed vineyards. The variety presented problems for winegrowers because it reached maturity about two weeks before other native varieties did. If a producer wanted to make a Nero d'Avola wine when its grapes were ready, the vinification was likely to take place under ambient conditions that were too warm. If he waited to harvest the grapes with those of other varieties, then the Nero d'Avola would be overripe and low in acidity. Nowadays vineyards are monovarietal and picked when each is ripe. The harvests are vinified separately and their products blended together later. Though Nero d'Avola is normally picked a week or two earlier than Frappato, a few wine estates prefer to vinify them together. For instance, Pierluigi Cosenza, the owner of Poggio di Bortolone in Vittoria, plants Nero d'Avola in a location that delays maturation and Frappato in one that speeds it up. As a result, their harvests coincide, and he can vinify them together. Nero d'Avola is now frequently blended with international varieties. Many of these are early ripening. Merlot, Syrah, and others tend to fully mature earlier than or at the same time as Nero d'Avola.

Traditionally, the maceration of Nero d'Avola lasted at most two days. Tachis during the 1990s recommended that producers who wanted to make Nero d'Avola wines of higher quality should increase the maceration period. This would allow them to extract more texture from the skin, giving their wines more structure. Still, Nero d'Avola juice typically receives several days less skin contact time than the juice of international varieties such as Cabernet Sauvignon and Merlot. The wine also typically sees several months less maturation time in oak barrel. Carefully stored, high-quality Nero d'Avola may maintain its quality for up to twenty years after bottling.

Nero d'Avola wines made on the western coast have the deepest color but also vegetal flavors. Since the unblended varietal examples seem incomplete, producers there frequently add other red varieties to these wines. In the center of the island, perched on hills south of the Madonie, there are only a few examples of Nero d'Avola producers, such as Montoni and Tasca d'Almerita at its Regaleali estate. The continental climate and higher elevations produce paler, more delicate wines. At five hundred meters (1,640 feet) and higher, Nero d'Avola has difficulty ripening. In highland areas stretching from Agrigento to Riesi, northwest of Gela, its wines have the most fruit and a pleasant underlying astringency. In the Vittoria area, they have a gentle character. In the Noto area, particularly near Pachino, they have an exotic ripeness and are sometimes pruney, sometimes gamy in smell, alcoholic, with a salty finish due to the high levels of sodium chloride in the soil. The climate there is very warm and moderated by the ocean on three sides. The two areas where varietal expressions of Nero d'Avola are the most distinct and have the highest quality are the contradas in the vicinity of Pachino and within the triangle formed by the towns of Butera, Mazzarino, and Riesi in the Riesi DOC. It was largely from grapes harvested at Butera that Giacosa constructed the great Duca di Salaparuta Duca Enrico wines of the mid-1980s to the mid-1990s. Duca di Salaparuta's

1984 Duca Enrico was the first bottled and widely marketed varietal Nero d'Avola. The Butera and the Pachino areas have calcareous soils, which favor the variety. The biggest difference between the two is their elevation: Butera is at about three hundred meters (984 feet), while Pachino is at fifty (164).

The most outstanding characteristic of Nero d'Avola in the mouth is its high acidity. Relative to that, its astringency is low. Federico Curtaz of Fessina, who worked for many years in Piedmont, makes a Nero d'Avola Ero from grapes harvested in Noto. He likens the variety to Barbera (quipping that "Barbera is the Nero d'Avola of the north"). Besides adding structure in the mouth, the high acidity controls bacteria during fermentation and helps resist oxidation. Varietal blends that include Merlot and Syrah provide some of the astringency that Nero d'Avola lacks.

Nero d'Avola wines are versatile, capable of functioning as the base for sparkling, rosé, and dessert wines. The variety can also make inexpensive young wine and "new" wine (released soon after vinification and called *novello* in Italy). Retail prices for Nero d'Avola vary from as low as sixty-five euro cents to thirty euro per bottle. Whenever the pricing of a brand (Nero d'Avola has become a varietal brand) reaches such extremes, the likelihood is that its image will become associated with the lower end of the range.

Sicilian producers have been concerned that mainland Italian bottlers of Sicilia IGT Nero d'Avola have been profiting at the expense of Nero d'Avola's image. In October 2011 the IRVV launched a regulatory initiative to burnish the variety's image in the market with a Nero d'Avola Sicilia Qualità certification. To qualify, producers must use a minimum of 85 percent Nero d'Avola in the blend, source the grapes from vineyards that have traditionally cultivated the variety, and adhere to strict viticultural and enological regulations, such as vine density constraints, yield limits, and dry extract, total acidity, and wine alcohol minimums. Most important, the wines must be not only produced but also bottled in Sicily. The IRVV checks wines seeking this certification to make sure that they meet or exceed minimum standards. With this initiative, Sicily has decisively drawn a line in the sand: no off-island bottlers need apply! This should give Sicilians more control over their ambassador variety.

Recommended producers and their wines:

Arfò Eloro Pachino
Cristo di Campobello *Lu Patri*
Barone Sergio *Sergio* Eloro
Brugnano *Lunario*
Calatrasi *D'Istinto*
Calì *Violino* Vittoria
Ceuso *Scurati* Nero d'Avola
COS *Nero di Lupo*

Curto *Fontanelle* Eloro

Cusumano *Sàgana*

Duca di Salaparuta *Duca Enrico*

Fessina *Ero*

Firriato *Harmonium*

Fondo Antico

Gulfi *Nerobaronj*

Gulfi *Nerobufaleffi*

Gulfi *Neromaccari*

Gulfi *Nerosanlorè*

La Lumia *Don Toto*

Maccari *Saia*

Marabino *Archimede* Eloro Riserva

Marabino *Rosa Nera* Eloro

Montoni

Montoni *Vrucara*

Morgante *Don Antonio*

Nanfro *Strade* Vittoria

Planeta *Santa Cecilia* Noto

Principi di Butera *Deliella*

Rapitalà *Alto*

Riofavara *Sciavè*

Rudinì *Saro* Eloro Pachino

Santa Tresa *Avulisi*

Savino *Nero Sichilli*

Tasca d'Almerita *Lamuri*

Zisola

SYRAH

Syrah is a variety first selected in the Rhone Valley and widely used in Australia (where it is called Shiraz). Sicily's great nineteenth-century ampelographer Baron Antonio Mendola listed Syrah in his collection of vines at Favara near Agrigento.[14] I have found no further references to Syrah in Sicily until the IRVV introduced it on an experimental basis in 1984 and 1985. After microvinifications were assessed, the IRVV advocated its use on the island. By 1995 Syrah was being used in several commercial Sicilian wine blends. Between 2000 and 2007 its surface area in Sicily increased by 738 percent. Syrah became the second-most-planted red variety in Sicily, after Nero d'Avola. There are about fifty-five hundred hectares (13,591 acres), representing 5 percent of the vineyard surface. Most of this is in western Sicily. Syrah grows well in warm, sunny climates and in sandy or clay-ferrous but not calcareous soils. It is very sensitive to drought, but it grows better at higher elevations away from the sea. At harvest, humidity can easily cause mold problems on the grapes. Normally Sicilian producers harvest it at a point of full grape skin maturity or even at the initial stages of overripening, which results in more complete pigment release; softer, denser textures; and alcohol levels between 13.8 and 14.6 percent in the wine. Wine flavor is similar to that of Australian Syrah, and very few Sicilian examples express the wood smoke, cedar, or tarry, vegetative character of Rhone Syrah. This is probably due to Sicily's warm temperatures, which are more like those of Australia's Barossa Valley and McLaren Vale than the northern Rhône Valley in France. Sicilians usually cultivate Syrah in hilly areas between 350 and 650 meters (1,148 and 2,133 feet) above sea level. Maceration usually lasts for ten days or more. The wine often matures in barrique for up to twelve months. Some growers and producers call it the brother of Nero d'Avola because of their similar growing habits and because they make good blending partners. They also say Syrah improves Nero d'Avola varietal wine, darkening it and giving it a denser and meatier smell. In the mouth, Syrah increases tactility that the palate perceives early as fullness and later as astringency. It can legally comprise less than 15 percent of many appellation wines labeled as Nero d'Avola. Some of the varietal Nero d'Avola samples that I have sampled taste more like Syrah than Nero d'Avola. Sicilian wine producers would be unwise to lose the vinous identity of Nero d'Avola, their calling card in the world of wine. In Sicily, Syrah is also commonly used in proprietary blends with Cabernet Sauvignon and Merlot.

Recommended producers and their wines:

Alessandro di Camporeale *Kaid*
Caruso & Minini Delia Nivolelli
Di Prima *Villamaura*
Fina
Planeta
Prinicipi di Butera
Rapitalà *Nadir*
Rapitalà *Solinero*
Sallier De La Tour *La Monaca*
Spadafora *Sole dei Padri*

MERLOT

There are about forty-seven hundred hectares (11,614 acres) of Merlot in Sicily, accounting for 4 percent of its vineyards. Trapani, Agrigento, and Palermo have more than 95 percent of these. Merlot is an international variety. From 1860 to 1874 the French expatriate Duc d'Aumale brought many cuttings from Bordeaux to the Zucco estate near Partinico.[15] Given that Merlot and Cabernet Sauvignon were the most important wine grapes in Bordeaux during this period, it is difficult to imagine that he did not include them. Zucco closed its operations when the duke's heirs sold it in 1923.[16] Isolated old Merlot vines in mixed plantings on Etna suggest another introduction, perhaps by Alexander Nelson Hood, who planted vines from Bordeaux there in the late nineteenth century. Merlot was reintroduced to Sicily in the middle of the 1980s. IRVV research in the early 1990s reinforced interest in it. Merlot integrates seamlessly in wine blends, adding color, body, and soft textures. It ripens earlier than most other red varieties. To accommodate its great need for water and to avoid harvesting in August, when there are risks of overripening and sunburn, higher-elevation plantings, up to seven hundred meters (2,297 feet) above sea level, are optimal. The Merlot vines for Salici, made by Baglio di Pianetto, are planted at 650 meters (2,133 feet). The 2004 harvest was in the last week of September. This is my favorite Sicilian Merlot because it is lighter and fresher than lower-elevation examples. Merlot is the third-most-planted red variety in Sicily, after Nero d'Avola and Syrah. From 2000 to 2008 its vineyard area increased by 664 percent. However, from 2008 to 2011 this dropped from 4,898 to 4,659 hectares (12,103 to 11,513 acres).

Recommended producers and their wines:

  Baglio di Pianetto *Salici*
  Cottanera *Grammonte*
  Cristo di Campobello *Lu Patri*
  Di Prima *Gibilmoro*
  Principi di Butera

NERELLO MASCALESE

At the time of his visit to Etna in 1774, Sestini noted the vine "Nigrello" in the Mascali area.[17] In English, this Latinate word means "little black one," which is exactly the same meaning for *nerello,* a word of Italian derivation. In 1839, Giovacchino Geremia mentioned "nerello mascalese" in a review of vine varieties found in the vineyards of Etna.[18] According to Daniela Bica's 2007 book about Sicilian vine varieties, *Vitigni di Sicilia,* Geremia's is the first citation of the name of the variety as it is spelled today.[19] It is unlikely that *nerello* referred to the size of the grape bunch (which is, on the contrary, quite large). More likely it described the color of the grape skin (which has a little black pigment). *Mascalese* refers to Mascali, a township north of the port of Riposto, which was the principal exit point for Etna wine during the nineteenth century. According to Giovanni Raiti, a local winegrower and amateur historian, farmers most likely originally selected Nerello Mascalese from vines growing in San Leonardello, a hamlet in the nearby township of Giarre. As of 2011 there were 3,698 hectares (9,138 acres) of Nerello Mascalese planted in Sicily, accounting for 3.28 percent of all Sicilian vineyards. Despite the recent success of Etna Rosso DOC, which requires at least 80 percent of the variety in the blend, 2009 through 2011 saw an overall decrease of about 270 hectares (667 acres) of Nerello Mascalese. The province of Catania is home to at least 60 percent of Sicily's Nerello Mascalese. It is sprinkled throughout the rest of the island, mostly for use as a *rosato* (rosé) wine. It used to be more diffusely planted in Sicily than Nero d'Avola. Increasingly, however, planting is focused on the northeast corner, particularly the north, east, and south slopes of Etna. The variety is notoriously sensitive to site. Only on Etna have great Nerello Mascalese wines been made. There the vines are planted on volcanic soils, usually at 350 to 1,050 meters (1,148 to 3,445 feet) where the ambient temperature varies 15°C (26°F) on average from night to day. It is rarely planted at the seaside. The harvest occurs from the end of September to the beginning of November, depending on elevation—the lower the earlier. Nerello Mascalese produces large yields. It must be short-pruned to reduce them and improve concentration. The wine is pale cherry red, with aromas of flowers, particularly violets, red fruit, tobacco, and spices, and in the mouth it is lean, with moderate alcohol, high sourness, and moderate astringency. In appearance the wine is very close to Pinot Noir. Nerello Mascalese is deficient in anthocyanins, the blue-purple pigments in grape skins that darken and give those hues to young wine. At the rim, the wine develops an orange tint at about five years. As is the case with Pinot Noir, this apparent oxidation need not impact wine quality. Long maceration on the skins during and after fermentation is risky because the pulp contains tannins, which dissolve in the presence of alcohol. Toasted new oak can easily overwhelm Nerello Mascalese's delicate aroma. In contrast, certain Nerello Mascalese wines from Etna exhibit a Nebbiolo character if they mature in large Slavonian or French oak barrels (*botti*) instead of barriques. Nerello Mascalese wines can age in bottle for ten to fifteen years, maybe more. Because modern vinification methods have been widely applied on Etna only since the early 2000s, a track record has not yet been established. Nerello Mascalese wines from other areas in Sicily do not age well in bottle. At least two clones are registered for use, NF5 and NF8, but many biotypes exist. More scientific selection needs to be done. In addition to high-quality red table wine, the variety makes good lower-cost, easy-drinking wine, sparkling wine, and rosato wine.

Recommended producers and their wines:

Antichi Vinai *Petralava* Etna Rosso
Benanti *Il Monovitigno*
Benanti *Rosso di Verzella* Etna Rosso
Benanti *Rovittello* Etna Rosso

Benanti *Serra della Contessa* Etna Rosso

Binoche *Setteporte*

Biondi *Outis* Etna Rosso

Calabretta Etna Rosso

Cavaliere *Don Blasco* Etna Rosso

Cavaliere *Millemetri* Etna Rosato

Cornelissen *Magma* Rosso

Cottanera Etna Rosso

Destro *Sciarakè* Etna Rosso

Duca di Salaparuta *Làvico*

Fessina *Erse* Etna Rosso

Fessina *Musmeci* Etna Rosso

Feudo Vagliasindi Etna Rosso

Firriato *Cavanera Rovo delle Coturnie* Etna Rosso

Girolamo Russo *Feudo* Etna Rosso

Girolamo Russo *San Lorenzo* Etna Rosso

Graci *Quota 600* Etna Rosso

Gulfi *Reseca*

Il Cantante Etna Rosso

Mannino *Donna Letizia* Etna Rosso

Murgo Brut Rosé Spumante V.S.Q. Rosé

Passopisciaro *Chìappemacine*

Passopisciaro *Porcaria*

Passopisciaro *Rampante*

Passopisciaro *Sciaranuova*

Tasca d'Almerita *Tascante*

Terre Nere *Calderara Sottana* Etna Rosso

Terre Nere *Feudo di Mezzo–Il Quadro delle Rose* Etna Rosso

Terre Nere *La Vigna di Don Peppino* Etna Rosso

ValCerasa Etna Rosso

Vigneri *Vinupetra*

CABERNET SAUVIGNON

As was the case with Merlot, the Duc d'Aumale and Hood likely had Cabernet Sauvignon among the cuttings that each brought to Sicily from Bordeaux in the nineteenth century. In the *Giornale Vinicolo Italiano* of 1890, the writer Clemente Grimaldi praised "a new type of wine" called Castello Solicchiato, produced by Baron Antonio Spitaleri, that was "pure" Cabernet Sauvignon and "had all the qualities, especially the smell, of a true Médoc."[20] This may be the first written proof of a Cabernet Sauvignon varietal wine made in Sicily. The IRVV vigorously studied and recommended the variety in the early and mid-1990s. Its vineyard acreage expanded dramatically from then until 2008, when it reached 3,922 hectares (9,691 acres). By 2011, however, this had decreased to 3,554 hectares (8,782 acres), or about 3 percent of Sicily's vineyard acreage. Cabernet Sauvignon is a red grape variety that resists heat, dryness, and disease in the vineyard and makes moderately dark, aromatic, tart, and astringent wine. Its bell-pepper and black-currant nose can easily dominate most varietal wines, but it is frequently blended at low percentages with Nero d'Avola or Merlot to add structure. The best Cabernet Sauvignon wine comes from the interior of the island at moderate elevations. Tasca d'Almerita Cabernets produced at Regaleali have a proven track record of excellence. I tasted a 1991 in December 2010. After almost twenty years, the color was very dark, the nose was loaded with black-currant smells, and the flavors in the mouth were elegant, lean, and tart, with fine astringency in the finish. At Vinitaly 2010 that spring, I had tasted a 2000 Tasca d'Almerita Cabernet Sauvignon. Also outstanding!

Recommended producers and their wines:

> Cantine Barbera *La Vota* Menfi
> Cottanera *Nume*
> Fazio
> Principi di Butera
> Spadafora *Schietto*
> Tasca d'Almerita Contea di Sclafani
> Viticultori Associati Canicattì *Aquilae*

FRAPPATO

In 1812, Sestini noted the use of Frappato in the Vittoria area.[21] Salvatore D'Agostino mentions in *Annuario della filiera vitivinicola siciliana* that Sestini was the first to write about Frappato.[22] In his *Giornale del Viaggio Fatto in Sicilia* ("journal of a trip in Sicily"), published in 1809, Paolo Balsamo describes its use in a blend, also from Vittoria, with Nero d'Avola.[23] It is likely that Frappato was first selected for propagation in Vittoria. Girolamo Molon in his 1906 work on ampelography cites an 1890 letter by Rosario Cancellieri from Vittoria that identifies Frappato as "the variety universally preferred" for wine production in the area, accounting for 90 percent of the surface area.[24] During the nineteenth century, Frappato wine from Vittoria was called the wine of Scoglitti after its port of export. Molon described Frappato as ideal for Vittoria's warm and dry sandy soils. He also noted that Nero d'Avola is a great companion for Frappato because it grows well in cooler and moister soils that are not suited for Frappato.[25] Its acreage in 2007 was 792 hectares (1,957 acres). This increased in 2008 (846 hectares, or 2,091 acres), only to fall back in 2010 (833; 2,058) and 2011 (803; 1,984). Frappato occupies less than 1 percent of Sicily's vineyards. The province of Trapani has almost four times as much Frappato vineyard surface as Agrigento or Ragusa. However, in the comune of Vittoria (in Ragusa) the variety excels and is the other half to Nero d'Avola in the Cerasuolo di Vittoria DOCG blend. The *terra rossa* (red sandy soil over limestone) and other sand-dominated soils a few miles southeast of the town of Acate help endow Frappato with extra aromatic lift and delicacy. It is easy to tell Frappato from Nero d'Avola vines because Frappato vines grow straight up, while Nero d'Avola ones grow out radially. In addition, Frappato is less vigorous. It has smaller bunch sizes and lower yields. Growers in Vittoria say that for Frappato, the predominant cane-pruning technique, Guyot, named after a nineteenth-century French proponent, is more effective than spur-pruning techniques, which are better for most other varieties in the area. While one bunch grows from a Frappato shoot, two grow from a shoot of Nero d'Avola. The harvest moment has to be well chosen. At full ripeness the bunches are delicate because they are tight and compact. The pressure of adjoining overripe grapes can break open their delicate skins and release their sweet juice to insects, yeast, and bacteria. The juice's time on the skins during fermentation is usually brief, less than four days. If the extraction is too rough, delicacy of texture is lost. Fermentation temperatures are best kept low, from 18°C to 20°C, to preserve fruit. In some years it is better not to conduct malolactic fermentation, which usually enhances fruit freshness and preserves sourness, adding pleasant zip to the wine. Maturation in new oak barrels can add woody aromas and flavors that easily overwhelm the wine's fruit and delicate texture. In addition, the oxidation that is more likely in barrel maturation shortens the life of Frappato wine, which is best consumed within a year or two of release. The wines are pale cherry red and lightly structured, very spicy and floral, and loaded with vivid cherry and pomegranate fruitiness. Frappato skins, like those of Nerello Mascalese, are relatively deficient in anthocyanins. Frappato wines average 13 percent alcohol by volume. They are sour, even more so than Nero d'Avola, and finish with both pleasant bitterness and light, delicate astringency. They have a tendency to oxidize rapidly. To appreciate Frappato, disregard conventions demanding that all great red wine must be dark, alcoholic, thick, and astringent. Giuseppe Romano, an enologist at Valle dell'Acate, was one of the first to showcase the variety, making the company's first varietal Frappato wines in 1991. Frappato performs well as a rosato. Paolo Calì also makes a white wine with it, Bianca di Luna. After about five months of maturation in stainless steel tank and three months aging in bottle, Frappato is ready for consumption and should be drunk within three years. Sicilian producers say that once bottled, Frappato can hold its quality up to five years. Though there is, by law, more Nero d'Avola than Frappato in Cerasuolo di Vittoria wines, Frappato's presence distinguishes them more than Nero d'Avola's does.

Recommended producers and their wines:

Arianna Occhipinti
Calì *Bianca di Luna*
Calì *Mandragola* Vittoria
COS
FiàNobile Vittoria
Valle dell'Acate *Il Frappato* Vittoria

NERELLO CAPPUCCIO

Nerello Cappuccio, also referred to as Mantellato, is native to Etna. The Italian word *mantella* means "mantle" or "cloak," which describes the way the variety's leaves hang over the vine. The first mention of it that I have seen is in an 1876 ampelography bulletin, which identifies it as Nerello Ammantellato.[26] Rarely is it planted on its own. In an older Nerello vineyard on Etna, composed of a mix of Nerello Mascalese and Nerello Cappuccio, it usually accounts for 15 to 20 percent of the vines. There are currently about 680 hectares (1,680 acres) planted there. The vineyard acreage of Nerello Cappuccio has been decreasing for several decades. The variety is very sensitive to powdery mildew. Nerello Cappuccio has smaller grape berries than Nerello Mascalese. Its varietal wine examples have a violet tint. Nerello Mascalese wine is redder. In the nose, Nerello Cappuccio wines tend to be floral and have red fruit smells. In the mouth they are coarser in texture and lower in acidity than Nerello Mascalese. Nerello Cappuccio varietal wines are best consumed before they reach five years of bottle age.

Recommended producers and their wines:

Benanti *Il Monovitigno*
Fessina *Laeneo*

PERRICONE

Perricone, called Pignatello in the province of Trapani, today occupies only about 330 hectares (815 acres) in Sicily, principally in the western provinces. Though it is an ancient Sicilian variety, its high point of popularity was during the late 1800s and early 1900s, when it was the most important red grape variety in the vineyards of the provinces of Trapani and Palermo. It was used in the production of Rubino Marsala. Mixed with white grapes, it made up the blend of a typical wine of local consumption, called Ambrato ("amber colored"), a rustic rosato. Its strongest association has been with vineyards south of Palermo, where it was used to make more sophisticated table wines. An Italian text on viticulture and enology published in 1883 describes Zucco Rosso as a well-regarded varietal Perricone.[27] In 1889, the British consul William Stigand, speaking of the wines from the Palermo area, stated that "the black grapes are almost exclusively of the kind called pignatello."[28] In his report on the vintage of 1889, published the following year, he notes that Salvatore Salvia in Casteldaccia, southeast of Palermo, made a red wine from Perricone. Salvia exported it with great success to France, Germany, and the north of Italy.[29] In 1896 a report published by the Italian Ministry of Agriculture, Industry and Commerce identified 100 percent Perricone wine as the Palermo province's vino da taglio and blends of "Perricone nero and Nerello" as the "ordinary wines of great commerce," or common table wine. The same page of the report also describes "very intense" "red-orange" wines made from a blend of Catarratto and Perricone. Catarratto and Perricone were commonly blended to make a coarse rosato wine.[30] After the phylloxera infestation of the early 1900s, Perricone began disappearing, first from the vineyards of Trapani and then from those of Palermo. Acreage began to decline rapidly during the 1930s. In 2000 it was close to oblivion, after which more vines were planted until its surface area stabilized in 2008. Throughout the island, small amounts are blended with Nero d'Avola to increase the latter's palate texture and lower its high acidity. For example, the grapes of a Perricone vineyard planted in 1959 at Tasca d'Almerita's Regaleali estate have been a component in the company's Rosso del Conte blend. Perricone has vigorous vines that produce a large quantity of grapes. Yields vary a great deal from year to year. Green harvesting is necessary to achieve equilibrium between foliage and fruit. It is harvested quite late compared to other varieties, for instance about fifteen days after Catarratto. Alcohol levels of the varietal wine are typically low to moderate, between 11 and 13 percent. If bunches are left on the vine to overripen, grape acidity drops rapidly as sugar climbs, resulting in alcoholic wines lacking in acidity. Higher elevations help sustain acidity levels but make late ripening more difficult. The grape skins' high polyphenol content endows the wines with deep color, astringency, and bitterness. Perricone wine tends to have a coarse texture. It has been touted as healthful because it contains high amounts of stilbenes, compounds with strong antioxidant properties. The wine, however, is not long lived. At Valledolmo, just south of the Madonie Mountains, Castellucci Miano features Perricone as its premier red variety. The grapes, harvested in October, are at eight hundred meters (2,625 feet) in elevation. This keeps their acidity high. To get the sugar needed for wine alcohol, Perricone grapes are sometimes dried indoors before being vinified. Mirella Tamburello, who works at her family winery in the heart of the Belice River Valley near Poggioreale, has been a longtime champion of the variety. She vinifies Perricone as a single-varietal wine under the Monreale DOC. Another longtime advocate is Stefano Caruso of Caruso & Minini. The vineyards of this estate are in the hills east of Marsala. Caruso takes the minority view that Perricone should not be matured in oak barrels and uses stainless steel tanks instead. In southeastern Sicily, Perricone makes wines that are lighter in color and less astringent. Producers there believe the vines are a different biotype and attribute these characteristics to it. There is as yet no consensus on what modern Perricone wine should taste like or how it should be made.

Recommended producers and their wines:

Caruso & Minini *Sachia*
Castellucci Miano *Maravita*
Castellucci Miano *Perric.One*
Feotto dello Jato *Vigna Curria*
Firriato *Ribeca*
Porta del Vento *Maque'*
Tamburello *Pietragavina* Monreale

NOCERA

This variety is cultivated principally on the plain and hillsides surrounding Milazzo that face the Tyrrhenian Sea. It is a minor variety in the Faro red wine blend (5 to 10 percent allowed), though before the twentieth century it dominated that blend. Virtually nothing is known about the origins of this variety. The first written mention of it that I know of is in the Italian Ministry of Agriculture, Industry and Commerce's publication *Notizie e Studi intorno Ai Vini ed Alle Uve d'Italia*, published in 1896.[31] In the last half of the nineteenth century, the Nocera wine from Milazzo, called simply Milazzo, had a reputation as high-quality vino da taglio because of its deep purple-crimson color, tendency to have a strong red tint at the rim of the glass, strong aromas, high alcohol, high acidity, and high astringency. French merchants preferred it above other Sicilian vini da taglio. With the steep decline of French trade in the late 1880s and the onset of the phylloxera epidemic in Sicily, Nocera vineyard surface there diminished after 1890 and declined steeply after World War II. Today there is very little planted. Ruggero Vasari, whose wine estate is just outside Milazzo at Santa Lucia del Mela, believes that Nocera needs to be blended with other varieties to make a complete wine. As proof, he produces an unimpressive varietal Nocera, which was the first modern one. Farther to the west of Milazzo, the wine producer Cambria, at Furnari, accords the variety more potential. Cambria uses two clones, Nocera Vulcanica and Nocera Milazzo, to make its 100 percent Nocera wine, Mastronicola, which first came on the market in 2011. The wine combines finesse and solidity and is definitely not the brute that Milazzo of a century before was reported to be. Alessio Planeta too has faith in the variety and would like to make a Mamertino DOC with 100 percent Nocera, provided that his proposed modification to the wine law is approved. The Planeta wine company has leased property in the Milazzo area with this intention in mind. The Mamertino DOC regulations currently allow 10 to 40 percent Nocera, the rest being principally Nero d'Avola. Planeta believes that with research the variety can be improved, by selecting the best biotypes, growing them better, and tailoring the vinification and maturation to bring out their salient characteristics.

Recommended producer and wine:

Cambria *Mastronicola*

SANGIOVESE

There are about 1,525 hectares (3,768 acres) of Sangiovese, most commonly found in central Sicily, making up almost 1.35 percent of Sicilian vineyards. Several DOCs allow it in blends. There are also some IGTs that allow varietal Sangiovese. It has a long history in Sicily, but no one knows when it was introduced from the mainland or elsewhere. Its high vigor and potential to produce high yields can be an asset. With all the great Sangiovese coming out of central Italy, there is little incentive to develop the variety as a star performer in Sicily.

PETIT VERDOT

During the mid-nineteenth century a small amount of Petit Verdot was planted in mainland Italy for use in Bordeaux blends. In Sicily beginning in the 1990s there were some experimental plantings of the variety in the provinces of Trapani, Palermo, and Agrigento. As of 1993, experiments with Petit Verdot began under the auspices of the IRVV. Tachis was very familiar with this variety and advocated its use in small amounts in blends. There are 225 hectares (556 acres) planted, mostly in Trapani, Palermo, and Agrigento. Until 2010, when it reached a high point, Petit Verdot acreage had been growing at a rapid clip. In 2011, plantings decreased slightly. Though in Bordeaux Petit Verdot ripens with difficulty and gives erratic results, in the warmer climate of Sicily it ripens regularly and gives consistent results. It is an extremely useful variety as a blender, providing color, complex spicy aromas, tannins, and acidity. Maturation in barrique helps smooth Petit Verdot's wild personality. Its youthful herbaceousness transitions with time into a balsam wood spice. The slowdown of plantings of this high-quality blending variety may be one sign that the Sicilian wine industry has taken a step back from investing in its infrastructure.

Recommended producers and their wines:

Baglio di Pianetto *Carduni*
Maurigi *Lù*
Poggio di Bortolone *Kiron*

PINOT NERO

Pinot Nero, internationally recognized as Pinot Noir, is the variety that most puts growers and winemakers to the test because it is difficult both to grow and to vinify with excellent results. There are 212 (524 acres) hectares in Sicily as of 2011, an increase of forty-two (104) over the previous year. This represents a high rate of increase over a small base. In Sicily, as elsewhere in the wine world, Pinot Nero garners attention disproportionate to the area it occupies. In the 1880s, Baron Spitaleri was producing Pinot Nero sparkling wine from vines he had planted on the slopes of Etna above the town of Biancavilla. Cuttings of Pinot Noir imported into Riesi in 1880 are believed to have introduced phylloxera into Sicily. By 1903 the variety was widespread in the province of Catania, and its vines were also in Siracusa and Agrigento.[32] However, Pinot Nero did not survive the phylloxera infestation. Its low yields and sensitivity to heat and disease convinced growers to plant other varieties in its place. But in 1985, Lucio Tasca had the desire to understand the best wines of the world. He had Pinot Nero planted at Regaleali. The clone produced lighter red wines suitable for sparkling, not still, wine. Subsequently, Tasca d'Almerita has used this Pinot Nero in a classic-method sparkling wine. Tachis parented a 2000 vintage Pinot Nero made from grapes harvested at eight hundred meters (2,625 feet) at Castiglione di Sicilia on Etna. He likened it to quality red Burgundy and encouraged Etna producers to take on the challenge of planting and vinifying the variety. In 2003 the IRVV suggested to Francesco Maurigi that he plant it at high altitudes near Enna. He did so, at 600 to 650 meters (1,969 to 2,133 feet) above sea level. South of Palermo at Ficuzza, Cusumano has Pinot Nero planted at seven hundred meters (2,297 feet). Buceci has it planted at Marineo a few miles to the north of Ficuzza. More wineries are making a go on Etna: Patria at Castiglione di Sicilia, Chiuse del Signore at Linguaglossa, Cantine Nicosia at Trecastagni, and La Gelsomina at Piedimonte. Duca di Salaparuta launched Nawàri, the first vintage being the 2005, from Pinot Nero grapes grown at seven hundred meters (2,297 feet) on the northern slopes. Tachis helped set up this vineyard when he was consulting for the winery. Pinot Noir has achieved the best results when planted at high elevations with concomitant high day-night temperature variation. Northern exposures are best because they limit the amount of sun that reaches the grape skins, which it can burn. Pinot Noir has a short growing season, the shortest of any red grape variety used for varietal wines. When the intention is to use Pinot Noir as a base for sparkling wine, it must be harvested before the skin fully ripens, to ensure high acidity levels. Based on the samples that I have tasted, the 2009 Duca di Salaparuta Nawàri best expresses the potential of what this variety can put into the glass. Perhaps Sicilians just need more time to master this difficult variety, and the vines need more time to send their roots deeper into the soil.

Recommended producers and their wines:

Duca di Salaparuta *Nawàri*
La Gelsomina
Maurigi *Terre di Ottavia*

GRENACHE NOIR (GARNACHA TINTA)

This variety was probably originally selected in Spain. The French have had such success with it that it is more frequently referred to as Grenache Noir than as Garnacha Tinta, its Spanish name. Given the long history of Spanish influence in Sicily, it is no wonder that Grenache Noir has a long history there. Cupani mentioned *Guarnaccia niura* in 1696, and around one hundred years later Sestini, discussing the wines of Vittoria, also noted the variety, using the same spelling as Cupani.[33] About a century later, in 1883, a bulletin of the Italian Ministry of Agriculture, Industry and Commerce listed Guarnaccia as one of the varieties in the province of Caltanissetta.[34] Grenache Noir was reintroduced in the late nineteenth century at Zucco in the vicinity of Partinico. When Giacosa first began working for Duca di Salaparuta during the 1960s, he noted a lot of Grenache Noir planted in the province of Agrigento. It is present in old vineyards on Etna at high elevations and in spots that accumulate cool air descending from the mountain. It ripens earlier than Nerello Mascalese. The British consul Stigand mentions that on Hood's estate, "the vine which has been selected as suited best to the soil and climate is the 'Grenache noir' of Roussillon."[35] This confirms that Hood sourced the cutting from a region of southern France. Grenache Noir is also found on Pantelleria, where it was likely brought from Tunisia. Abraxas blends it with Syrah and Carignan to make Kuddia di Zè. Italians call Grenache Noir *Alicante,* which is confusing because of the simultaneous presence of a tinted variety, Alicante Bouschet, traditionally used, mostly in the South of France, to darken wine. In 2011 the main cultivar list of the IRVV, "Sicilian Viticulture in Numbers," noted that the island had 279 hectares (689 acres) of Alicante Bouschet. This could very well mean one, the other, or both together. At any rate, there is not much Grenache Noir planted in Sicily.

Recommended producer and wine:

Vigneri *Vinudilice*

7

VITICULTURE IN SICILY

Sicilian winegrowers demonstrate a strong and sensitive attachment to the soil and to their vines. Before the 1990s they had difficulty keeping pace with improvements in enology and the commercialization of wine. Their viticultural practices, however, have evolved alongside techniques practiced for centuries in the traditional wine-producing countries of Europe. Since the end of the nineteenth century, Sicilian viticulture has adapted to the infestation of phylloxera from the early 1880s to 1920, the modernization of the bulk wine industry from the late 1950s to the mid-1980s, and the development of a quality sold-by-the-bottle wine industry from the late 1980s to the present day.

Before the twentieth century, Sicilians largely planted their vines mixed with other crops. Beyond established quality wine–producing areas such as existed in France, southern Germany, and other isolated areas, this practice was widespread, particularly in poorer farming communities. It was an effective use of space if the plants were positioned so that each got sufficient light, ventilation, and root space. Where conditions were windy, which is often the case in Sicily, surrounding plants and walls served as windbreaks. Polyculture, the interspersing of different types of plants in a growing area, provided farmers with more security than monoculture. Vines grew alongside vegetable plants, fruit trees, and cereals. If a malady, a pest, or unfavorable climatic conditions affected one plant type, there would still be others that were less or not affected. Polyculture also gave peasant farmers a measure of self-sufficiency and had positive effects on the family diet.

TRADITIONAL VITICULTURE: PRE-1950 ROOTS

During the nineteenth century, as the Marsala and Mascali wine industries developed and Sicilian wine exports increased, true vineyard monocultures began to be planted. In Marsala, for example, only 5 percent of the vineyards were specialized in the late 1800s. Of the new vineyards that were planted there at the end of the 1800s, however, about 35 percent were specialized. Other crops were often planted in strips next to those early specialized vineyards. The expansion of vineyard monocultures was more rapid where vineyards were planted on flat land or rolling hills, such as at Marsala. In other areas, such as Etna, where landholdings were smaller and there are severe slopes and rocky conditions, the changeover was more gradual. Even today, fruit trees commonly dot Etna's terraced vineyards. Here the construction of terraces supported by rock walls claimed land for vineyard use at the expense of much more labor. By the twentieth century, only where there was sufficient low-cost labor could terraced vineyards be maintained against the destructive forces of gravity, rain, root growth, and animal activity. Creating new vineyards on terraces was simply not profitable.

THE PHYLLOXERA INFESTATION

The phylloxera infestation came to Sicily in the early 1880s, more than a decade after it arrived in France. Phylloxera, officially named *Daktulosphaira vitifoliae,* is a microscopic louse that attacks vine roots. It causes vines to die after several years of infestation. The insects spread rapidly in the mixed sand-clay-silt soils that cover most of the island. Though phylloxera was reported in all Sicilian provinces within five years of its known introduction, most of the devastation occurred later, at the end of the nineteenth and the beginning of the twentieth century. Because the volcanic soils on Etna, Pantelleria, and the Aeolian Islands are rocky and sandy, they were and remain less hospitable to phylloxera, which prefer moister and richer soils. In these areas there are still vines, usually isolated, that remain on their original roots (as opposed to the phylloxera-resistant American rootstock eventually planted everywhere else). On Etna as many as 15 percent of the vines are on their own roots.

Before phylloxera appeared, planting a vine entailed burying one end of a one-year-old branch, called a cane, into the ground. This occurred in the winter or early spring, during or at the end of vine dormancy. With the first spring heat, dormant buds on the unburied part of the cane turned green and then sprouted, forming green branches called shoots, which bore infant leaves and what would become bunches of flowers. Below the ground, the cane began developing its root system. It took about four years for the vine to give its first substantial harvest. When a vine in an established vineyard died and needed to be replaced, during the winter, farmers buried all but the apex of a cane from an adjacent vine, running it underground to the vacant spot. At the apex, the most light-sensitive part of the cane, buds came to life at the first period of sustained warmth. With growth above the ground, the cane rooted its buried part, though it continued to be linked to the parent vine for several years, if not longer. This prephylloxera system of replacing individual vines, called layering or *provignage* (*propaggine* in Italian), is still practiced today on Etna, Pantelleria, and the Aeolian Islands.

After phylloxera's landfall in France, researchers there, in the United States, and in other countries began to look for a cure. Though they failed to discover how to eradicate phylloxera or cure infected vines, researchers in France and the United States by the early 1870s had devised a strategy that enabled *Vitis vinifera,* the parent of all European vine cultivars, to grow in phylloxera-infested soils. They grafted *Vitis vinifera* vinestock onto the roots of adequately resistant indigenous American vine species. Because the American vines had evolved in the presence of phylloxera, they had developed an ability to heal from and withstand the insects' attacks on their roots. During the late nineteenth century, France, Italy, and other affected countries grafted *Vitis vinifera* vinewood onto American rootstocks. Researchers found that the grafts between different combinations of *Vitis vinifera* cultivars and various American vine species each had unique characteristics, which expressed themselves differently according to the climate and soil where the grafted plants grew. Researchers could therefore develop rootstocks that were the product of multiple crossings between American vines and *Vitis vinifera* to amplify variables such as success of the graft, adaptability to site, vigor, and disease resistance. They selected the most successful rootstocks and sent them to private nurseries for propagation and release to the public. Beyond resistance to phylloxera, Sicily needed rootstocks that adapted well to the particular characteristics of its soils. The topsoils are very dry during the growing season due to a lack of rain. Also, many of its soils are high active lime soils, with a high pH, from pulverized rocks containing calcium carbonate. Many American vine types develop a physiological disorder, chlorosis, in such soils. A third condition is the high levels of salinity in the soils of the southeastern half of the island. At varying concentrations for different vines, salts can be toxic. Sicily therefore needed rootstocks that not only were resistant to phylloxera but also could perform well in dry, calcareous, and salt-rich soils.

In 1888 the Palermo Royal Nursery of American Vines was established, with branches at Marsala, Milazzo, Catania, Caltagirone, Noto, and Piazza Armerina. Its purpose was to devise a Sicilian solution to phylloxera. Federico Paulsen, an agricultural expert from Rome, was put in charge. He was to create one of the two most important Sicilian rootstocks, 1103 Paulsen, a rootstock with good resistance to drought, high active lime, and salinity. In 1894 Antonio Ruggeri from Messina, working in the Ragusa area for a Vittoria- and Siracusa-based nursery research facility, began a series of hybridization experiments that led to Sicily's most used rootstock, 140 Ruggeri. Affectionately called Ruggeri Veloce ("Speedy Ruggeri") by growers, this rootstock has particularly high vigor in deep, dry, and very high active lime soils. These two interspecific crossings provided full phylloxera protection, registered high rates of successful grafting onto Sicilian native vinestock, and were well adapted to the island's growing conditions. During the late nineteenth century, Sicily made great progress in the fight against phylloxera. Private Sicilian vine nurseries facilitated the enormous viticultural changes that had to occur if Sicilian viticulture was to survive. The Cali Fiorini bothers of Catania, Giuseppe Di Grazia of Messina, and Giuseppe Zirilli Lucifero of Milazzo propagated early phylloxera-resistant varieties, such as Rupestris du Lot and Berlandieri X Riparia 420A, and sold rootstocks grafted onto vine varieties to Sicilian growers for planting. In 1908, the government authorized the free distribution of American rootstocks and vine budwood to farmers. In the early 1930s, 1103 Paulsen and 140 Ruggeri were introduced and became widely used in Sicily. Today both rootstocks are used throughout the world. The Sicilian effort to combat and solve the phylloxera problem was an unqualified success.

In 1880, during the high point of the nineteenth-century planting boom in Sicily, the surface area of its vineyards totaled 321,718 hectares (794,982 acres). This area was reduced to 176,000 hectares (434,905 acres) in 1905 and dropped even further, to a low point of 169,200 hectares (418,102 acres) in 1920. During the first two decades of the twentieth century, many phylloxera-stricken vineyards were not replanted. The least likely to survive were those at higher elevations, on steeper slopes, and on poorer soils. These sites were lower yielding but, on average, produced better-quality wine grapes. The market for Sicilian wine, however, did not support the costs of farming them.

After 1920, with phylloxera solved, World War I over, and the Italian economy improving (until 1925), vineyard acreage rebounded. However, more-fertile and flatter areas were planted with higher-yielding, more-disease-resistant, and easier-to-grow varieties, which also substituted in those vineyards that were replanted. Vine variety diversity in vineyards decreased. The Depression of the 1930s and the Second World War stymied the development of more vineyard planting. During the first half of the twentieth century the only area in Sicily that showed a substantial rebound in vineyard planting was the plains in the province of Trapani. These vineyards supplied the Marsala industry. After World War II the plains and low-incline sites of Agrigento were widely planted, also to supply the Marsala industry. As tractors and other vineyard machinery became available in the 1950s, the amount of labor required to farm a given area of land decreased. Many workers left Sicily's vineyards and farms for employment in the industrial north of Italy. Viticultural areas, particularly difficult-to-farm ones such as the Aeolian Islands, were abandoned. Most of the farmers and other inhabitants emigrated to Australia. Agriculture was perceived as an activity solely for those on the lowest rung of society, who were unable to escape Sicily.

ALBERELLO

Until the 1950s, though vines had been grafted onto rootstocks and new plantings were increasingly specialized, viticulture was essentially conducted in the same way as at the turn of the century. The vine-training system used almost exclusively in Sicily was alberello. Combined with Sicily's warm, sunny, and dry climate, it was ideally suited for the production of the concentrated, high-alcohol wines used as the base for Marsala and the vino da taglio that Etna and southeastern Sicily became associated with before 1970. This system enables vines to produce high-extract and high-sugar grapes, although at the high costs of hand labor and low yields. Greek settlers arriving in the eighth century B.C. had most likely brought it to the island.

Alberello means "little tree" in Italian. The vines take the shape of dwarf trees. Each trunk is about twenty to twenty-five centimeters (eight to ten inches) high and is often dug into a small pit. At its head, the trunk divides into three or four branches that rise into the air like arms to a height of about sixty-one centimeters (two feet). Each branch carries one spur, a short cane the size of a small finger. Each spur has two or three buds. At the beginning of each season, the green parts of the plant erupt from the buds. The trunk and the branches are kept from year to year as the support for vegetation and fruit, unless there is a need to replace the branches because of disease or physical damage. Alberello is called a head-trained system because it uses the top of a vertical trunk as the starting point for annual pruning. Before the start of growth in the spring, while the vine is still dormant the farmer removes the wood that grew during the previous season, returning the vine to its seasonal starting configuration, with the exception of new bud-bearing spurs and, in some systems, one or more new bud-bearing canes. The farmer selects the healthiest spurs closest to the trunk. In the alberello system, each vine is small and carries a small crop load. Because the spurs—and hence the buds—are approximately equidistant from the roots, they receive nutrients and other plant substances more or less simultaneously. Bunches also tend to ripen simultaneously, which helps farmers bring in a uniformly ripened harvest. Provided that vines are short enough or are planted far enough apart, they are open to light from all directions of the sky.

Because the vegetation is low, the vine benefits from a layer of warm air that builds over the surface of the ground throughout the day. The darker the soil, the more radiant heat it absorbs and the warmer this layer becomes. This added warmth means the grapes ripen faster than they would in other training systems. The warm conditions also increase the evaporation of water through the ripened grapes' skin, elevating the sugar level of the grape berries to such high degrees that 18 percent alcohol wines are possible.

The low-lying canopy of leaves also preserves the humidity that rises from the ground, making alberello ideal for dry growing conditions. Sicily has little rain during the growing season and low atmospheric humidity. The canopy moisture is good for the plant, provided the weather is dry and windy enough to limit the development of fungus growth. However, insects find the canopy a protected place where they can avoid detection. Fruit and insects sheltered by leaves are difficult to reach with chemical sprays.

Vine density varied depending on locality. In areas such as Marsala, where vineyards were on flat ground, densities were about thirty-five hundred vines per hectare (1,416 per acre). Mountainous areas where the soil was fertile, such as on Etna, averaged ten thousand vines per hectare (4,047 per acre). At this density, only a man or a small draft animal such as a mule can negotiate the short distance—one meter (about three feet)—between vines. The greater the density, the shorter the vines need to be so that they do not shade one another. Short vines are also more resistant to wind damage. Sicilian growers may avoid wind damage by sheltering their alberello vines in shallow pits or on the leeward side of stone walls or other windbreaks. Tying the canes and shoots growing from the permanent branches to support poles or other branches also helps limit wind damage.

Save for the allowance of small engine-driven cultivators (*motozappa*), alberello is not adaptable to mechanization. Its pruning, training, and harvesting involve back-breaking labor. Other training systems introduced into Sicily mostly during the 1960s involve far fewer human-hours. During the 1970s there was a dramatic decrease in alberello vineyards. By 1984, only 54 percent of the vines in Sicily were trained in alberello. By 2010, this had dropped to about 8.5 percent. Moreover, mechanical methods of concentrating musts, the early 1990s development of synthetic sources of tartaric acid, and increasingly effective policing of illegal wine shipments have diminished the vino da taglio market in favor of lower-alcohol, fresher wines that are better achieved with higher-trained, row-vine systems. Nonetheless, Salvo Foti, an enologist working in the Etna area, is dedicated to preserving alberello viticulture in Sicily. He has created an association of winegrowers, I Vigneri, dedicated to using this system.

Various permutations of alberello exist in different places on Sicily, due in part to climatic differences. For example, the system unique to the island of Pantelleria is *alberello basso strisciante*. *Basso* means "low," referring to the height, about ten centimeters (four inches), of the branches. *Strisciante* means "crawling" and describes how the branches, about four to six of them with one or two buds per spur, move out horizontally from the head to a distance of about one meter (three feet). Vines are planted about two meters (seven feet) apart. They look like spiders crawling across a stonescape. Each vine grows in a pit dug twenty to thirty centimeters (eight to twelve inches) into the volcanic soil. This shelters the shoots, leaves, and fruit from high winds and is similar to systems used on the Greek island of Santorini and the Spanish island of Lanzarote. The pit also collects rain and dew, making this moisture accessible to the roots. The lower planting densities on Pantelleria—2,500 plants per hectare (1,012 per acre)—mean each vine can collect more moisture. In *alberello marsalese,* practiced in the vicinity of Marsala, a short cane carrying three or four buds is tied to a spur on another branch, forming an arc. This cane is replaced each year. The other branches carry two-budded spurs. During the summer, shoots grow out from the buds and droop, causing the leaves and fruit to splay on the ground. Some farmers support the vine, its vegetation, and its fruit with a stake. Mazara del Vallo has a similar version, called *alberello mazarese*. The cane from one branch is strung under other branches. Marsala and Mazara del Vallo are two of the driest and windiest areas of Sicily, which makes it possible to allow the vegetation and fruit to lie on the ground without being damaged by fungus attack. In the vicinity of Alcamo, there is another version of alberello. A pole helps support the trunk and one cane that emerges from the trunk. A spur on the trunk carries two buds, and the cane carries six to eight. During the growing season, the pole supports the green shoots, the vegetation, and the fruit and protects them from wind damage.

MODERNIZATION: LATE 1950S TO MID-1980S
GUYOT AND CORDONE SPERONATO

Like alberello, Guyot, named after a French scientist who promoted its use in the 1860s, is a head-trained system. Guyot pruning found its way to Sicily during the late nineteenth century via the French technicians working at estates such as Zucco, Duca di Salaparuta, and Castello Maniace. Unlike alberello, it relies on long canes instead of short spurs to carry buds. Also, wires and stakes form parallel rows and support the vines and their vegetation and fruit. Guyot vines can be mechanically harvested but not mechanically pruned, which requires experience and skill.

By the 1950s, mechanization was introduced to Sicilian viticulture. The distance between the parallel rows of vines in Guyot training accommodated tractors, harvesters, and other farming machinery. As alberello vineyards decreased, average vine density decreased, to about twenty-seven hundred vines per hectare (1,093 per acre). At the same time, the increasing loss of trained vineyard workers to northern Italy encouraged the introduction of cordon-spur (*cordone speronato*) training. This row-training system requires less pruning skill than Guyot and can also accommodate mechanical pruning. Both systems create a thin vertical canopy along the row. The increased elevation of the bunches and vegetation above the ground reduces the concentration of sugar and increases the total acidity in the grapes, resulting in less-rich and sourer wines.

TENDONE

During the 1970s the *tendone* system of vine training became widespread, particularly in western Sicily. Tendone is the training of vines on an extended, over-the-head pergola. Provided that vines in tendone are planted in fertile soil, they can support the production of higher yields per area than are common for lower systems of training. The resulting wines tend to have low alcohol. While the system can produce lively, fresh white wines in hot, sunny climates, it does not usually produce quality full-bodied red wines. Tendone was introduced when the demand from both the vino da taglio and the Marsala industry for concentrated high-alcohol bulk wine had diminished and export markets wanted fruitier, fresher bulk wine. The Marsala industry found it less expensive to add concentrated rectified must to tendone's low-potential-alcohol musts. During the 1980s the high volume of production per hectare made possible by tendone was ideal for the wine-for-distillation industry financed by European Union subsidies. Nowadays this system is rarely used for wine grapes.

GRAFTING

After phylloxera invaded Sicily, winegrowers needed to employ grafters or learn how to graft. Before phylloxera, they selected and propagated the vines that they preferred in their vineyards. The process of selecting vinestock on site is called mass selection. After phylloxera, they needed to graft their selections onto rootstocks, provided by nurseries, containing American vine species genes. Between the onset of phylloxera and the 1980s, on-site grafting, called dry grafting, was common. Teams of grafters roamed Sicilian vineyards. In some areas, such as Etna, where there was a strong winegrower tradition, vineyard workers did their own dry grafting. This entails grafting vinestock onto root-stock that has already been planted in the vineyard for that purpose. Since the 1980s, nurseries have increasingly taken over the job of grafting, which they do with grafting machines. This is called bench grafting. The most prestigious nurseries are not in Sicily. Nowadays when Sicilian producers want to plant a vineyard, they usually place an order of several vinestock-to-rootstock grafts with a nursery. The nursery does the grafting and sends the bench grafts to the winegrower, who plants them. Winegrowers may, however, instead send vinewood from their own vineyards to the nurseries for bench grafting. This is the way that they most often practice mass selection. More commonly, growers, with the help of a nursery or a consultant, select both a clonal selection of their chosen variety and a rootstock that will be grafted to it. The nursery makes the graft and sends the grafted vinestock back for planting.

IMPACTS OF INDUSTRIAL VITICULTURE

Though irrigation was initially introduced to Sicily during the Muslim occupation, Sicilian vineyards did not employ systematic mechanized irrigation until the 1960s. It was adopted more rapidly in western than eastern Sicily. Irrigation is particularly helpful in sustaining young vines during drought. It also helps maximize and stabilize grape production. Appellation laws in the European Union regulate irrigation because its use can lead to overproduction. Also during the 1960s, petrochemical companies developed and vigorously sold synthetic fertilizers, pesticides, herbicides, and fungicides. These products, along with the planting of varieties such as Trebbiano Toscano and the use of training systems such as tendone, allowed farmers to sustain vineyards at higher yield levels, as much as thirty to forty metric tons per hectare (26,765 pounds per acre). By comparison, today's average is eight metric tons per hectare (7,137 pounds per acre). Tractors and other machinery increased vineyard soil compaction, reducing drainage and removing air from the topsoil. This shortened the life of vines and made them increasingly dependent on irrigation and fertilization, depleted soil resources, and destroyed organisms above- and underground. The destruction of the Sicilian vineyard ecosystem is only now being reversed, by farmers and wine producers employing sustainable, organic, and biodynamic viticulture.

VITICULTURE FROM THE LATE 1980S

By the end of the 1980s, Sicilian wine producers realized that their bulk wine industry had no future, faced with declining per capita consumption at home and elsewhere in southern Europe and more efficient, and hence lower-cost, bulk wine production in New World countries. Forward-looking Sicilians realized that they had to enter the world of quality wine, in which wine was sold by the bottle. Viticultural technology had to be revamped to achieve more-concentrated wines than had been produced in the 1970s and 1980s and fresher and better-balanced wines than had been produced in the 1950s and early 1960s. Vineyards in tendone were transformed to use Guyot and cordone speronato. Guyot has been the most popular. Vine density in new vineyards has been between four and six thousand per hectare (1,619 and 2,428 per acre). By inserting new rows between existing ones, winegrowers have been able to increase the vine density of vineyards formerly planted in tendone. This change has been driven by the belief (not scientific fact) that to produce higher-quality wine grapes, more vines should each carry less fruit in a given area. By the time these changes were made, tractors were narrower, and some could even straddle rows. Though mechanical harvesting is used more and more, most vineyards are still harvested by hand.

During the 1990s, vineyard technologies arrived in Sicily for the most part from points north, where climates were cooler and wetter. Initially enological consultants from the north advised Sicilian vineyard owners to practice techniques such as defoliation—to increase airflow around and through bunches—and to get direct sunlight on grape skins to speed up their phenolic maturation (the development of compounds such as tannins). It took a succession of dry, hot vintages, running up to the hottest and driest in recent memory, 2003, to show Sicilian vineyard owners and the rest of Italy, which suffered the same heat and drought, the risks of these practices. Sunburned grape skins endow wine with a raisin flavor that destroys the varietal character of the grape, obscures vineyard character, and homogenizes wine style. In an effort to protect their grapes from the sun, many Sicilian producers now irrigate in May and June to increase vegetation and then turn off the tap except for periods in July, August, and September with a dangerous combination of sunlight and high temperatures. About three weeks before harvest some producers strip off the leaves around the fruit on the side of the row not exposed to the sun. This provides more ventilation to the bunches without increasing their sun exposure. Only when vines are having difficulty ripening their red grapes do winegrowers remove leaves to expose the bunches to direct sunlight.

One practice that could be used more often, particularly in white wine production, is night harvesting. When grapes are night-harvested, they come in at cooler temperatures. This preserves precursor aroma compounds in the skins, which results in more-aromatic wines. Moreover, acidity levels in grapes build up at night and decrease throughout the day. Although night harvesting decreases the high energy costs of refrigeration, this hardly offsets the added costs of paying workers overtime wages. The expense of equipment and setting up a vineyard for night harvesting are also high. Nevertheless, Donnafugata has night-harvested some of its Chardonnay vineyards since 1998. Feudo Arancio also harvests at night.

VINE DISEASES AND DISORDERS

Because Sicily is dry and winds there are common, fungus disease is usually kept at bay. Powdery mildew, called oidium in Europe, unlike most other fungus diseases, does not need moist, windless conditions for propagation. It depends on wind. Sicily is a windy island. Powdery mildew is a common and serious problem in Sicilian vineyards, but it can be held at bay by periodic applications, about four per year, of a mixture of sulfur, lime, and water.

Downy mildew, called peronospera, is a highly virulent fungus that proliferates rapidly in warm and humid conditions. It rarely affects Sicilian vineyards. But once every twenty years or so, it becomes a severe problem. For this reason, Sicilian winegrowers are not well prepared to deal with it. Two infamous attacks occurred in 1957 and 1972. More recently, in 2007 and 2011, attacks significantly reduced yields. Winds and high day-to-night temperature changes protect locations that are frequently humid and warm, such as the north and east faces of Etna, from downy mildew. Sicilian growers used to protect their vines with regular applications of a small amount of copper added to a sulfur spray. This gives extremely limited protection. Sulfur and copper applications are allowed even in sustainable, biologic, and biodynamic viticulture. When, in the early 1990s, synthetic fungicides that quickly destroyed downy mildew became available, Sicilians stopped the prophylactic spraying of copper-sulfur solutions.

Some vines in areas of Sicily with high active lime soils suffer from chlorosis, a disorder, caused by an iron deficiency, that slows the production of chlorophyll. The best protection is to put vines on lime-tolerant rootstocks such as 140 Ruggeri. Applications of ferrous sulfate also fend off the disorder.

THE IMPACTS OF YOUNG VINES

Sicilian vines are young. The average age of vines in a vineyard, save for some rare ones on Etna, is rarely more than fifty years old. The average age of vines in Sicily's well-established vineyards is fifteen years old. Vines reach their production prime at eight years old. After that time, their yields decline, at first slowly, then more rapidly. With increased vine age, however, the grapes, all other things being equal, make better and better wines. Older vines with deep roots can tap into Sicily's abundant underground water resources. They do not need irrigation. Deep in the subsoil, their rootlets can drink in what is the essence of *terroir*, mineral salts dissolved in water. In my experience, the tactile structure of wine gets finer with greater vine age. With increasing vine age and more-attentive cultivation practices, the raw materials for Sicilian wines should become better and better.

ECO-FRIENDLY VITICULTURAL PROTOCOLS

Since 2000 there has been increasing interest in protocols that minimize the destructive impacts of modern grape cultivation on the environment. Modern viticulture is necessarily monocultural because only monocultures have, at least until now, delivered high-quality, regular yields, at lower costs than those of polycultural systems. But monoculture relies on human intervention. Restoring biological diversity and some of nature's adaptive ability involves instituting protocols that can be expensive and time consuming. Inevitably they involve ethically driven small steps. The planning and implementation of all these protocols involve a great deal of attention to detail. This greater attention alone results in better crops and better wine. Sicilian wine producers, particularly in dry and windy areas like Marsala and Menfi, champion the idea that their growing environments make their viticulture naturally more eco-friendly. Adhering faithfully to rigorous organic and biodynamic protocols, however, entails taking risks that could compromise the quality of the crop or reduce its volume in certain years.

ORGANIC VITICULTURE

Beginning in the mid-1990s the organic (*biologica*) viticulture movement began to attract the attention of Sicilian wine producers. In part, this interest was a response to the demands of the German and Austrian markets, which asked for organic products. EU regulations precisely define what chemical cultivation additions, such as herbicides, fertilizers, and pest and disease antidotes, can be applied in organic viticulture. Clever solutions have been created to compensate for restrictions on antidotes that are disallowed. For example, Santa Tresa in Vittoria and Marabino in Noto use pheromones (in this case female insect hormones) instead of pesticides to stifle the reproduction of harvest moths (*tignola*), their most serious insect problem. Certified organic estates can print "*Vino ottenuto (o prodotto) da uve da agricoltura biologica*" ("Wine obtained [or produced] from grapes from organic agriculture") on their labels. There are as yet no regulations that pertain to organic vinification. Bosco Falconeria, a small estate in Partinico, is one of Sicily's pioneers, beginning its efforts to go organic in 1985 and becoming certified in 1989. Another early adopter is Salvatore Ferrandes on the island of Pantelleria. Tenuta del Nanfro in Caltagirone started using organic viticulture in 1998. COS has officially been organic since 2004.

SUSTAINABLE VITICULTURE

By 2005, *sustainable* had become a buzzword in the Sicilian wine industry. New World wine industries and academic institutions launched the concept of sustainability in viticulture in the early 1990s. This basically means minimizing the negative impact of modern grape cultivation on the environment. During the 1990s, sustainable viticultural protocols—such as Low Input Sustainable Agriculture (LISA) in North America and Australia, Sustainable Winegrowing New Zealand (SWNZ), and France's *lutte raisonnée* ("reasoned struggle")—came into existence. In their infancy, they focused on how to minimize chemical additions in vineyards. Meteorological data obtained in the vineyard or by local research stations are analyzed against the degree of microbial and insect pressure to determine minimal doses of chemical additions. The precise targeting and timing of the additions maximize their efficacy. Precise targeting involves pairing vineyard management protocols with technologies of application. For example, treatments of grape bunches should be applied in a precise zone unobstructed by leaves. Planting nitrogen-fixing cover crops between rows diminishes the need for synthetic fertilizers.

Quality Sicilian wine producers are increasingly focused on the impact of all their activities on the environment as a whole. The EU has subsidized solar panel installations and other sustainable projects at several Sicilian wine estates. Donnafugata and Feudo Arancio have been leaders in the use of sustainable practices and the promotion of the concept of sustainability. At the 2010 Vinitaly, Tasca d'Almerita announced its partnership with Milan's Catholic University of the Sacred Heart in a sustainable program called SOStain. Planeta has more recently become a partner in SOStain. Large wine companies preferentially adopt sustainable viticulture and, more generally, sustainable business activities over organic or biodynamic protocols.

BIODYNAMIC VITICULTURE

Biodynamic viticulture is the application of the principles of the Austrian philosopher Rudolf Steiner to grape cultivation. At a 1924 conference, he presented his ideas to agronomists who subsequently translated them into a system of agricultural practices. The macrocosm, the microcosm, and their elemental forces figure into the rationale for biodynamic viticultural activities, as for all other such activities. Examples of biodynamic practices are spraying dilute nettle tea on vines and timing certain activities to coincide with cosmologic events, such as pruning or planting during a descending moon. Organic and sustainable practices are used as long as they accord with the philosophy. There are several organizations that certify biodynamic agriculture. In the mid-1990s the Pachino producer Hans Zenner and his son, Dó, became the first practicing biodynamic winegrowers in Sicily. Interest in and adoption of biodynamic viticulture had begun to grow in Sicily by 2005. Other early adopters were Abbazia Santa Anastasia and COS.

THE FUTURE IMPORTANCE OF ECO-FRIENDLY PROTOCOLS

The above protocols are all holistic and extend, to varying degrees, beyond viticulture into some, if not all, aspects of wine production, distribution, and marketing. They also extend in varying degrees to issues such as global warming, air pollution, water pollution and availability, and the limits of carbon-based energy sources, such as oil. The United Nations has issued a strategic policy called Global Impact that sets sustainable standards for businesses. The goal is to establish networks of compliant businesses and organizations that not only support the policy but preferentially conduct business with one another. The alcoholic beverage–purchasing monopolies of the governments of Finland, Sweden, Norway, Iceland, and the Faroe Islands have signed an agreement that, starting in 2013, will give preferential trading status to the industries of other countries in compliance with Global Impact. Northern European countries are important export markets for Sicilian wine producers. Because of the increasing political concern over sustainability, the Sicilian wine industry is likely to benefit from adopting sustainable and other eco-friendly protocols.

8

ENOLOGY IN SICILY

During his travels through Sicily in the late eighteenth century, Johann Wolfgang von Goethe observed that the "oil and the wine are also good, but would be even better if prepared with greater care."[1] Sicilian winegrowers throughout history have maintained a deep connection to viticulture that has kept them in step with existing viticultural technologies. Their understanding of enology, however, lacked the sophistication found in mainland Italy and certainly in France and Germany. This deficiency is consistent with Sicily's historic inability to transform its high-quality raw materials into finished products. Only after the mid-1990s did Sicilian winemaking practices reach parity with those of the sophisticated wine industries of the world.

EARLY SICILIAN ENOLOGY

While the grapes the ancient Greeks grew resembled the grapes we eat today in look and taste, their wines bore little resemblance to present-day ones. From what we know about their techniques, their wines must have quickly oxidized after alcoholic fermentation. They covered wine oxidation and other flaws with the addition of seawater, spices, and other substances. The problem of oxidation and flaws due to a lack of hygiene confronted not only the Greek Sicilians but also the Romans and all of the European wine cultures that followed. It was not until after Louis Pasteur, in the mid-nineteenth century, studied the role of microbes and oxygen in fermentation and maturation that producers could make great technical strides in controlling wine production.

Italians have always regarded the French as the masters of wine production. Though the French imported an enormous quantity of raw Sicilian wine during the nineteenth century, they had neither invested in nor educated the Sicilian wine industry. Italian private and public institutions were studying and reporting about French enology then, but their writings had little impact on what was practiced in Sicily, although several Sicilian nobles, members of that era's sophisticated and cosmopolitan class, imported French technology and hired French consultants. After the 1990s, Sicilian producers paid attention to Australian viticulture and enology since they recognized that Australia had a climate similar to theirs and had developed sophisticated technology that transformed harvests into easy-to-sell, international-style wine.

Sicilian wine technology evolved much more slowly than that of the rest of Europe. One example of a missed opportunity occurred in 1802, when the Sicilian physician and poet Giovanni Meli, in a letter to Saverio Landolina Nava of Syracuse, recommended a vinification methodology that the Prince of Butera and the Prince of Cattolica had successfully used.[2] Meli described terra-cotta and cement vats at the villa of the Prince of Butera at Bagheria, a town close to Palermo. Each vat had a small hole at the top and a wooden hatch near the base. The method of fermentation he described was to let the skins, stems, and pulp macerate for fifteen days, to drain the wine off the skins, to clean out the vats, and to put the wine back in until it was ready for sale. These vats could be hermetically sealed, to limit the access of oxygen. Meli saw the value of this for fermentation and maturation at a time when most technicians in Sicily believed that wine needed unrestricted contact with air. Landolina Nava separately described a red wine producer working in the Faro area who had conical open-topped oak fermentation tanks of a design similar to one still used in Bordeaux.[3] At the end of a nine-day maceration period, at the moment when it lost the aroma of fruit juice, this producer racked the wine off its sediments. The equipment and methods that Meli and Landolina Nava described became commonplace in twentieth-century enology. Unfortunately, their efforts to advance Sicilian enology had little impact in their time.

Before the twentieth century most Sicilians drank amber-colored white wines, copper-tinted *rosato* wines, or red wines that were coarse textured, alcoholic, and slightly sweet. These wines were probably oxidized, if not faulty in other ways. The nobility preferred imported table wines of all types, most of which were made in France. Except for Giuseppe Alliata, they had little interest in consuming local wine besides Marsala, let alone making it. During the late eighteenth century and the first half of the nineteenth century, foreign markets, most importantly the British, imported Marsala and Sicilian table wines, principally red. The table wines that they wanted were fresher, less alcoholic, and drier than the ones Sicilian commoners preferred. Besides Marsala, Sicily's most recognized wine was a very sweet white, Moscato di Siracusa.

The nineteenth century saw a worldwide explosion in wine consumption and wine trading. The traditional winemaking areas of Europe were in regions where vintage quality and harvest volume varied from year to year. Sicily became an important source of *vino da taglio* ("cutting wine"). It was mostly red and was used by northern Italian and French producers as an additive to reduce wine variation and to give wines a competitive edge with respect to depth of color and degree of alcohol and astringency. Vino da taglio was dark violet, high in alcohol, high in astringency, and sometimes slightly sweet. When the French imported Sicilian vino da taglio during their phylloxera crisis, they preferred to buy it as freshly fermented as possible, even when it was still fermenting and slightly sweet. If the wine was transported in the last stages of fermentation, the remaining active yeasts would preserve it until it reached cellars in France. The French also wanted wines rich in tannins, which would better preserve the wine during shipment. Once it was in France, technicians cleaned up and otherwise adjusted the wine by racking it off the lees and fining, filtering, and sulfiting it. As a result, the Sicilian producers of vino da taglio did not develop expertise in stabilizing, blending, or aging wine. At the same time, from the late nineteenth until the mid-twentieth century many Sicilians developed a taste for vino da taglio, which they called *superalcolici*. This demand retarded the development of fine Sicilian table wine (*vino da pasto*) because it pushed the Sicilian wine ethos toward alcoholic and rough wines. French and northern Italian merchants returned in the mid-twentieth century for more of the booster vino da taglio, but its trade began diminishing in the 1970s and petered out during the 1990s.

It was the English who invested in Sicilians and the Sicilian wine industry. They introduced the technology for producing fortified wines. The base wines that were needed for Marsala were high in alcohol and oxidized. Delicacy of texture was not an important factor for these wines. However, when English merchants bought unfortified Sicilian table wine for resale, they sought more delicate ones, both red and white. The evolution of wine technology and changing consumer preferences began to marginalize the fortified wine market after the middle of the twentieth century. The most durable "technologies" that the English brought to Sicily turned out to be wine entrepreneurialism and the know-how to conduct international trade.

Before the twentieth century there were few Sicilian vineyards planted to single varieties, let alone to just white or just red vine varieties. Red and white grapes were often harvested and vinified together, creating a range of wine colors from golden to amber to pale red. In the Marsala area, the table wine of farmer families was *ambrato*, made from a mix of red and white grapes. According to *Notizie e Studi intorno Ai Vini ed Alle Uve d'Italia* (1896), the Palermo area, for example, was known for "golden" wines made from blends of Catarratto, a white grape, and Perricone, a red one.[4] The historic Etna red wine blend contained white grapes from white vine varieties that were planted in small numbers among the Nerello Mascalese and Nerello Cappuccio, the principal red varieties. At the end of the eighteenth century, King Ferdinand III of Sicily sent the Apulian wine technician Felice Lioy to Sicily to improve its abysmal wine production. Lioy worked in the northwest from 1789 to 1812. Among other recommendations, he proposed the separate harvesting and vinification of white grapes and red grapes. His prescriptions, presented in his book *Memoria per la manipolazione dei vini* (1800), became a catechism for wine producers, particularly Benjamin Ingham, who thirty years later included Lioy's advice in an instructional booklet used at his Marsala house.[5] When white grapes were harvested separately from red ones, there was the possibility of making both white and red wines, as well as rosatos (which during the twentieth century came to be made from red grapes alone). The separate vinification of red and white grapes became increasingly common during the nineteenth century.

At harvest time, workers brought baskets of grapes to *palmento*s. A *palmento* was the area where freshly harvested grapes were crushed and where the juice underwent alcoholic fermentation. In western Sicily, larger farm complexes called *baglio*s housed the palmentos. The walls of the palmento were very thick, to buffer rapid temperature changes. Stone floors transmitted the cool temperature of the earth. Palmentos in some regions, such as Etna, were built to make use of gravity: their reception area was elevated, and subsequent processes occurred at lower elevations.

Rarely were grapes preselected before processing. One such rarity was noted by the British consul William Stigand, who described the grape bunches at the Hood estate at Castello Maniace being destalked "on a series of dressers, such as are used in the Gironde."[6] Harvesters traditionally carried their loaded baskets up opposing stairways that ran along the outer wall of the palmento and converged on one or two open windows. Through these windows they unloaded the baskets onto a stone floor that sloped down gradually to shallow fermenting tanks hollowed into the floor. These tanks had walls of calcareous stone fitted together with a calcareous terra-cotta mortar. They were of the size needed to accommodate the annual volume of each grower's harvest.

The most common grape-processing method used in the palmentos was called *pesta-imbotta* or *pestimbotta*, which means "to crush and put in cask." The crushing of fresh grapes (red, white, or both together) was done rapidly and before fermentation occurred. Once the harvesters had dumped the bunches onto the palmento floor, a team of crushers trod the grapes underfoot. Until the middle of the twentieth century, they wore leather shoes with soles fitted with metal studs. The soles did not have heels. The pressure of crushing was spread out and extended throughout the bottom of the foot. The studs bruised the stems and skins and ruptured the seeds. Usually the shoes were not cleaned before or after use. During the late nineteenth century, some producers making fine wine required pressers to wear soft-soled moccasins or use bare feet. Prince Baucina at La Contessa even insisted that pressers clean their feet before getting to work. A handful of producers, such as Henri d'Orleans at Zucco and Alexander Nelson Hood, had teams of workers who destemmed the grapes by hand. Thus bitter substances in the stems were discarded before alcohol could extract them. At Zucco, La Contessa, and Corvo at Casteldaccia, machines pressed white grapes before fermentation. These machines were of French construction and delicately pressed the grapes, allowing the resulting wines to be delicate in texture.

Commonly during the pestimbotta process, the crushers would sprinkle a white powder (calcium sulfate, referred to as gesso) on the bunches and crushed grapes. This was also added later, during alcoholic fermentation. Gesso increased the strength of the acidity, making the wine sourer and helping to preserve it from bacterial attack. During the late nineteenth century this practice was discontinued because gesso was thought to be harmful when consumed. Later this usage was shown to be harmless, though by that time tartaric acid had made gesso obsolete.

The pestimbotta process was essentially the same for white and rosato production. It was modified for red winemaking. The basic pestimbotta method intermixed white and red grapes. After the pressing of the grapes underfoot, the juice was fermented off its skins in a tank built into the ground. For more sophisticated wine, the white grapes were separated from the red and there was a distinction between white, rosato, and red wine production. White wine production had less aggressive crushing and pressing and few, if any, pressed bunches added to the fermentation that followed the initial pressing. The juice from the pressed grapes drained into a tank, where it underwent the tumultuous part of fermentation. After a day or two, when most of its sugar had transformed into alcohol, the juice was transported or drained into barrels, in which it finished fermenting. In 1800, Lioy described how unfermented juice was continuously mixed with juice in more advanced stages of fermentation in the must.[7] This suggests that in the late eighteenth and early nineteenth centuries the common fermentation process was continuous rather than a batch process and saw wine continuously drained from the tank and put into barrel. More sophisticated vinification was done in batches so that all the grapes in the vat were at the same stage of fermentation.

White wines were amber colored, due to the initial skin contact and oxidation. In eastern Sicily, where the grape mix was red dominant, a wine made with no skin contact after the initial crush was called a *pistammutta,* dialect for *pestimbotta.* A pistammutta wine was essentially a rosato. After the grapes were pressed, their juice fermented tumultuously for one or two days in tank and was then put into barrels, where it completed fermentation. This wine was for local consumption. Today Alice Bonaccorsi and Rosario Pappalardo pay homage to pistammutta with their Etna rosato RossoRelativo. They place freshly harvested Nerello Mascalese bunches in a cool area for twenty hours. During that time, color seeps from the skins into the pulp. Then they machine-press the grapes, ferment the juice without temperature control, and bottle it. Though it is difficult for me to mentally reconstruct the flavor of a nineteenth-century Etna pistammutta, the RossoRelativo I tasted was drier, much cleaner, and less bitter than I imagine a nineteenth-century rosato would have been.

When red wines were desired, as was often the case in eastern Sicily and the export market, the pestimbotta process was modified. Pressed red grapes were added to the fermenting must. The amount of the pressed grapes added to the fermentation vat in the palmento and the length of the maceration in tank depended on the style of wine desired by the purchaser or the locals who would consume it. The pressers waded into the mass of fermenting skins and juice to increase the extraction of color and tannins. They were known to clutch or be tied to ropes that dangled from the ceiling. This was to keep them from falling into the must due to asphyxiation as the carbon dioxide (CO_2) gas that fermentation emitted replaced the air. Red wines with increasingly more color and structure were commonly referred to as "twelve-hour," "twenty-four-hour," and "forty-eight-hour," for the amount of time that the fermenting must had been in contact with the crushed grapes. The traditional vini da taglio were closest to forty-eight-hour. If its red grapes were deeply colored and very ripe, forty-eight-hour wines could be dark and concentrated. Nero Pachino vini da taglio sold to merchants for blending were forty-eight-hour wines.

The juice liberated from the mound of grapes crushed underfoot drained through stone-carved channels, down a tube, and out a spout into the shallow fermenting tank below. After the chorus of workers singing traditional harvest songs had sufficiently stomped on the bunches, on the call of their leader they would rearrange the smashed bunches into a shallow pile using a hoelike instrument and stomp on them some more. At a certain point they would mound the mush of skins, stems, and seeds; place a board or thick straw mat on top; and, lifting one foot and then the other onto the board or mat, use their combined body weight to squeeze the mush. The pressers would repeat this sequence three times. Sometimes they would do it again later in the day. Before the juice drained into the tank, it was roughly sieved to remove seeds and other debris.

Collected in the shallow vat, the must commenced fermentation. If the ambient temperature was sufficiently high, within a day the fermentation became tumultuous. This initial phase of the fermentation would usually last up to forty-eight hours, with the crushers wading into the tank to distribute the grape skins evenly across the must, thereby increasing the color and flavor extracted from the skins. When the desired degree of maceration had occurred, the fermenting juice was drained off the sediments. On Etna the fermenting wine was often drained into a second, deeper and larger vat constructed in the ground. Workers next transported the wine by means of clay jars, wooden or animal skin buckets, or other receptacles and poured it into barrels, usually made of chestnut. Where gravity could be used, they simply directed the must or wine into barrels using channels. The barrels where the now gently fermenting wine was transferred were in another room or another building, called a *dispensa* or *cantina*. In some places, such as Syracuse, where the palmento was in or next to the vineyard, the dispensa was some distance away, usually in a clutch of farm buildings associated with the owner's domicile. In such cases the must was put into small barrels, loaded onto wagons, and transported to the dispensa, where it was drained into larger casks. The casks on average had capacities of twenty to thirty hectoliters (528 to 793 gallons), but some held one hundred hectoliters (2,642 gallons) or more. They were rarely cleaned and were prone to leakage. Early barrel-cleaning machines first came into use in Marsala in the mid-nineteenth century. Zucco had two by the 1880s. Leaks were repaired with plaster of Paris or some other filler.

Until the juice finished fermenting, the casks' bungholes were left open to allow carbon dioxide gas to escape. The completion of alcoholic fermentation, when all or nearly all of the grape sugar had transformed into alcohol, largely depended on ambient conditions. If the temperature remained warm enough, fermentation completed soon, from several to a dozen days after onset. If winter temperatures arrived too soon, it would slow down or stop, likely to restart the following spring when the ambient temperature rose. In practice, when the winemaker noticed that the wine had become clear and bubbles were no longer rising, he hammered a wooden stopper (bung) into the bunghole of the cask. This helped keep fruit flies away, kept objects from falling in, and reduced evaporation. Little was known or understood about malolactic fermentation until well into the twentieth century. This bacterial fermentation turns the sharply sour malic acid into the softer-tasting lactic acid and leaves the wine less vulnerable to deleterious bacterial infections. It is gentle in the sense that it is difficult to notice. The wine becomes cloudy due to the creation of carbon dioxide gas and the disturbance of sediments. When it is limpid again, malolactic fermentation has stopped. Sometimes, however, malolactic fermentation stops without transforming all of the malic acid into lactic acid, leaving stability compromised. At cool locations, such as on Etna, malolactic fermentation likely occurred on its own in the spring, when outside temperatures were high enough to warm the dispensas. In warm places, such as Menfi or Pachino, it was likely to commence during the finale of alcoholic fermentation and finish quickly thereafter. When both yeast- and bacteria-induced fermentations had completed, the wine was much less vulnerable to microbiologic degradation and hence more stable for transport and storage. Fortified wines, because of their high levels of alcohol—about 20 percent—were totally microbiologically stable. Probably few other Sicilian wines, however, reached microbiologic stability until the middle of the twentieth century.

Vino da taglio was seldom racked (i.e., drained from cask off sediments into empty barrels) because it was sold just before or at the end of alcoholic fermentation. If the wine remained in the dispensa, it would be racked once after the winter in preparation for sale. During the late nineteenth century, racking occurred more often as the culture of wine improved and more quality vini da pasto began to be produced. Racking is a natural way of stabilizing and clarifying wine, though too much in the presence of air can allow excessive oxidation. Commonly the finer wines were racked four times, the last during the summer after the harvest. There was, however, no topping up of casks to speak of. This would have reduced the oxidation of the wine. Casks were often left half full. Under normal conditions the wine would be sold before the next harvest, in order to use the dispensa space and the casks efficiently. However, the finest Sicilian producers, such as Baucina, d'Orleans, and Hood, matured their wines in cask for up to three and a half, five, and seven years, respectively.

Within the greater wine world, the burning of sulfur in empty casks was widespread. This was conducted during the racking operation, when wine was moved from one container to another. Sulfiting was known to remove bad smells from casks not in use. What was not fully understood in the nineteenth century was that burning sulfur creates sulfur dioxide (SO_2) gas, which has strong antioxidative, antienzymatic, and antibacterial properties. It kills wild vineyard yeast and reduces the activity of ambient cellar yeasts and selected yeasts. Burning sulfur in casks between rackings was standard practice at the best châteaux in Bordeaux in the eighteenth century. While some Sicilian producers making fine vino da pasto burned sulfur in their casks between rackings, most did not. Instead they used a cosmetic alternative called the *stufa* ("oven"). They boiled fruits and spices such as orange peel, cinnamon, and carob seeds in water and poured the hot liquid into empty barrels. The wood absorbed the water, whose aromas covered the objectionable ones of spoilage yeast and bacteria.

A lack of hygiene was the norm for nineteenth-century Sicilian wine production. Surfaces that came in contact with grape juice or wine were cleaned neither before nor after vinification. There was a belief among Sicilians that the fermentation process had such a forceful cleansing power that it did not need to be protected by sanitation. Tartaric salt accumulations in casks were never scraped away. As a result, palmentos and dispensas became breeding grounds for microbial infections that obscured the true character of wine made in them. This uncleanliness continued in some areas of Sicily well into the twentieth century.

During the vinification process, sediments and whatever skins and stems were left over from the crushing underfoot—whether unfermented, half fermented, or fully fermented—were pressed for their remaining liquid. Nothing went to waste. Even the dry grape skins were soaked in water and refermented to make family table wine. There was an area in the palmento dedicated to this final pressing. These pressings varied in character and quality. Early vinification equipment had copper and bronze parts, which contaminated wine with cupric salts. When exposed to light, these give white wines a reddish brown tint. Such contamination might have played a role in the color common to Sicilian white wines. In the mid-1870s, mechanical steel-and-wood presses, mostly imported from France, began to replace the traditional palmento press (*conzo*), which employed a massive tree trunk that spanned the length of the palmento and was attached to a huge stone counterweight. Initial pressings were dark and pleasantly astringent but not so bitter. Successive pressings produced successively paler, bitterer, more rudely astringent, and lower-acid juice or wine. This liquid was either added to already fermenting juice or wine or left to continue its fermentation and maturation separately.

Producers added carob juice, cooked must, or cane sugar to the fermenting must if they wanted to increase the sugar content and therefore the potential alcohol content of their wine. Another solution for increasing alcohol strength was simply adding grape spirits. Lemon juice was added to increase acidity. The blood of bulls and other animals was commonly used in fining wine to remove impurities. In the late nineteenth century, producers of fine wines did this with egg whites, which they would whisk into a foam and add to casks. At the Baucina estate the white wines were racked and fined with egg whites eight times before bottling. The blood or egg whites combined with tannins and debris, settled in the lees at the bottom of the cask, and were removed during the racking process. The commercial bottling of fine Sicilian vino da pasto began in the late nineteenth-century. Otherwise, the wine was sold by cask or in bulk.

The type of red wine production in which the stems and skins of the grapes stayed in contact with the fermenting juice was called *ribollito* in certain parts of Sicily. This skin contact lasted up to a week or more. Domenico Sestini used the word *ribollito* to indicate such extended macerations.[8] *Ribollito* is the past participle of *ribollire*, meaning both "to reboil" and "to boil intensely." On Etna such macerations were not uncommon. The term *ritornato*, meaning "sent back," was used in the Caltanis-setta area for essentially the same process. In southeast Sicily, a fermentation vat was called a *ritorno*. Sestini and others noted that ribollito wines resisted degradation. The added tannins from such long macerations would have helped preserve the wine from oxidation. Ideally, the fermentation would have completed without the interruption of a draining off the skins. By contrast, the draining off the skins with twelve-hour, twenty-four-hour, and forty-eight-hour wines would have left them with unfermented sugars, which would have been vulnerable to spoilage yeasts and bacteria. These yeasts and bacteria were plentiful in the unclean dispensas typical of Sicilian wine producers. These wines would certainly have been ruined by the time they reached the cellars of overseas buyers. Jessie White Mario, in her article "Prodotti del Suolo e Viticoltura in Sicilia" ("Products of the Soil and Viticulture in Sicily"), published in 1894, noted a wine jury's contemporaneous assessment of Sicilian wines that had been imported into the United Kingdom for a wine fair: "As soon as we had begun to taste, we were in agreement that the wines were more or less in a state of fermenta-tion; shortly after we had to remove the wines from the competition because they had no commercial value: some were even so ruined that they were not saleable."[9] Sicilian winemakers have suggested to me that *ribollire*'s literal meaning "to reboil" referred to a fermentation reinitiated after it had stopped. However, the outcome of such a "reboil-ing" performed in the conditions typical of nineteenth-century Sicilian wineries would have been putrid and undrinkable wines. The vinification method used by the Prince of Butera that Meli described in 1802 resembles ribollito. One wonders how much better nineteenth-century Sicilian wines would have been if producers had read, digested, and acted on Meli's observations.

LATE-NINETEENTH-CENTURY FINE WINE PRODUCTION

The late nineteenth century saw the emergence of a quality wine industry in Sicily. The principles of modern enology, as practiced in northern Europe, were introduced. A small group of forward-thinking producers began adopting such techniques and enter-ing their wines in international wine fairs. Modern Sicilian enologists know little, if anything, about the history of this early quality wine industry. During that period two of the earliest enological schools in Italy were established in Sicily. The State Technical

Agricultural School (La Scuola Enologica) at Catania was created in 1881. Its primary role was as a school of viticulture and enology. Several years after its inception it created a Scuola Enologica, which eventually became the Istituto Tecnico Agrario Statale "F. Eredia," specializing in viticulture and enology. As of 1885, Marsala had a Regia Scuola Pratica di Agricoltura ("Royal Practical School of Agriculture"), which offered instruction in viticulture and enology. In 1931 it became the Regio Istituto Tecnico Agrario "Abele Damiani." Starting in 1947, this school has offered a special degree in enology and viticulture. Since the late 1990s it has collaborated with the School of Agriculture (Facoltà di Agraria) of the University of Palermo to offer a specialized university degree in enology and viticulture. There were also three experimental vinification centers, one in Riposto, founded in 1888, one in Noto, founded in 1889, and one in Milazzo, founded in 1903.

A DELAYED EMBRACE OF THE TWENTIETH CENTURY

The Sicilian wine industry declined steadily during the 1890s and continued to deteriorate until the end of World War II. Unsurprisingly, this period saw little innovation in Sicilian vinification. But beginning in the 1960s, Ezio Rivella brought modern vinification techniques to Tasca d'Almerita, Settesoli, and Duca di Salaparuta. At about the same time, refrigeration equipment and stainless steel became available to wineries. During the 1970s and 1980s the rapid development of cooperative wineries brought new technologies and equipment to Sicily, principally in the west, where the cooperative movement was stronger and more widespread. The work of the Istituto Regionale della Vite e del Vino (IRVV, "Regional Institute of Vine and Wine") and its consultant Giacomo Tachis helped to instill a modern European winemaking ethos in Sicily. Before Tachis's arrival in the early 1990s, concrete and large chestnut casks (botti) had been the only maturation vessels there. His influence brought French barriques into common use for the maturation of red wine. Sicily had been known more for its white wines than its reds. Its reds did not have a reputation for having rich—what Tachis called supple—tannins. According to the quality of the red grape skins and the style of red wine desired, he encouraged producers to adjust the vigor and duration of maceration. For the highest-quality red wines, he sought high dry extract levels. Provided that the tannins in the grape skins were fully developed, these could be achieved with pumpovers and macerations that continued for two weeks or even longer, beyond the end of alcoholic fermentation.

In the early 1990s Carlo Corino, working at Planeta and Settesoli, brought an Australian perspective and Australian techniques to Sicily, and then, in the late 1990s, the Australian Kim Milne, a master of wine and a flying winemaker (via metal, not feathered, wings), consulted for Firriato. In 2000 Calatrasi hired a team of three Australian enologists, Brian Fletcher, Lisa Gilbee, and Linda Domas. Planeta barrel-fermented in new oak barriques a Chardonnay that it released in the mid-1990s. This wine captured the attention of Italian and foreign journalists, who equated its creamy texture and thick, burned-caramel and toasty flavors with top-quality white wine. Firriato's Nero d'Avola Harmonium, thick, ripe, and oaky, also recalls the style of wine for which Australia was known. The fascination with new-oak-flavored wines spawned a decade of heavy oaking, which sent Sicilian wine away from its roots but toward something else it undeniably needed: international acceptance and acclaim.

MAINLAND ITALIAN CONSULTANTS

The increasing influence of consulting mainland Italian enologists, most of whom also worked in Tuscany, brought Sicily more in touch with modern international vinification and another step away from coming to terms with its roots. Tachis was trained only in enology, though he acquired viticultural knowledge throughout his career. Most consulting enologists today are also trained in viticulture. In Sicily, Carlo Ferrini, Riccardo Cotarella, and Donato Lanati were the principal consulting enologists—three of the most important in Italy—who followed in the wake of Tachis. They brought not only their international reputations, credibility, expertise, and connections to enological suppliers (of machines, tanks, barrels, yeast, additives, packaging, etc.) but also an understanding of how essential viticultural science was for wine production and connections to viticultural suppliers (irrigation installation companies, agrochemical manufacturers, and nurseries).

Sicilians admired Tachis for his understanding of their history and his often-expressed love of the island and its culture. Ferrini, Cotarella, and Lanati have been more difficult for Sicilian enologists to accept as anything but outsiders. Not that these mainland-based enologists do not express a genuine passion for the island and respect for its people. However, none of them show Tachis's mastery of Sicilian history. Because they have established relationships with viticultural and enological suppliers in northern Italy and France, they direct their Sicilian clients to buy from these and not Sicilian vendors. This offends some Sicilians. What irritates Sicilian enologists most, however, is not the behavior of these foreign enologists but that of the Sicilian wine producers who employ them. Sicilian enologists believe that the producers who forsake them for foreign consultants refuse to acknowledge their hard work and skill. One Sicilian producer who did just that told me that he had upgraded from a Fiat to a Ferrari.

In 2003, Ferrini became the head enologist of Donnafugata following Tachis's departure, and Cotarella took over at Abbazia Santa Anastasia. Around the same time, Ferrini got the plum job in Sicily: Tasca d'Almerita hired him. Moreover, he followed two Tuscan clients, the owners of Castello di Fonterutoli and of Sette Ponti, to consult for their Sicilian outposts, Zisola in Noto and Maccari in Pachino, respectively. Cotarella was the coach behind Morgante as its wines moved from obscurity into the spotlight. Lanati, however, had been in Sicily earlier than either Ferrini or Cotarella. Salvatore Geraci in 1990 sent a bottle of wine from his vineyard south of the city of Messina to this Piedmont winemaker. Lanati liked it better than the Barolos he was sampling. He suggested that Geraci produce it commercially. Thus the now-famous Palari was born, and Lanati had his first Sicilian client. Emiliano Falsini, a Tuscan enologist associated with the Matura Group, recently replaced Lanati at the Graci Etna estate. The success of Girolamo Russo, Falsini's most famous client, also on Etna, has attracted attention to Falsini's work.

HOMEGROWN CONSULTANTS

Salvo Foti stands out, by himself, as Sicily's greatest homegrown consulting enologist. Curiously, his expertise did not evolve from the goings-on at the IRVV experimental station at Virzi in the 1990s or its spin-offs. In the 1980s, after getting a technical degree in enology, Foti began working with wine producers in various areas of Sicily. In the early 1990s he got his specialist degree in enology at the University of Catania. He has a strong attachment to Etna. As a child he helped his grandfather farm a small vineyard there. Until 2012 his pivotal client at Etna had been Benanti, with whom he had been working since the 1990s. More recent is his association with Gulfi, a winery near Vittoria that excels in single-contrada Pachino wines. Foti manages a group of one to two dozen skilled Etna-based vineyard workers. The group calls itself I Vigneri ("The Winegrowers") after a trade guild of similarly skilled workers named the Maestranza dei Vigneri ("Winegrowers Guild") that dates back to 1435. Foti had articles of constitution drawn up for I Vigneri in September 2009. In addition to their duties tending alberello vines, these workers spend the off-season rebuilding the historic lava terraces in Etna's vineyards. In 2010 they built an *enoteca* in Randazzo to showcase the wines of the I Vigneri winegrowers and producers. Foti himself owns a small wine estate, also called I Vigneri. Beyond Benanti and Gulfi, his consulting clients tend to be small, even micro-, producers. They also identify themselves under the I Vigneri banner. Foti's perspective goes beyond the wine business. His mission is to preserve, manifest, and perpetuate the relationship between land, vine, and human. He believes in alberello, dense vine spacing, and the avoidance of systemic sprays and synthetic soil additions. One can always identify a Vigneri vineyard by these characteristics and the chestnut poles that support the vines. Foti's vinification techniques vary from mainstream ones that assure control through a modest degree of intervention to artisanal, which usually assumes minimal intervention. He has tended to rely on barriques for red wine maturation. Foti has written two books about the wine culture of Etna. More than any other person, he has fostered an awareness of its unique wine culture.

While the force of Foti erupts from the east, the other major Sicilian force, the duo of Vincenzo Bambina and Nicola Centonze, who incorporated their partnership as B&C Enologists, blows across the island from the west. Both went to the Marsala School of Enology and finished their studies in northern Italy, Bambina in Piedmont and Centonze in the Veneto. Their business partnership alone reveals a spirit of association that is new to Sicily. With some clients, they split the work. With others, one or the other takes primary responsibility. As a young enologist Bambina worked under Tachis at Donnafugata. Yet Tachis's perspectives did not inspire him. Bambina espouses a viticulture and enology of the south. He believes that vines grown in Sicily should not be stressed as is commonly done in traditional European viticulture. Vine care should ensure that a robust, green canopy protects the vine from too much sun exposure and that the vine has enough water to avoid hydric stress. He is not a fan of monster wines or the drastically small yields and late picking that their pursuit encourages. With respect to vinification, he avoids excessive extraction, preferring elegantly styled wines. The wines of two of his clients, Fondo Antico and Brugnano, express this style best. While Bambina energetically states his case, Centonze is self-effacing. He quietly listens to what his clients want and organizes the work to achieve that end, carefully weighing what course is best. The wines of Abraxas from Pantelleria show his meticulous attention to detail.

Another Sicilian enologist's star has been rising. After fourteen years of being in charge of enology at Tasca d'Almerita, Tonino Guzzo went off on his own. Since then he has dramatically improved the wines of a cooperative, Viticultori Associati Canicattì. His work manifests a flair for the unusual, such as making a *passito* Perricone at Castellucci Miano and botrytis Grillo at Gorghi Tondi. His greatest triumph is high-altitude Catarratto at Castellucci Miano. Other Sicilian consulting enologists whose work has been impactful are Giovanni Rizzo, Vito Giovinco, Antonino Di Marco, Giuseppe Romano, and Salvatore Martinico.

NO- OR LOW-SULFITE WINEMAKING

There are some off-road vinification trends worth noting, though they are by no means limited to Sicily. One such is no-sulfite winemaking. Because some people are allergic to sulfites and there is consumer resistance to them, there are wine producers who have been trying to refrain from adding sulfites to wine. However, this is a risky practice because sulfites protect wine from oxidation and the activity of microbes that cause wine degradation. Since white wines do not enjoy the antioxidative protection of the tannins of red wine, they are more at risk. Sweet, low-alcohol wines are even more at risk, since sugar is particularly vulnerable to both yeast and bacterial infection. In Sicily the leaders in no-sulfite winemaking have been the Belgian wine merchant Frank Cornelissen and the Etnean Giovanni Raiti. Cornelissen refrains altogether from adding sulfites to his wines. At Giuliemi, Raiti, with the help of the enologist Pietro Di Giovanni, produces Quantico white wine and red wine. Salvo Foti has also been making two low-production (about one thousand bottles) no-added-sulfite wines, Vinudilice, a *clairette,* or light red wine, and Vinujancu, a white wine.

WILD, AMBIENT, AND SELECTED YEASTS

Sulfite additions are inextricably connected to the subject of vineyard, winery, and selected yeast activity during winemaking. Sulfites subdue and kill vineyard yeast, so-called wild yeast, that arrives at the winery on the skins of freshly harvested grapes. Many producers prefer to eradicate vineyard yeast strains because they cause higher levels of volatile acidity in the wine. Producers who do not add sulfites to their fresh juice let vineyard yeast carry fermentation until ambient yeast strains that inhabit the winery take over and lead fermentation to completion. Such producers say they use natural yeast. The other path is to add sulfites and then selected yeast. Though selected yeasts are "natural," it is more difficult to argue that they are wild. They come from companies that select, propagate, and sell specific strains. Their use takes wine away from the terroir of both the vineyard and the winery and results in fruitier wines that are usually more appealing to consumers. Their predictable behavior gives winemakers more control over outcomes. Because red wines are less dependent on the fruity smells imparted by yeasts and because consumers tolerate volatile acidity more in red than white wines, the use of vineyard and winery yeast is much more common in red than white wine production. It is rare to find producers of white wines who forgo the use of selected yeast. However, Cornelissen, Foti, Giuliemi, COS, Bonaccorsi, Guccione, Barraco, Porta del Vento, and Marabino all use vineyard and winery yeast in white wine fermentation.

SKIN CONTACT IN WHITE WINE PRODUCTION

If producers macerate white grape skins in warm fermenting juice à la red wine production, they take further risks. White skins contain phenolic compounds that are unstable and oxidize rapidly, thus causing wine to brown. They also contain bitter and astringent substances that add coarse texture to wine. For at least a decade Cornelissen and COS have been fermenting on white grape skins. COS does this in clay jars called amphorae. Cornelissen uses thousand-liter (264-gallon) high-density polyethylene tubs. Some varieties, such as Chardonnay, have the structure, acidity, and alcohol to work better in this kind of fermentation than a variety such as Inzolia, which is lacking in acidity. Chardonnay also benefits from lees contact more than most other varieties. The mannoproteins released by degenerating yeast cells in the lees mute bitterness and astringency released from the skins by the increasing concentration of alcohol. For its Èureka Chardonnay, Marabino has been experimenting with fermenting 60 percent of the Chardonnay on its skins and 40 percent off them. Marco Sferlazzo at Porta del Vento near Palermo ferments Catarratto for two weeks on its skins without temperature control, relying on indigenous yeasts and not adding sulfites. Alice Bonaccorsi, in the town of Randazzo on Etna's north face, ferments ValCerasa Etna Bianco on its skins, calling the white wine Noir. At Marsala, the Barraco estate makes a Catarratto and a Zibibbo that spend five and thirteen days, respectively, in contact with the skins. At Terzavia, Renato De Bartoli makes Catarratto Lucido wine by fermenting the juice on the skins with temperature control and indigenous yeasts. He also makes a 100 percent Moscato from late-harvested grapes, which he calls Dolcemamà. He ferments this too on its skins but leaves the wine sweet and with 14 percent alcohol. The sweetness covers any bitterness extracted from the skins. Similarly, the production of Passito di Pantelleria includes fermentation in contact with the dried grapes.

AMPHORAE

The off-road hardly ever taken is the use of amphorae for vinification and wine maturation. In the late 1980s, Josko Gravner in northeast Italy, unhappy with the standardization and hyperstabilization of contemporary wines, began researching and experimenting with the ancient Greek and Roman technique of fermenting in terra-cotta amphorae. One part of the world still fermenting in amphorae is the Republic of Georgia (formerly part of the Soviet Union). Historians believe that this area could have been the origin of *Vitis vinifera* more than five thousand years ago and that people who live there have been making wine in jars and amphorae ever since. After Georgia broke away from the Soviet Union and had its civil war, Gravner visited to witness how its wine was made. He is one of the leading innovators in Italian wine.

A year after Gravner made his pilgrimage, Cornelissen, fascinated by Gravner's wine philosophy, also went to Georgia. When he returned, he fermented Etna reds and whites in amphorae. Fifteen of his first seventeen wines turned into vinegar. The problem was that the terra-cotta walls of the amphorae were permeable to oxygen gas, which attacked the wine. Cornelissen's solution was to coat their insides with epoxy resin, to both limit oxygen transfer and make them easier to clean. Now he matures Magma and MunJebel, two red wines, in four-hundred-liter (106-gallon) resin-coated amphorae that he has buried in the ground inside his cantina. He covers each amphora with a basalt lid. He thinks that porcelain amphorae would be even better than his coated terra-cotta ones, as they would be easier to clean and even less permeable to oxygen. Cornelissen does not seem wed to any formula. He is an intuitive winemaker. Yet he is not against taking cues from modern science.

At the same time that Cornelissen was first adopting the use of amphorae, the COS team of Giambattista Cilia and Giusto Occhipinti was also experimenting with them. They use 225- to 400-liter (59- to 106-gallon) amphorae that they have buried in the ground. Larger than four hundred liters, they say, generates too much heat. After experimenting with Tunisian-, Sicilian-, and Spanish-made amphorae, they have found the Spanish ones most to their liking. Because the amphorae are made of clay, Cilia believes they pick up the flavor of the surrounding soil. Unlike Cornelissen, who ferments in open tubs, Cilia and Occhipinti let both red and white wines ferment in amphorae. They also mature their wines in amphorae, like Cornelissen, but they came up with a different solution to the oxidation problem. They leave the wine on its lees in the amphorae after fermentation. In the lees are live yeasts that scour the wine for oxygen. Their activity balances the passage of oxygen through the amphora walls and into the wine. To solve the problem of oxidation through the lid, they line the top rim with clay caulk and clamp discs of steel onto it. During the March or April following alcoholic fermentation, Cilia and Occhipinti take the wine off the lees but leave it in the amphorae. They bottle during the summer, after the wine has had ten months in the amphorae. COS uses 400°C (752°F) vapor to disinfect them. Ultraviolet light is another option. COS ferments Grecanico, Nero d'Avola, and Frappato in amphorae. It makes both a red and a white Pithos. *Pithos* is the Greek name for a storage amphora. Cilia says that examples of red Pithos have remained in perfect condition for ten years. He and Occhipinti work in a different way than Cornelissen with amphorae. They take their inspiration more from history, though they, like him, use modern strategies to solve the problems associated with amphorae use.

One other producer in Sicily uses amphorae. At his small farm, Serragghia, on the island of Pantelleria, the winegrower Gabrio Bini uses amphorae to make a dry Zibibbo wine, called Serragghia Bianco. The flavors of the wines of Bini and the other producers who use off-road techniques do not conform to the tastes of consumers and many wine critics. Tasting them challenges us to change how we appreciate wine.

SPARKLING WINE

Sparkling wine production may appear an odd fit for its warm climate, but Sicily has high-elevation sites on Etna, in the center, and along its northern edge. There is even a little-known history of sparkling wine production on the island. From 1881 to 1901 there were notices in several publications of a well-made traditional method (*metodo classico*) style sparkling wine from a company on Etna owned by Baron Antonio Spitaleri. The varietal base was Pinot Nero. The next notable Sicilian sparkling wine appeared in 1971, when Duca di Salaparuta began producing a Martinotti (Charmat, or tank) method Brut Riserva. A producer of Sicilian "Champagne" contemporaneous with Spitaleri was the winery of Fratelli Favara e Figli at Mazara del Vallo. Less is known of its efforts.

As of 1974, Giuseppe Milazzo in the province of Agrigento was making metodo classico wine. Tasca d'Almerita released its first metodo classico wine in 1990. Since 1991 Murgo has made its metodo classico brut from grapes grown on the slopes of Etna. Today about twenty Sicilian producers are making a total of five hundred thousand bottles of sparkling wine, a small percentage of Italy's massive three hundred fifty million bottles of such wine. Some of these bottlings amount to as few as two thousand bottles. Others, such as those of Duca di Salaparuta, can amount to two hundred thousand. Sparkling wine is produced through either the Martinotti (or Charmat) method of conducting the second fermentation in tank, followed by filtration with the addition of a dose of sugar and bottling under pressure, or metodo classico, which involves second fermentation in bottle, maturation of the wine for months or years in bottle on the yeast sediment, removal of the yeast sediment, addition of a dose of sugar, and bottling. Sicilian producers use many different grape varieties, both international and native, to make the base wines. Murgo is the market leader of metodo classico wine, with about ninety thousand bottles. Though Sicily is not known for its sparkling wines, its many high-elevation areas allow producers to make them every bit as well as producers at higher latitudes.

9

AT THE HEART OF SICILY

Cool, dry north winds howled. They swirled around us. We looked up at a vast blue sky punctuated by white clouds racing overhead. An undulating golden carpet of wheat spread out to the mountains that defined the edges of the valley below. From the top of a ridge we looked eastward and down on Feudo Montoni, a white square cut into an island of green. Vines in a sea of wheat. Clumps of trees sprung up here and there like tufts of grass.

Fabio Sireci's voice rang out above the winds. "The trees near the vineyards are euca-lyptus. Giacomo Tachis smelled them in our Nero d'Avola. We are at the heart of Sicily, where the provinces of Agrigento, Palermo, and Caltanissetta meet." His right hand pointed over my shoulder and to the southwest, at a high mountain not far off. "From Mount Cammarata you can see the Mediterranean Sea and the coastline of Africa." His hand swung to the east. A volcano rose menacingly on the horizon. "You can even see Etna today." He pointed down. "That's Valledolmo running along the slopes of the Madonie Range. My grandfather Don Rosario lived there. He bought Feudo Montoni at the beginning of the last century.

"There is always wind at Montoni. Today it's a cool, dry *maestrale* wind. When the scirocco blows on a summer day, it's a convection oven. The temperature can rise to over 40 degrees [Celsius (104°F)]. But if you move into the shade, you don't even break into a sweat. At night in the summer, you need a sweater."

Fabio is a *vignaiolo*, what we, following the French, call a vigneron. The word identi-fies someone who labors in all aspects of wine production, from growing the vines to making and merchandising the wine. He or she has a particularly strong connection to, a respect for, the soil and nature. A vignaiolo commonly works about ten hectares (twenty-five acres) of vines, making and selling enough wine to support a family. The family helps with the work. Vignaioli (the plural of *vignaiolo*) are rare in Sicily, even when the definition is stretched. Montoni, for example, comprises about twenty-five hectares (sixty-two acres) of vines. Though Fabio engages in nearly every aspect of the work, he needs the help of full-time employees: Pietro in the vineyards, Pino on the tractors, and Andrea in the office. Francesco Spadafora, a vignaiolo near Alcamo, works his own farm, Spadafora, in a similar manner. He has ninety-five hectares (235 acres) of vineyards. At the other extreme are the nanovignaioli. You find them on Sicily's volcanic islands. On Pantelleria, two husband and wife teams, Salvatore and Dominica Ferrandes of Ferrandes and Giacomo and Solidea d'Ancona of Solidea, each own and work about two hectares (five acres), though they may also rent small parcels. Generational transmission adds dimension to the meaning of the word *vignaiolo*. One piece of land supports generations of vines and generations of vignaioli.

On our left, near the very top of the ridge, was a vineyard swaying in the wind. Fabio: "That is Sauvignon Blanc. I sell these grapes to Duca di Salaparuta. They told me they wanted them to give perfume to their wine. Further down the slope our Catarratto is planted; below that, Grillo. The soil gradually changes from sand- to clay-dominant. The sand gives wine elegance, perfect for white wines. The clay gives structure, perfect for reds. Below the baglio, iron compounds make the clay reddish."

A gust pushed us back. Fabio turned and motioned us back to the Jeep. In the relative quiet inside, he continued. "This was the granary of the Romans. Not far from here, Sicily's three primordial valleys meet: the Val di Mazara from the west, the Val Demone from the northeast, and the Val di Noto from the southeast. Arabs in the eleventh century at what is now Vallelunga established Regaleali, 'the farm of Ali,' where today the Tasca d'Almerita family has their winery. After the Arabs came the Normans. King Ruggero gave this land to his wife. Later different Aragonese nobles possessed the land. In 1469 one of them built the Montoni baglio. They chiseled that year into a rock at the winery. Over a century later the Vatican commissioned Andrea Bacci, the physician to Pope Sixtus V and a professor of botany, to visit Sicily to discover its best wines. He came here or very near here. He found vineyards and he tasted the wine, red wine. In his *De Naturali Vinorum Historia,* Bacci wrote about the 'unheard of fertility of vineyards where stout vines grew as big as tree trunks.' He described the wine as 'very strong, deep red, with the most pleasant smell and flavor, and a capacity for long aging.'[1] Considering that the wines of those times were made without good hygiene, what Bacci tasted must have been incredible. And the Vatican today is one of our best clients!" He laughed in amazement. "As far as everybody can tell, a vineyard has always been here. To find another you have to go nine miles. Wheat was very valuable throughout much of the history of Sicily. Yet there have always been vines here. That means a lot. My grandfather Don Rosario bought Montoni and its vineyards in the early 1900s.

When Don Rosario died, his nine-year-old daughter, my mother, was left an orphan, and Feudo Montoni, hers by inheritance, was without someone to manage it. After my father married my mother in the late 1960s they came back to Montoni and restored it and eventually passed it on to me."

We drove down the ridge past vineyards and the baglio, then more vineyards. We passed the low point in the valley and drove up to another vineyard. Fabio told us these vines were five years old. Pietro, the vineyard man, was waiting for us. Under his blue Montoni baseball cap, white whiskers jumped out like flames. He stood with his tanned, muscular arms crossed against his chest, a black dog, Nerrone ("Big Black One"), and a hoe at his side. Nerrone's size did not live up to his name. Pietro was sixty-one years old. He had worked at Montoni for ten years. Fabio recounted an incident that occurred during the 2009 harvest. Chunks of ice fell like knives from the sky. A severe hailstorm destroyed a piece of the vineyard. Flies swarmed over and on the bleeding Nero d'Avola. Wild yeast and bacteria were finishing the job. Pietro had carefully nurtured and trained these vines. He stood there crying. Nerrone pawed his leg. Their eyes met. Pietro was certain that Nerrone was comforting him, trying to tell him that he had to look forward. Fabio told us that when he is not at Montoni, he feels safe knowing that Pietro is there. Pietro feels the spirit of the place.

The Vrucara vineyard one-third of the way up the hillside of vineyards is the source of Fabio's most structured Nero d'Avola wine. The vines are old, averaging eighty years. The grasp of their innumerable rootlets goes deep, some fifteen meters (forty-nine feet) into the reddish soil, a blend of 80 percent sand and 20 percent clay tinted by iron oxide and peppered with fossil seashells, the murmur of a prehistoric era when Montoni was submerged under water. The depth of the roots insulates the vines from drought, from ground-level fluctuations of sound, compression, temperature, and moisture, and from surface vineyard treatments and soil additions. The rootlets absorb a sap of water and minerals that is primarily held by the clay. This sap rises up to the grapes and leaves a faint print of the soil in the wine. Documents chart the human history of Montoni ownership. The DNA of Vrucara vines charts the vines' history. The reputation of the site as ideal for vines and its isolation from other vines make it possible that the genetic identity of the Vrucara vineyard is a direct path into the distant past. Does this path lead back to Andrea Bacci? Fabio suspects that the Vrucara Nero d'Avola is a unique biotype significantly different from the "original" one that experts believe was selected near the town of Avola on the southeastern coastline of Sicily. He posits: "Could the Vrucara biotype be a selection of Nero d'Avola that predates that of Avola?" He shrugs. He suspects that his Catarratto, selected from an old mountain vineyard, is unique too. He propagated it from seventy-five-year-old vines.

Vrucara Nero d'Avola looks and tastes different from the other Nero d'Avolas in Sicily. Vrucara wine is paler. Its smell lacks the dried grape character of Nero d'Avola wine made in the Noto zone. Along with the typical berry scents, Vrucara wine smells of laurel. Tachis identified dried rose petals and eucalyptus in it. The 2008 vintage smelled less oaky than the 2007. Fabio has been increasing the size of the barrels in an effort to decrease this smell. In the mouth the wine is less viscous, less hot, with a clearer, more obvious thread of sourness than Nero d'Avola wines from other areas of Sicily. The astringency is finely textured, arrives late, and lingers on and on.

These characteristics could result from many factors. The continental climate of the vineyard means high diurnal temperature excursion. The cool nights preserve total acidity, thereby enhancing sourness. The high elevation (400 to 750 meters [1,312 to 2,461 feet] above sea level) and persistent winds delay and lengthen the harvest period. The harvest occurs in early to mid-October, weeks later than in most other areas. The grapes finish ripening in cool weather. This preserves aromatic precursors in their skins. During ripening, light more than heat drives photosynthesis. Ripening occurs slowly, allowing for a gradual selection of the finest and ripest grapes.

How the wine is made also modifies its flavor. Fabio allows the vineyard and winery yeasts and then the winery bacteria to drive fermentation to completion. As a result, Vrucara is less fruit driven and more vinous. He leaves the skins in contact with the fermenting juice or wine for as much as one month. Though this reduces fruitiness, it adds underbrush smells. More tannin is extracted too. If the tannin compounds are well developed, the wine astringency has a pleasant vibrating dryness that lasts and lasts. If the rest of the attributes are in balance, this astringency is a sign of quality and potential longevity. Finally there is the finishing period, twelve months in mostly new, 225-liter (fifty-nine-gallon) oak barrels or some larger barrels and casks. During its maturation, Fabio racks the wine according to smell and taste as it moves further away from the purple appearance, tutti-frutti smells, and coarse texture of its youth. Vrucara terroir evolves as it moves from subsoil to vine to berry to wine and to our lips.

The best way of maintaining the genetic identity of a vineyard while improving its performance is to select and propagate individual vines with desired characteristics. This process is called mass selection. In mass selection, terroir itself is the testing ground for individual vine performance. It is the arena for the selection process. The process occurs over generations of vines and people in a certain place. Very few wine producers or grape farmers in Sicily perform mass selection. Instead they select vine types from nursery catalogues, a process that is less precise and does not preserve the genetic identity of the existing vineyard. Mass selection is an essential activity of the vignaiolo. Though it can be achieved using the services of a nursery, the best way to do it is on-site. If the vignaiolo does not have enough skill to graft in the field, he must hire a professional. Grafters work in teams. One member, the head (capo), organizes the team and is the point person in contact with the vineyard owner. The owner and the capo agree on either a daily or a per-graft rate. The owner plants the American rootstock that he purchased from a nursery well before the arrival of the grafters. He then provides them with cuttings (bacchettini, canes ten to fifteen centimeters [four to six inches] long and each with two or three buds) from the individual Vitis vinifera vines he has selected from his vineyard. The grafters will attach the Vitis vinifera to the rootstock.

Field grafting is a dying trade in Sicily. Nurseries offer services that take its place. Young people do not want to enter the trade. They associate agriculture with poverty and older generations. Sicilian grafters are usually about seventy years old. Though they are on pensions, they continue to work, out of habit and friendship.

Fabio had asked the capo of his grafting team to meet with us. On our arrival at the baglio, Don Calogero was waiting for us. Sicilians show respect for older people by using the title *don*. Fabio thinks that Don Calogero is about eighty years old. He is the capo of a squad that numbers, according to the job, from five to fifteen grafters. He is responsible for the quality of the work. By law, at least 90 percent of the grafts have to take. If this is not the case, Don Calogero and his workers must do a *ripasso*, which means regrafting the unsuccessful grafts. This is not a simple issue. The failure of a graft can be caused by either the grafter or a vineyard worker. In a ripasso, Don Calogero determines which grafts are his team's responsibility to redo. The rule is that if the implanted bud is still green (i.e., living), it is not their fault. The graft might not have developed because it was inadvertently buried during the growing season, left without irrigation during a dry period, or bruised by a rock or clump of dirt thrown by a tractor. If the failed bud is brown, it has died. This indicates that the grafter is at fault. He might not have properly cut out the bud or inserted it into the rootstock. There might have been a bad match between the bud and the rootstock. The determination of fault is a sensitive issue. Resolution depends on the relationships Don Calogero has with the vineyard owner and the owner's workers. Fabio couldn't recall a failed graft that was the fault of Don Calogero's team. Fabio has unwavering trust in and respect for Don Calogero.

Fabio had prepared the ground for the meeting: he had made clear that we were knowledgeable, respectful journalists who wanted to record for posterity Don Calogero's work. Without this introduction, Don Calogero likely would have done no more than introduce himself. The fact that he was willing to go further and demonstrate his craft showed us that Don Calogero respected and trusted Fabio. It is unusual for an older Sicilian man to esteem a younger one.

We met Don Calogero under the gate of the baglio. He was of average height, thin and wiry. Under his bald pate, white hair shot out from the sides of his head. His hands trembled and his head bobbed. Fabio later told me that Don Calogero shakes when he is emotional. Sicilian men are not supposed to show emotion. He also avoided direct eye contact with me. I interpreted this as shyness. Fabio mentioned that Don Calogero is wary of strangers. They may wish to steal the secrets of his work.

Don Calogero explained that he had learned field grafting from his father when he was a boy. Don Calogero had worked for a squad hired by Giuseppe Tasca from 1953 to 1959. From 1959 to 1975 he worked for another property owner. Then he left this job to form his own squad. I asked him what it takes to be a good grafter. He replied, "A knowledge of grafting technique, seriousness, honesty, collegiality, and a willingness to ask the capo for help if they need it. I select the ones who come with me. They must be good. Otherwise they stay at home."

We sat down on a bench under the gate of Montoni. Don Calogero explained how he grafts. "Grafting takes place from mid-July until the end of September. Before mid-July the *marza* [a scion, a piece of vinewood and bark carrying the bud to be grafted onto the rootstock] is too tender and green. The *linfa* [fluid or sap underneath the bark] is not yet able to adhere to the rootstock because its consistency is too watery. The trunk of the rootstock too has to be ready to receive the marza. Its linfa should have nearly the same consistency as that of the marza. The cuts have to be clean and the fit has to be perfect. Then I wrap an elastic band around the graft. This presses the marza against the cut in the rootstock. I slip a leaf from the rootstock under the elastic, over the graft. This protects the graft from abrasion and light and preserves humidity at the point of the graft."

He swung around to a wooden case sitting next to him on the bench. It looked like my father's well-worn medical bag. Don Calogero explained: "This is a *cassettino*. Each grafter has his own. Cabinetmakers make them to order. This is Pino's." Pino is the tractor man who was standing nearby in a blue mechanic's jumpsuit. Don Calogero had given the cassettino to Pino as a gift. Don Calogero lifted up a green bacchettino from one of its compartments. "If this were August, I would soak this for a day before using it. Since it is July, the linfa has enough water in it."

From another compartment of the cassettino he pulled out a snub-nosed knife. "This knife is very, very sharp." To show us, he shaved the hair off the back of his hand.

He then took the knife in one hand, grasped the bacchettino in the other, and wedged the cane against his chest. He slid the blade to a bud on the bacchettino. His hands stopped trembling. He made one slice, a crosscut, above the marza and one below. The marza, a flap of bark with a little erect bump, innocently waited. He placed his thumb against the wood above the marza. Then slowly from below, he slid the knife blade under the marza and cut it off. The slice looked like a fingernail. On the convex side was the bud.

Don Calogero: "The wood is still too tender. The cut was not perfect. The wood must be white, not green." He turned over the slice and pointed to the center of the concave side at the point where the bud was. "The inside of the marza must be white with a brown heart. Within fifteen days the bacchettini will be perfect for the rootstock."

Fabio whispered to me: "Observe Don Calogero's force, his sensitivity, his love."

Pino handed Don Calogero a yearling rootstock that Pino had removed, roots and all, from the vineyard. Don Calogero explained that the grafting would be done in the vineyard. The rootstock vine would be in the ground, not dug up like the one brought to us. Normally, out in the vineyard, he pins the rootstock against the ground with his foot. His patient still, the surgeon wields his scalpel.

With shears he cut off all the shoots emerging from the rootstock trunk. Just under where the first had been, he made a crosscut, this time brandishing a pointed knife, and then an incision. He lifted up the bark on either side of the incision, remarking, "Like the bacchettini, the rootstock is too green. The bark doesn't open up easily." He picked up the fingernail-shaped marza. He inserted it firmly into the incision and then wrapped a red rubber band over it and attached a leaf. "Next spring a green shoot will grow out of the bud."

Don Calogero continued: "If the marriage is right, the two will become one. You will never be able to pull the top of the plant off the roots. If the marriage does not take, the next year the rootstock will reject the marza or will be weakly attached to the plant above. If the marriage is bad, you can pull the vine from its roots even after ten years."

Throughout this demonstration, Don Calogero had made comparisons between the work of this team and that of a team from Marsala that Tasca d'Almerita had hired. He told us that while his team could achieve 220 to 230 grafts per man per day, the Marsala team could do five to six hundred. Waving his trembling finger, he asserted that his team's grafts had a much higher success rate. The Marsala grafters cut out a much smaller marza. It formed a less successful union. He referred to the Marsala grafters as *quelli* ("those"). The presence of these quelli violated his world.

Our parting with Don Calogero was graceful, humble, and respectful. We had learned a lot about Montoni, but we had not yet met Fabio's father, Elio Sireci. That had to wait until more than a month later, in early September.

It was Elio who restored Montoni after it had been adrift for decades. When he married Fabio's mother in 1967, he promised her that if they had children, he would "pull the thorns at Montoni and plant flowers." The thorns in this case were not only the weeds but also the former *mezzadri* (sharecroppers) and others who lived on and farmed Montoni as if it were their own.

Before the 1950s, mezzadri had been the labor that worked the *latifondi* in this area. During the 1950s, agrarian reform laws enabled the government to appropriate large parcels of land from the owners of *latifondi*. The government divided the land into smaller parcels, which it gave to mezzadri and other poor people. Regaleali in nearby Vallelunga lost 700 of its 1,220 hectares (1,730 of 3,015 acres). During those years, Montoni drifted without leadership or management, while Fabio's mother, Adele Belliotti, its owner, grew up in Palermo. Though Montoni was too small to be directly affected by the agrarian land reforms, former mezzadri lived on the property and farmed it as squatters.

We arrived at Montoni late in the evening. Fabio introduced us to his father and mother. It was evident that Elio was very ill. He told us that as soon as his wife had become pregnant (with Fabio's sister) during their honeymoon, he had focused on restoring the property to his family. He showed us a photo of Montoni as it was in 1967: there was a little village of huts and tents on the property.

Elio explained: "There were eighteen former mezzadri who were living on the property and farming it. It was terrible. I told them that the property was ours, but they refused to move. A ringleader had everyone in the palm of his hand. He carried a scepter. He told the rest that I would be gone like a young captain who gave orders, then threw up his hands and left. The ringleader told the mezzadri: 'Stay where you are. He will be gone in ten months.' I assured him I would be making a career out of being a captain."

Elio paused, removed his beret, took a difficult breath, and continued: "I brought legal action against them. The case went all the way up to Rome, where it was ruled in my favor. The ruling became the precedent for a national law. Instead of having them forcibly removed, I paid them to leave. After that, they told me they had paid for fertilizers. I paid for that too. By midnight I was Montoni's only captain.

"I surprised them. I went around and met everyone and developed a friendly relationship with everybody. I brought them work. I was always mannerly and honest and hardworking. These same people now show me special respect. They admire me. When I meet them now, they kiss me and hug me.

"My wife and I had a lot to do. Many things were stolen. We had no electricity, no water. We transformed everything. I bought the first tractor in the area and renovated the baglio to house it and other tractors that I bought afterward. I restored the vineyards. I sold their grapes to Settesoli, Duca di Salaparuta, and Tasca. They earned medals with my grapes. Giuseppe Tasca once told me that he would make wines that the world would notice."

Fabio: "But Giuseppe Tasca taught us much. Papa knew how to manage the property, but Giuseppe Tasca helped him understand the agronomic part. Tasca taught us where to plant grapes, how to train them, and when to harvest. Tasca made wines that were technically correct. Papa bottled wine every year for friends and the family. The wines were good but not at the level of Tasca's."

Elio: "Fabio grew up in the vineyards and in the cellar. He began to bottle Montoni. Now Montoni wins awards around the world. He goes to Japan. The Japanese invited him to dinner to show Montoni wines. I wish I could help him now. "

Fabio: "You are helping. You are helping."

Elio's spirit wanted to leap out of his chair and get to work, but he breathed unevenly and heavily. It was time for us to go.

Fabio drove us to our farm lodging (called an *agriturismo*). During the drive he told us, "My father and I have been carried here by the wind. It is our family duty to maintain Montoni, to be socially responsible, and, through responsible agriculture, to preserve its nature." We learned eight weeks later that Elio had passed away soon after Fabio completed the harvest in the autumn of 2010. His spirit lives on in Fabio and in the vines of Montoni.

10

UNDERSTANDING SICILIAN WINE BY PLACE
The Three Valleys

Because wine is an agricultural product, its identity is bound to place. There is, however, no simple and logical way to discuss Sicilian wine from a regional perspective.

Sicily is divided into nine provinces (*province*, the plural of *provincia*): Agrigento, Caltanissetta, Catania, Enna, Messina, Palermo, Ragusa, Siracusa, and Trapani. These are also the names of their respective capital cities. When listening to Sicilians, one has to infer from the context of the discussion whether they mean the province or the city. Municipalities or townships (*comuni*, the plural of *comune*) make up each province. A township has the same name as its principal town. For example, Linguaglossa is the principal town in a township of that name. In some cases, such as Noto, the principal town is large enough to be considered a city. Here too one has to infer from the context whether the township or the town/city is intended. *Frazioni* (the plural of *frazione*) are smaller political entities within comuni. "Hamlet" is the most accurate translation for *frazione*. *Contrade* (the plural of *contrada*) are small places that have historical or cultural significance. A contrada is not an official political subdivision. It is a quarter or neighborhood. Historically Sicilians have not named specific vineyards. They refer to them by contrada and ownership. Vineyard and winery locations are usually classified by province and comune. Statistics are collected based on these political units. A combination of history and politics created them, rather than agriculturalists interested in connecting product identity to origin.

An alternative to a political address is an appellation one. Italian appellation law was created to connect wine identity to place through the development of appellations of origin. The laws also regulated all aspects of wine production. These regulations, called *disciplinari* (the plural of *disciplinare*), are protocols of production. They are designed to ensure minimum standards of quality and style for each designation and to protect appellation names from fraudulent use.

The most recent appellation system resulted from a revision of Law 930, instituted in 1963. The revision, Law 164, in 1992 defined four basic legal categories for wine, commonly referred to by the acronyms DOCG (Denominazione di Origine Controllata e Garantita, "Guaranteed Denomination of Controlled Origin"), DOC (Denominazione di Origine Controllata, "Denomination of Controlled Origin"), IGT (Indicazione Geografica Tipica, "Geographic and Typical Indication"), and vdt (vino da tavola, "table wine"). Vino da tavola may be sold in bulk or by the bottle. It is the most common type of wine but by law cannot indicate place beyond the country of origin. Of these categories, DOCG has the most stringent quality control production regulations, followed by DOC, IGT, and vdt, which is largely unregulated except for basic type and quantity of production.

Consumers, however, have started to see new acronyms on many labels. As of 2010, the new Italian wine regulation Law 61 accepts EU-wide changes that harmonize members' appellation systems. Basically, DOCG and DOC wines are associated with a new category, DOP (Denominazione d'Origine Protetta, "Protected Denomination of Origin"). IGTs are associated with IGP (Indicazione Geografica Protetta, "Protected Indication of Origin"). Producers have the choice of using the old or the new acronyms. Vdt is now referred to as *vini senza DOP e IGP* ("wine that is neither DOP nor IGP"). Varietal and vintage labeling are allowed for some wines in this category. Others simply state wine color. Vini senza DOP e IGP will largely be sold in Europe as vdt has been in the past. Export markets such as the United States will likely see only DOP and IGP wine categories. It is possible that a wine producer may resort to the vini senza DOP e IGP category if, for some reason, he or she has not followed the disciplinare of a DOP or IGP. Or he or she might do so for personal or marketing reasons. But this situation has been rare and will likely remain so in the future.

Most of the wine regulations are very confusing and are not relevant to the interests of consumers. This book is written at a time when wine laws are in transition. Current wine law recognizes both the old and the new nomenclature. Producers have the choice of using one or the other on wine labels and in their promotional materials. Since the market at the time of writing still concerns itself primarily with the old nomenclature, I use them in this book. Legal details can bog down discussion to the point where they impede understanding of important ideas. I include them only when necessary.

The appellation concept attempts to outline geologic, climatic, and historic bound-aries along with appropriate production protocols. However, power politics during the appellation application process frequently misdirects appropriate and sincere inten-tions. Many appellations end up rarely used. Regulations are often diluted and homog-enized so that they are acceptable to everyone (and no one). Many producers within DOCs have preferred to label their wines as IGTs to take advantage of that category's more flexible regulations. They also recognize that if the DOC name has no visibility in the marketplace, it does not help them sell the wine. Because branding can be made proprietary by registering brands with the government, producers preferentially identify their wines by brand and by the appellation that gives them the balance of flexibility and market recognition that best suits them. In Sicily at the time of the writing of this book, that appellation is most often Sicilia IGT. For wine in the marketplace by 2013, it will be Sicilia DOC, given that the future popularity of the Terre Siciliane IGT is less likely. Within Sicily only a few DOCs have name recognition. The best examples are Marsala, Etna, and Cerasuolo di Vittoria (actually Sicily's only DOCG). Producers will continue to use and promote well-known DOCs. Those who can label wines as DOCs that are not well known and will likely remain so, such as Delia Nivolelli or Salaparuta (not to be confused with the producer Duca di Salaparuta), are likely not to do so but rather to label by brand under the Sicilia DOC. None of the handful of subregional IGTs, such as Camaro and Fontanarossa di Cerda, are likely to develop any traction in the marketplace. Producers are unlikely to use them too. Wine law provides criteria for decommissioning underused appellations due to lack of use. Some will disappear. Appellations, unlike political boundaries, frequently overlap one another. Producers can choose which to use if their production fulfills the requirements of two or more. Though this may be good for the producer, it makes the education of the consumer much more difficult. The assumption of the consumer is that everything on the label means something and has value. However, learning about the details of what is on the label drains a lot of the fun and passion from wine appreciation without appreciably enhancing understanding.

To attain a legal Italian appellation status, producers must draw up a proposal that outlines appellation borders, standards of production, and allowed wine typologies. They present this application to the Ministry of Agriculture in Rome, which assesses the proposal. The standards to be met for the approval of a DOCG application are more rigorous than for DOC. At the time of writing, there is one DOCG in Sicily, Cerasuolo di Vittoria. It graduated from DOC to DOCG status in 2006. This made a difference in the quality of the wines. The market held producers to a higher standard, and almost overnight they became known for serious red wine. Other DOC appellations in Sicily should also apply for or more actively seek the DOCG designation. To do so, producers must draw up a disciplinare that features more stringent quality control regulations than their current DOC disciplinare includes. They then submit it in the form of an application to the Ministry of Agriculture in Rome. If approved, their DOC becomes a DOCG. There are currently twenty-two DOCs in Sicily. Marsala DOC producers should submit the Vergine category. Pantelleria producers should submit the Moscato di Pantelleria DOC and Passito di Pantelleria DOC categories. Because of its historic importance, producers of Moscato di Siracusa should rally together to apply for DOCG. Producers on the island of Salina should propose a Malvasia delle Lipari Passito DOCG. Those on Etna should take steps to gain a DOCG for both Etna Rosso and Etna Bianco. In the

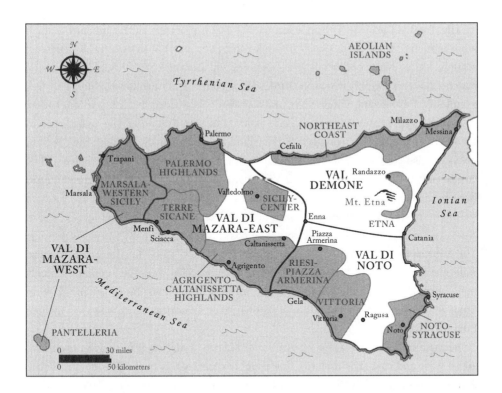

Wine areas of Sicily's three valleys

more distant future, Noto should work toward a DOCG for red wine. Faro was famous in the nineteenth century for its red wines and has a terroir with the potential to produce great wine, but there should be more Faro DOC producers before such an application can be made. Having a clutch of appellations at the prestigious DOCG level would improve the average standards of Sicily's historic wines and would raise the image of its wine industry.

While knowledge of Sicilian provinces and legal appellations is helpful in understanding Sicilian wine, there is a political and administrative subdivision of Sicily that predates the provinces and, of course, the appellations. The division of Sicily into the Tre Valli probably happened before 1000 A.D., during the period of Muslim rule. Though *valli* (the plural of *valle*) in Italian translates to "valleys" in English, its original usage in Sicily likely derived from the Arabic *wali*, which means "magistracy." That it is impossible to identify three principal valleys makes this derivation seem all the more likely. The Tre Valli were Val di Mazara, Val di Noto, and Val Demone. The borders of each became more defined as the terminology became more widespread during the sixteenth century. The valli were officially referred to until land reforms in the early nineteenth century initiated the division of Sicily into provinces.

The Tre Valli provide a format for a territorial exploration of the modern Sicilian wine industry. They divide Sicily into a western section, Val di Mazara; a southeast section, Val di Noto; and a northeast section, Val Demone. The city of Enna in the island's center is roughly where the three valleys converge. The following three chapters examine Val di Mazara, Val di Noto, and Val Demone, divided by each territory's most salient geographic and cultural characteristics. Taken in that order, the valli represent the stages of the Muslim conquest of the island. By design or by accident, the Tre Valli divisions also correspond to one way of carving Sicily into three geologic pieces. The largest valley, Val di Mazara, contains the Sicani and Palermo Ranges and the southern flank of the Madonie Range, all of which are calcareous. A calcareous, mineral salt–rich sedimentary stratum spreads out south of them like a skirt. The second largest, Val di Noto, has the Hybleaen Mountains and their coastal areas. Here hard limestone prevails. The Nebrodi Mountains, the Peloritani Mountains, and Mount Etna dominate the third valle, Val Demone. The Nebrodi are largely sandstone. The Peloritani contain the only metamorphic rocks on the island. The Taormina fault line cuts the Peloritani off from Etna, which is a geologic formation of its own. Most historical maps, however, include Etna in Val Demone.

Because of the much larger size of Val di Mazara, I discuss it in the context of two areas: west and east. The dividing line roughly corresponds to the Freddo and Belice Rivers. The Freddo flows north from the hills between Salemi and Calatafimi to the Tyrrhenian Sea. The Belice flows from the Sicani Mountains southwest to Menfi. West of the Freddo and Belice Rivers is Val di Mazara–West. This area more or less contains the province of Trapani. Within the Val di Mazara–West section, I discuss the island of Pantelleria, the Marsala DOC, and the coastal and inland highland areas that, although they are within the Marsala DOC borders, grow grapes dedicated to making unfortified wine. As a category reference for these unfortified wines, their territories, and their producers, I use the term *Western Sicily*. The Marsala DOC and Western Sicily, therefore, have the same borders. Marsala is of such great historical importance and so complex that it needs to be discussed on its own. Val di Mazara–East lies east of the Freddo and Belice Rivers. Just east of the Belice, it contains the Terre Sicane zone, with vineyards that extend from the coastline at the cities of Menfi and Sciacca up to the Upper Belice Valley, just south of the Sicani Mountain Range. To the east of the Terre Sicane zone is a broad swath of coastal highlands, what I call the Agrigento–Caltanissetta Highlands. This ends at the Salso River, which empties into the Mediterranean at the southern coastal city of Licata. The northern part of Val di Mazara–East, east of the Freddo River, includes what I call the Palermo Highlands, which contains the overlapping DOCs of Alcamo and Monreale, and Sicily-Center, the area south of the Madonie Mountains.

Val di Noto is the southeastern corner of the island. It comprises the land enclosed by the Salso River on the west and the Simeto River and its tributary, the Dittaino, to the north. Beginning along the southern coast east of the Salso, the highlands to the north and west of the coastal city of Gela extend north to the Riesi DOC and the city of Piazza

Armerina. To the southeast of this Riesi–Piazza Armerina zone is the Vittoria zone. Moving farther southeast along the coast there is the wine area around Noto, and then the vineyards near the city of Syracuse. I call this area the Noto-Syracuse zone. In chapter 12, I discuss the wine areas around Noto and Syracuse separately, because the former is well known for red wine and the latter for sweet white wine. The northern border of Val di Noto is the Dittaino River where it flows east from near the city of Enna to the Simeto. The Simeto empties into the Ionian Sea south of the city of Catania.

Val Demone is the smallest of the Tre Valli. It includes the flanks of Mount Etna, which I refer to as the Etna zone. The next wine zone I call the Northeast Coast. It comprises the foothills and coastal areas that skirt both flanks of the Peloritani Mountains (one southeast toward the Ionian Sea, the other north toward the Tyrrhenian Sea) and, moving west, a narrow band of coastline and foothills at the base of the Nebrodi and Madonie Mountains facing the Tyrrhenian. The Aeolian Islands comprise another zone. By far the most important island in this archipelago, winewise, is Salina.

11

VAL DI MAZARA

Val di Mazara is the largest of the three historic regions of Sicily. It includes Palermo, the capital city of the Norman Kingdom of Sicily in the twelfth century and of modern-day Sicily. Val di Mazara extends from the intensively cultivated vineyards of western Sicily to the island's interior, home to little more than vast tracts of high plains and steep hills that are blanketed by wheat fields and punctuated with isolated vineyards. In contrast with Val di Noto and Val Demone to its east, Val di Mazara historically was more influenced by the cultures of the Phoenicians and the Muslims than the Greeks. The vast landholdings known as latifondi also dominated it to a greater extent, from the Roman era through the nineteenth century. The two principal wine areas in the region are Val di Mazara—West, which comprises the island of Pantelleria, Marsala, and Western Sicily, and Val di Mazara—East, which includes the Palermo Highlands, Terre Sicane, Sicily-Center, and the Agrigento-Caltanissetta Highlands.

VAL DI MAZARA—WEST
PANTELLERIA

Legend has it that the Phoenician lunar goddess, Tanit, enamored of Apollo, attracted his attention by pouring Pantelleria wine instead of ambrosia into his goblet. Giacomo Casanova, the eighteenth-century adventurer, is said to have offered Pantelleria to his lovers. One sip of a modern-day Passito di Pantelleria convinces me that such tales are not far-fetched. The sweet wine of Pantelleria is Italy's most extravagant dessert wine.

MAP 2.
Val di Mazara—West

Though Pantelleria may seem to be off the beaten path, its strategic position in the Strait of Sicily was not overlooked by Benito Mussolini, who saw it as Italy's unsinkable aircraft carrier in the center of the Mediterranean Sea. He armed it to the gunnels, built an airport, ringed the island with roads, and refurbished the principal port at the town of Pantelleria. Unfortunately this attracted the Allies, who bombed it ferociously, leveling the town of Pantelleria and forcing the island's inhabitants to leave and take cover on Sicily and elsewhere in Italy. The Panteschi (the plural of *Pantesco*), as the Pantellerians are called, have seen more or less the same parade of occupiers as Sicilians on the main island. The Muslims left the most visible footprints: the white-domed stone houses called *dammusi,* the circular stone *giardini arabi* ("Arab gardens") that are built to shelter citrus trees from the relentless winds, and Arabic-sounding and -looking names such as that of the contrada Bukkuràm, meaning "rich in vines."

Pantelleria is closer to Africa than to Europe, being sixty kilometers (thirty-seven miles) northeast of the Tunisian coast and one hundred kilometers (sixty-two miles) southwest of Sicily. With eighty-three square kilometers (fifty-two square miles) of surface, it is the largest of Sicily's offshore islands. Geologically speaking, Pantelleria is an infant. Not more than two hundred thousand years ago, successive eruptions pushed lava rock two thousand feet up from an undersea plain to create the jagged and craggy rock formations that characterize the island today. Its baroque shape and black-green volcanic rocks glistening in the azure Mediterranean waters suggest its epithet, the Black Pearl. The Panteschi, some seven thousand strong, impress even Sicily dwellers with their individualism. The winegrower Fabrizio Basile crowed to me that he does not feel Sicilian at all. But although Sicilians have difficulty uniting under a common cause, when Panteschi get together the results can be explosive.

Pantelleria's name evolved as its occupiers came and went, from the Punic-Phoenician *Yrnm* to the Greek *Kòsuros* or *Kòssoura* and to the Latin *Cossura* or *Cossyra*. The Muslims called it Qawsarah, phonetically related to *Cossura*. A Byzantine monastery dating from the sixth century A.D., Patelarèas or Patalarèas, is believed to be the origin of the modern name. Another theory is that *Pantelleria* derives from the Latin word *tentorium* ("tent"). It is no coincidence that on the island, the name of the walled area where grapes are laid out to raisin under an awning or sunshade is called a *stenditoio con le tende* ("drying area with awnings"). Beyond the mysteries of etymology, there can be no question that the drying of grapes into raisins (*uve passe,* the plural of *uva passa*) and the production of *passito* wines (made from dried grapes; from the verb *appassire,* meaning "to wither") have an ancient history here.

The passito wines of Pantelleria entered commerce in the late nineteenth century. They were even exported to England and the United States. In the early twentieth century Italian merchants sought out Pantelleria's fine raisins and sweet wines. To serve their needs, the Panteschi planted more vineyards. Vineyard surface reached its zenith in the 1920s, with more than fifty-eight hundred hectares (14,332 acres). More than three-quarters of the vines planted were Zibibbo.

Phylloxera arrived in 1928 and devastated vineyards throughout the next decade. Replanting on rootstocks began five years later, but World War II derailed progress. During and after the war the emigration of numerous Panteschi decimated the agricultural labor force. In the 1950s, vineyard surface was half that of the 1920s. Improved technology increased yields per hectare, resulting in total yields for the island that nearly achieved the levels of the 1920s. A great demand for passito wine set off a boom from 1965 to 1970. But decline set in again during the 1970s. Markets turned to seedless grapes for both eating and baking. Countries such as Greece, Turkey, and Cyprus could supply raisins at lower cost. Merchants preferred to buy dried Zibibbo grapes from Pantelleria and vinify the wine in Marsala and other Sicilian production facilities or in northern Italy. *Zibibbo* is another name for the variety Moscato di Alessandria. Piedmont merchants, long familiar with another member of the Muscat family, Moscato Bianco, became major purchasers and vinifiers of Pantelleria Zibibbo. Panteschi sold their best grapes to the table grape market and their best raisins to the confectionery industry. They used their worst grapes and raisins in the wines they drank. These were called *ambrati,* named for the murky amber of the liquid. Flaws obscured the wines' quality.

Consistent with Muslim inheritance custom, heirs have divided land on Pantelleria for centuries. This creates a highly fractionalized pattern of land ownership. The prevalence of small land parcels makes economies of scale impossible and adds to labor costs. The island's rugged terrain also requires time-consuming and expensive manual labor. Because manufactured goods—and even drinking water—have to be shipped or flown to the island, the cost of living is higher than on Sicily's main island. Irrigation is not feasible, because Pantelleria has virtually no water resources other than its thermal springs. For all these reasons, Pantelleria wine costs more than comparable Sicilian wine. Panteschi winegrowers needed to make wines with cachet so that sophisticated and wealthy consumers would be willing to pay more for them. Their moment arrived in the 1990s, when Italians became wealthier and began purchasing more expensive wine. Celebrities, among them the Italian fashion designer Giorgio Armani and the French actress Carole Bouquet, built vacation homes on the island, bringing more attention to it. They and a growing number of other affluent tourists increasingly visited the island—if not by yacht then by plane from Palermo or Trapani or by ferry from Palermo, Trapani, or Mazara del Vallo. For this breed of wine lover, the Italian wine market provided Super-Tuscans, Barolos, Angelo Gaja wines, and Brunello di Montalcinos, but no iconic "super" sweet wine.

What Marco De Bartoli failed to achieve for Marsala, he achieved, or almost achieved, for Pantelleria. In the early 1980s he saw the potential of the island's wines and began experimenting in Marsala with raisins that he bought from a grower on Pantelleria. His first vintage of Bukkuram, a passito, was the 1984. With it and the others that followed, De Bartoli set new standards of quality and style for Passito di Pantelleria. The name *Bukkuram* and the design of its label evoked the island's Arabic past. The wine was golden and clear, infused with the exotic flavors of flowers and fruits commonly associated with Arabic gardens. Its texture was smooth and syrupy, and it had just enough sourness to make a clean exit. In the same year that De Bartoli came out with Bukkuram, the Pantesco winegrower Salvatore Murana made his first Martingana passito. Both wines bear the name of the contrada where their grapes were grown.

Gabriella Anca and Giacomo Rallo, the owners of the Donnafugata wine company on the main island of Sicily, needed dessert wines to complement their range of dry wines. In the late 1980s they rented a farm on Pantelleria with seven hectares (seventeen acres) and a winery. Based on their knowledge of what consumers wanted and on the advice of Sauternes and Tokay producers, they directed their enologists to craft fresher, fruitier, and tarter versions of Pantelleria wine. They launched a passito, Ben Ryé, in 1989. Its freshness and higher acidity set it apart from the Passito di Pantellerias of other producers. Donnafugata enriches the base wine of its passito with dried grapes grown at some of the higher altitudes on the island, where the harvests are later. These give higher acidity to the wine. Kabir, a Moscato di Pantelleria, came later. It is a sweet late-harvest wine made from grapes dried on the vine after fully ripening. The 2010 Kabir was about 11.6 percent alcohol, reducing its weight but enhancing its freshness.

Donnafugata owns the most vineyard surface on the island. As of 2008, the company sources grapes from some sixty-eight hectares (168 acres). It also buys grapes. All told it is the second-largest producer on the island, after Pellegrino.

Before building its winery in Marsala in 1992, the Pellegrino Marsala house consulted the Sauternes expert Denis Dubourdieu about how to improve Pantelleria wine. Based on his experience with similar French products, such as Muscat de Frontignan and Muscat de Beaumes de Venise, he helped Pellegrino achieve a style of Zibibbo passito that emphasized lightness and purity. Pellegrino's Passito di Pantelleria Nes, which it sells under the Duca di Castelmonte brand, expresses this more natural style. It has hints of orange and cedar in the nose and is more viscous than sweet on the palate.

I attended a wine conference on the island in 1995. Pantelleria then seemed on the edge of fame. At the meeting, tempers flared when the discussion came to what methods should be allowed for drying grapes. Traditionally grapes dried in the open air in the sun. The DOC regulations specify this method and allow for exceptional protection of drying grapes during inclement weather. Since 1951, however, drying machines had also been in use on the island. Essentially, these are fans that blow humidity away from the harvested grapes. This is particularly important in the first few days of drying because a great deal of water evaporates from the stems then. The resulting humidity provides an ideal environment for rapid mold growth. Over the years, many drying machines with a variety of systems for controlling ambient humidity have been used. Tubular polyethylene tents (serre, the plural of serra) were introduced in the mid-1980s for all types of fruit production in Sicily. They not only sped up the rate of desiccation but also protected the grapes from inclement weather. While the drying machines were used in open air and reduced the temperature around the grapes, the tunnels increased the temperature during the drying process. At the 1995 conference, De Bartoli, then the president of the Istituto Regionale della Vite e del Vino (IRVV, "Regional Institute of Vine and Wine"), argued that the law should be changed to allow methods that were not traditional but still respected grape quality. Panteschi winemakers, however, suspected that merchants wanted this flexibility so they could industrialize production. I learned at that meeting how argumentative Panteschi can be. The current law bans drying machines but allows drying in polyethylene tunnels when weather threatens the drying process. Since there are no specific regulations determining what is and is not threatening weather, drying in tunnels is commonplace. Furthermore, the law allows tubular tents for general use as long as they have openings along the sides to let air flow through. The fractious chatter that I heard in 1995 about who was really drying grapes under the sun and who was taking quasi-legal shortcuts still occurs today.

Moscato di Pantelleria DOC and Passito di Pantelleria DOC are the vinous crown jewels of the island. The regulations governing them are similar. Both must be made from late-harvest Zibibbo dried in the sun while still attached to the vine, with some additional grapes dried off the vine. In practice, Moscato di Pantelleria is lighter and less sweet than Passito di Pantelleria. To get the extra sweetness and concentration for

Passito di Pantelleria, producers add more grapes that have been dried off the vine. These contain less water, so their sugar content is higher and the compounds in their skin and pulp are more concentrated. Beyond Moscato di Pantelleria DOC and Passito di Pantelleria DOC, there is a more expansive appellation, Pantelleria DOC, which includes six wine types, from sparkling (*spumante*) to fortified (*liquoroso*). DOC regulations for all of these require bottling in Sicily. There is a long history, however, of Marsala houses in Trapani and merchants from northern Italy, particularly Piedmont, buying Pantelleria grapes and raisins and making wine according to their own specifications and needs. Well into the 1990s Panteschi winegrowers were suspicious that extra-Sicily bottling was occurring and that wines illegally labeled as Moscato di Pantelleria DOC and Passito di Pantelleria DOC were infiltrating commercial networks. They also suspected that Marsala houses were making Pantelleria wines of all types with grapes from other sources. Rumors continue. Some Panteschi have lobbied for a law that would make it obligatory to bottle all Pantelleria wines on their island. This would help ensure that such wines were made with 100 percent Pantelleria grapes. It would also encourage people to associate these wines with Pantelleria and its wine community rather than Marsala and its wine community. Current law requires all DOC wines to be vinified on Pantelleria. Producers must bottle Moscato and Passito di Pantelleria DOC wines on Pantelleria, except that certain grandfathered producers may bottle them elsewhere in Sicily. If producers wanted to change the appellation status for both Moscato di Pantelleria and Passito di Pantelleria or only the latter from DOC to DOCG, the issue of obligatory vinification and bottling on Pantelleria would become even more contentious. DOCG regulations generally obligate bottling within the boundaries of the appellation.

On the other hand, many Panteschi do not want to lose the business of Marsala merchants. The house of Pellegrino alone processes more than half the wine grapes from the island. Marsala merchants do not see how quality would increase by bottling Moscato di Pantelleria and Passito di Pantelleria on Pantelleria. It would certainly increase their production costs. They would be forced to duplicate facilities and forgo economies of scale. Plus, shipping wine in bulk is less expensive than shipping it in bottle. For these reasons, the movement among some producers to require on-island bottling has not gone far. On the other hand, Pantelleria wine law requires that the addition of distillates to liquoroso versions of Moscato di Pantelleria DOC and Passito di Pantelleria DOC occur on the island. Pellegrino, a large producer of these versions, built a vinification facility on Pantelleria in 1992 expressly to conduct this fortification. It has also continued to bottle off-island. De Bartoli and Murana too have built wineries and bottle their wine on the island. In 2006 Donnafugata built a winery inside a Pantelleria dammusi, but it had no room for a bottling line. A Sicilian company with a sizable presence on the island, Miceli, has its bottling facility off-island, in the township of Sciacca. In fact, most Pantelleria wine is bottled off-island. Notwithstanding the requirement that Moscato and Passito di Pantelleria DOC wines be bottled on Pantelleria, the law exempts those producers that had bottled such wines for at least one year in Sicily prior to its enactment to bottle such wines off-island. During our visit to Pantelleria, ex-agricultural minister Calogero Mannino, owner of Abraxas, expressed frustration with this loophole that allows off-island bottling of its two crown jewels: "La deroga è piu grande della regola!" ("The exception is greater than the rule!"). As an on-island bottler—and an architect of Italy's Wine Law 164—he knows that bottling on Pantelleria cements the identity of these wines to that of the island.

Another issue that has both history and currency is the way in which fortified Pantelleria wine negatively impacts the market for Moscato and Passito di Pantelleria. For centuries merchants have fortified wines to make them seaworthy. In 1992 Pellegrino began producing a fortified Moscato di Pantelleria. Now it produces a Pantelleria Moscato Liquoroso and a Pantelleria Passito Liquoroso under the Duca di Castelmonte brand. Miceli also produces liquoroso wine, as do several other merchants, mostly in Marsala. The production costs of fortified versions of Pantelleria Moscato and Passito DOC are much lower than those of unfortified versions. Retail prices show the difference. Sweetness levels mirror those of unfortified versions. The alcohol levels of Pantelleria Passito Liquoroso and Passito di Pantelleria are close, 15 and 14.5 percent respectively. In general, fortified and unfortified wines taste very similar. Producers of unfortified Moscato and Passito di Pantelleria are concerned that consumers cannot easily recognize the difference, though labels state *liquoroso* when applicable, along with the higher alcohol percentage. Pantelleria wine producers not making the liquoroso versions, among them many Panteschi, also claim that the cheaper versions are trading on the reputations of their "natural" counterparts.

At the 1995 conference, Murana and other local producers expressed hope that Panteschi could achieve something special in the wine world. This quickly erupted into heated arguments among Panteschi and between Panteschi and non-Panteschi. On the heels of that conference, some producers accused others of illegal wine sophistication. In 2004 a Pantesco winegrower made allegations to authorities against several other producers that resulted in court cases. At the beginning of 2009, eleven out of the seventeen accused were absolved. The resolution of the accusations against the other six was postponed. Not only are the island's vineyards fractionalized, but so are its inhabitants. Few Pantesco restaurants feature local wine. This demonstrates the lack of island self-determination. It is easier to make money from tourism than from agriculture or wine production. The average age of those who work in the vineyards is more than sixty years. There awaits no next generation of Panteschi winegrowers. At a meeting in 2010, Murana told me that all the hopes he had nurtured during the 1980s and early 1990s have evaporated.

Putting the problems of the Panteschi aside, their island is an exciting location for viticulture. More than fifty volcanic vents, now extinct, have formed conical hills of volcanic debris. These geologic formations are called *kuddie* (the plural of *kuddia*) or *cuddie* (the plural of *cuddia*). Their names, mostly Arabic in origin, identify the localities that surround them. Wine producers also name their wines after kuddie. In doing so, they identify the location of production. The island's many thermal springs, some of whose temperatures reach 100°C (212°F), evidence volcanic activity, which is diminishing. Its highest point, Montagna Grande, reaches 836 meters (2,743 feet) above sea level. The sharp inclines of jagged-edged volcanic rocks have forced humans over the centuries to build terraces to create cultivatable patches of soil.

The greenish black rocks that dominate and characterize the island are made of pantellerite. They have a low pH and are rich in sodium. The rocks erode into porous sandy soils. The pumice in these soils is filled with tiny cavities that absorb dew at night. Because these soils are light and soft and drain well, contact with them rarely damages low-lying vine vegetation. They are also very fertile.

Pantelleria's climate is maritime-Mediterranean, with hot summers and mild winters. The average annual temperature is 19°C (66°F). Temperatures average 11°C (52°F) in the winter and 25°C (77°F) in the summer. The island gets about three hundred millimeters (twelve inches) of rain per year spread over fewer than fifty days, mostly between November and February. July is a parched month, with an average of two and a half millimeters (0.09 inches) of rain. The island has few streams, but dry stone and gravel beds become torrents during the winter. One important factor is the wind, which blows at an average of twenty kilometers (twelve miles) per hour more than 320 days per year. Different exposures on the island are subject to winds from different directions. Winds can be very strong from mid-May to June, knocking off tender shoots and impairing flowering. The vines are dug into holes and trained low to the ground to get cover. The scirocco is feared most. Along with its winds, it can bring so much heat that the vines become comatose and the grapes wither on the vine. At Scauri, a port on the southwest coastline, Donnafugata loses one harvest in three because of the scirocco.

Zibibbo became increasingly popular from the beginning of the twentieth century. Its triple use—for table grapes, raisins, and wine—strengthened market demand. Zibibbo accounts for 90 percent of the vines planted on the island. The white grape varieties Catarratto and Inzolia and the red grape varieties Perricone and Alicante (Grenache Noir) make up most of the balance. *Alberello pantesco* is the training system of tradition and choice. On the wind-shielded plains of Ghirlanda and Monastero, some row training on wires is employed.

The normal harvest begins during the second decade of July and ends during the last decade of September. There is a small second harvest in October, of buds on secondary shoots (*femminelle,* the plural of *femminella*). The small bunches (about ten grapes each) of tart, low-alcohol grapes (*racemi,* the plural of *racemo*) yield a refreshing table wine consumed locally. The earliest-harvested grapes are reputed to make the best passito wines. They come from the warmest areas, at low elevations and close to the sea. These grapes have higher sugar and are in perfect condition. The weather remains sunny, hot, and dry for the drying period, from the first harvest in early August to the end of September. The yields at such sites, however, are low, about forty-five quintals per hectare (4,015 pounds per acre). Higher and cooler sites make better dry table wine. The highest vineyards on the island are at about four hundred meters (1,312 feet) for white grapes and three hundred meters (984 feet) for red grapes.

If it takes the same amount of grapes to make five bottles of normal dry wine as one bottle of Passito di Pantelleria, where does that missing volume go? Water vapor escapes through the drying grape skins, concentrating all the other grape constituents. Traditionally winegrowers laid out the grapes on mats or nets in an area (*stenditoio*) enclosed by walls. The walls collect heat, raising the ambient temperature by about 10°C (18°F). The drying process is faster at higher temperatures. The faster it is done, the less chance there is that the insects, weather, mold, or other factors will compromise the raisins. Many producers cover their grapes at night to protect them from nighttime humidity and dew. An awning or other covering at the ready also serves to protect the grapes from inclement weather. Drying grapes have to be monitored carefully. Just as a chef flips an egg in a frying pan, a winegrower must turn over each bunch regularly, to ensure even drying and to check for fungus. During the drying period a stenditoio smells like hot apple pie.

There are two degrees of drying, *passolata* and *passa Malaga*. Passolata grapes are semidried, spending one to two weeks under the sun. Twenty-five to 40 percent of their juice is sugar. The little juice still inside the berry is just enough to macerate the skins in and to vinify the skins and juice. Passolata grapes look as wizened as Amarone grapes. The processes for drying them are similar to those used in the Veneto region for Amarone production. After three to four weeks of drying, fresh grapes become fully dried raisins, called *uva passa Malaga*. Though they are soft and pliable, they do not contain enough liquid but must instead be either soaked in juice or wine or tossed into a fermenting must for maceration. Aromatic compounds are at peak concentration at this point. Further drying decreases the aromas. Grapes can be dried for as long as three to four weeks, at which point 55 percent of their syrup becomes sugar. After such extreme drying, grapes are one-quarter of their original weight. During the drying process, aromas transition from orange and muscat to dried figs and dates.

Though the Pantelleria climate is rather steady, there are still occurrences that can alter the quantity and quality of the harvest and drying periods. Excessive drought in 1982, 1988, and 2003 reduced yields. In 1996 and 2007 downy mildew decimated yields. It can occasionally rain during the drying period. Francesca Minardi of Azienda Vinicola Minardi told me that rain during the drying period in 2004 forced her to vinify her drying grapes sooner than planned.

Using serre reduces the drying time dramatically. These enclosures intensify the heat. Three to four days is sufficient for passolata and seven to eight days for passa Malaga. By law, producers may use serre with air vents, whose drying period is longer than that of unvented tents but shorter than drying in open air. It is easy to understand why many producers use these enclosures. Another way to speed up the process is to first immerse grapes in hot water mixed with caustic soda. The bath removes their bloom, thus speeding up the evaporation of the juice. However, this also reduces aromatic compounds. The skins of grapes treated this way appear paler, hence their name *uva passa bionda,* meaning "blond dried grape." The DOC does not allow this use of caustic soda.

Though machines can destem the harvested grapes, this grows increasingly difficult as they become more raisined. Traditionally women destemmed raisined grapes while sitting around a large table. By hand is still the commonest way to destem uva passa Malaga.

The traditional method of making Passito di Pantelleria is to add uva passa Malaga to fresh Zibibbo grapes in fermentation. This is very similar to how Hungary's sweet Tokaji Aszú wines are made. The raisins add flavor and sugar. When fermentation reaches the desired residual sugar and alcohol levels, the wine is drained and the skins pressed. There are, however, many different options that Pantelleria winegrowers can use to alter the process and the end result. Passolata grapes can be used. Some producers cold-macerate harvested grapes for up to three weeks. Some winegrowers rehydrate the paste of the fermented skins in wine and then press it to extract more fruit sugar, which they add back to the fermenting must or wine.

After fermentation the sweet wines are clarified and stabilized using static cold sedimentation aided by fining agents. Before bottling they are usually sent through diatomaceous earth filters. During these processes, concrete, stainless steel, fiberglass, or oak barrels are used as containers. Concrete vats exist in older wineries. If they have no cracks, they can be excellent containers. Stainless steel tanks are easiest to clean, and micro-oxygenation can reduce their tendency to give wines pungent, vegetal smells. Fiberglass tanks are more common on Pantelleria than in other wine-producing zones. Concern about styrene, a hazardous chemical, is reducing their use. Large oak barrels generally have been phased out. They are too difficult to keep clean. Some producers use a percentage of new, small-format barrels in their mix of maturation vessels. These give flavor and oxygenate the wines somewhat. Most producers do not mature their sweet wines for long periods after fermentation. De Bartoli, on the other hand, matures Bukkuram in used barriques for two years before bottling.

Because Moscato di Pantelleria and Passito di Pantelleria are not only the island's most prestigious categories but also its most widely recognized throughout the world, I have focused this discussion on them. The Passito is darker, golden amber, with a strong scent of raisins, dates, and dried apricots. The Moscato is more golden and has some fresh apricot aroma mixed in with the dried. It also has some floral scents. The Passito is more viscous, sweet, and alcoholic than the Moscato. Moscato Liquoroso and Passito Liquoroso lack the concentration of the unfortified versions. They are available in many markets, and consumers interested in understanding Pantelleria wines should be aware of the difference.

Murana, the island's most famous native wine producer, makes an aromatic dry wine, Gadì, from Zibibbo racemi that he collects in October from several sites. His farm center is at Mueggen, which he calls "an island within an island." It is an isolated plateau in the interior at an altitude of four hundred meters (1,312 feet). Here Zibibbo is harvested in mid-September, several weeks later than at his other sources. These grapes are used in Turbè, a light Moscato di Pantelleria whose sweetness is balanced by its 13 percent alcohol. Mueggen and Khamma are both Passito di Pantellerias that move the alcohol and the sweetness up a degree. Martingana is a single-vineyard wine from the southeastern coast. The vineyard was planted in 1932. The old vines there can ripen their grapes in the area's extreme warmth of August. Murana selects the best grapes from this vineyard and dries them outdoors for thirty to forty days.

Three artisanal producers, Salvatore Ferrandes, Fabrizio Basile, and Salvino Gorgone, each farm several hectares and make tiny quantities of wines. Ferrandes, whose father also grew grapes and made wine, is building his own winery and will be installing a bottling line. His wines are concentrated, very sweet and viscous, and loaded with the smell of honey and dates. He was proud to tell me that they contain 170 grams per liter (twenty-three ounces per gallon) of sugar; the minimum by law is 110 grams (fifteen ounces per gallon). He says that for every Passito di Pantelleria he makes, he could make five bottles of dry wine. To help fund his passito production, Ferrandes grows, harvests, and sells the island's prized capers. During my visit, his teenage son Adrian accompanied him and demonstrated a genuine appreciation for the fruit that his father grows. Time will tell if he will be in the next generation of this vanishing breed. Basile is also the son of winegrowers. His grandfather too was a grape grower. His father helped Basile set up his winery, where he also intends to create a small restaurant. His Shamira Passito di Pantelleria 2007 is delicate and light. Gorgone, like many Panteschi winegrowers, has another job that helps support him, one that serves the brisk tourist trade. He is a builder. He farms only three hectares (seven acres). His wines have a pure, fresh, and lively taste, the hallmarks of the modern style. He has a brand-new winery, Dietro L'Isola, but uses another facility on the island for bottling.

Abraxas espouses a style somewhere between those of Donnafugata and Murana. Its Passito di Pantelleria is very spicy. Scirafi, the Abraxas second-tier Passito di Pantelleria, is based on first pressings, rather than the tarter, more delicate free-run juice, and on the addition of less-dried grapes during vinification. The former Italian agricultural minister Calogero Mannino, famous for his advocacy of the Italian (and Sicilian) wine industry, established Abraxas in 1999 as an oasis where he could escape the intrigues of the political world. Abraxas has twenty-six hectares (sixty-four acres) of land, making it one of the largest growers on the island. Four hectares (ten acres) are in the contradas of Bukkuràm and Scirafi at 125 meters (410 feet), a warm site ideal for making Passito di Pantelleria. Twenty-two hectares (fifty-four acres) straddle the Mueggen and Randazzo contradas. These vineyards are at three to four hundred meters (984 to 1,312 feet) in one of the coolest sites for viticulture on the island. The vineyards here are sizable and flat, allowing for wire training and some mechanization. Beyond its Passito di Pantellerias, Abraxas makes a dry white wine and several red wines. The white is Kuddia del Gallo, a 70 percent Zibibbo, 30 percent Viognier blend. It combines the exotic smells and fat, rich, slightly bitter tastes of both vine varieties. Abraxas is the island's red wine leader in quantity and quality. My favorite is Kuddia di Zè, a blend of 50 percent Syrah, 30 percent Grenache, and 20 percent Carignan.

Due to the high cost of production and the paucity of land suitable for still dry wine production on Pantelleria, it is unlikely that we will see many dry wines from there on the international market. The first such was De Bartoli's Pietranera, first released in 1990. This dry, cold-fermented Zibibbo remains the reference point for varietal Zibibbo. Giacomo Tachis believed that Pantelleria could produce top-quality red wines. At the 1995 conference, he told me that while the north of Italy made tart and hard-textured wines that needed long aging in barrique to soften, the Pantelleria climate could achieve suppleness without barriques. He pointed to the sunny sky: "That is Pantelleria's *barricaia* [a maturation room containing barriques]." Tachis thought that the ultimate skin ripeness achievable in Pantelleria's cooler zones could naturally produce deeply colored, rich, supple red wines. He suggested the use of Carignan, based on his experience with the variety in the similar growing environment of Sardinia. Varieties introduced into Tunisia during its French colonial period could be a source of vine wood for producers interested in making Rhône-style wines, which the Italian wine industry has not mastered. I hope that Abraxas's red wines move in this direction. Its high-altitude site, its state-of-the art boutique winery, built in an isolated Italian army barrack from World War II, and the combined expertise of its consultant Nicola Centonze and full-time enologist Michele Augugliaro are assets that can help it achieve this feat.

On Pantelleria we find both winegrowers and entrepreneurs. Will there be a next generation of native winegrowers? What is likely is that outside wealth will create boutique estates that present the mystique and the image but not the reality of the Pantesco winegrower. That wealth, though it may preserve the wine, will not represent its spirit. Murana told me that Pantelleria wine production is becoming "a sport of the rich for the rich."

Other recommended producers and their wines:

Cantine Rallo Passito di Pantelleria
Carole Bouquet *Sangue d'Oro* Passito di Pantelleria
Case di Pietra *Niká* Passito di Pantelleria
D'Ancona e Figli *Cimillýa* Passito di Pantelleria
Miceli *Entellechia* Passito di Pantelleria
Miceli *Yanir* Passito di Pantelleria
Serragghia di Giotto Bini Moscato di Pantelleria
Solidea Passito di Pantelleria

MARSALA

A century troubled by two world wars and one Great Depression did little to support Marsala, a product that depends on international trade and economic stability. After

World War II, Marsala producers increasingly combined their wine with the flavors of nuts, fruits, spices, and eggs to attract more customers with different tastes. Food industries and consumers purchased these "Marsala"s for culinary preparations and for the enhancement and preservation of various foods. The popularity of the so-called Marsala Speciali caused the image of Marsala to transition from sophisticated beverage to commodity product indirectly consumed as an ingredient. The most challenging problem that Marsala—like Sherry and Madeira, its two prototypes—has faced has been the shift in consumer tastes from oxidized fortified wines to fruity table wines.

The market deterioration has been dramatic. As of 1921 there were about fifty enological companies in Marsala. After World War II there was a proliferation of Marsala companies, mostly small, that capitalized on commercializing the wine and priced it so as to undercut the established Marsala houses. By 1950 there were 226 such operations. By 1970 about a hundred Marsala producers remained. There were only fifteen in 2010, when a bottle of Fine Marsala could be purchased for as little as one and a half euro. The final slap was the "Is Marsala a bluff?" debate that took place on a Sicilian wine blog, "Cronache di Gusto," from April to June 2010. Will Marsala survive?

Though John Woodhouse modeled Marsala after Madeira, Benjamin Ingham moved its style more toward that of Sherry. He incorporated Sherry techniques such as maturation by *solera,* a system that homogenizes wine quality and style by systematically blending younger with older wine. As with Sherry, in Marsala production, grape spirit is added to a fully fermented dry white wine. Though red grapes were used to make ruby Marsalas during the nineteenth century, and though the 1984 revision of the Marsala production *disciplinare* reinstated a ruby version, *rubino,* made mostly with red grapes, Marsala is largely a fortified white wine. Before the mid-nineteenth century the triad of Catarratto, Inzolia, and Grillo dominated Sicilian vineyards. Inzolia proved to be too vulnerable to powdery mildew, which attacked in the mid-nineteenth century. Grillo largely took its place until the end of the nineteenth century. Grown in alberello, Grillo grapes are harvested when their sugar is high and can be naturally vinified into 14 to 17 percent alcohol wines. From 1900 to 1920, when phylloxera necessitated the replanting of vineyards, farmers opted to plant the higher-yielding Catarratto instead of Grillo. Catarratto produces lower-alcohol wines than Grillo. Rectified concentrated grape juice can be added to Catarratto musts to increase the base wine alcohol degree. More grape spirit can to be added to fortify the wine. Purists perceive this greater reliance on added grape sugar and spirit as a move away from connection to place and toward a concocted industrial product. Catarratto wine tends to oxidize rapidly, darkening as it does so, but this is just what Marsala producers want, particularly for the styles identified by the word *ambra* ("amber"). To encourage oxidation even more, they splash the base wines in open air during the racking process. After World War II, the quality of Marsala's base wines deteriorated. Since 1984 the white variety Damaschino has been allowed in Marsala production. Its high yields and low-alcohol wine do not endear it to purists.

Once they have made and blended the base wines, Marsala producers add grape spirit to make Vergine. This, the purest type of Marsala, has no other additions. To the Fine and Superiore styles, producers can add coloring and flavoring products. Fine and Superiore evolved when early Marsala producers needed to adjust the appearance, smell, and taste of immature Vergine to suit the preferences of a buyer. Brand names originally devised for particular markets became the internationally recognized names for styles of Marsala, for example Italy Particular (IP), Superior Old Marsala (SOM), London Particular (LP), and Garibaldi Dolce (GD). Each producer has its own recipes for styles and brands, and every one must satisfy the Marsala DOC regulations. Each recipe, called a *concia,* prescribes additions of grape spirit, *sifone* ("sweet fortified wine"), *mosto cotto* ("cooked must"), and rectified concentrated grape juice. Before a producer blends in these additions, he must declare to regulatory authorities which lots will become what regulated types of Marsala. Changes to this declaration cannot be made. Hence a wine declared as a Fine must remain a Fine even if it matures for many years in barrel without additions, like a Vergine. When they add grape spirit, producers must take into account the concentration or dilution that other additions and evaporative rates during maturation will cause. Before bottling they can make a final spirit addition to meet the 17 percent alcohol by volume minimum required for Fine and the 18 percent minimum for other styles.

Understanding the various ingredients of the concia is essential to understanding what makes Marsala. To make sifone, also called *mistella,* spirit from late-harvested grapes is added to fermenting grape juice, cutting its fermentation short. Sifone provides sweetness and a syrupy texture. During Marsala maturation, it also enhances the development of specific aromas. In Marsala Superiore, the percentage of sifone in the concia is greater than that of the dry base wine, perhaps even double it. Sifone accounts for the greatest percentage of constituents in the dolce version of Superiore, particularly the type labeled *oro* ("golden"). Mosto cotto provides another range of aromas, similar to burned sugar or caramel. Its principal function, which purists look down on, is to tint Marsala dark brown, a hue that could otherwise be achieved by long maturation in barrel. Mosto cotto is principally used in Marsala labeled *ambra.* Rectified concentrated grape juice can be added to fine-tune the sweetness and viscosity of Marsala. Purists frown upon it too. By law, sifone, mosto cotto, and spirit used in Marsala must be derived from grapes grown in the Marsala DOC.

The difference between Fine and Superiore is maturation time. A Fine needs to mature one year, the first four months of which may be in a nonwooden container. For the eight remaining months, the container must be wooden. The Superiore must age at least two years in wood. There is a longer-matured category of Superiore, Superiore Riserva. It must mature in a wooden container at least four years before being bottled. For all Marsala styles, oak and cherry are the two wood types allowed. The barrels are never entirely filled. This allows a steady oxidation of the wine. A cool, somewhat humid, and dark environment is best for maturation. Fine, Superiore, and Superiore

Riserva can also be labeled to indicate color: *oro* for golden, *ambra* for amber, and *rubino* for ruby. The labels for residual sweetness level are *secco* (dry, less than forty grams per liter [five ounces per gallon]), *semisecco* (semidry, between forty and one hundred grams per liter), and *dolce* (sweet, more than one hundred grams per liter [thirteen ounces per gallon]). Fine and Superiore labeled *ambra* must contain at least 1 percent mosto cotto. Fine and Superiore rubinos must have at least 70 percent Pignatello (a variety called Perricone in the Palermo area), as well as Nero d'Avola or Nerello Mascalese.

If the producer were to add only grape spirits to the base wine and then age it for at least five years, he could release it as a Vergine. After five more years he could release it as a Vergine Riserva or Vergine Stravecchio. If producers use the solera maturation system, then they can print *Vergine Soleras* or simply *Soleras* on the label. In a solera system, younger wine systematically replaces older wine that has been removed from barrels for bottling or further blending. Thus Soleras do not carry a vintage year, whereas some Vergines do.

Marsala Vergine should be pale gold, with an intense nutty nose accented with citrus. In the mouth, it should be soft and savory. Dry Oloroso Sherry has a bitter finish that Marsala Vergine does not. Unfortunately, a minuscule amount of Vergine is produced. As of 2010, Marsala Vergine accounts for only 0.7 percent of production, while Marsala Superiore represents 18.6 percent, and Marsala Fine has the largest share, 80.7 percent.[1] Vergine wines can be splendid. Some develop a *rancio* or leathery smell with age. Some tasters like this smell. Some do not, me included. The clean smell I prefer may be less exotic than one with a rancio character, but for me it is more pure. In general, the more Grillo in the blend of a Vergine, the paler the color, the spicier and nuttier the smell, and the more viscous and finely astringent the texture.

If a specific year appears on a wine that says *Soleras* on the front or back label, it must refer to something other than the age of the wine. Some houses use their founding year as part of the branding on the front label. Examples are Pellegrino 1880 and Intorcia 1930. If aging in barrel exceeds the minimum amount required by law, producers sometimes specify so on the label. Ten years is the minimum aging period for the Vergine Riserva category. A wine labeled *Vergine Riserva 20 anni* has had an additional ten years of maturation.

The government revised the Marsala wine production regulations and labeling in 1984. The new law, referred to as 851, attempted to restore tradition to Marsala. After World War II, Marsala merchants sourced grapes from beyond the borders of the province of Trapani, in the provinces of Palermo and Agrigento. The new law restricted such sourcing to the province of Trapani, excluding the township of Alcamo, Favignana (one of the Egadi Islands), and Pantelleria, all in the province. In addition, Marsala wine had to be produced and bottled within the new boundaries. The law also restricted the use of cooked must and, most important, banned Marsala Speciale, the Marsala flavored by spices, fruits, and so forth that had gained popularity after World War II. One popular egg, or zabaglione, style that used to be known as Marsala all'Uovo had its supporters even among expert tasters. It was left in the disciplinare as *cremovo zabaione vino aromatizzato* or *cremovo vino aromatizzato*, with a requirement of at least 80 percent Marsala. The word *Cremovo*, not *Marsala*, dominates the front label of such wines. Products with 60 percent or more Marsala may have the phrase *Preparato con l'impiego di vino Marsala* ("Prepared with the use of Marsala wine") on their label. If made with less than 60 percent Marsala, the product may still list the wine among the ingredients. These and other changes helped put Marsala back on a more traditional track.

Periodically wine journalists criticize the Marsala houses for the low quality of Marsala wine and the continually worsening image of the industry. Many have been the remedies proposed to restore the industry to good health. Some suggest decreasing the legal yield limits (presently one hundred quintals per hectare [8,919 pounds per acre] for whites and ninety quintals per hectare [8,028 pounds per acre] for reds), raising the minimum alcohol levels allowed for base wines, and banning the use of cooked and concentrated must. Some say producers have chased the low-cost Fine market at the expense of developing the traditional and quality side of the industry. Most Fine is sold to the food industry expressly for flavor enhancement and preservation. But if quality were higher across the board, would more Marsala be sold? Unfortunately, current consumer flavor preferences limit any possible improvement in the market. Marsala was conceived for a world without refrigeration, in which the need for asepsis was not widely understood and transportation challenged the stability of what was purchased. The world has changed. Although most of the fruits and vegetables in our supermarkets now come from thousands of miles away, they are still fresh when we buy them. Modern consumers regularly appreciate the flavors of fresh fruit. They prefer fruity to oxidized wines.

The Marsala industry as a whole should not try to remake its image. Unless the world drastically changes, a remake will not succeed. The core identity of Marsala must be preserved, just like our finest art and historical monuments. That core identity comes from the Marsala of the late eighteenth and early nineteenth century, when Vergine was its defining style.

Though Woodhouse fortified his Marsala and subsequent wine law has obligated fortification, there is no reason why it should not be optional. Pre-1960s wine producers in Sicily regularly produced wines with between 14 and 17 percent alcohol. The crucial factors that made and still make this possible are Grillo, alberello, and Marsala's warm, dry, and windy climate. Cellar maturation in dry conditions raises the alcohol content even higher. The minimum alcohol percentage at bottling for Marsala Vergine should be set lower, at 16 percent, to allow for unfortified versions bearing a new Marsala Vergine DOCG label. Producers of the Marsala Vergine DOCG would be required to state whether the wine was fortified or not. If fortification were an option, not a rule, those producers who wanted to challenge themselves by forgoing fortification could point the way toward a Marsala that more truly represented and featured the wine of origin. Unfortified Marsala Vergine would bring Marsala back to its pre-Woodhouse, genuinely Sicilian roots.

Casano (founded 1940). This small family-run house has vineyards that supply 50 percent of the grapes needed for its Marsala and three table wines. Third-generation siblings Francesca and Francesco Intorcia are breathing new life into the company. The smart design of its website demonstrates how Marsala could better present itself to the world.

Florio (founded 1833). The ILLVA di Saronno drinks group, which has owned Florio since 1998, purchased the Duca di Salaparuta winery in 2001. ILLVA consolidated both companies into Duca di Salaparuta, retaining the facilities and brands of each. Florio is now an umbrella brand for Marsala made by the Duca di Salaparuta company. The labels use the branding *Cantine Florio 1833*. These wines mature at the Florio baglio, seaside at Marsala. The quality of Florio Marsala has remained stable through these transitions. Florio, like other Marsala producers, has a range of branded products, including Marsala, fortified wines, and wines from the islands of Pantelleria and Salina. It sources the grapes for its Marsalas from along the coast, just like the early Marsala industry. Moreover, Florio bases the blends for its Marsala Superiore Riservas and Vergines on Grillo grown in alberello. They age for eight years in oak barrel. Their pale golden color, clean nutty bouquet, and rich, savory palate are characteristics of the pure style that I appreciate most. These Marsalas are pure, solid, and elegant. Florio makes two excellent Vergines, Terre Arse and Baglio Florio. The Donna Franca Marsala Superiore Semisecco Ambra, matured for fifteen years, blunts the spice and power of the Vergines with an edge of sweetness.

Marco De Bartoli (founded 1978). Born into the elite Marsala merchant world, the mercurial Marco De Bartoli raced cars during the 1970s while working at the Pellegrino and Mirabella Marsala houses. Warned by scrapes with disaster on the roads and disillusioned with how the Marsala industry chased profits rather than quality and identity, he retired to take the reins of his family's farm at Samperi. While Marsala houses were going out of business in the late 1970s and early 1980s, he was buying up the finest reserves, creating a collection that would give his Marsala that je ne sais quoi of character. He was the most outspoken supporter of the Grillo variety. His most controversial wine (there were many controversies that swirled around him) was Vecchio Samperi Ventennale 20 anni. It was 100 percent Grillo. He kept his yields so low (twenty hectoliters per hectare [214 gallons per acre]) that his base wines naturally reached about 16.5 percent alcohol. After twenty years in a solera system, which raised the alcohol level through the evaporation of water from the wine, the wine was bottled at roughly 17.5 percent alcohol without the addition of grape spirits. Because the alcohol percentage was less than the legal minimum of 18 percent, De Bartoli was not allowed to label this wine as a Marsala but as a vino liquoroso (which was not true, since it was never fortified). Because Vecchio Samperi was 100 percent wine, it represented the terroir more truthfully than any Marsala could. It also was closer to the type of wine, vino perpetuo, that the inhabitants of Marsala made before the arrival of John Woodhouse in 1773. In the summer of 2010 De Bartoli told me, "A good wine must have an alcohol grade high enough to age well. There need to be good vineyards. But since 1963 the law permits the possibility of making Marsala from grapes that would make a wine of about 8 percent alcohol. This makes shit, big shit. It cannot age. In 1980 I first released Vecchio Samperi. This was a real Marsala, but I was not allowed by law to identify it as Marsala on the label. The wines were very well received. Despite the great reputation of Vecchio Samperi, it was not easy to sell. I sold very little because of the reputation of Sicily, of Marsala, and of Pantelleria. However, I am not of Sicily, Marsala, or Pantelleria. I am De Bartoli, who makes Samperi and Bukkuram. This is the moral of the fable. I am a producer of quality wine, not Sicilian wine. I went outside and they treated me as if I were an outlaw. I had a sack of problems and they made a party out of it. But it does not bother me. To live in Sicily is not easy." In March 2011, De Bartoli died at the age of sixty-six years. He was an artist working in the world of business and politics. His two sons, Renato and Sebastiano, and his daughter, Josephine, are now in charge of the family business.

Martinez (founded 1866). Fifty percent of the production of this small, family-owned house is Marsala. The other half is other types of fortified wines. The company owns no vineyards, preferring to buy base wine. Its Marsala wines emphasize purity and delicacy. The Vergine Riserva "Vintage 1995" is pale, with a delicate nose of dried fruits and orange rind and a delicate though persistent finish. Paler still and so complex in the nose (strong toasted hazelnut smells) that it seems to be sweet when it is in fact dry is the Exito, Vergine Riserva 1982.

Pellegrino (founded 1880). The house of Pellegrino, officially Carlo Pellegrino & C., experienced great growth in the 1930s. It adapted to the difficult Marsala market of the 1980s by establishing a line of table wines. It is a big and dynamic family-owned operation. About 40 percent of the wines it releases are Marsala, an enormous commitment considering the market. The Marsala wines are labeled Cantine Pellegrino 1880. About one hundred of its three hundred hectares (247 of 741 acres) of vineyards are dedicated to Marsala production. The balance principally supplies its Duca di Castelmonte line of unfortified wines. The Riserva del Centenario 1980 that I tasted in 2010 was an exotic Vergine, amber-red, with smells of dried fruits, nuts, and cedar and a rich, full palate. The Superiore Riserva Grillo had a pure nutty, caramel taste. Pellegrino makes a dependable line of Superiores.

Other recommended producers and their wines:

Cantine Buffa Marsala Superiore Riserva Ora Dolce
Cantine Buffa Marsala Vergine
Cantine Intorcia Marsala Vergine Soleras
Cantine Rallo Marsala Soleras Vergine *20 anni*

WESTERN SICILY

I have defined this wine zone so that it roughly corresponds to the one authorized to make Marsala. In the western coastal lowlands running from the town of Trapani to Sciacca, the climate is hot and arid, with winds blowing off the Mediterranean Sea. Along the coastline the breezes are cooling and provide humidity to the soil and vines. It is sunny for an average of 250 days a year here. During all but the winter months, there is very little rainfall along the coast. In many spots this plain is densely planted to vineyards. Woodhouse most likely sampled wines from the Birgi Vecchi and San Leonardo contradas along the coast just to the north of Marsala. He later sourced most of his grapes from the township of Petrosino, halfway between Marsala and Mazara del Vallo. Locals connect Petrosino's potential for great Grillo with its unusual subsoil, *sciasciacu,* in which marine fossils are embedded in calcareous detritus. In particular, the contrada Triglia Scaletta has a reputation for fine Grillo. The best soils for Grillo are loose, porous, and low in fertility, with a moist calcareous crust, rich in mineral salts, underneath. Coastal areas are also ideal for Grillo because it thrives in the sun and heat. The salt in the air and the subsoil gives Grillo wine a sapid taste. Many of the best vineyards along the coast have terra rossa topsoils. Patches of this red soil blanket the comunes of Castellammare del Golfo, Marsala, Petrosino, Mazara del Vallo, and Campobello di Mazara.

To the east the elevation of rolling hills increases steadily up to the highlands that extend from Mount Erice in the north to Castelvetrano, northwest of Menfi, in the south. Mount Erice, rising to 750 meters (2,461 feet), condenses much of the humidity borne on winds coming off the Tyrrhenian Sea. Its hillsides have the highest rainfall in Western Sicily. Lower elevations are very dry. Thankfully there is subterranean water available for irrigation. To the immediate northwest of the centrally located town of Salemi, vineyard altitudes range from four to six hundred meters (1,312 to 1,969 feet). In the vicinity of Salemi, the soil tends to be calcareous clay, rich in potassium but poor in nitrogen and available phosphorus. The deficiency of nitrogen and phosphorus slows growth, leading to low-alcohol wines. Interior hilly areas in the comunes of Buseto Palizzolo, Calatafimi, Fulgatore, Gibellina, and Partanna have similar soils. Clay soils become hard during dry spells and crack open. The surface they form needs to be constantly broken up. Easier to farm are the loose and fertile *terre brune,* "brown soils," in the comunes of Balata di Baida, Buseto Palizzolo, Fulgatore, Poggioreale, and Salaparuta (not to be confused with the firm Duca di Salaparuta).[2] At the higher elevations common in the interior hills, rainfall is higher and the clayey soils absorb water, making them cool and moist throughout the summer. In addition, winds rising up the hills release their moisture to vines as morning dew. The principal variety planted here is Catarratto, which produces a high-acid, moderate-to-low-alcohol wine. Chardonnay grown here has given good results. Fessina, an estate based at Rovittello on the north face of Etna, sources Chardonnay grapes from a vineyard it owns at Segesta, about twenty kilometers (twelve miles) north of Salemi. This vineyard faces northwest and is at six hundred meters (1,969 feet) on rocky, calcareous clay soil. The wine Nakone, one of the finest Chardonnays made in Sicily, matures on its lees for five or six months with no new-oak contact. Franco Giacosa sourced Inzolia from Salemi for the Duca di Salaparuta wines of the 1970s, 1980s, and 1990s. Duca di Salaparuta continues to source Inzolia from this area and has purchased an estate here, Risignolo, as a source for Kados, its 100 percent Grillo wine. The eastern edge of the Western Sicily zone is near the comunes of Poggioreale, Gibellina, and Salaparuta. These townships lie between the Freddo and Belice Rivers in the upper Belice Valley.

Catarratto Comune accounts for about 40 percent of the vines, of both red and white varieties, in the province of Trapani. The other white varieties, in order of most to least planted, are Grillo, Grecanico, Inzolia, Catarratto Lucido and Extralucido, Trebbiano Toscano, Chardonnay, Zibibbo, Pinot Grigio, Viognier, Damaschino, Malvasia Bianca, and Sauvignon Blanc. In the 1930s, Grillo occupied about 60 percent of the vineyards near the coastline. Now it is rare, particularly inland. Catarratto Extralucido is found more in the interior, particularly in the Alcamo area. Its high acidity results in a very tart white wine. The red varieties, from most to least planted, are Nero d'Avola (more than 7 percent of the vineyard area), Syrah, Merlot, Cabernet Sauvignon, Frappato, Nerello Mascalese, Petit Verdot, Alicante Bouschet, and Perricone. Most of the Nero d'Avola was planted in the 1990s. No one red variety has excelled in Western Sicily. Historically Perricone was the most important red variety in the zone, but it has become rare. Together with Carignan, also very rare, if existent at all, in Trapani now, it was the base of the red blend for vini da taglio, red wines, and rosatos.

There are several DOCs in this sizable zone. The operatic-sounding Delia Nivolelli is an appellation for various wine types using various vine varieties. Its basic rosso focuses on Nero d'Avola, Perricone, Merlot, Cabernet Sauvignon, Syrah, and Sangiovese. Its bianco has a more indigenous blend, featuring at least 65 percent Grecanico, Inzolia, and Grillo. Then there are varietal wines, which must meet the 85 percent variety minimum imposed by the DOC. The Delia Nivolelli DOC encompasses a large area, nearly surrounding the town of Marsala but not including it. In 2004 the Erice DOC superseded the Colli Ericini IGT. Some of this DOC's vineyard sites are on the slopes of Mount Erice close to the sea, but the appellation reaches well inland to the south, halfway down the island, overlapping the Delia Nivolelli DOC. In general, because of the high altitude of the vineyards in the appellation, between 250 and 500 meters (820 and 1,640 feet),

Erice DOC wines tend to be lower in alcohol and higher in acidity than other western coastal wines. While Erice Bianco requires at least 60 percent Catarratto in its blend, Erice Rosso requires more than 60 percent Nero d'Avola. The DOC also features a wide range of indigenous and international varietal wines in a plethora of styles. The western edge of the Alcamo DOC creeps over the Freddo River. This appellation is described in the Palermo Highlands section below. The Salaparuta DOC lies in the upper Belice Valley at the eastern limit of the Western Sicily zone. At least 65 percent of its bianco must be Catarratto, while the same minimum of Nero d'Avola is prescribed for its rosso. Most of the wines in Western Sicily have been bottled and released to the market under the regionwide Sicilia IGT.

Tasca d'Almerita buys nearly all the grapes grown on Mozia, just north of Marsala in the lagoon along the coastline. This island is the site of an ancient Phoenician city and trading outpost. Shards of Phoenician pottery are so common in the vineyards that they make up part of the topsoil. The island is just offshore from Birgi Vecchi and San Leonardo. Tachis selected budwood from very old vines for these vineyards when they were replanted on rootstocks about a decade ago. Tasca d'Almerita buys its grapes from the Whitaker Foundation, which was established by Joseph Whitaker, a descendant of the nineteenth-century Marsala producer Ingham. The foundation administers the island and cares for its archeological treasures. Harvested grapes are loaded into small boats and transported to Sicily's shoreline. Trucks transfer them to Tasca's facility in Vallelunga for processing. The wine Mozia is 100 percent Grillo. It is light and soft with a salty finish. The vines need more age to produce more-concentrated wine. On the island of Favignana farther to the west, in the Egadi Islands, Firriato has a five hectare (twelve acre) experimental vineyard, in which it has planted Grillo, Catarratto, Perricone, and Nero d'Avola.

Across Western Sicily a high percentage of the grape crop is consigned to cooperatives. Along the west coast are the larger ones, particularly Colomba Bianca, Cantine Europa, and Cantina Sociale Birgi. Many retirees and elder professionals farm small plots of land and sell their grapes to cooperatives. The cooperatives principally sell juice and wine in bulk but are increasingly bottling it as they attempt to move away from the bulk market. Many of the other wine companies in the area are Marsala houses that have diversified into bottled unfortified wine. Merchant-owned and cooperative wineries have long dominated Western Sicily. Given the history of wine production and the great surface area dedicated to vineyards here, it is unfortunate that there are not more small and medium estate wine companies in the area to own vineyards, make wine, and commercialize it.

Barraco.   Seven kilometers (four miles) from the sea in the township of Marsala, Nino Barraco makes fifteen thousand bottles of artisanal wine a year. One is a five-day skin contact Grillo white wine. Tasted at Vinitaly 2012, the 2010 smelled of almonds, hazelnuts, and diesel and had a salty tang in the finish. A thirteen-day skin contact dry

Zibibbo was darker, with a strong floral and citrus nose and an astringent and bitter mouth. Barraco also makes a pale Pignatello (Perricone) that supports my experience throughout Sicily that there are at least two biotypes of Perricone used there: one for dark, astringent wines and another for paler, less-astringent ones. His best red wine was a 2010 Nero d'Avola. It was dark and had a strong bouquet of cherries, watermelon, and chocolate and a ripe, alcoholic, and astringent mouth. The 2006 Milocca is a passito Nero d'Avola. Its cedary cherry cough syrup nose leads into a sweet but astringent Port-like palate.

Caruso & Minini.   Though the Caruso & Minini winery is in a renovated hundred-year-old baglio in the city of Marsala, its 120 hectares (297 acres) of vineyards are in a spot in the hills between Marsala and Salemi at about 350 meters (1,148 feet) in elevation. In 2004, Mario Minini combined his business expertise managing a winery in the north of Italy with Stefano Caruso's dream to give flavor to the grapes that his family had been growing and selling to merchants for more than one hundred years. Other Minini and Caruso family members help out. According to Stefano, the focus of the wines is purity of flavor. The texture of the 2011 Grillo Timpune that I tasted in April 2012 was round but tactile. It had fermented for ten days in five-hundred-liter (132-gallon) oak and acacia barrels and then been left on the lees. The 2011 Cusora, a Chardonnay and Viognier blend fermented in stainless steel, showed the success of those varieties in the rich, cool soils of the inland hills. It had tropical aromas and a soft body. With 13 percent alcohol, it was refreshing to drink. Typically Sicilian Chardonnay and Viognier wines have higher alcoholic content. Stefano Caruso is one of Perricone's most outspoken advocates. The variety has a long history in the Marsala-Salemi area. Growers used to call it Catarratto Rosso. Caruso ferments and matures it in stainless steel tanks to make Sachia. The 2009 vintage was deep reddish purple, with a mouth bursting with the smells of fresh cherries. A 2008 Syrah Riserva, Delia Nivolelli DOC, was opaque purple, with a balsamic nose and a round, soft mouth finished by lingering fine-textured astringency.

Marco De Bartoli.   De Bartoli makes excellent Marsala-style wine and one of Sicily's best dry Grillo wines at the family farm, Samperi, outside the city of Marsala. The Grappolo del Grillo is barrel fermented, which gives it an aroma of grilled nuts. In 2010 De Bartoli told me that his 2008 "will be better in ten years."

Fazio.   Brothers Girolamo and Vincenzo Fazio asked Giacomo Ansaldi to help restructure what had been a cooperative winery. It now bears their family name. They brought Ansaldi on board as a partner and as the full-time enologist. He advised the brothers that the future of the industry would be tied to the English-speaking world. Hence the winery is officially named Fazio Wines. Vincenzo spearheaded efforts to register the Erice area, where the winery is located, as a DOC. The DOC began with the 2005 vintage. Most of the Fazio wines, however, are bottled under the Sicilia IGT designation. A Müller-Thurgau derived from grapes grown at 450 to 500 meters (1,476 to 1,640 feet) has garnered attention with a nose more scented with flowers and spices than German or Alsace examples. The alcohol level of 12.5 percent, lower than that of most other Sicilian wines, helps ensure its refreshing character. At the 2011 Vinitaly, Fazio introduced a sparkling version. My favorite varietal wine from Fazio is its Cabernet Sauvignon, which has the grape's dusty vegetal smells and characteristic fine astringency. The PietraSacra Nero d'Avola Erice DOC has tobacco scents and a fine astringent texture as well. The whites, always spicy, include two Inzolias, one bottled as an Erice DOC and the other as a Sicilia IGT, and Grillo and Catarratto Sicilia IGT wines.

Fina.   Owner Bruno Fina worked as an IRVV enologist for ten years. This was during Tachis's consultancy. The two men developed a close working relationship. In 2005 Fina started a winery, Fina Vini, in the suburbs northeast of Marsala. His own vineyards supply 20 percent of the grapes he vinifies. His extensive knowledge of the terroirs of Western Sicily, combined with friendships and business contacts with many growers, enables him to carefully select the grapes he buys. The high quality of the fruit shows in the wine. He sources Fiano from high altitudes (four hundred meters [1,312 feet]) in the Contessa Entellina appellation near Menfi. The 2009 Fiano was very expressive, with lemon and peach scents. Its mouth is viscous yet tart. From the hills of the Calatifimi-Segesta area, Fina sources Viognier to make a spicy wine similar to the Fiano. When making Grillo, he blends the sea salt notes of grapes grown along the coast with the more aromatically fruited and sourer grapes from higher altitudes in the interior. Caro Maestro ("Dear Master"), a wine that he dedicates to Tachis, is a full-throttle blend of Cabernet Sauvignon, Merlot, and Petit Verdot matured for two years in barrique and six months in bottle before release. The vintage that I tasted was opaque blue-black with mint and cinders in the nose. In the mouth, berry flavors enveloped a sheath of sourness and fine astringency. Fina's 2006 Syrah was one of the best Sicilian Syrahs that I have tasted. It was as dark as a moonless night. Slight smoke rose up with berry smells. The mouth was thick and wild with alcohol, bitterness, and astringency.

Firriato.   Firriato has grown quickly since it was established in the mid-1980s, becoming one of the largest wine producers in Sicily, owning 320 hectares (790 acres) of vineyards and making more than five million bottles of wine annually. Besides holdings in Trapani, the winery owns eleven hectares (twenty-seven acres) of vineyards on Etna. During the late 1990s it quickly built up its northern European markets. During this rapid growth phase, the owners Salvatore and Vinzia Novara Di Gaetano hired Australian and New Zealand enologists. Their wines began to display an international style. The wines have been driven by concepts rather than place of origin, though the Etna wines prove they can do otherwise, and their Favignana project could also yield place-specific results. Lately the company has turned to the Tuscan consulting enologist

Stefano Chioccioli. Harmonium Nero d'Avola is deep purple-black, with burned oak and blackberry fruit, and is extremely soft and thick in the mouth. Camelot, a Cabernet Sauvignon–Merlot blend, has more astringency than the Harmonium. This gives it more structure. The Firriato winery is in Paceco just east of the city of Trapani, but it purchases its grapes from throughout Sicily.

Fondo Antico.　Giuseppe Agostino Adragna, a personable commercial manager, and Lorenza Scianna, a young enologist who combines technical skill, enthusiasm, and energy, breathe professionalism and excitement into the Polizzotti family's winery, Fondo Antico. Sensing the shift from international to indigenous varieties, the company discontinued its international wines except for Syrah. Fondo Antico's calling card is Grillo, particularly its Grillo Parlante (50 percent of production, 150,000 bottles per year). Although the winery is in Birgi, a coastal area, its vineyard elevation ranges from fifty meters (164 feet) near the coast to 250 (820 feet) meters on inland hills. Grillo Parlante tastes fresh and lively without giving up the sapidity that characterizes coastal Grillo. Il Coro Grillo has the tactile edge of wood contact without an oak scent because the barrels used are made of acacia wood. Fondo Antico's Nero d'Avola comes from cool clay soils. The resulting red and rosato (Aprile) wines are fresh and lively. Unforgettable is a 2007 Memorie Clairette, made by pressing fresh Nero d'Avola grapes and fermenting the red-tinted must in barrique. It was both delicate and complex.

Gorghi Tondi.　The Sicilian wine industry has been a man's world until the past twenty years. Two sisters, Annamaria and Clara Sala, manage the Tenuta Gorghi Tondi estate for their family. The company's thirty-five hectares (eighty-six acres) of vines, all in contrada San Nicola in Mazara del Vallo, are divided into vineyards that run up to the Mediterranean and several that lie adjacent to small saltwater lakes in a World Wildlife Fund nature reserve. Grillo dominates the varieties planted seaside in red sandy soils. Nero d'Avola and Chardonnay, two varieties strongly associated with calcium carbonate, are planted in vineyards that abut the lakes, which are karstic (that is, connected to one another and to the Mediterranean by underground streams and caverns set in limestone). At the 2012 Vinitaly, I tasted a citrusy-salty Grillo wine, the 2011 Kheirè, from the sandy-clay soils. The 2011 Rajàh, a dry Zibibbo, was more aromatic, with rich grapefruit and orange smells, and was also saline. The estate also makes a Chardonnay and a Nero d'Avola from the high–calcium carbonate, silt-dominant soils by the lakes. There is a one hectare (two and a half acre) Grillo vineyard planted next to one of the lakes in a spot protected from the offshore winds. Here the *Botrytis cinerea* fungus gradually attacks the overmature Grillo. Due to unusual local climatic conditions, this fungus, which most of the time destroys grape quality, here enhances it. The result is Grillo D'Oro Passito, Sicily's finest botrytis wine. There aren't many like it, due to the island's dry, windy climate. The 2008 had a nose of dried fig, caramel, and ripe grapefruit and was characteristically viscous in the mouth.

La Divina.   At La Divina, a boutique winery in a renovated Florio baglio in view of the island of Mozia, Giacomo Ansaldi makes two dry wines—a white, Abbadessa, a blend of Grillo and Zibibbo, and Cipponeri, a blend of Nero d'Avola and Perricone. Both are ripe and extracted in style. The Abbadessa is deep golden yellow, with strong orange and tropical fruit smells, and viscous with a savory bitter edge. The Cipponeri is deep in color and has a lusty red fruit nose and a thick, rustic mouthful of textures. Ansaldi also makes one sweet, late-harvest wine, Aruta. It is amber and made from dried Zibbibo grapes vinified and aged in oak. All three wines are in very limited production and only available at his *relais*-restaurant, Donna Franca.

La Terzavia.   Renato De Bartoli, Marco's son, has been developing his own brand, La Terzavia. He vinifies the wines at Samperi, the family estate southeast of Marsala, using Grillo from the hills there to make a nondosage metodo classico sparkling wine.

Other recommended producers and their wines:

Cantine Rallo *Aquamadre*
Cantine Rallo Bianco Maggiore
Cantine Rallo *Perla Dell'Eremo* Müller Thurgau
Duca di Salaparuta *Bianca di Valguarnera*
Duca di Salaparuta *Calanìca* Inzolia-Chardonnay
Duca di Salaparuta *Kados*

VAL DI MAZARA—EAST
PALERMO HIGHLANDS

The Palermo Highlands had two periods of promising developments in its local wine industry. In the late eighteenth century, King Ferdinand III of Sicily from his throne in Naples sent the agricultural specialist Felice Lioy to help improve the production of wheat, oil, wine, and other products. Lioy visited farms in the towns around Palermo. He observed agricultural practices and offered advice to farmers. Unfortunately, his counsel was met with indifference and resentment. In 1799, with Napoleon Bonaparte threatening Naples, Ferdinand fled to Palermo. The following year, the Real Cantina Borbonica ("Royal Bourbon Winery") was built in the town of Partinico southwest of Palermo. It had a sophisticated design that allowed horse-drawn carts to drive up ramps and deliver their baskets of grapes at the top of stone vats. Once the grapes were unloaded into the vats, workers crushed them. While the fermenting must was still warm, it was drained into casks and regularly refilled with must that had been set aside. Today this process is called topping-up. Lioy was the enological force behind these innovations. In 1802, Giovanni Meli described closed fermentation tanks in use in Bagheria by the Prince of Butera and in Misilmeri by the Prince Cattolica, but this practice seems not

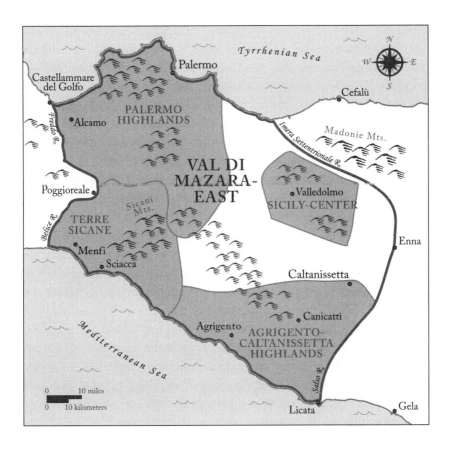

MAP 3.
Val di Mazara—East

to have spread.[3] With Ferdinand's final return to Naples in 1815 and his death in 1825, the Real Cantina Borbonica fell into disuse. The local wine industry returned to its pre-Lioy practices.

In the second half of the nineteenth century, the hills to the southwest, south, and southeast of Palermo became the site of a nascent high-quality wine industry. A fertile plain called the Conca d'Oro ("Golden Shell") rings the city. The Conca d'Oro is about one hundred square kilometers (thirty-nine square miles) and lies between the mountains that encircle Palermo and the Tyrrhenian Sea off Sicily's north coast. Since the time of the Norman kings, the Conca d'Oro has been celebrated for its luxuriant gardens and citrus groves. It is where the wealthy noble families of Palermo built their lavish country villas and gardens in the nineteenth century. These families typically garnered an income from large agricultural holdings in various other parts of Sicily. They spent most of their time and money on the pleasures and pursuits of life in and around Palermo, returning to check on the operation of their rural farms perhaps a few times per year, or perhaps never at all.

Among the handful of serious winegrowing families here were some who sought to re-create the lighter, fresher, and cleaner wines from Europe. The hills surrounding Palermo harbored promising sites to achieve these styles. French technicians worked in the cellars of Edoardo Alliata's Casteldaccia winery southeast of Palermo and in those of Henri d'Orleans at Zucco just north of where the Real Cantina Borbonica had been in operation. The wines of Alliata and d'Orleans were highly praised and exported widely. Other producers invested in new French winemaking equipment and achieved similar results. They had more success with white wine production than red. During the nineteenth century much of this wine was consumed in Palermo and its environs. Yet again, this period of enological growth almost evaporated later, at the beginning of the twentieth century.

During the twentieth century, land costs and Palermo urban sprawl pushed quality wine production well outside the city and its suburbs. Moving west and south of Palermo, among scattered mountains there are areas with elevations between 200 and 850 meters (656 and 2,789 feet) that are well suited for viticulture. In 1901 the Tasca family won an award with their wine Camastra, made at the Villa Camastra on the southwestern edge of the Conca d'Oro. Production of this wine was quite limited and was eventually discontinued in 1922. While the Tascas' Regaleali estate in the center of Sicily was making wine well enough by 1871 to win an award at a Sicilian wine competition, it was not until the late 1950s that Giuseppe Tasca d'Almerita and his wife Franca Cammarata began to modernize the vineyards and winery there. In the wake of the destruction caused by the Belice earthquake of 1968, in the early 1970s the Guarrasis of Rapitalà and the Spadaforas rebuilt their families' winemaking facilities. These sites were where younger generations of motivated family members embraced the challenge of quality wine production. Francesco Spadafora exemplifies this transition. Despite owning a sizable estate of ninety-five hectares (235 acres), he, in the tradition of a French vigneron, personally oversees the production of his wine from the vineyards to the cantina.

Besides the blue bloods of Palermo there were also "red bloods," entrepreneurial families that followed in the wake of the nobles, themselves becoming notable wine producers in the Palermo Highlands. An example is the Cusumano family. The youngest generation of Cusumanos, the brothers Alberto and Diego, has developed a state-of-the-art winery on the shoulders of the family bulk wine operation, Cadivin, on the southern side of the Palermo Highlands near Partinico. It sources grapes not only from growers throughout the island but also from its four hundred hectares (988 acres). Calatrasi is another powerhouse, developed by the brothers Maurizio and Giuseppe Micciche in 1980. In 1992 Maurizio built the family grape and wine business to new heights by purchasing two hundred hectares (494 acres) of land at six hundred meters (1,969 feet) in elevation near Corleone. In 1998 he entered into a joint venture with BRL Hardy. Calatrasi formed a joint venture with a Tunisian winery in 2000, purchased vineyards in Apulia, and then in 2010 formed Calatrasi Mediterranean Domains by assembling a diverse group of international strategic partners.

In other cases, family members with an agricultural background have pooled their labor, vineyards, and financial resources to create estates with a boutique profile. One example is the three brothers who joined together to create Alessandro di Camporeale in the town of Camporeale. Brothers Vincenzo, Giuseppe, and Antonio Melia collaborated to build the Ceuso estate between Alcamo and Segesta. It is rare in Sicily, though, to find a group of unrelated Sicilians who have each contributed capital to form a joint stock company. One such anomaly is the Feotto dello Jato estate near the town of San Giuseppe Jato southwest of Palermo. It has seven investors.

In Sicilian, *foreign* can mean "from mainland Italy." There have been few such people in the Palermo Highlands. Most notable is the Venetian investor Paolo Marzotto, who in 1997 purchased Baglio di Pianetto due south of Palermo. Cooperatives are also few in number compared to the many in western and southwestern Sicily. The Cantina dell'Alto Belice, with its eight thousand members and 160,000 hectares (395,369 acres), is one of the largest. The Palermo Highlands are characterized by isolation. It takes usually an hour or so to drive from one producer to the next. Besides the numerous other difficulties facing Sicilians during the first half of the twentieth century, one wonders how much the strong grip of the Mafia on this area may have stifled the development of free commerce. One winery with an unusual profile is another cooperative, Libera Terra Mediterraneo, with its brand Centopassi. It was born using land confiscated from the Mafia south of San Giuseppe Jato. It is a symbol of defiance to the Mafia.

The hills south of Palermo get more than average rainfall for Sicily, nearly all of it falling from September to May. In the interior, winds vary according to topography. Elevations of up to seven hundred meters (2,297 feet) combined with northern exposures predispose some areas, such as Ficuzza, to white wine grapes and vines with short gestation periods, such as Pinot Noir and Merlot. Other areas, such as Alcamo, Camporeale, and San Giuseppe Jato, have recently had good results with red wines, particularly Syrah. The soils are clay dominant, although the tops of slopes tend to be sandier. Some soils are calcareous, as in the Piana degli Albanesi. Others, such as those at Ficuzza, are slightly acidic, due perhaps to higher levels of precipitation.

Inzolia and Catarratto are the traditional white varieties. Catarratto in particular has long been associated with the townships of Alcamo and Camporeale. Until the mid-1980s, these townships supplied Marsala with base wines for Marsala production. They also made copious amounts of nonaromatic and low-alcohol wines, which were shipped by rail, boat, or truck either west to Marsala or east to Messina and thence to Reggio Calabria and the rest of Italy. The Vermouth industry was the destination for much of this wine. This business was particularly brisk during the 1950s and 1960s. From about 2005, Grillo has been increasingly planted for white wines. In the nineteenth century, Perricone was the most important red variety. During the twentieth century, Nero d'Avola replaced it, though Perricone remained in use as a blender to add color and texture to Nero d'Avola wine. International varieties were introduced in the Palermo Highlands at Zucco and La Contessa in the nineteenth century, but they were discontinued during the early-twentieth-century devolution of the Sicilian wine industry. During the 1980s, Hugues Bernard, the French husband of Gigi Guarrasi, introduced French varieties at Rapitalà, and estates such as Disisa set up experimental plantings of many international varieties in collaboration with the IRVV. In the 1990s, the IRVV's experimental station at Virzi near Camporeale became the experiment center and command post for viticultural and enological innovation. From there emanated the spirit that once again revitalized the Sicilian quality wine industry.

There are two DOCs in the Palermo Highlands, Alcamo and Monreale. The northeastern slice of the Marsala DOC overlaps the Alcamo DOC (but not the township of Alcamo). The Alcamo and Monreale DOCs also overlap. The western half of the Alcamo DOC is home to the dark black soils formerly considered ideal for white wines but not reds. The Melia brothers at Ceuso have disproved that assumption with their strong, powerful reds. Until 1999, Alcamo was a DOC reserved for white wine only. Simply called Alcamo white, it had to contain at least 80 percent Catarratto of the Comune or Lucido types. A modification to Alcamo DOC wine law in September 1999 dropped the varietal minimum to 40 percent and added a Classico (at least 80 percent Catarratto) designation. It also added Rosso based on at least 60 percent Nero d'Avola supplemented by other red varieties. The Rosso Riserva category required two years of maturation before market release. Varietal Alcamo DOCs were allowed, as were Spumante ("Sparkling"), Novello ("Early Release"), and Vendemmia Tardiva ("Late Harvest").

The eastern half of the Alcamo DOC is the western one-third of the Monreale DOC. Producers in this overlap can choose either appellation, provided that their wines meet the legal production requirements. Like their counterparts elsewhere in Sicily, most simply use the Sicilia IGT designation. Since about 2000, Alcamo in particular has become known as the source of some of Sicily's most successful Syrah wines. These come mostly from the area around the town of Camporeale (also in the Monreale DOC). Giuseppe Tasca of Tasca d'Almerita believes that the reason for Camporeale's success with this variety is that at harvest time there is the right amount of heat and very little chance of precipitation. The 2008 Sallier de la Tour La Monaca Syrah that I tasted at Vinitaly 2011 combined the complexity of cool-climate Syrahs with the body of warm-climate ones. Tasca d'Almerita manages the vineyards of Sallier de la Tour and harvests and transports the grapes to Regaleali for vinification.

The Monreale DOC takes its name from the town of Monreale just outside Palermo, which is famous for its cathedral containing strikingly beautiful mosaics from the Norman period. The international fame of the cathedral should provide promotional support to the DOC, though no vineyards are near it. Most of the dozen or so wine estates in the Monreale DOC are clustered around the towns of San Giuseppe Jato and Camporeale. San Giuseppe Jato is about thirty kilometers (nineteen miles) from Monreale and the Palermo city limits. Camporeale is farther away. Monreale Bianco must have a minimum of 50 percent Catarratto and Inzolia; Monreale Rosso, a minimum of 50 percent Nero d'Avola and Perricone. There are also Rosato, Vendemmia Tardiva,

Rosso Riserva, and Bianco Superiore typologies (the last requires more than 12.5 percent alcohol and more than six months of maturation before release). Monreale varietal wines, white and red, are also allowed for a wide range of varieties. Monreale does, however, uniquely include the possibility of a Perricone DOC. Just as the Monreale DOC has staked its territorial claim to the Cathedral of Monreale, it has staked a varietal claim to Perricone. The Tamburello winery has made a strong, sustained effort to associate itself and Monreale with Perricone. Its Pietragavina Perricone is identified as 100 percent Perricone and bottled as a Monreale DOC wine. Feotto della Jato makes a single-vineyard Perricone, Vigna Curria, under the Sicilia IGT denomination.

Alessandro di Camporeale. The brothers Rosolino, Antonino, and Natale Alessandro are known for their high-powered Syrah wine, named Kaid. The ones I sampled were dark, thick with ripe smells, heavy, and richly textured. In addition to the normal Kaid, there is a Vendemmia Tardiva Kaid, which adds lust to power in the form of residual sweetness. A Sauvignon Blanc has few of the vegetal tones typical of the variety. Vincenzo Bambina, the company's consulting enologist, explained the reason. "This," he says, "is a real Sicilian Sauvignon Blanc, one that expresses the intense light of Sicily." The company is integrating acacia wood staves with oak ones in the composition of its barrels.

Baglio di Pianetto. A former chairman of the board of the group that owned the Santa Margherita brand and the scion of a family that made a fortune in the textile industry, Paolo Marzotto brings business savvy to a wine project that is more than just idle play. Despite his seventy-plus years he races around as if he were a young entrepreneur in search of his first business success. His granddaughter Ginevra Notarbartolo, however, is increasingly visible. Baglio di Pianetto's high-elevation site, at 650 meters (2,133 feet), is planted to Inzolia, Viognier, Merlot, Nero d'Avola, and Petit Verdot. The wine Ficiligno blends the aroma of Viognier with the structure of Inzolia. A varietal Viognier, Ginolfo, subtly shows the grape's floral smells in the context of modest oak nuances and body. The company's most outstanding and most underrated wine is the Merlot Salici, which unites woodsy and earthy nuances with a tart, rich mouthful. For those who like red wines with thick, bristling tannins, the Carduni Petit Verdot will satisfy. Marzotto's preference is to match savory with savory. Accordingly he recommends serving the Carduni with dark chocolate or aged wild game.

Brugnano. To vinify their grapes from family and rented vineyards near the coastline at the northwestern Gulf of Castellammare, the brothers Francesco and Salvatore Brugnano have enlisted the help of Vincenzo Bambina and Nicola Centonze. The hand of these two talented consulting enologists is evident in the elegance of Brugnano's wines. My favorites are the V90 Vinovanta Catarratto, Lunario Nero d'Avola, and Naisi, a 75 percent Nero d'Avola–25 percent Tannat blend. The Nero d'Avola provides the cherry fruit; the Tannat, woodsy spices and a long astringent finish.

Ceuso. Ceuso is the epitome of a family collaboration. Antonino Melia works the fifty hectares (124 acres) of vineyards. His brother Vincenzo, who recently retired from his position as the manager and coordinator of the IRVV research winery in Marsala, is the viticultural specialist. Giuseppe, another brother, is the on-site enologist. Their brother-in-law Francesco Vallone handles the books. Vincenzo worked closely with Tachis, who became his mentor and friend, from 1995 to 2007, during Tachis's consultancy for the IRVV. One can see his impact not only in the style of the wines, which are blends of indigenous and international varieties, but also in the outfitting of the winery, which reminded me of the winery of Tachis's most famous client in Tuscany, Tenuta San Guido. Though Sicily was known for white wines, Tachis believed that its potential for red wines was even greater. Indeed, the Melia brothers have transformed an area known for Alcamo white into one that makes sculpted, powerful red wine blends. You can taste the power of the fertile black soil of Alcamo in their wines. Ceuso bottles have only proprietary labeling. After the lightweight and good-value Scurati white and red Sicilia IGT, the wines become dark, rich, and densely textured. Fastaia is a Bordeaux blend of Cabernet Sauvignon, Merlot, and Petit Verdot. The Petit Verdot adds some balsam in the nose and astringency in the mouth. The calling-card château wine, Ceuso, is 50 percent Nero d'Avola, 30 percent Cabernet Sauvignon, and 20 percent Merlot. It is richer and riper than the Fastaia. Ceuso Custera is a single-vineyard wine released with bottle age. The 1999 that I tasted in July 2010 had the red-orange rim of a mature wine and a dense nose of cinder, licorice, and celery. Ceuso red wines are usually big in the mouth. The bottle age of the 1999 Custera had made its palate more delicate.

Disisa. The Di Lorenzo family has owned this estate since 1860. Its vineyards are at four to five hundred meters (1,312 to 1,640 feet) on clay soil in the Belice and Jato River Valleys in the Monreale DOC. From 1800 to 1850 the land had a special authorization to make wine. A winery was constructed during the 1930s and vineyard surface was increased. White bulk wines made from Catarratto, Inzolia, and Grillo were produced. During the 1970s, the bulk wine market deteriorated. Disisa's owners, inspired by the international varieties that they had planted in collaboration with the IRVV, set the estate on a path of focusing on their commercial use. As of 2009, however, it began replanting its vineyards of international varieties with indigenous ones. The red wines have more-focused flavors than the whites. In particular, a 2008 Tornamira, a blend of 50 percent Syrah, 25 percent Merlot, and 25 percent Cabernet Sauvignon, had a bell pepper–scented nose and a long, fine, astringent finish. The Vuarìa Monreale DOC, a 100 percent Nero d'Avola from the same vintage, had its tart edges rounded off by barrique.

Duca di Salaparuta. The pioneering wine producer Duca di Salaparuta was sold in 1961 to Ente Siciliano per la Promozione Industriale (ESPI) and again in 2001 to ILLVA di Saronno, a northern Italian drinks company, the producer of Disaronno Originale. In 2003, ILLVA named its Sicilian group Duca di Salaparuta and placed the brands Duca di

Salaparuta, Corvo, and Florio under it. The discussion here concerns itself with the first two. For much of the modern era the Duca di Salaparuta branch has been in talented enological hands. From 1968 to 1997 they were Giacosa's. In 1998, Angelo Paternò replaced Giacosa as technical director, then served until June 2001. From the 2001 harvest to May 2008, Carlo Casavecchia took over. Stefano Salvini filled the position until leaving it in mid-2012. From the mid-1960s to the mid-1970s and from 1991 to 1997, Ezio Rivella of Enoconsult had a consulting role. Tachis was a consulting enologist from 1996 to 2006. Casavecchia played a major role in important acquisitions to ensure that the highest-quality vineyard sources would be available to Duca di Salaparuta. In 2003 the company purchased two holdings: Suor Marchesa, in the same area in the comune of Butera where Giacosa had sourced the heart of Sicily's first varietal Nero d'Avola (Duca Enrico), and Vajasindi, on the north face of Etna in the township of Passopisciaro. Later it purchased an estate, Risignolo, in Salemi. Duca di Salaparuta sources grapes for its largest brand, Corvo (in red and white), from all over the island. It generally makes its prestige wines with grapes from outside the Palermo Highlands. The historical premises at Casteldaccia, fifteen kilometers (nine miles) east of Palermo, house the managing headquarters, a maturation cellar, and a wine museum. The company has s modern vinification facility in the seaside village of Aspra, just outside Bagheria.

Fatascià. The owners of Fatascià are Stefania Lena and her husband, Giuseppe Natoli. Their lives were shattered when the indictment of Lena's father forced them to leave Abbazia Santa Anastasia. She had been the enologist at that estate near Cefalù, where she had worked with Tachis and the Umbrian consulting enologist Riccardo Cotarella. At the time of the indictment, her father's plan had been to unite Abbazia Santa Anastasia and Fatascià, which he owned then. After leaving Abbazia, Lena focused her attention on Fatascià, as did her husband and older brother, responsible for sales and marketing. The estate owns thirty hectares (seventy-four acres) in the townships of San Giuseppe Jato, San Cipirello, and Contessa Entellina. At the 2012 Vinitaly, the banana nose of the 2011 Grillo varietal wine indicated its youth. In the mouth it was round and salty. Lena had us guessing about the varietal mix of the 2011 Enigma. She gave us a hint: 90 percent of it was Grillo. The wine was too aromatic and bitter for a 100 percent Grillo. Fran got it right when she selected Zibibbo as the other 10 percent. Lena's 2007 Rosso del Presidente, a Cabernet Franc–Nero d'Avola blend, was more refreshing and had finer astringency than the 2010 Aliré, a blend of Syrah and Nero d'Avola. While Fran and I were tasting these wines, several people in the Sicilian wine industry came to Lena's booth to enter into friendly conversation with her. They offered support and encouragement for her efforts.

Porta del Vento. Porta del Vento is the brand of a winery named for its proprietor, Marco Sferlazzo. He makes the wines with his own hands on his ten hectare (twenty-five acre) estate at six hundred meters (1,969 feet) in the contrada of Valdibella at Camporeale.

The soil is rocky with a sandy subsoil. Sferlazzo focuses on the two most distinctive varieties native to the area, Catarratto, exclusively its Lucido and Extralucido biotypes, and Perricone. He also has Nero d'Avola. At Vinitaly 2012, I sampled a vertical tasting of his Catarratto wines. The 2010 was pale amber and had a nose of green tea. The 2009 showed the difficulty of this rainy vintage and the vulnerability of low-sulfite winemaking. It was darker amber with some oxidized apple smells. The 2008, however, came back on the path taken by the 2010. It smelled of quince and nuts and was very sour. The 2007 was paler but nuttier than its older brother. I tasted a 2010 Maquè rosato made with Perricone. It smelled of ripe plums and was very tart and unusually bitter and astringent. A 2010 Maquè Perricone had flesh to balance its astringency. It was one of the best Perricones that I have ever tasted. It is a no-sulfite-added wine fermented on its skins for thirty days. Sferlazzo's 2010 Ishac, a Nero d'Avola, was a deep purple and expressed perfectly ripe fruit. The finish buzzed with acidity and fine astringency.

Rapitalà.   Tenute Rapitalà is a wine estate in the comune of Camporeale with 160 hectares (395 acres) of vineyards at a site whose elevations range from three to six hundred meters (984 to 1,969 feet). Clay is at the bottom and sand is at the top. The harvest lasts twenty days from bottom to top. *Rapitalà* is a translation of *Rabidh-Allah,* which means "River of Allah." The Guarrasis, an old Alcamo family that resided in Palermo, made and sold bulk wine from the grapes on this estate, mostly the locally dominant Catarratto variety, before the 1968 Belice earthquake destroyed the farm buildings. Also in that year, Gigi Guarrasi married Hugues Bernard, a naval officer at the time but also the son of a winemaker. Bernard spearheaded the rebuilding of the winery with the aim of making a French-style Sicilian wine. In the mid-1980s he planted Chardonnay and Sauvignon Blanc and purchased French barriques. Later in that decade he planted Pinot Noir and Syrah. In 1998 he formed a partnership with Italy's largest winery group, Gruppo Italiano Vini (GIV). GIV has the major share. Bernard died in 2006. Today Laurent Bernard, his son, is the company's president and brand manager. He is a self-proclaimed "engineer-psychologist" with an understanding of every detail of the property and how to manage its forty-odd employees. At his right hand is the winemaker Silvio Centonze, who has worked at Rapitalà since 1990. The predilection of the site for white grapes and the skill of Centonze show brilliantly in Rapitalà white wines: the Fleur Grillo, from recently planted Grillo vines; Piano Maltese, 45 percent Grillo, 45 percent Catarratto, 10 percent balance of Chardonnay and Sauvignon Blanc; and Casalj, 70 percent high-elevation (up to six hundred meters [1,969 feet]) Catarratto blended with 30 percent Chardonnay. In April 2012, I had a vertical tasting of Chardonnays branded Grand Cru, from the 2007, 2006, and 2005 vintages. The 2007 harvest was small due to a downy mildew infection, but the remaining crop was ripe and concentrated. The wine was tight, powerful, and had many years left in it. The 2006, from a year too warm for lively white wine, showed just that. It was rich but lacked length in the mouth. The 2005 was the deepest gold and had the mushroom nose of mature Champagne. Though the 2007 had more promise, the 2005 was ready to drink and delicious. The 2010, which I did not taste, was the twentieth vintage of Chardonnay for the estate. Rapitalà's red wines, though fine for Sicily, could be better. Of them, I prefer the honest and direct midslope Campo Reale Nero d'Avola; a more refined Nero d'Avola from higher up the slope, Alto Nero d'Avola; an even higher-elevation Nero d'Avola, Solinero, which gains body from a dose of lower-elevation Nero d'Avola; and a medium-to-high-elevation Syrah named Nadir. When I visited Rapitalà, I saw Laurent Bernard gazing over the slope of the vineyards, his eyes gleaming. I imagined that he could hear distinct flavors oozing from the elevations as if they were the notes of a musical scale.

Spadafora. Owner Francesco Spadafora fondly remembers his visits as a boy to his family farm in Virzi, a neighborhood of the town of Camporeale. His father, Pietro, a friend of Diego Planeta, offered to let the IRVV use his winery for its experimental vinifications. The IRVV was there from 1990 to 2000. Spadafora recalls his excitement at being in the crucible of the transformation of the Sicilian wine industry. "Here wine changed," he declared. The experience added intellectual structure to his attachment to the place and fondness for agricultural life. By the late 1980s Spadafora found himself devoting his time to the vineyards at Virzi. He started the wine estate in 1988 when his father gave him the land. He has ninety-five hectares (235 acres) of vineyards at 250 meters (820 feet) with sand-dominant soil. Though he helped to establish the Monreale DOC with Mirella Tamburello, he bottles all his wines under the Sicilia IGT. Spadafora brings the passion and energy of a small winegrower to his banner wine, the 100 percent Syrah Sicilia IGT Sole dei Padri. His other notable wines are Schietto Grillo and Schietto Cabernet Sauvignon, both Sicilia IGT. The Don Pietro red and white Sicilia IGT blends are consistently satisfying.

Other recommended producers and their wines:

Cossentino *Lioy* Rosso
Guccione *Gibril* Nerello Mascalese
Guccione *Perpetuo di Cerasa*
Guccione *Rosso di Cerasa*

TERRE SICANE

The viticultural area between the Belice and Platani Rivers is focused on the Belice, which has its source in the mountains of San Giuseppe Jato south of Palermo and moves south-southwest to empty into the Mediterranean just west of the town of Menfi. The official wine road, Terre Sicane (in full, Strada del Vino Terre Sicane), covers nearly all of the Belice-Platani area. Beyond this to the southeast, the Duca di Salaparuta winery sources Inzolia from the townships Ribera and Cattolica Eraclea for its Colomba Platino wine.

Though historians celebrated this area as producing some of the finest wines in the classical age, in subsequent periods grapes became a secondary crop and wine production a tertiary industry until the post–World War II period, when Marsala merchants scavenging for cheaper and cheaper raw material invaded. With the market for wheat and meat from livestock diminishing due to international competition, grapes looked promising. Just as the bulk wine market began falling away in the late 1970s, the Settesoli cooperative grew to fill the void. Another needed boost was Donnafugata, which, after its creation in 1983, renovated the family vineyards and built its principal winery at Contessa Entellina. The arrival of a family with such enormous marketing talent has helped move the image of the entire area in a positive direction. Then came the meteoric ascent of the Planeta winery during the 1990s. This set the stage for the creation of smaller, family-run estates during the 1990s. To get better grapes, winegrowers cut yields by as much as 75 percent. Wineries were fitted with stainless steel tanks equipped for temperature control. Settesoli and Planeta were quick to implement the results of successful IRVV experiments. Both companies had the enological guidance of Carlo Corino, fresh from his work in Australia. Tachis had been with Donnafugata since the early 1990s, right after his consultancy for the IRVV began. According to Alessio Planeta, "Menfi is the laboratory where the new wines of Sicily began." Terre Sicane is the New World of the Sicilian wine industry.

During the post–World War II bulk wine market boom, the Terre Sicane area was fertile ground for the cooperative movement. In 1958 the largest and most dynamic cooperative, Settesoli, was created. Today it has 1,841 farmer-members with six thousand hectares (14,826 acres) of vineyards. Two other large cooperatives are Cellaro in Sambuca, founded in 1969, and Corbera in Santa Margherita Belice, founded in 1971.

There has been a modest development of family-owned wineries in Terre Sicane. For the most part these families supplied grapes to Marsala merchants and local cooperatives following World War II. With Planeta, which was a member of Settesoli before and after its first release, as their local success story and emboldened by the 1995 to 2001 Sicilian wine boom and the added stimulus of EU financial assistance, about a dozen families decided to make, bottle, and sell their own wine. Pietro Barbera was one of the founding farmers of Settesoli. He made his own wine in 1995 and 1996, but his winery, Cantine Barbera, got off the ground with the construction of a state-of-the art winery in 2000. The Di Prima family in Sambuca had similarly grown and sold grapes before it started bottling in 1999. Agareno was founded as a collaboration of eight farmer families. Feudo Arancio's owners come from farther afield. In 2002, Gruppo Mezzacorona, the well-respected cooperative from Trentino–Alto Adige, built the winery for its Sicilian brand, Feudo Arancio. Today it is the largest private landholder of vineyards in Sicily, with six hundred hectares (1,483 acres) shared between Sambuca in the province of Agrigento and Acate in the province of Ragusa. Young Italians, mostly Sicilians, run the pristinely clean winery that looks down on Lake Arancio and the town of Sambuca. In the mid-1990s the Miceli company, created during the 1970s by the Palermo wine entrepreneur Ignazio Miceli to promote and distribute the wines of leading Sicilian estates, planted thirty-five hectares (eighty-six acres) of Viognier, Chardonnay, Syrah, Cabernet Sauvignon, Cabernet Franc, and Tannat in the vicinity of Selinunte along the coastline to the west of Menfi on the advice of Attilio Scienza. After the death of Ignazio, his cousin Pippo Lo Re and a partner, Gianni Tartaglia, took over the estate. It is now sixty hectares (148 acres) and produces more than one million bottles annually from its own and purchased grapes. The winery uses both international and native varieties. Miceli also rents a cooperative winery space between Menfi and Sciacca and has an outpost on Pantelleria.

The climate in Terre Sicane is hot and arid, though there are some cooling breezes that affect coastline areas. Wine producers elsewhere in Sicily refer to the harvest period of Menfi as being the earliest on the island. Because harvests come in at warm temperatures, wine acidities tend to be lower than at most other locations in Sicily. Donnafugata and Feudo Arancio have both introduced night harvesting to reduce the temperature of harvested grapes and offset this problem. The winds, particularly the scirocco, can be strong enough to break young shoots. Dry, hot, and windy conditions lower disease pressure, making organic and biodynamic viticulture more viable. *Sustainable viticulture* is a phrase in vogue in the Menfi area. Unfortunately water is scarce. One sees no alberello training here, proof that its viticulture boom happened after World War II.

The soils are on marine terraces of sedimentary origin. Underneath the topsoils are marl deposits. Soil color varies from dark to reddish to yellowish brown. While at lower elevations the soils are mixes of clays, silts, and sands, higher elevations also have sandstone and some rocky areas. There are fluvial patches of rounded stones near the Belice River. The soil is generally calcareous. Though they show great potential to make quality wine, intensive farming over a long period has left some soils so depleted that it will be difficult to restore them. Settesoli has vineyards on the coastline that go as high as 350 meters (1,148 feet). There is a high range of hills dividing Menfi from Sambuca. Di Prima has a vineyard there, Pepita, at five hundred meters (1,640 feet). Donnafugata's Contessa Entellina vineyards, farther inland between Sambuca and Corleone, range in altitude from 250 to 550 meters (820 to 1,804 feet).

Before the 1980s, 90 percent of the vines planted were white varieties, mostly Catarratto, Trebbiano, and Inzolia. Since the 1980s, producers have ripped out much of the Trebbiano because the bulk market, for which it was planted, has been deteriorating. As a foreign grape that makes low-aroma, lightweight wines, it has no future in Sicilian quality white wines. Nero d'Avola has dominated the red varieties, but its performance here has not identified it as a superstar. It makes basic wine, on the vegetal side. Since the 1970s, Settesoli has been a major force in determining the varieties selected for new plantings. The cooperative's policy has been to tell its farmer-members what varieties to plant based on its analysis of market demand. During the 1980s and 1990s, Settesoli told its growers to plant the international varieties Chardonnay, Cabernet Sauvignon, Merlot, and Syrah and paid them more to do so. Despite the success of Planeta's Chardonnay, the climate is too hot and dry for this variety. Viognier came later, is better suited to the Menfi area, and has been quite successful, particularly for Settesoli, which pioneered the development of the variety. Planeta has championed Grecanico. While Planeta's Cometa Fiano has received critical acclaim, it is a small production. However, Settesoli grows 70 percent of the Fiano in Sicily. While Fiano was brought from Campania for the IRVV-IASMA (Istituto Agrario di San Michele all'Adige) studies conducted at Settesoli in the late 1980s, Grecanico has long been present on the island, but its tendency to produce low-alcohol wines made it unpopular. Syrah has been promoted as the subzone's ideal red variety, but results so far have not yet proved this contention. The Cabernet Sauvignon and Merlot from this region are certainly good, but its climate is too warm to make a Bordeaux-style Cab or Merlot.

DOCs here first proliferated in the mid- to late 1990s: Contessa Entellina, Sambuca, Santa Margherita di Belice, Menfi, and Sciacca. Most of the wineries use the Sicilia IGT denomination, and the DOC typologies are so liberally drawn that they lack distinction.

Cantine Barbera. Marilena Barbera, aided by her mother, directs the family winery, which has fifteen hectares (thirty-seven acres) at Belicello near the seashore at the mouth of the Belice River. They have seven hectares (seventeen acres) of international varieties and eight hectares (twenty acres) of native ones. Some of their vineyards are forty years old. At the winery, I compared two 2009 Inzolias, one from fifteen-year-old vines growing on clay soil and another from forty-year-old vines growing on calcareous soil. The first was bottled as a Sicilia IGT, the second as a Menfi DOC Inzolia Dietro le Case. While the IGT had a limited range of smells, mostly fermentative in character, the DOC had green vegetal smells, was thicker in texture, and had more body. Old vines on the right soil make the best wines. At the La Vota vineyard, in deep, sandy soil in a loop of the Belice River, Cantine Barbera has planted Cabernet Sauvignon. The wine La Vota, a Menfi DOC, had a capsicum nose, a characteristic that I like if it is not extreme (this was not) and if it is balanced by a thick, juicy mouth (which it was). Alba Marina is a Catarratto passito. The Catarratto bunches were twisted when ripe, cutting them off physiologically, but not physically, from the plant. The grapes dried while still attached to the vine, which supplied enzymes to the skins that unlocked a wide array of smells. A touch of oak balanced the aromas of citrus, apricot, and ripe banana. The high acidity of Catarratto helped reduce the heavy sensation of the residual sweetness. The result was a rich but delicate dessert wine.

Di Prima. Davide Di Prima of the Di Prima winery follows in the footsteps of his great-grandfather, who started growing grapes here a hundred years ago. His great-grandfather, however, never would have seen Lake Arancio spreading out below the winery. In his time it was a river. It was dammed during the 1950s to store irrigation water. Davide's father, Gaspare, was the president of the nearby Cellaro cooperative winery. Di Prima started bottling a percentage of his family's grapes in 1999. The family still sells some of its production to cooperatives. There are thirty-seven hectares (ninety-one acres) across three sites: one at 325 meters (1,066 feet), below the winery, looking down on Lake Arancio; another at 425 meters (1,394 feet); and a third, Pepita Roccarossa, a former IRVV experimental site, at more than five hundred meters (1,640 feet). Di Prima's 1999 Syrah attracted critical attention and became its calling card. A 2006 Villamaura Syrah that I tasted in 2010 was dark, minty, camphory, balsamic, rich, and densely textured. It was an extreme wine, very powerful or too powerful, depending on your taste. The Pepita Rosso (there is also a Bianco), a 50–50 Syrah–Nero d'Avola blend, was redder, less thick in the mouth, and just as astringent, but with more acidity. The Gibilmoro Chardonnay that I tasted was too oaky. Di Prima told me he was reducing the oak contact. Pepita Bianco is a 50–50 Inzolia-Chardonnay blend.

Donnafugata.   Donnafugata, officially Tenuta di Donnafugata, makes stylish wines with names and labels that project fanciful images of Sicilian culture. The wines are always impeccably made. If criticism could be directed at them, it might be that they are not distinctly place driven. They lack the quirky noses and asymmetric palates of artisanal wines. Giacomo Rallo and wife, Gabriella, have been gradually transferring the management of the estate to their son, Antonio, now in charge of wine production, and their daughter, Josè, in charge of marketing and communications. Tachis, the estate's consulting enologist from 1992 to 2000, had a strong hand in the design of its two most famous dry wines, Tancredi, a Nero d'Avola strongly accented with 30 percent Cabernet Sauvignon, and Mille e Una Notte, a Nero d'Avola with "a small percentage of other varieties," bottled as a Contessa Entellina DOC. Tancredi, created in 1990, has the Tachis taste, but Mille e Una Notte, created in 1995, has more of a Carlo Ferrini one. Ferrini was Donnafugata's head consulting enologist from 2003 to 2009. In flavor, Tancredi makes a clear nod to Bordeaux, while Mille e Una Notte whispers a mysterious blend of things enmeshed in strong but seamless oak. That is more Ferrini. As of about 2010, Mille e Una Notte has been getting less maturation in oak and more in bottle. Though Ferrini belittles his prowess in white wine vinification, Josè Rallo credits him with excelling in making Donnafugata's white wines—six labels, each with a personality of its own.

Feudo Arancio.   Mezzacorona from the Trentino area of Italy bought this farm of 280 hectares (692 acres) in 2001 to provide warm-climate varietal wines to the United States and other export markets. The company name is Feudo Arancio–Nosio. The winery is loaded with refrigeration technology, which must come in handy, since Sambuca can be a very hot place during the summer. The staff at the time of our visit in 2008 was very young, on average under thirty years of age. The two wines that left a memory were Hedonis (70 percent Nero d'Avola, 30 percent Syrah), dark and impenetrable in appearance, with pigment in its legs and a thick, oaky palate, and Hekate, made from Muscat of Alexandria grapes dried on the vine for four to six weeks before fermentation, a sweet, syrupy, but fresh wine exuding floral and citrus smells.

Planeta.   The Planeta winery began at the site of the family's fortified baglio at Ulmo, a neighborhood of Sambuca. For many years the family had gathered here to help with the wheat harvest. It became more active during the 1970s and 1980s, as a farm that supplied Settesoli with grapes from ninety hectares (222 acres), mostly of Catarratto, Trebbiano, Grecanico, and a small amount of Sangiovese. In 1985 fifty hectares (124 acres) of experimental vineyards were installed. Among the twenty varieties planted were Nero d'Avola, Grecanico, and numerous international varieties. Merlot, Nero d'Avola, and Grecanico excelled there. Planeta the wine estate was born in 1995. Its first wine, the 1994 Planeta Chardonnay, was an instant success. In 2000 Planeta built a winery at Dispensa, in the township of Menfi. Here it focuses on red wine made with French varieties. Planeta is developing a Merlot, designated by the contrada of origin, Ulmo. It is also developing a Syrah, designated by the contrada, Maroccoli, a site at four hundred meters (1,312 feet) in Sambuca. It has augmented its Fiano from Ulmo with Fiano from Gurra, a Planeta vineyard near the shoreline at Menfi. At Gurra the chalky soils and extra heat increase the floral smells and reduce the bitter tastes of Cometa, Planeta's barrel-fermented Fiano. The La Segreta red and white wines are fine for the everyday dinner table. Tight and tart, Alastro is a Grecanico varietal wine made from the grapes of a twenty-five-year old vineyard at Ulmo. Alessio Planeta plays the pivotal role of directing the estate, though his uncle Diego still has the final word. Alessio makes most of the enological decisions. His cousin Francesca, Diego's daughter, focuses on public relations, and Santi, Alessio's brother, on sales in the Italian market.

Settesoli.   This cooperative began selling wine in the mid-1960s. Its first wines were white blends of Inzolia, Catarratto, and Grecanico. Diego Planeta became its president in 1973, at a time when the industry was in grave crisis. Cooperatives were turning toward making wine to be distilled and sold to the European Union. Planeta realized that this was a dead end. He had to point Settesoli in the direction of a positive outcome. In 1986, Scienza organized a collaboration between the IRVV and the IASMA, the foremost research institute in Italy. Planeta volunteered the vineyards of Settesoli farmer-partners to be the sites of experimental vineyards. He put two technicians at the project's disposal. Soon there were about forty experimental vineyards at various Settesoli sites in and about Menfi, planted with about fifty different native and nonnative varieties. At the same time, Planeta involved the Settesoli vineyards in a program that coordinated the IRVV research with a zonation study carried out by the Servizio Geologico dell'Assessorato all'Agricoltura ("Geological Service of the Sicilian Department of Agriculture"). These studies pushed the cooperative to the forefront of Sicily's quality wine revolution.

Settesoli compared the studies it was involved in with marketing ones. It paid growers more to plant particular varieties in particular soils using particular rootstocks. In this way, the whole company was directed toward the world market. The most promising international varieties, according to Scienza, were Fiano, Chenin Blanc, Chardonnay, Cabernet Sauvignon, Merlot, and Syrah. Thanks to the IRVV's vinification studies and wine blend analyses at Virzi in the Palermo area, Settesoli knew early on which of these varieties made good wines on their own and how they functioned in blends. Seventy percent of the vineyard sources for Settesoli are concentrated within twenty kilometers (twelve miles) of the town of Menfi. The cooperative awards its growers for low yields, the sanitary condition of the grapes, and attaining targeted sugar and pH levels. All the wines bear the name of the contrada where the grapes were grown. Fifty percent of the production is red wine. Fifty percent is white. Only four wines come in contact with oak during processing. All Settesoli branded wines have varietal designations except Seligo, which is a blend of Grecanico and Viognier. Settesoli Nero d'Avola is the most sold Nero d'Avola in Italy. The company uses the Sicilia IGT almost across the board. Menfi DOC is used for "meditation" wines (*vini di meditazione*), which are likely to be dessert wines. MandraRossa is the quality brand exported to major foreign markets. My pick of the MandraRossa line is the Chardonnay, which is round and satisfying. Settesoli has developed a strong market for its wines in the United Kingdom. It collaborates with its importer there to present another quality brand, Inycon. In 2012, Vito Varvaro succeeded Planeta as the cooperative's president.

SICILY-CENTER

South of the Madonie Mountains, bounded by the Platani River on the west and the Salso River on the east, and north of the mountainous area surrounding the city of Caltanissetta is Sicily-Center, the heart of the island, where the three provinces of Palermo, Agrigento, and Caltanissetta converge. Mountains protect this area of high hills and low valleys on all sides. Here the earth and the sky take on larger dimensions than normal. Valleys separate steep slopes covered with wheat. Vineyards are rare. Roads damaged by landslides languish without repair. They wind endlessly, seeming without direction.

The few producers who make wine here are separated by both significant distances and valleys and mountains. The high elevations, the surrounding high hills and mountains, and the great distance from the sea give this area Sicily's only true continental climate. Storms riding the prevailing winds from the north-northwest during the summer months cannot carry their humidity beyond the Madonie Mountains. However, the scirocco can bring convection-oven summer heat from the south. When this happens, the dark soils absorb the heat, making the surface an inferno. During the night the temperature plunges. Elevation and exposure can moderate overall temperatures. Vineyards usually lie between four and nine hundred meters (1,312 and 2,953 feet). Harvests begin here in mid-August, a month later than for the same varieties planted on the southern coast, and finish at the end of October. Higher elevations and more northerly exposures mean colder all-around temperatures. This makes Sicily-Center a marginal area for viticulture. Perhaps this is why historically there have been so few vineyards there. Extreme day-to-night temperature variation makes the area extremely interesting for white wines.

At lower elevations the soils are predominantly clayey with varying amounts of iron, providing a reddish tint, and varying amounts of calcium carbonates, making pastel reds, browns, and grays. Bands of reddish calcareous clay loaded with marine fossils point back to a time when this area was under water. This is ideal soil for Nero d'Avola and other red varieties that like calcium carbonate. The clay holds enormous amounts of water. If the cracked crust of dried clay is broken up regularly, the old vines with deep roots have no water problems. An artificial lake harboring irrigation water or a lucky find of an underground water source is necessary where soils drain more freely and vines are young. At higher elevations, sandstone and sandy soils dominate. These soils are better for white varieties than for red.

There are three outstanding producers here: Castellucci Miano, Montoni, and Tasca d'Almerita. The DOC Contea di Sclafani that these producers have created for themselves is like virtually all other Sicilian DOCS, a little bit of this and a little bit of that. Though the DOC is large, these three wineries are within about ten kilometers (six miles) of one another in the vicinity of the towns of Valledolmo and Vallelunga.

Contea di Sclafani Bianco must be at least 50 percent Grecanico, Catarratto, and Inzolia, with other allowed white varieties rounding out the blend. Rosso must be at least 50 percent Nero d'Avola and Perricone, plus other allowed red varieties. There are also a rosato and a varietal wine designated DOC. These generic regulations do little to define an area with such a singular identity. Catarratto Comune excels here. It feigns Riesling at nine hundred meters (2,953 feet) and higher. Inzolia provides body in blends with Catarratto. Nero d'Avola is lighter in color, more tart, less meaty, with fine astringency. Perricone provides color and texture. Nerello Mascalese makes a pale wine. It is the base of the Contea di Sclafani Rosato, a wine that finds favor in Valledolmo, a town with its back to the Madonie. There is Ciliegiolo too, a variety common along the southern Tuscan coastline. Tasca d'Almerita has achieved great results with Chardonnay and Cabernet Sauvignon.

Castellucci Miano. This producer was a cooperative until 2005. Now under the management of Piero Buffa and the enological supervision of Tonino Guzzo, this estate at Valledolmo has taken off. Vineyards as high as one thousand meters (3,281 feet), old vines, and alberello training provide the foundation for some special wines. That specialness is achieved with the Catarratto variety. At one thousand meters, the harvest sometimes occurs in early November, in the rain or the snow. Shiarà is the Catarratto wine from these unique vineyards, most between 800 and 950 meters (2,625 and 3,117 feet) high. The oldest vintage I tasted, 2005, had developed Riesling-like petrol aromas. A more recent vintage, the 2009, had the pungent, flinty smell of Sauvignon Blanc. Shiarà is the most exciting Catarratto wine produced in Sicily. For its red wines, the estate focuses on Perricone. Guzzo dries the grapes before vinification. He makes an Amarone-style wine, Maravita, concentrated and astringent, and a lighter wine, named Perric.One, using the ripasso method (fermenting with the addition of skins already used for the Maravita). The dried fruit in the aroma of these two wines will appeal to those who appreciate Amarone.

Montoni. Fabio Sireci commutes from Palermo several days per week to manage his estate, Feudo Montoni. The vineyards are on the east-facing slope of a valley that runs north to south, creating a channel for winds. The elevation of his twenty-five hectares (sixty-two acres) of vineyards ranges from 450 to 750 meters (1,476 to 2,461 feet). A comparison between Feudo Montoni Catarratto and Grillo varietal wines clearly shows the more angular nature of the Catarratto. Sireci also makes a Sauvignon Blanc varietal wine. The star here, though, is Nero d'Avola. It features in two wines, the estate Nero d'Avola and a single-vineyard wine, Vrucara. Both are pale reddish and, though without the big fruit common to Sicilian Nero d'Avolas, have a persistent fine astringency that many others lack.

Tasca d'Almerita. The patriarch Lucio Tasca keeps a watchful eye over the estate Conte Tasca d'Almerita, which his sons, Alberto and Giuseppe, now direct and manage. Besides the four hundred hectares (988 acres) of vineyards at Regaleali, northeast of Montoni at Vallelunga in Sicily-Center, the company owns vineyards on Salina and Etna. It also buys grapes from the island of Mozia off Sicily's western coast and rents vineyards at Camporeale, where it produces wines under the Sallier de la Tour label. The company believes in estate-bottled wines. It has plans to build wineries on both Salina and Etna. Tasca d'Almerita offers a remarkably consistent range of wines with respect to quality standards. One of the advantages that Regaleali has over most competitors is vine age as high as forty years. For the most part, vines in Sicily are less than fifteen years old. The vineyards here lie between 400 and 750 meters (1,312 and 2,461 feet) above sea level on diverse soils. The red wines from this estate, particularly the ones in which French varieties play a major or supporting role, are well constructed and stylish. Tasca d'Almerita every year uses two thousand barriques made by nine different cooperage companies. Every year, the company buys six hundred new barriques, then uses them for three years. In search of a seamless whole, the consultant Ferrini crafts the flavor as wines from the different barrels are blended and the brands are constructed. My preferred wines are the Cygnus, a Nero d'Avola–Cabernet Sauvignon blend; Camastra, a Nero d'Avola–Merlot blend; and the famous Cabernet Sauvignon, the best one produced in Sicily.

Rolling hills dominate the area between the Platani and Salso Rivers. Although this was a famous area for wine in the time of the ancient Greeks, throughout much of history it was known for wheat production. During the early nineteenth century the mining of sulfur became the most important industry here, with wine production a distant second. The province of Caltanissetta responded to the vini da taglio wine boom of the 1870s by doubling the vineyard acreage it had in the 1850s. The province of Agrigento had its vineyard boom when it almost tripled acreage from 1949 to 1984. This corresponded to the post–World War II need for Marsala base wine and following growth of coopera-tives. The fact that a high percentage of the vines, particularly in Caltanissetta, were trained in tendone indicates that much of the grape production there has been directed toward growing table grapes. There is a lot of table grape production along the coast too. During the 1950s and 1960s, wine merchants roamed the countryside, looking for inexpensive sources of bulk wine. After the 1960s, cooperatives formed, freeing small farmers from the tyranny of the merchants. Most grapes grown in the area are still consigned to cooperative wineries. Morgante understood in the early 1990s that it had to make the transition from supplying grapes to making and bottling quality wine. Its wines have realized the potential of the area, at least for red wine production. A handful of other estates have made the change from bulk to bottle.

Red grapes cover the high hilly areas between and north of the cities of Agrigento and Caltanissetta. Nero d'Avola has been the area's dominant red variety. Sangiovese was planted during the 1970s because of its high yields. During that decade, this area produced mostly rosatos. Inzolia was and is the most important white variety in the hills. During the 1960s and 1970s, there was a well known but very basic white wine, Akragas, made in the vicinity of Agrigento. *Akragas* was the city's ancient Greek name. This wine, which was sold both for direct local consumption and for use as vino da taglio, was made with Inzolia, Catarratto, and Pizzutella, a minor variety. Closer to the coastline, the grapes are mostly white. Catarratto is the traditional grape. Locals believe that the Greeks brought it here. Much of the wine made from Catarratto has been sold for vermouth production. The area's other important white grape is Inzolia. During the 1970s, Trebbiano was heavily planted, mostly in tendone. The wines it made were light and vapid, good for gulping or distillation. The red grape along the coast is also Nero d'Avola.

Though most of the vineyards in the Agrigento-Caltanissetta Highlands range from four to six hundred meters (1,312 to 1,969 feet) high, there are vineyards along the coastline too, some at sea level. The vineyards are scattered throughout the countryside, indicating the fractionalized nature of landholdings. The zone is very arid and hot during the summer. The areas high up in the hills benefit from greater daily temperature excursion. Right along the coast, during the day there is a cooling onshore breeze. But the scirocco can be ferocious here. In May and October it frequently comes for four-day periods, bringing 70 to 80 percent humidity, which it gathers over the Mediterranean Sea, and sand, which it picks up in the Sahara Desert. Up in the hills the soils vary from reddish clayey, usually selected for red grapevines, to white calcareous, usually chosen for white grapes. Some areas are very rocky. Heading toward the coastline, the soil is increasingly clay dominant. There are calcareous clays here too. In general, the calcium carbonate content of the soil in the Agrigento-Caltanissetta Highlands increases from west to east.

The exceptional estate of these highlands is Morgante Vini in the town of Grotte, about twenty kilometers (twelve miles) to the northeast of Agrigento. When Fran and I made our visit, we thought we had taken the wrong road because parts of it were unpaved and looked bombed out. The only other machines on the road were heavy construction vehicles. When we arrived at our destination, Carmelo Morgante, a son of the patriarch Antonio Morgante, explained that although there was a better access road, the one we had used was the more direct one. "What is normal here is not normal elsewhere. This part of Sicily works in ways that even I don't understand." He jokingly referred to the nearby city of Favara as "the Republic of Favara." Carmelo showed us Morgante's vineyards, taking us to some of the many small parcels that make up its sixty hectares (148 acres). We were at roughly four hundred meters (1,312 feet). The soil was mostly clayey, with some whiter areas where more calcium carbonate was present. The major inflection point for the estate, Carmelo explained, was the late 1980s and early 1990s, when local growers suddenly realized the bulk wine market was dying. It was time to change or become obsolete. Antonio understood that the change was coming but believed that his sons, Carmelo and Giovanni, were better equipped to adjust to it. He put them in charge of the winery, and in 1989 the two brothers made their first vinifications. Visiting Vinitaly and tasting the wines there, they realized how little they really knew about making wine. They began to search for someone who could help them. Carmelo met Cotarella and was convinced that he was the answer. Cotarella at the time was reluctant to pick up a Sicilian client, but Carmelo pursued him. After a year of supplications, Cotarella consented, on the condition that the brothers meticulously follow his instructions from the vineyards to the bottling line. They have done just that. The first vintage bottled under his direction was the 1998. Carmelo oversees the winery and the business. Giovanni takes care of the vineyards. Morgante makes three wines, Scinthilì, a light red Nero d'Avola with only two days of maturation on the skins, normal Nero d'Avola, strong but a bit coarse and rustic, and Don Antonio. Don Antonio, with its dark, opaque appearance, toasted-oak nose, and thick but fine-textured mouth, is simply the most exotic and delicious bottle of wine with *Nero d'Avola* on the label.

Twenty kilometers (twelve miles) to the west is the town of Canicattì. Accenting the last syllable makes it sound like the refrain in a Sicilian folksong. One cooperative there, 480 farmers and one thousand hectares (2,471 acres) strong, stands out: Cantina Sociale Viticultori Associati (CVA). In the past ten years it has made great strides in improving the quality of its wines. Many attribute this to the work of its consulting enologist, Tonino

Guzzo. Not too far to the northeast, on a direct line between the cities of Agrigento and Caltanissetta, is Masseria del Feudo Grottarossa. This estate, owned by the brother and sister Francesco and Carolina Cucurullo, has one of the oldest Chardonnay vineyards in Sicily. Planted in 1985, it was an experimental plot associated with IRVV research. Masseria's first commercial wine was the 2002 Haermosa, a Chardonnay. It is barrel fermented. Recent vintages are strongly lees accented.

South of Agrigento along the Mediterranean shoreline is the D'Alessandro winery. It is just a few kilometers from the Valley of the Temples, a UNESCO World Heritage Site with the well-preserved ruins of several Greek temples. D'Alessandro's vineyards rise from sea level to five hundred meters (1,640 feet). Its Inzolia vines are trained in tendone, which protects the grape skins from the hot sun (the bunches are below the canopy) and helps lower wine alcohol by reducing fruit sugars. I tasted the 2011 Inzolia in April 2012. It had a pleasant but strong banana and fresh straw nose. With some months of bottle age, the wine should lose the banana, a fermentation smell. The mouth was low in acidity and sapid. The wine tasted of the mineral salts in the soil and the salty sea air. Grillo has been planted here for the past five years. D'Alessandro's 2010 Grillo had citrus and untoasted almond in the nose and was richer and heavier in the mouth than the Inzolia. A 2010 Catarratto was the darkest of the three white wines, due in part to its one year more of bottle age. It was also the most aromatic, with strong pear and straw smells. In the mouth, the wine's sourness gave it length and edge. A 2010 Nero d'Avola and a 2009 Syrah were both vegetal in the nose, a sign of underripe skins. It may be too warm here to ripen these varieties properly. A 2009 Syrah–Nero d'Avola blend did not show this underripeness, perhaps because the barrique that it matured in rounded out those smells. D'Alessandro's best wines are the whites. It is a young estate, born in 2006.

Due east, toward the hills ten kilometers (six miles) shy of the Salso River and near the town of Campobello di Licata, is Milazzo, one of Sicily's twentieth-century pioneers of metodo classico production. Giuseppe Milazzo uses Inzolia, Chardonnay, and Pinot Bianco in his sparkling wines. He grows some of the Chardonnay in tendone, to preserve scent, acidity, and lower alcohol levels. His Maria Costanza bianco is a still wine made with Inzolia, Chardonnay, and Nero d'Avola vinified without the skins. The Maria Costanza rosso is 100 percent Nero d'Avola. Baglio del Cristo di Campobello is farther south, toward the seaside town of Licata, and ten kilometers (six miles) from the sea. One of its vineyards abuts a gypsum mining area, which shimmers in the evening light. Baglio del Cristo di Campobello makes an aromatic Grillo, called Lalùci, that smells as brilliantly as gypsum shines. On the plain of the mouth of the Salso River, at about seventy meters (230 feet) above sea level, is La Lumia (in full, Tenuta Barone Nicolò La Lumia). Bottling began here in the late 1980s. On the advice of Tachis, Nicolò La Lumia increased the maceration time of his Nero d'Avola to eight days, beyond what was typical for the area. The resulting wine, the 1992 Signorio, was atypically astringent. It was released in 1995 after three years in stainless steel. Torreforte, a Nero d'Avola that is fermented on its seeds and skins, needs even more time to soften. Dried Nero d'Avola grapes are added to the fermentation of another La Lumia wine, Limpiados, to extend maceration and increase the alcoholic content to 15 percent. The estate's Nikao, made from late-harvested, raisined grapes, is a passito Nero d'Avola. Less exotic is the Don Toto, a round, plump, ripe-tasting Nero d'Avola.

12

VAL DI NOTO

Val di Noto encompasses the southeastern corner of Sicily. Historically it was associated with more intensive agriculture than was Val di Mazara. Today Val di Noto –particularly the city of Ragusa—is considered the most entrepreneurial area in Sicily. In the wake of a massive earthquake in 1693 that devastated southeastern Sicily, the ancient towns of Noto, Ragusa, Modica, Scicli, Caltagirone, and Palazzolo Acreide embarked on an ambitious rebuilding campaign. They are now part of a UNESCO World Heritage Site celebrated as the culmination of baroque architecture in Europe. The ancient city of Syracuse on the Ionian Sea, founded by Corinthian Greeks in the eighth century B.C., also has a UNESCO World Heritage designation. The four principal wine areas in Val di Noto are Riesi–Piazza Armerina, Vittoria, Noto, and Syracuse.

RIESI–PIAZZA ARMERINA

The Salso River defines the southwestern border of Val di Noto. The highlands to the east and the west of the river share geologic similarities. Both swaths of hills have calcareous alluvial soils that were mined for minerals, particularly sulfur. According to several leading Sicilian enologists, the area just to the river's east bounded by the towns of Riesi, Butera, and Mazzarino is the golden triangle for Nero d'Avola. Ideal vineyard elevation there is between two and four hundred meters (656 and 1,312 feet). There is a DOC for this area, named after Riesi. The limits of the Cerasuolo di Vittoria DOCG and the Vittoria DOC overlap the comunes of Butera, Riesi, and Mazzarino

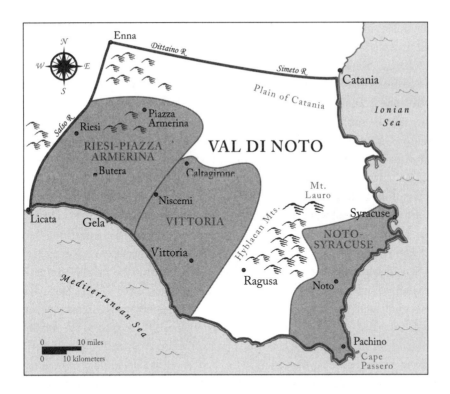

MAP 4.
Val di Noto

without substantial geologic justification. The Vittoria appellations extend across the low, fertile plain of Gela to grasp the core of the Riesi DOC. In doing so, they cross a sediment-filled depression that runs from Gela to Catania. On the eastern side of this is the African tectonic plate, represented by the Hyblaean Plateau. On the western side is the Maghrebian thrust belt, hills and mountains thrust up by the meeting of the African Plate and the Calabrian Arc.

Little is known about this area's wine history before the twentieth century. The contrada of Iudeca near the town of Butera had a reputation for quality wine grapes in the late nineteenth century and for at least the first half of the twentieth, but the locally consumed wines were poorly made. Then, in January 1979, Franco Giacosa, prospecting for wine for the Corvo blend, visited a cooperative winery there, the La Cooperativa La Vite of Riesi. He sampled the Nero d'Avola of the 1978 vintage, the first one the cooperative had vinified. He saw in this rough-and-ready sample Nero d'Avola's capacity to make great wine. During the 1980s and most of the 1990s, Butera wines became the heart of Duca Enrico, Duca di Salaparuta's and Sicily's first varietal Nero d'Avola. As needed, Giacosa blended in Nero d'Avola wines from Gela and Pachino to give more body and spice. West of Gela along the coastline, he found very ripe Nero d'Avola in the low hills between Manfria and Butera. Because the Butera area was higher and therefore cooler and farther from the moderating impact of the sea, its Nero d'Avola was a stronger bright blue-red and made a wine with fresher flavors. Giacosa identified the area's small-rock-peppered, pale gray calcareous marl soil as ideal for the variety. This soil type is locally called *trubi*. The golden marl soils of the Iudeca contrada were another favorite source for Giacosa.

In 1997 Giacosa left Duca di Salaparuta to work for Zonin, a large family-owned wine producer from the Veneto that owns vineyard property in many areas of Italy. Giacosa alerted Zonin that there was a huge baronial property, Deliella, for sale halfway between Riesi and Butera. In the same year, Zonin purchased this 310 hectare (766 acre) estate, of which 130 (321 acres) were already planted to vines, and renamed it Feudo Principi di Butera. Other protagonists in the Sicilian wine world evidently were watching the situation closely. Several years later Cusumano purchased 120 hectares (297 acres) in contrada San Giacomo in the nearby town of Mazzarino. Cusumano uses the grapes from these vineyards in its varietal Nero d'Avola and a higher-cost Nero d'Avola, Sàgana. Fazio also bought land in the Deliella contrada in Butera. Even following Giacosa's departure, Duca di Salaparuta continued to buy grapes from Riesi. It recognized the quality and individuality of the site. In the late 1990s and early 2000s Duca di Salaparuta's Terre d'Agala wine was based on Riesi grapes. In 2003, Duca di Salaparuta bought about two hundred hectares (494 acres) at contrada Suor Marchesa in Butera. Its Passo delle Mule has the Butera Nero d'Avola profile: medium-deep red, ripe but fresh fruit, rich, sour, and with a delicate but evident astringency.

The Riesi DOC was created in 2001. It comprises the towns of Riesi, Butera, and Mazzarino and defines the typologies for rosso, rosato, bianco, superiore, novello, and vendemmia tardiva. The Riesi Rosso DOC regulations give equal importance to Cabernet Sauvignon and Nero d'Avola. At least 80 percent of the Riesi Rosso DOC blend must be from one or both of them.

Maurigi. Twenty years ago the Palermo nobleman and agricultural entrepreneur Francesco Maurigi bought the Tenuta di Budonetto estate. Budonetto is just outside the village of San Cono about twenty kilometers (twelve miles) west of the Riesi-Butera-Mazzarino triangle and ten kilometers (six miles) south of the city of Piazza Armerina. It is more similar in climate and elevation to Sicily-Center than to nearby Riesi. The climate is continental. Elevation is between 560 and 700 meters (1,837 and 2,297 feet). At such altitudes, the average diurnal temperature range is between 10°C and 12°C (18°F and 22°F). While on hot summer days, temperatures can reach 46°C (115°F), on the same night they might plunge by 20°C (36°F). In winter, temperatures can go below freezing, and it snows occasionally. Mountains to the north shield Budonetto, but it is open to winds from the south. It is very dry during the summer months. The soil is deep calcareous sand. Maurigi has three wells and is well supplied with underground water. When he bought the estate twenty years ago, he planted eggplants, peppers, and other vegetables. During the 1990s the wine industry boomed, and Maurigi planted fifty-five hectares (136 acres) of vines. In 1996 he built the winery. The first commercial production was the 2001 vintage. The emphasis is on the international varieties—Viognier, Sauvignon Blanc, Petit Verdot, Cabernet Franc, Pinot Noir, Syrah, Merlot, and Cabernet Sauvignon. Maurigi produces the best Sauvignon Blanc, Coste all'Ombra, that I have had from Sicily. The 2009 that I tasted in the summer of 2010 was pale gray-green, with grapefruit and mint in the nose. The mouth was pure and crystalline, with refreshing sourness. A 2010 that I tasted in March 2012 had a slight late-harvest color, smell, and texture. The musky fennel, pine, and licorice nose was intriguing. Beyond the Sauvignon, varietal wines dominate the menu: Granny Cabernet Franc, Lù Petit Verdot, Terre di Ottavia Pinot Noir, Terre di Sofia Chardonnay, and Le Chiare Viognier. Though my favorite among the reds was the Granny Cabernet Franc, for its soft, easy-to-drink character, the Terre di Ottavia Pinot Noir is one of the best Pinot Noirs produced so far in Sicily. The great thing about these wines is that each is dramatically different from the others and very well made. Terre di Maria, Saia Grande, and Bacca Rossa are red wines with different blends of varieties. Bacca Bianca is an Inzolia with small percentages of Chardonnay and Grecanico. The team of agricultural consultant Lucio Brancadoro and consulting enologist Giovanni Rizzo has done superlative work here. The area around Budonetto has great potential for white wines, sparkling wines, and Pinot Noir.

Principi di Butera.   Feudo Principi di Butera now has 180 hectares (445 acres) of vineyards on rolling hills. Giacosa believes that three hundred meters (984 feet) is perfect for Nero d'Avola. The color of each slope's soil changes through a range of pastel hues from gray to brown to red. Nero d'Avola and Syrah are planted on the whiter soils. These soils are low in organic matter and rich in calcium and magnesium carbonates, which curbs the vigor of Nero d'Avola and Syrah. Cabernet Sauvignon and Merlot are planted on darker slopes, where the soil is richer. The Bordeaux varieties work splendidly here. The area is windy, which helps keep down disease pressure. The calcium carbonates and clay reduce the need to irrigate. In some places, the calcium and magnesium carbonates are so concentrated that they clog the irrigation system. There is water about one hundred meters (328 feet) underground, but at some locations it can be found fifteen meters (forty-nine feet) deep. According to Giacosa, Butera delivers less exceptional results in growing white grapes for white wine. Only 20 percent of the grapes on this farm are white. Since the 2010 vintage, the Bordeaux consultant Denis Dubourdieu has been fine-tuning the balance of vegetation to fruit on each vine. Fewer bunches are left on weak plants, and more on stronger ones. Leaves that do not get sun are removed. About eight to ten leaves are left for every bunch. Excess bunches are cut off. Experimental wines show improvement. The results can be tasted in the 2010 Deliella, a 100 percent Nero d'Avola. An experimental Syrah had deep color and a distinct nose of smoke, licorice, black pepper, and tar, typical to Syrah. The Principi di Butera Riesi

Rosso is 80 percent Nero d'Avola and 20 percent Syrah. The Bordeaux varieties work splendidly on this soil too. My favorite wine from the estate is Symposio, a blend of 65 percent Cabernet Sauvignon, 30 percent Merlot, and 5 percent Petit Verdot. It has a fine long astringency associated with perfectly mature Bordeaux red varieties. The Principi di Butera wines show appropriate levels of ripeness and are never overworked in the cellar. Giacosa retired in 2011. He is one of Sicily's wine pioneers.

Statio Agraria Philosophiana.   So far only sizable companies have invested in the Riesi-Butera-Mazzarino triangle. I hope that it will see more start-ups, such as Stato Agraria Philosophiana, named after the contrada of origin, Sofiana, in Mazzarino. It is a few kilometers from the Villa Romana del Casale at Piazza Armerina, famous for its colorful, well-preserved floor mosaics. Sofiana has its own Roman ruins. In 2006 Nando Marano and his sons, Eugenio and Luigi, began focusing on setting up their property for wine production. The vineyards are at five hundred meters (1,640 feet). The Ver Rubens 2010 Nero d'Avola Riesi DOC was one of the fruitiest red wines that I have tasted from Sicily. Ver Florens 2011 Perricone Riesi DOC was very spicy in the nose, with a fine, astringent finish. Only six thousand bottles of each wine were produced.

VITTORIA

The Romans called the plain between the Dirillo River and the Ippari River to its southeast the Plaga Mesopotamica Sicula, meaning "the plain between two rivers in Sicily." They highly regarded the wines from this area. When the city of Vittoria, just north of the Ippari, was founded in the early 1600s, land grants of two hectare (five acre) parcels were made to farmers on the express condition that they plant one exclusively to vines. To this day the properties with vineyards are modestly sized. Each such property has a clutch of buildings, of which at least one is a traditional cantina known as a palmento. Domenico Sestini described Vittoria as "a land where the vine flourishes" in his 1812 presentation to Florence's Accademia dei Georgofili.[1] When the Sicilian agricultural economist Paolo Balsamo toured the area in the early 1800s he described the blend of the Nero d'Avola and Frappato varieties and declared the wine of Vittoria to be "among the best of those that are produced in Sicily."[2] The high point of growth for the area's wine industry was the middle of that century to the late 1880s. Vittoria's port, Scoglitti, was the exit point for its wine, also simply called Scoglitti. During this period the docks there were improved. Along with the ports of Milazzo and Riposto, it was the most important exit point for Sicilian wine, most of which went to Malta for consolidation and transport to northern Italy and other destinations. Much of Vittoria's wine was red vino da taglio, made by the pestimbotta method, twenty-four hours for pale red wines and forty-eight for the more popular red wines.

The late 1880s to mid-1890s trade war with France crippled the industry. In 1893 the Licata-Syracuse railway line was constructed, connecting Vittoria to Catania, Messina,

Reggio Calabria, and points in mainland Italy. A railway station was built at the northern edge of the town of Vittoria. This became an important locus of commerce, around which merchants located their premises. Though the English, Austro-Hungarian, and German markets helped sustain the industry until the first years of the twentieth century, Scoglitti wine came to an end with the phylloxera infestation. Farmers here simply did not replant in the new century. Decline set in, lasting until the 1970s. The traditional vineyards that had supplied the merchant houses are mostly just north of the rail line at the town of Vittoria. They spread out on the flat plain that extends northwest to the town of Acate, north along the Dirillo River Valley, and finally northwest again beyond Pedalino to the town of Chiaramonte Gulfi, which rises up on the foothills of the Hyblaean Mountains.

The Cerasuolo di Vittoria DOC came into existence in 1973. Before then, *cerasuolo* had been used in various places in Italy to mean a cherry-colored wine. The word derives from *cerasa*, which means "cherry." An Italian gastronomy touring guide published in 1931 refers to the *cerasuoli* of Vittoria as brilliant cherry red, highly perfumed, robust, alcoholic, and excellent for aging. It also mentions a kind of vino da taglio called *vini pestimbotte*.[3] During the 1960s the retired army colonel and chronicler of Sicilian wine and cuisine Giuseppe Coria was one of the pioneer producers of modern Cerasuolo di Vittoria at his Villa Fontane. The first regulations specified at least 40 percent Frappato, at most 60 percent Nero d'Avola, and a maximum 10 percent Nerello Mascalese and/or Grossonero, an indigenous variety that has largely been grown as a table grape. The regulations were amended in 1991 and again in 2005, when Cerasuolo di Vittoria became Sicily's first DOCG. The present regulations specify between 50 and 70 percent Nero d'Avola and between 30 and 50 percent Frappato and forbid the use of Nerello Mascalese and Grossonero in the DOCG blend.

On the positive side, the DOCG tightened up stylistic variation within the category. More stringent production requirements and a tasting committee that guaranteed wine quality eliminated some embarrassing examples. On the negative side, the changes lessened the importance of the Frappato variety. The intention was to ensure that Cerasuolo di Vittoria wines had deeper color and a longer life in bottle than Frappato-based wines were likely to have. That Frappato is limited in the blend is unfortunate because it is distinctive and unique to the area. Lighter-weight, Frappato-driven wines would have moved Cerasuolo di Vittoria away from the Nero d'Avola wines, particularly the Sicilia IGT Nero d'Avolas, which have dominated the Sicilian wine selection. The blend that makes Cerasuolo di Vittoria distinctive is 50 percent Frappato and 50 percent Nero d'Avola. Because varietal Frappato using the Vittoria DOC is highly sought after by the trade, winegrowers are replanting the variety. Unfortunately this has diminished its availability for Cerasuolo di Vittoria DOCG wines. Until enough Frappato is replanted, producers may be using less than they list on technical sheets and might even be making Cerasuolo di Vittoria DOCG wines with more than 70 percent Nero d'Avola, which would not be in accordance with regulations.

The new DOCG recognizes two zones. The original 1973 DOC borders contain what is today the DOCG Classico zone: all the land within the townships of Vittoria, Comiso, Acate, Chiaramonte Gulfi, and Santa Croce Camerina in the province of Ragusa; Niscemi and Gela in the province of Caltanissetta; and Caltagirone, Licodia Eubea, and Mazzarrone in the province of Catania. If the grapes come from this zone and the resulting wine matures at least eighteen months in the winery, the wine may be called a Cerasuolo di Vittoria Classico DOCG. Wines from vineyards in Vittoria but beyond the Classico zone, including parts of the city of Ragusa and the townships of Riesi, Butera, and Mazzarino across the Gela-Catania depression, may be labeled Cerasuolo di Vittoria DOCG without the Classico descriptor provided they mature a minimum of nine months in the winery. The borders of the Cerasuolo di Vittoria DOCG are also equated with a new DOC, Vittoria, approved in 2005. There are five topologies of wine in the Vittoria DOC: Rosso di Vittoria, Frappato di Vittoria, Nero d'Avola di Vittoria, Inzolia di Vittoria, and Novello di Vittoria. International varieties are not allowed for either the DOCG or the DOC category.

The heart of the Classico region, roughly contained in a triangle linking the towns of Acate, Vittoria, and Roccazzo, encompasses a plateau between 175 and 300 meters (574 and 984 feet) in elevation. The town of Chiaramonte Gulfi is at a higher elevation, along the edge of the Hyblaean Mountains. A disconnected area around the town of Santa Croce Camerina has a tradition of making Cerasuolo di Vittoria. It too is part of the Classico zone and has terra rossa soil. As at most other places in Sicily, the climate is hot and arid. Vines are under hydric stress. Producers usually turn on the emergency irrigation system about two or three times each growing season.

Historically the wine trade has identified vineyards by their contrada. Sestini mentions Santa Tresa, Pettineo, Fossa di Lupo, Spedalotto, Capraro, and Montecalvo.[4] Others that have come to my attention are Bastonaca, Bonincontro, Casazza, Fontane, Mortilla, Quaglio, Roccazzo, Sabuci, and Salmè. In the future, I hope that regulations will allow the use of contrada names on the label so that interested tasters can begin to study the relationship between soil and wine flavor.

Not only Frappato but also the high sand content of the soil gives lightness to Vittoria wine. At Salmè, the soil is dark brown and its sand content very high. Salmè wine is intensely perfumed, light, and delicate. Where the soil is redder (as terra rossa), at Bastonaca, Pettineo, and Bonincontro, the wines become darker and stronger. At Bastonaca the terra rossa is forty to fifty centimeters (sixteen to twenty inches) thick and about 80 percent sand. At the bottom of this reddish soil is a ten centimeter (four inch) thick layer of yellow sand that contains iron. Under this is calcareous rock that is soft and crusty and absorbs water like a sponge. It is difficult for vine roots to break through this whitish red rock (*calcario-spugnoso*, meaning "calcareous-spongy"). If it is close to the surface it is best broken up so that roots can penetrate deeper, particularly to secure a constant source of water. Some say that Frappato needs terra rossa because otherwise it makes wines that are too delicate and light bodied. On the sand of Salmè the Frappato is featherlight and delicate. Valle dell'Acate in the Dirillo River Valley has soil with more silt and clay and lacks the white calcareous crust underneath. This soil is more vigorous and makes fuller-bodied Frappato. Zones close to the sea are on sandy soils with a calcareous crust underneath. Their vineyards tend to produce paler and lower-alcohol wine. Areas farther from the sea and at higher elevations, such as Chiaramonte Gulfi at 450 meters (1,476 feet) and Licodia Eubea at five hundred meters (1,640 feet), often have calcareous, clay-dominant soils. Their wines tend to have higher acidity and more astringency.

The almost thirty producer-bottlers in Vittoria are generally small and do everything from growing the grapes to selling the wine. Because there are no dominant cooperatives or merchants, they all have a similar perspective. A high percentage of producers belong to the consortium Consorzio Tutela Vino Cerasuolo di Vittoria, a factor that helped them gain DOCG status. Planeta, because of its international presence, has helped promote Cerasuolo di Vittoria throughout the world.

Arianna Occhipinti.   Arianna Occhipinti, a niece of the COS co-owner Giusto Occhipinti, is one of Sicily's few genuine winegrowers. Her enthusiasm and the creativity expressed in her wines are making her a sensation. Her fluency in English has helped her in the U.S. market. She owns seven hectares (seventeen acres) of vines in the Fossa di Lupo contrada. She also rents several more hectares. She brought her farm to life in 2004, the year after making her first wine. She steers away from barriques, instead using large casks and stainless steel tanks, though she would like to eventually swap out the steel for cement. She believes in using indigenous yeasts, fermentation and maceration on the skins for white wines, and unusually long macerations for reds. These are risky maneuvers. Her white SP68 (named for the provincial road on which her winery is located) is half Zibibbo and half Albanello, a white variety, now rare, that was widespread during the nineteenth century in Pachino, Syracuse, and Noto. Albanello was important in the blend of Ambrato di Comiso, an extinct Marsala-like wine sweetened by the addition of mosto cotto. To make her white SP68, Occhipinti vinifies and macerates on the skins for twelve to fifteen days, lets the wine settle for six months, and tanks and bottles it without filtration. The 2011 I tasted in 2012 was slightly amber, with a Moscato nose and a pleasantly bitter and sapid taste. Her 2011 SP68 red was 70 percent Frappato and 30 percent Nero d'Avola. This wine gets twenty days of maceration on the skins and six months of maturation in stainless steel tank. Her most notable wine is her Il Frappato. She macerates the grapes for fifty days! Then the wine goes into twenty-five hectoliter (660 gallon) Slavonian oak casks for fourteen months before bottling. The 2010 had some leather nuances from the old cask and was tart and light in the mouth. Siccagno is her Nero d'Avola, which is made with more or less the same technique as Il Frappato. The 2009, though lacking freshness in the nose, was tart and tightly structured, traditional in style. Passonero is a passito of Nero d'Avola grapes that undergo twelve days of drying outside on cane mats. Occhipinti covers them at night. She ferments the wine for seven days on the skins and then matures it for sixteen months in used barrique. She waited some years before issuing her first Cerasuolo di Vittoria, called Grotte Alte. The 2006 macerated for forty days on its skins and then matured for four years in large oak casks. Occhipinti is finding her style through her wines. They express her open mind and curiosity while respecting the history and culture of Vittoria wine.

Avide. Avide owns fifty hectares (124 acres) and entered the wine market in 1982. Its core vineyard site is at 225 meters (738 feet) in elevation in the contrada of Bastonaca. Avide has high percentages of Frappato in its Cerasuolo di Vittorias. The Black Label Cerasuolo di Vittoria is a 50–50 blend. It is fruity, tarry, and astringent. Released later, Avide's banner Cerasuolo is Barocco, 60 percent Frappato and 40 percent Nero d'Avola. This was the first Cerasuolo di Vittoria that made an impact on me. I tasted the 2003 in 2010 and the 2006 in 2012. With age the wine gets exotically spicy and tarry yet round and ready to drink. Similarly complex and spicy but with a longer astringent finish is the Sigilio, a 50–50 Nero d'Avola and Cabernet Sauvignon. As with the Barocco, I tasted the 2006 in 2012. These two 2006 wines had about a year of barrel aging and two of bottle aging before release. They demonstrate the increased spiciness and polished textures in the mouth that only the long maturation of high-quality wine can bring. Avide also makes an interesting Inzolia threesome. The Herea is dry, soft, and slightly salty. Riflessi di Sole, a Vittoria DOC wine, is barrique-fermented for six months and then aged in bottle for another six. The Inzolia picks up color, aroma, and astringency from the oak without being overwhelmed. Lees contact gives it softness. Giovanni Rizzo, the consulting enologist, grew up on Pantelleria. At Avide he has engineered a Pantelleria-like passito wine using sun-dried Inzolia grapes. He ferments Inzolia wine and raisins and then matures the wine in barrique for one year. The result, Lacrimae Bacchi, is golden, with honey and dried figs in the nose and a mouth much more delicate and less luscious than a Passito di Pantelleria.

COS. COS began in 1980 as a partnership of three young friends, who were inspired to create a new culture of wine in Vittoria and Sicily itself. The *S* in COS comes from the last name of Cirino Strano, one of the founders, whose sister Pinuccia succeeded him from 1985 to 1995. Pinuccia has since left, but the three initials remain. Cilia and Occhipinti are both hands-on owners. They are twins in commitment and vision but distantly related with respect to personality. Occhipinti tends to travel abroad more, representing COS to the world. His quiet intensity immediately charms listeners and tasters. Cilia's studious and exuberant love for his work equally captivates. The blend of Occhipinti and Cilia has been dynamic. They were instrumental in securing the DOCG for Cerasuolo di Vittoria and have been leaders for their zone in other ways. In the 1980s their company was one of the first in Sicily to buy barriques for maturation. In 2003 they decided to turn their backs on barrique. When wood's micro-oxidative effects are needed to tame a wine, particularly Nero d'Avola, which tends to be reductive, they use thirty hectoliter (793 gallon) casks.

They were early adopters of organic and biodynamic viticulture. They prefer concrete vats to stainless steel, a growing preference among producers concerned with the way steel induces reduction in wine. Along with Frank Cornelissen, in 2000 they were the first in Sicily to use four hundred liter (106 gallon) amphorae instead of tanks and barrels. They call their 100 percent amphora wines Pithos. *Pithos* means "amphora" in Greek. Unfortunately, DOCG regulations forbid the use of clay containers for vinification. For this reason, COS does not bottle a Cerasuolo di Vittoria under the Pithos label. COS uses the minimum of sulfites needed in its wines. By sulfiting less, winegrowers cede a good measure of control to yeast and bacteria. This can mean more floral and spice or more earth and leather scents in the nose, depending on the dominant yeast and bacteria.

Cilia, Occhipinti, and the COS team farm twenty hectares (forty-nine acres) on the terra rossa of Bastonaca. They make a spicy, peppery, tart, moderately astringent, cherry-fruited Frappato. They ferment it half in amphora and half in cement tank. There are two Nero d'Avolas, both named after the location of the vineyards. Nero di Lupo, from the Fossa di Lupo contrada, is lighter and fresher. The other, Syre, from the locality of Sciri, is derived from older vines planted in alberello, with corresponding lower yields. These factors give it more power. The maturation period for Syre is two to three years, while for Nero di Lupo it is nine months. Syre as a result is less fruity, rounder, and more nuanced. Ramì is Inzolia and Grecanico fermented on their skins for ten days and minimally sulfited. There is Pithos white and Pithos red. Grecanico has been chosen for Pithos white because it strongly resists oxidation. When using clay jars it is important to protect the wine from oxidation. Pithos succeeds. When I tried it, it did not change its aroma for a day after it had been opened. The nose is of apple and caramel and the palate is sour and astringent. Pithos red is a Cerasuolo di Vittoria incognito, in the sense that the blend (i.e., the content) is consistent with the law (even if the container is not). It is spicy but round and soft. The white Pithos deviates more from the modern style for white wine than the red Pithos deviates from modern reds.

Daino.   Daino is a wine producer in the vicinity of Caltagirone, near the northern limit of the Cerasuolo di Vittoria DOCG. Amid old cork oak trees, Gianfranco Daino grows his vines in alberello in sandy terra rossa at 325 meters (1,066 feet). The combination of alberello and terra rossa produces deep colored and powerful red wines. The standout is Suber, a blend of 50 percent Nero d'Avola with 30 percent Grenache Noir and 20 percent Frappato, here referred to as Alicante and Nero Capitano, respectively.

Feudi del Pisciotto.   Feudi del Pisciotto is at 250 meters (820 feet) on the outskirts of Niscemi, a hill town looking west over the plain of Gela. The owner is Paolo Panerai, a publishing magnate and the owner of Castellare in the Chianti Classico region and of Rocca di Frassinello in the Maremma on the south Tuscan coast. He assembled the two hundred hectare (494 acre) estate by buying parcels from fourteen different owners. He planted vines in 2002. The first vintage released was the 2007. The property includes a large private home, eventually to be renovated and transformed into a luxury hotel, and a huge, fully restored eighteenth-century palmento. Thirty-three hectares (eighty-two acres) of vines planted in 2002 skirt the modern winery, which is adjacent to the palmento. There are some areas of Feudi del Pisciotto where the topsoil is sandy and rocky and others where clay is dominant. Calcareous rocks are found in abundance. The property extends over the western edge of the Cerasuolo di Vittoria DOCG appellation. The winemaker Alessandro Cellai, who crafts the traditional-style wines of Castellare, uses modern technology here, such as cryomaceration, skin contact in the presence of dry ice (solidified carbon dioxide). The estate produces three times as much red wine as white. It has two lines, Baglio del Sole and the Designer series. The Baglio del Sole are well-made wines using local varieties: an Inzolia-Catarratto blend, a 100 percent Inzolia, and a 100 percent Nero d'Avola. The Designer wines are named for famous Italian fashion designers. They create the graphics for the labels. The flavors and textures within are as bold as the colors and lines on the outside. Because the grapevines are young, the barrels recently purchased, and Cellai new to the area, it will take him several years to refine the powerful statements that these wines make. Of the Designer wines that I tasted, the one that I preferred was the Ferrè Passito. I sampled the first vintage, the 2009. To make this wine, late-harvested Gewürztraminer and Semillon are dried for six weeks, then pressed, fermented, and matured for nine months in barrique. Giacomo Tachis, who had studied dessert wines of all types, including how they are made, always wanted to create a sweet wine with these specifications. Cellai confided in me that Tachis, his mentor, would approve of Ferrè Passito.

FiàNobile. FiàNobile is the joint effort of two winemaking families, the Corallos and the Alias. Francesco "Ciccio" Alia, a lover of history who passed away in August 2011, and his younger partner, Corrado Corallo, a trained viticulturalist, shared the work of running the estate. Like Calì, FiàNobile has vineyards in Salmè. I first met Alia at the estate of his neighbor Calì. He brought over an Ambrato di Comiso that was made in 1960 and had spent fifty years in three hundred liter (seventy-nine gallon) casks. As wine had evaporated over the years, more had been periodically added, just as is the case in vino perpetuo. It was amber, with nutty and dried fig aromas and a sweet, luscious taste. The alcohol degree was 17 percent. True to the terroir, FiàNobile's Frappato is reddish brown, with red currants, boiled cherries, and crushed black pepper in the nose and a crisp, slightly bitter, refreshing mouth. Alia mentioned that it should be consumed within three years. Though the Cerasuolo di Vittoria is fine, it is the Aidda Cerasuolo di Vittoria Classico—with its spicy notes of cedar and cloves erupting from red berry fruits and its elegant mouth—that balances strong acidity, alcohol, and astringency.

Gulfi. Vito Catania, born in 1951 in Chiaramonte Gulfi, made his fortune in the chemical industry in northern Italy but brought it back to his hometown in 1998 to start the

Gulfi winery. The hill town, its buildings shining limestone white, stands sentinel over the Romans' Plaga Mesopotamica Sicula and its wine towns Comiso, Vittoria, and Acate. Catania enlarged vineyards that he had inherited there. Their elevation is from three to five hundred meters (984 to 1,640 feet). The soil is calcareous clay with white calcareous stones, quite different from the yellow to red to brown sands that coat the plain. Between the higher elevation, whiter soils, and greater distance from the sea, this is a cooler area with greater extremes of temperature. It gets more rain too. The Cerasuolo di Vittoria has deeper color than wines from vineyards near Vittoria. It is less spicy, with strong red fruit smells. It is astringent, tart, and elegant in style. Gulfi makes one of the few Carricantes in the zone, Carjcanti. The vines grow between four and five hundred meters (1,312 and 1,640 feet), several hundred meters lower than most sites on Etna. They also grow in clay peppered with limestone rock, very different than the black volcanic soils of Etna. Despite these differences, the flavor of Carjcanti is not so dissimilar from that of a Carricante from Etna.

Nanfro. To the north of the Classico zone but still in the Cerasuolo di Vittoria DOCG, four kilometers (two and a half miles) from the town of Caltagirone, Concetto Lo Certo farms twenty-seven hectares (sixty-seven acres) of vineyards. His estate is Antica Tenuta del Nanfro. The elevation is between 350 and 450 meters (1,148 and 1,476 feet). The subsoil is sandstone. The soil combines sand with humus and is cool and moist, a fertile mix. Since 1998 Nanfro has been organic. In the late 1990s and early 2000s its red wines had leather in the nose, a consequence of using very little sulfites but interpreted as a flaw by many tasters. Lo Certo subsequently worked with the consulting enologists Vincenzo Bambina and Nicola Centonze, from 2005 through 2011. The wines made under their supervision express fresh fruit without animal scents. The red wines have a Beaujolais-like freshness. They are never tiring to drink. Lo Certo's Vittoria DOC wine, Strade, a 100 percent Nero d'Avola, is in this style. Respiri is a Nero d'Avola–Syrah blend. The ripe Nero d'Avola fruit in this wine is balanced by a dusty nose and a drying texture on the palate, perhaps from the Syrah. Lo Certo's Sammauro Cerasuolo di Vittoria is more serious, with a strong floral, fruity, and peppery character, but soft and silky in the mouth. In his white wines he relies on Inzolia. His Strade Bianco is 100 percent Inzolia. It has an exotic orange rind character, a sign of slight overripeness, yet it is dry on the palate. He makes a true late-harvest Inzolia, Riserva dei Sensi, which has banana and orange marmalade smells and a sweet palate.

Paolo Calì. The most perfumed and delicate wines of Vittoria come from Paolo Calì. One of his two vineyards in the contrada of Salmè has singular soil, fine dark brown sand sprinkled with marine fossils. The sand goes six meters (twenty feet) deep. It is extremely infertile. Underneath the sand is a layer of calcario-spugnoso. The sand's dark color makes it so hot that vines must be cordon rather than alberello trained. The cordon gets the grapes higher off the ground. Calì's other site has paler soil, which is mostly clay and silt. Osa is the estate's rosato. It is intensely aromatic and has a bitter edge. The red fruit and rose nose of Frappato Mandragola also has a peppery note. This wine is very tart and slightly bitter, toniclike. The Cerasuolo di Vittoria Manene is pale ruby-orange, with a powerful red berry and ripe apricot nose and similar toniclike mouth. In its freshness and elegance, the Violino Nero d'Avola has the high aromatic notes and lightness on the palate befitting the sound of a violin rather than the sonorous cellolike tones and richness of a more typical Nero d'Avola wine.

Planeta. Planeta has a winery and thirty-four hectares (eighty-four acres) of vineyards on reddish sandy soil near the mouth of the Dirillo River dedicated to Cerasuolo di Vittoria production, one hundred thousand bottles per year. Planeta makes two cerasuoli. The Red Label is a blend of 60 percent Nero d'Avola and 40 percent Frappato. Maceration lasts eight days. The wine undergoes malolactic fermentation in stainless steel tank and is then bottled. The result is a light, fresh, slightly saline, and easy-to-drink red. The Cerasuolo di Vittoria Classico is Dorilli, named after the company's farm on the banks of the Dirillo. It remains twelve days on the skins and then matures twelve months in five hundred liter (132 gallon) barrels. Given its higher percentage (70) of Nero d'Avola, longer skin contact, and maturation time in oak, this is a richer, more concentrated, and more ageworthy wine than Red Label Cerasuolo.

Poggio di Bortolone. For more than one hundred years, Cosenza family members have been the proprietors of Poggio di Bortolone. The owner during the 1980s, the father of the red-haired Pierluigi Cosenza, made the transition from alberello to wire training in the vineyard and from vino da taglio to vino da pasto in the cellar. He put the first Poggio di Bortolone in bottle, the 1982 vintage. The estate's fifteen hectares (thirty-seven acres) of vineyards are on yellow-ochre to brownish red calcareous-sandy soil between 200 and 270 meters (656 and 886 feet) at Roccazzo within sight of the hill town of Chiaramonte Gulfi. This part of the Vittoria appellation, Pierluigi told me, has always been the Nero d'Avola dominant end. Because of the high demand for Frappato wines, he planted more Frappato vines and released his first varietal example, a 2010 vintage. In April 2012 I tasted a 2008 and a 2009 Cerasuolo di Vittoria Classico side by side. They were 60 percent Nero d'Avola and 40 percent Frappato. The harvest conditions were dry and sunny in 2008, compared to wet and cool in 2009. The 2008 wine was softer, with less acidity and more length. The 2009 was tart and astringent. One outstanding Cerasuolo di Vittoria Classico is Il Para Para, named after a torrent that runs across the vineyard of the same name. I also tasted its 2008 in April 2012. Though there are single-contrada cerasuoli, a single-vineyard one is a rarity. The vines in this one are old and reach deep into sand mixed with rounded stones. After vinification, Il Para Para sits in stainless steel tank for three years before spending eight months in *tonneaux* (large barriques). Only five thousand bottles of this exotic, superripe wine are made. Even better is the Pigi (Pierluigi's nickname), a 40 percent Cabernet Sauvignon,

60 percent Syrah blend. It is made in the same manner as Il Para Para but is much more durable. A dark, dense ruby, loaded with balsamic, mint, crushed black pepper, and cassis in the nose, and tart, tart, tart in the mouth, the wine remained fresh for three days after being opened. Cosenza was one of the first Sicilian producers of a 100 percent Petit Verdot. He and his father, now deceased, planted the vines in 1996 on the advice of the Istituto Regionale della Vite e del Vino ("Regional Institute of Vine and Wine"). The 2008 was true to the variety: powerful and dense, with a spicy, woodsy nose. Not so elegant, but a good cutting wine for fatty foods.

Santa Tresa. Santa Tresa makes wines with great character and style. Massimo Maggio, an enologist who also directs the Maggio family estate, Maggio Vini, entered into a partnership in 2001 with Stefano Girelli, a wine entrepreneur from northern Italy. Their fifteen hectares (thirty-seven acres) are planted in the contrada of Santa Tresa, adjacent to Bastonaca. Here we are in the heart of the Cerasuolo di Vittoria, on terra rossa. At the time of our visit in 2010, Maggio was using the Maggio Vini winery to process the grapes. He plans to have a winery built at Santa Tresa. Rina Lanca is a 70 percent–30 percent Grillo-Viognier with a banana-grapefruit nose and a fat, slightly coarse mouth. Nivuro is a 70 percent–30 percent Nero d'Avola–Cabernet Sauvignon blend. It is dark, has a mulberry and ginger nose, and is slender and elegant. The pomegranate and burned sugar nose of ripe Nero d'Avola dominates the Cerasuolo di Vittoria. Very dark is the Avulisi, a single-vineyard wine from a site planted in 1964 to Nero d'Avola. The oak in the nose is strong and needs some time to yield the fruit within. The mouth is thick but finishes with a delicate astringency.

Terre di Giurfo. The combination of clay-limestone soil and an elevation of five hundred meters (1,640 feet) up the valley of the Dirillo River provides this estate with cooler soils and ambient temperatures. The wines have more weight, richness, and acidity than those from other estates in the Acate-Vittoria-Roccazzo triangle. Tasted at Vinitaly 2012, the 2011 Belsito Frappato was spicier and richer in body than most Frappatos. The consulting enologist Giuseppe Romano's doting on Terre di Giurfo's 2011 sweet late-harvest Frappato earned it the name Uniku, meaning "little one" in Sicilian dialect. The 2011 vintage was pale ruby red, with apricot aromas and zippy acidity to balance its *dolcezza.*

Valle dell'Acate. With a hundred hectares (247 acres) of vineyards, Valle dell'Acate is one of the largest producers of Cerasuolo di Vittoria Classico. It is in the valley of the Dirillo River. The river is small and sluggish, though in Greek times it was navigable by small boats. The valley channels the breeze that runs east and west, back and forth between the sea and the interior highlands near Vizzini. The altitude of the vineyards varies from 90 to 250 meters (295 to 820 feet). Most of the vineyards face south. The only wineries that join Valle dell'Acate alongside the Dirillo are Planeta, near the mouth of the river at a low elevation, and Terre di Giurfo, which is upriver at five hundred meters (1,640 feet). The soil color at Valle dell'Acate varies greatly, from honey to gray to red. The soils are calcareous and range from clay dominant at lower elevations to sand dominant at higher ones. The Jacono and Ferreri families own Valle dell'Acate. The force behind the estate since the 1990s has been Gaetana Jacono. She is in the sixth generation of the Jacono family that has made wine. She convinced her father to take the risk of bottling the whole production of the estate. She has been a highly visible member of the younger generation of Sicilians who during the 1990s helped push Sicilian wine out of its bulk wine past. Also active in the direction and promotion of the estate is Francesco Ferreri. Valle dell'Acate produces three white wines. Beyond a well-made, basic Inzolia Vittoria DOC and the rounder and richer Bidis, a Chardonnay-Inzolia blend touched by twelve months in oak barrel, there is Zagra, which is 70 percent Grillo. Grillo is rarely used in the Vittoria area. The 2009 Zagra I tasted in May 2010 was golden and had a late-harvest orange marmalade nose. The mouth was rich, viscous, soft, slightly saline, and dry. The first Frappato that I ever tasted was that of Valle dell'Acate in the late 1990s. Typically it is pale red and smells of wild forest berries and freshly crushed black pepper. The mouth is light, fresh, and zippy. Drink it within two years of release to get its full impact. The Valle dell'Acate estate has been and remains a champion of varietal Frappato. Its Cerasuolo di Vittoria Classico is a well-made ambassador for the DOCG. Its most sophisticated wine is Tanè, Sicilian dialect for Gaetana. This wine is a blend of 90 percent Nero d'Avola and 10 percent Syrah, but of the Syrah grapes only the pulp is used. Omitting the Syrah skins decreases the Syrah smell and, therefore, better preserves the wine's Sicilian identity. Matured in barriques, half new, half one year old, the wine combines an oak-enhanced bouquet with a power and acidity in the mouth. The enthusiasm and skill of the consulting enologist Giuseppe Romano have helped ensure that Valle dell'Acate wines are excellent year after year.

NOTO

After an earthquake in 1693 destroyed the medieval city of Noto, a new town of the same name was constructed about eight kilometers (five miles) to the south to replace it. The construction is regarded as a masterpiece of the Sicilian baroque style of the eighteenth century. This Noto became important for wine production during the nineteenth century. At the beginning of the twentieth century, phylloxera devastated the area around it, which never recovered. Before phylloxera, the vineyards were mixed. When they were replanted, they were dedicated to one grape, Nero d'Avola. In the early 1970s, many of the surviving vineyards were transformed into citrus groves.

Twenty kilometers (twelve miles) to the south, on a triangular spit of land at the southeast extremity of Sicily, is the township of Pachino. The Ionian Sea is to the east and the Mediterranean Sea to the south. About 95 percent of the wines produced here are red wines. In the areas around and between the village of Pachino, the city of Noto, and Avola, a city to the north on the Ionian Sea believed to be the home of the original Nero d'Avola vine selection, they used to go by the name Pachino. Pachino was the classic vino da taglio. It was known for its intense color and was much sought after to give a "healthier" appearance to the wines of the north.

Pachino locals have always preferred twenty-four-hour and forty-eight-hour wines, made by the pestimbotta process. They drank these even with the local fish cuisine. On the other hand, there were local markets, such as Modica near Ragusa, that preferred pistammutta with no maceration time, which makes a rosato. After the 1950s, French and Piedmont merchants were the major buyers of Pachino wines. They sought Nero Pachino, the darkest, ripest, and most concentrated forty-eight-hour wine. It had very high alcohol, as high as 18 percent, and some sweetness. In taste it was similar to Ruby Port. The township's warm, ventilated climate was ideal for this type of wine: ripe grapes naturally dried on the vines, thereby concentrating their constituents. They also retained most of their acidity, helped by the area's calcareous soils. The combination of high alcohol and high acidity made Pachino valuable for blending and improved its stability during transport.

Nero d'Avola has deeply colored skins, which give good color to wine, but the use of alberello and late harvesting increased the extractability of pigments from the skin of other grapes (and the sugar content of the resulting wine). Merchants, particularly those from France, convinced growers to plant nonnative varieties to boost color. Principal among these vinous interlopers was Jacquez (Jacquet), locally called Giakè, a *Vitis aestivalis* and *Vitis vinifera* hybrid known as LeNoir in the United States. This variety produces a deep crimson and tannic wine. The European Union, however, does not allow the use of Giakè grapes in wine production, because American vine species were involved in its hybridization. During the past thirty years these interloping varieties have been uprooted. The Pachino vineyards are now nearly 100 percent Nero d'Avola.

In palmentos, many of which still dot the countryside and now usually house equipment and supplies, local farmers formerly vinified their grapes according to the prescriptions of Italian brokers called *scagni*. The scagni brought local tasters, *assaggiatori*, and paid based on taste and alcohol content—the higher the more expensive. The scagni then sold the wines to merchants with very specific demands. There were, for example, some in the French Beaujolais region who wanted pale red wines to improve or stretch their Beaujolais.

After being interrupted by the First and Second World Wars, the vigorous trade of Pachino wine recommenced during the 1950s and remained important until the 1980s. In the 1960s and 1970s French traders had such a strong presence that, according to Antonino Di Marco, the president of the local Strada del Vino ("Wine Road"), Pachino was "like a French colony." But in the 1980s the bulk wine market began collapsing and the French left. The EU sponsored the grubbing up of vines to encourage a transition to vegetable and citrus production. *Pachino* became the name for a cherry tomato.

Unfortunately, this tomato, not even indigenous to Sicily, has hijacked the name of a unique Sicilian wine and wine zone. The recently restored, immense Rudinì winery, built in 1897, has been turned into a museum for the public. It memorializes the importance of Pachino's former wine industry. It is called Cattedrale del Lavoro Pachinese ("Cathedral of Pachino Work"). The first floor contains a palmento area, where the grapes were trodden underfoot upon their arrival, a room for crusher-destemmers and other vinification machines, a cavernous room with rows of open-topped vinification vats, a room where filtration took place, a pressing station, a small enological station, and an office. Below the ground floor of the winery, huge stone cisterns were dug by hand out of hard calcareous stone. The merchants' quarters, now abandoned and in ruin, can still be seen at the port of Marzamemi, the principal exit point for Pachino wine. From vacant, crumbling buildings, long lines of rusty pipes exit and slope down to the harbor, where tanker ships once waited to drink their fill of Pachino. Now-abandoned train tracks and stations once served tanker trains with northern Italian destinations.

From the late 1990s through the first years of the twenty-first century, a handful of both Sicilian and non-Sicilian Italian producers sourced grapes from, bought vineyards in, and built wineries in the vicinity of Pachino, anticipating that this would become a, if not the, classic region for Nero d'Avola wines. Duca di Salaparuta frequently bought Nero d'Avola grapes here. From 1999 to 2001 Pachino Nero d'Avola was the heart of the Duca Enrico blend. In 1996 Vito Catania, Sicilian by birth but a resident of northern Italy, began the Gulfi project. In 1998 the entrepreneurial Planeta family bought sixty hectares (148 acres) nearby. In the same year, the Veneto wine entrepreneur Paolo Marzotto bought seventy hectares (173 acres) as a southeast outpost for his Palermo-based Baglio di Pianetto project. In the late 1990s Giuseppe Benanti, the proprietor of the Benanti winery at Etna, bought vineyards in the zone. In 2000 Antonio Moretti, the proprietor of the Sette Ponti winery in Tuscany, did the same. In 2001 Angelo Paternò bought sixty hectares (148 acres) to set up Tenuta dei Fossi. As a former enologist for Duca di Salaparuta, he was familiar with Pachino and its wines. At this point there are no large plots left to buy near the village of Pachino, where the best contradas for wine grapes are located. In 2003, some twenty kilometers (twelve miles) north of Pachino, just outside the city of Noto, Filippo Mazzei of Tuscany bought seventeen hectares (forty-two acres). The key protagonists in orchestrating many of these purchases were Salvo Foti, the consulting enologist for Gulfi and Benanti, and Antonino "Nino" Di Marco, an agent for Planeta, a consulting enologist for several estates in the provinces of Ragusa and Siracusa, and the owner of his own Pachino estate, Terre di Noto. The Modica di San Giovanni family, a noble family of Noto, owns a large piece of land, three hundred hectares (741 acres) in all, centered on the contrada of Bufalefi. This includes forty-five hectares (111 acres) of vineyards. The average vineyard owner, however, has only one and a half hectares (four acres). During the late 1970s and 1980s the local cooperative Elorina helped liberate growers from the grip of merchants' agents. Beset by the financial problems that most Sicilian cooperatives face, it has a low profile. The company Vini Rudinì (no relation to the Rudinì family that built the Rudinì winery in 1897) produces the most wine. In addition to owning fifty hectares (124 acres) of vineyards, it buys the production of four hundred small growers.

Latitudinally south of Tunis and with two coastlines, Pachino is on average the warmest spot in Sicily. During July and August its average daily high temperature is more than 30°C (86°F). At fifty meters (164 feet) or so above sea level at Pachino, the Nero d'Avola harvest usually occurs around September 10. At 130 meters (427 feet) at Zisola just outside Noto, the harvest takes place at the end of September. Because of the proximity of the Mediterranean and Ionian Seas, there is little both day-to-night and seasonal temperature variation. The extended growing season ensures complete ripening. Due to the long growing season and the warm temperatures, some grapes raisin on the vine as others finish ripening. Because of this mix, Pachino wines frequently have raisin nuances and have been known to reach 18 percent alcohol. However, these *superalcolici* no longer exist, since EU wine law has prohibited "wines" containing more than 16 percent alcohol for decades.

Winds here come from all directions, but the prevailing one is the *ponente*. When the scirocco blows, it brings humidity. There is virtually no rain during the growing season. The seas on two sides make this a humid growing environment, though constant winds keep down the incidence of mold. As in the rest of Sicily, only in years, such as 2007, with periods of sustained rainfall and warmth is the perilous downy mildew a problem.

The core vineyard area is within a triangle formed by the towns of Ispica, Pachino, and Noto. There are few vineyards in the vicinity of Noto. Driving from anywhere along the Ispica-Noto line toward Cape Passero at the extreme southeast of Sicily, one sees few vineyards until reaching some low hills. Then vineyards are everywhere. Southeast of these hills, the contradas that have earned reputations for producing the best grapes— Bufalefi, Buonivini, Baroni, and Maccari—are more or less in a line pointing southeast toward the town of Pachino. The gently sloping vineyards undulate until flattening out near the coastline. At this point the area of the famous wine contradas ends. Here, as in Vittoria, contrada identification is not legal on wine labels, though some producers embed contrada names in proprietary wine names or the names of their estates. It would be a step forward to make their controlled use legal, as this would give more meaning to the concept of place and, ultimately, terroir.

The principal soil type is brown and calcareous, with a clay content of about 25 percent. The whiter the soil, the higher the calcium carbonate content. The whiter soils, *terrabianca,* are usually at the tops of hills. The grapes mature earlier there, and yields are low. Special rootstocks must be used to improve the uptake of iron from the high-lime soil. *Palomina,* or *colombo,* is a gray soil that approximates the trubi soil at Butera. *Terra forte* is a darker, high-clay soil. *Terra nivura* is a black soil that contains more humus and retains humidity. It is the richest of the soils. Because of its darkness, direct sunlight warms it up quickly. The dark soils have more loam, which makes them more vigorous. Vines tend to bear more grapes on terra nivura. The topsoil is about fifty to sixty centimeters (twenty to twenty-four inches) deep. Below it is a layer of calcareous rock called *balata*. As in Vittoria, this rock layer absorbs water, including humidity. Roots can move through the balata by means of fissures. Water is deep below. It drains down from the Hyblaean Mountains. The only cost of this water is that of drilling a well and pumping it out. Alberello is the principal training method here. Farmers frequently rake or plow their vineyards to raise the moisture from the subsoil. This also destroys surface cracks that would otherwise allow oxygen to attack the roots.

The Eloro DOC became law in 1994. It overlaps the boundaries of the provinces of Ragusa and Siracusa. On the Ragusa side it includes the town of Ispica. On the Siracusa side it includes the municipality of Noto at its eastern limit and extends north to Noto Antica, the old city of Noto, which was destroyed by the 1693 earthquake and subsequently deserted. Eloro Rosso must contain at least 90 percent Nero d'Avola, Frappato, and Pignatello (Perricone). The more specific subzone wine Eloro Pachino has to be produced with grapes from the township of Pachino, more than 80 percent of which must be Nero d'Avola. A commission tastes all Eloro Pachino wines. There is also a riserva category for Eloro Pachino, which prescribes at least two years of maturation, including at least six months in oak barrel. Eloro Nero d'Avola has to contain at least 90 percent Nero d'Avola. These regulations reflect the region well. The problem has been that the name Eloro does not have the cachet of the area's main tourist destination, the baroque city of Noto. The fact that the Eloro DOC straddles two provinces has also impeded provincial sponsorship of projects. The Noto DOC was created in 2008 and restricted to the townships of Noto, Rosolini, Pachino, and Avola, all within the province of Siracusa. Producers in the overlap of the Eloro and Noto DOCs, which includes most in this region, now have the choice of which to subscribe to for each of their wines. The trend is to use the Noto instead of the Eloro DOC. Unfortunately, the law for Noto Rosso insists on a minimum of only 65 percent Nero d'Avola. Noto DOC should be synonymous with Nero d'Avola wine. There are many other typologies of Noto DOC, the most important being Moscato di Noto and Moscato di Noto Passito, alternatively called Passito di Noto. Moscato di Noto was formerly its own DOC (approved in 1974) before being absorbed into the Noto DOC. Its various permutations share the strong floral smell of the Moscato Bianco grape and have varying levels of sweetness. Sparkling versions are less sweet than normal versions, which are less sweet than passito versions. Liquoroso, or fortified, versions, also sweet, are allowed but rare.

One hundred percent Nero d'Avola wine from Pachino has moderate to deep depth of color, more red than blue. It is spicy and smells of dried fruits. High acidity is the norm. Astringency is not strong unless the alcohol has dissolved tannins from seeds, stems, or oak into the wine. Additions of other varietal wines to Nero d'Avola can fundamentally alter its look, smell, and taste. Most expensive Nero d'Avola wines mature in barrique, as much as one-third being first-use barrique. This imparts a burned, toasty nose that competes or marries with, depending on your point of view, that of the Nero d'Avola. Inexpensive Nero d'Avola matures in stainless steel tank or concrete vat. The low pH of Nero d'Avola, combined with natural or added sulfites, can make it smell vegetal and slightly putrid when bottled from stainless steel tanks, a sign of reduction that may disappear with some oxygenation or aging in bottle.

There were many wines from around the city of Noto in the eighteenth, nineteenth, and twentieth centuries. In the early nineteenth century, Paolo Balsamo reported in *A View of the Present State of Sicily* that in Sicily, "they make the best wines at Noto; which may readily be believed when the nature of the soils is considered, which are hot and light, and above all, the nature of the climate, which is so soft." He identified Albanello as the variety singled out for praise by Noto's winegrowers, who used it to make a sweet wine.[5] Because Albanello wines have a high pH (about 3.6), some modern-day producers have suggested that in the past it was used in blends to raise Nero d'Avola's low pH (about 3.2). Salvatore Marino, the winemaker for Marabino, comes from a family that has been in the Pachino wine industry for generations. He told me that there was some Catarratto Mantellato planted in Pachino in the middle of the twentieth century.

Though Moscato di Noto was known during the nineteenth century, by the beginning of the twentieth century there was no longer a distinction between it and Moscato di Siracusa. Sweet Moscato wines from this area were increasingly simply called Moscato, without place identification other than the address of the producer. The wines were also increasingly fortified. The phylloxera epidemic devastated the area around the city of Noto, and vines were not widely replaced there as they were at Pachino. There is no Moscato di Noto made in the vicinity of the city of Noto, at least that I know of. But in the Noto DOC, in the vicinity of Pachino, there are. Producers there today have revived Moscato di Noto and nearly all have one in their product line. The Felice Modica estate Moscato is from the grapes of local seventy-year-old vines.

The most frequently heard comments about Moscato di Noto focus on how the grapes are dried for the passito version. Moscato Bianco, unlike Zibibbo (Muscat of Alexandria), has a delicate, thin skin that burns easily when subjected to direct sunlight. Even if it doesn't burn these grapes, direct sunlight darkens their skin and hence the wine; turns the wine's flavors toward dried fruits, spices, and burned sugar; and accelerates oxidation. Drying the grapes indoors at cooler temperatures preserves the yellow-gold of the skin and the wine and the aromas of fresh fruits and reduces oxidation. Fruity aromas and sweetness in the nose can optimally balance the volatile acidity caused by oxidation that does occur. Barone Sergio, for example, for its Kaluri, dries the grapes in the sun, leading to a darker wine and pushing its smell toward dried apricot and honey. At the other extreme, Planeta, for its Passito di Noto, dries the grapes indoors in a dehumidified area for forty days at 23°C (73°F). This long, cool drying process extracts flavor from the skins. As Alessio Planeta declares, "In this wine, technique is important."

For the less sweet (nonpassito) Moscato di Noto, producers late-harvest the grapes. The point at which they stop fermentation determines the residual sugar and alcohol content of the wine. If they ferment the grapes in a pressurized vat, they can leave some fizz in the wine. For example, Baroque by Rudinì has 9.5 percent alcohol, 0.9 grams per liter (0.1 ounces per gallon) of residual sugar, and slight carbonation. The style is reminiscent of Moscato d'Asti. Roselle cryomacerates grapes for twelve hours at 5°C (41°F) before cold-fermenting them for its Moscato di Noto. This wine, whose carbonation is left at the detection threshold, has more alcohol (11 percent) and more sweetness than Rudinì's Baroque.

Curto. Giombattista Curto, a judge, is the proprietor of the family estate Curto, which dates back to 1670. The winery is at a villa just outside Ispica, but the twenty-four hectares (fifty-nine acres) of vineyards are in the vicinity of Pachino. Francesca, Curto's daughter, now manages the estate. Fontanelle Eloro DOC is made from the grapes of fifty-year-old vines. It is an earthy and elegant wine. Less classic but also well made is Ikana, a Nero d'Avola–Merlot blend to which the Merlot adds black fruit and an aroma of cinders.

Gulfi. Though the Gulfi winery is at Chiaramonte Gulfi in Vittoria and makes excellent Cerasuolo di Vittoria, its focus is single-vineyard wine from Pachino. Gulfi has vineyards in many of the best contradas. To avoid stepping over the legal line regarding contrada names on labels, its four wines named for the contrada of origin have the prefix *nero* ("black"). They are NeroBufaleffj, NeroMaccarj, NeroBaronj, and NeroSanlorè. The *j* at the end is a substitute for the contrada's *i*, which helps to distinguish the wine name. *Sanlorè* is Gulfi's way of identifying the contrada of San Lorenzo. These four vineyards are, in some cases, just several hundred meters (about a thousand feet) from one another. As a group they present an ideal way to explore flavor differences resulting from differences in exposition, soil, vine age, and the reality that, although vinified and fermented in the same manner, each evolves differently. I compared the 2006 vintage of these four wines at Vinitaly in April 2011. The year 2006 had warmer than normal growing conditions. I preferred the NeroBaronj because it had the freshest fruit, as much blue berries as red, and a layer of fine astringency underneath its rich body. My second choice was the NeroBufaleffj, which was softer and rounder in the mouth than the NeroBaronj. The nose of the NeroMaccarj went too much toward dried fruit. The wine with the ripest fruit, to the point of smelling like raisins, was the NeroSanlorè.

It is challenging, educational, and fun to speculate on how mesoclimate, exposition, and soil impact wine flavors. The following is how I rationalized my experience of the flavors of these wines. Baroni and Bufalefi are both at fifty meters (164 feet) in altitude, while Maccari is at thirty (ninety-eight feet) and San Lorenzo at ten (thirty-three feet). Baroni has clay-calcareous soil so white that it shines in the light. This makes it cooler than other soils. Its calcium carbonates stabilize vine growth because they allow it to harbor water even during dry periods. As a result the grapes should have a fresh taste and high acidity. At Bufalefi the soil changes within a short distance from black to white calcareous clay to red sand. Because of the close proximity of these different soils, blending vinification lots would homogenize the impacts of each soil. At Maccari the soil is calcareous clay but darker than that at Baroni. The darker soil means higher topsoil temperature, increasing vine vigor as long as the temperature is not excessive. The Gulfi vineyard at San Lorenzo is fewer than seven hundred meters (2,297 feet) from the sea and ten meters (thirty-three feet) in elevation. Its soils are loose and sandy, dark brown, with elevated iron oxide content. The proximity to the sea makes this overall the warmest site, with the lowest day-to-night temperature variation. The result is very ripe wines with a tendency toward overripeness. There are many more factors that could, in any given year, have more significant impacts than what I have mentioned. Because of the slight incline of the vineyards, the impact of exposition on grape character is relatively minor. All Gulfi vines are trained in alberello. In general, the Gulfi Pachino wines are concentrated and powerful. They mature in barrique.

Marabino.   Owned by a group of investors, Marabino began in 2002. All twenty-seven hectares (sixty-seven acres) of its vineyards are around its winery in the contrada of Buonivini. All of the vines are on wires except those in the prized 3.7 hectare (9.1 acre) Archimedes vineyard, whose forty- to eighty-year-old bush vines lean on poles (*alberello impupato*). This vineyard gives its name to Marabino's most important wine, Archimede, an Eloro Pachino Rosso Riserva Nero d'Avola aged in sixty-hectoliter (1,585 gallon) casks. The director of the estate is Pierpaolo Messina, the son of one of the owners. Messina has put Marabino on a biologic, biodynamic, and minimal-sulfite-addition path. He does not like new-oak barrels, particularly barriques. He tolerates the fifty that he has because they are useful for some of the wines, particularly the Noto DOCs, which have an international style. The Pachino native Salvatore Marino, Marabino's enologist, is charged with making sure that the wines are appealing and stable. Though this forces him to be more conservative than Messina (the wine industry blames enologists for wine flaws), he thrives on engineering solutions to Messina's challenging direction. Though Marino grew up in Pachino, he has worked in wineries in California, New Zealand, and Australia. He combines an intimate understanding of Pachino with an international perspective. Maturation in large casks for one year gives Archimede a pure, elegant character. Spices in the nose, high acidity, and fine astringency characterize the wine. Most producers, not only in Pachino but in all of Sicily, use barriques (for two or three years of maturation) to make darker, softer, and richer but less elegant and less long-lived wines. Beyond Archimede, I have been impressed by Marabino's Nero d'Avola rosato, Rosa Nera Eloro DOC, and Eureka Chardonnay. This is not white wine country. It is too warm. Yet Marino does a masterful job with Eureka. He is pushing it away from new oak and sulfites and doing some skin contact as well. Quite a challenge for warm-climate Chardonnay!

Planeta.   The Planeta Pachino project has been Alessio Planeta's personal challenge. During the harvest and vinification period he spends half his time here, though it accounts for just one-tenth of Planeta's production. For the red wines he uses a selected yeast, NDA21, which was sourced from a palmento in Noto and then propagated in a lab. He gets the benefits of selected yeast—most important, its predictable behavior—while letting terroir drive alcoholic fermentation. Planeta bottles in Menfi. Santa Cecilia, Planeta's top Pachino Nero d'Avola red, was bottled as a Sicilia IGT before being switched to Noto DOC. Planeta's other wine from this zone is its Passito di Noto DOC. It is a pale straw yellow. The nose is a bowl of oranges and peaches with flowers and vanilla bean thrown in. The mouth has some refreshing acidity to balance the sweetness. Of all the Moscato di Noto passitos produced in the appellation, this is the least traditional in style.

Riofavara.   Since 1994 Massimo Padova and his sister, Marianta, have transformed their family's century-old business from servicing the bulk wine market to bottling its own wine with its own brand, Riofavara, on the label. Massimo manages the winery. Though it and some vineyards are in Ispica, Riofavara also has vineyards closer to Pachino. The company makes five wines, including a refreshing Moscato di Noto called Notissimo. Padova's two best wines are Nero d'Avola Eloro DOCs, Spaccaforno and Sciavè. Spaccaforno is a moderate red-brown. The nose is spicy, with lots of mature red fruit and a whiff of rusty iron. Sourness and astringency dominate the mouth. Sciavè includes the grapes of some sixty-year-old vines that have very low yields, two to three hundred grams (seven to eleven ounces) per plant per year. They grow in a soil formation called Tellaro, which has a topsoil of calcareous stones mixed with silt on a marl subsoil. This soil absorbs water and releases it to the roots during the dry summers. Padova blends these grapes with those from a vineyard near the winery to get an average per-plant yield of one and a half kilograms (two pounds), normal for high-quality wine. Sciavè has new oak and some spicy red fruit in the nose. The mouth is textural, something to chew as well as drink.

Tenuta dei Fossi.   After many years of working for other wineries, including Duca di Salaparuta, Angelo Paternò purchased vineyards and built a winery in the San Lorenzo contrada close to the Ionian Sea. He maintains the following rules of production: alberello in the vineyard and cement vats in the winery. The manner in which cement vats retain and exchange heat has allowed him to avoid refrigeration. Initially he focused on the indigenous varieties Nero d'Avola, Moscato Bianco, Inzolia, and Grecanico, but as of 2007 he has added Tannat, Merlot, Syrah, Chardonnay, Viognier, and Semillon to his vineyards and cellars.

Terre di Noto.   From 1980 to 1986 Nino Di Marco, originally from the Marsala area, worked as an agent in the Pachino wine trade for an Emilia-Romagna cooperative. It sold the wine he bought to merchants in France and northern Italy, particularly Piedmont. He stayed in southeast Sicily, becoming the most influential and capable consulting enologist in the area. He invested in his own winery, Terre di Noto, in Pachino in 1989. It comprises thirty-five hectares (eighty-six acres). He sells some of his grapes and wines to other producers and vinifies the remaining crop to sell under his own label. His dream is to dedicate more and more time to Terre di Noto. Di Marco has not used barriques for the past four years, preferring tonneaux. He is a master just as much of white wine production as of red. He makes an excellent Inzolia white, Balata, which has peach and banana in the nose and a dry, tart, but slightly sapid mouth. He also makes a red Balata, a blend of Nero d'Avola, Cabernet Franc, and Cabernet Sauvignon. The Cabernets dominate the nose. The wine is refreshingly tart and light. His Noto DOC Nichea, though pale red, is richly but finely astringent.

Tridente Pantalica. Dó Zenner makes Terra delle Sirene Nero d'Avola from the grapes of vines that he lovingly tends. It has a nose of leather and red fruits. The mouth has a persistent and fine astringency. Zenner knows and understands every vine in Tridente Pantalica's six hectare (fifteen acre) vineyard in Bufalefi. He uses the Riofavara winery and Massimo Padova's logistical assistance for vinification. In 1985 he and his adoptive German parents Hans and Nina first experimented with vinifying their own grapes. In 1987 they decided to start a winery. Hans and Dó were among the first in Italy to embrace biodynamic viticulture. Since the mid-2000s Dó, Vietnamese by birth, has managed more and more both the vineyard and the winemaking.

Zisola. Filippo Mazzei, of the family that owns Castello di Fonterutoli in Tuscany, bought a fifty hectare (124 acre) estate that he calls Zisola in the contrada of the same name just outside Noto. It is an isolated outpost of wine production in an area now dedicated to citrus production. The white calcareous rock challenges vines to find nutrition. There are seventeen hectares (forty-two acres) of vineyards. Wells supply water in May and June, which lets the vines grow enough leaves to shade themselves from the brutal sun in July and August. Mazzei has an expert team: Luca Bici, the Fonterutoli enologist; Carlo Ferrini, the consulting enologist from Tuscany; and Gaetano DiPino, the Sicilian farm manager. Nero d'Avola, Cabernet Sauvignon, Syrah, Petit Verdot, and Cabernet Franc are planted in alberello at Zisola. On the day of our visit Ferrini set up a battery of barrel samples of the same wine from at least twenty-five different barriques. The barriques had different forests of origin, coopers, and toast levels. Ferrini's first strength is his feel for the vineyard. His second is his ability to balance a wine through blending, much of which comes from his knowledge of barriques' impact on taste. At Zisola, Mazzei provides Ferrini with the resources and freedom to nurse and construct great wine. Ferrini loves the estate, the city of Noto, and Sicily. There are two wines, Zisola and Doppiozeta. Zisola is a varietal Nero d'Avola. It is darker than most Nero d'Avolas. The nose is very ripe, with brambly berry fruit and pomegranates. Cedar comes from the barrique. The mouth is solid and thick, with soft astringency. In April 2012 I tasted the 2007 Doppiozeta, a blend of 60 percent Nero d'Avola, 30 percent Syrah, and

10 percent Petit Verdot. It was opaque, with ripe berry fruit and toasted oak smells, and thick and tactile in the mouth. Though not sweet, it reminded me of a vintage Port. *Doppiozeta* means "double Zs" in Italian. It is the core of MaZZei.

Other recommended producers and their wines:

Arfò *Vignale* Eloro
Baglio di Pianetto *Cembali* Nero d'Avola
Barone Sergio *Kaluri* Passito di Noto
Barone Sergio *Sergio* Eloro Nero d'Avola
Benanti *Il Drappo*
Felice Modica *Dolcenero*
Feudo Maccari *Saia* Nero d'Avola (a stylish and delicious wine made with the
    guidance of the consultants Carlo Ferrini and Gioia Cresti)
Rudinì *Baroque* Moscato di Noto
Rudinì *Saro* Eloro Pachino

SYRACUSE

Syracuse is more important for its historical than its modern role in the Sicilian wine industry. Pollio Siracusano, named after King Pollis, reputed to be one of Syracuse's earliest rulers, was Sicily's first famous sweet wine. The eighteenth- and nineteenth-century archaeologist and classicist Saverio Landolina Nava suggested a correspondence between it and Moscato di Siracusa, the famous sweet Sicilian wine of his day.[6] How similar they were cannot be determined, because of the lack of historical detail surrounding Pollio Siracusano.

Because the province of Siracusa before 1927 included the present province of Ragusa, pre-1927 data does not reveal provincial distinctions between the two. However, we know that as a viticultural area, the province of Siracusa was dealt an almost mortal blow by phylloxera. After 1910, production plummeted and vineyard surface declined.

An occasional palmento can be found in the Hyblaean Mountains at high elevations, as high as 650 meters (2,133 feet) at Castelluccio. This indicates that before phylloxera, there were vineyards in the interior highlands. The presence of volcanic soils alongside calcareous ones could provide interesting terroir for cool-climate wines from this area. After phylloxera, only some vineyards on the coastal plains remained. Despite their arid condition during the growing season, these plains have ample underground water reserves. The calcareous soils there produce high-acid Nero d'Avola wines. Since there is no DOC for red wine, let alone Nero d'Avola wine, in the province, Nero d'Avola must be bottled as a Sicilia IGT in Siracusa.

Syracuse's calling card, Moscato di Siracusa, was Sicily's most expensive and rarest wine in the eighteenth and nineteenth centuries. There are references to both white and red Muscat wines from Syracuse during this period. In his notebook in 1775, Thomas Jefferson compared the cost of Syracuse wine to that of Madeira, one of the most prized wines of his day.[7] Cyrus Redding, the great nineteenth-century English wine taster and chronicler, in his *A History and Description of Modern Wines,* published in 1860, connects Syracuse with "a red muscadine, equal to any other in the world, if not superior."[8] It is difficult to know what he meant by "red muscadine." In *Il Vino Pollio Siracusano,* written in 1802, Landolina Nava refers to one type of Moscato Rosso present in Syracuse. He did not think highly of its potential.[9] There is a great deal of genetic diversity among biotypes of Moscato, some of which have red skins. *Notizie e Studi intorno Ai Vini ed Alle Uve d'Italia,* a description of Italian wines and vines published in 1896 by the Italian Ministry of Agriculture, Industry and Commerce, describes Moscato di Siracusa as being made with Moscato Bianco. At the end of the nineteenth century, it vied on the international wine market with the famous Muscats of Lunel, Frontignan, and Setubal. There is no mention of Moscato Rosso in *Ai Vini ed Alle Uve.* It describes Moscato di Siracusa as clear, golden yellow, syrupy sweet, mildly perfumed, and rich in dry extracts. The reference to high dry extracts supports Jefferson's observation that the Syracuse wine he enjoyed had an unusually high amount of sediment. *Ai Vini ed Alle Uve* describes the production process of the late nineteenth century: "The grapes were harvested at the end of August and were either dried on the vine or removed and dried in the sun for eight to ten days. After the stems were removed, the grapes were trodden underfoot. Fermentation on the skins and seeds proceeded for twenty-four to thirty-six hours before racking and pressing" (translation mine).[10]

An Italian gastronomic touring guide published in 1931 notes that Moscato di Siracusa was made from the grapes of vines grown on the plains of Syracuse and the hills of Noto. It describes the wine as one of the most famous *vini liquorosi* in Italy for drinking at the end of a meal. The Italian word *liquorosi* implies sweetness and suggests fortification. The guide also mentions the wine's alcoholic degree of 14 to 16 percent.[11] Italian wine law officially recognized Moscato di Siracusa as a DOC in 1973. In 1992, Antonino Pupillo, a modern-day producer, decided to resuscitate the appellation. It was on the verge of extinction due to a combination of lack of use and misuse. The following year Pupillo made some experimental plantings of Moscato, which resulted in the production of a wine in 1997 that was granted the Moscato di Siracusa DOC. This wine ensured the survival of Moscato di Siracusa. Today there are about seven producers who make Moscato di Siracusa DOC. They have small productions and are, essentially, hobby producers.

Unlike the production laws for Pantelleria, which are lengthy and detailed, the ones for Moscato di Siracusa are brief. They describe only one typology of wine. Beyond identifying Moscato Bianco as the only variety that can be used, the key regulation requires the grape juice before vinification to have the potential to make a wine of at least 16.5 percent alcohol. The finished wine must realize at least 14 percent alcohol. The residual sugar in the wine is the unfermented sugar from the juice. To account for the high concentration of sugar in the grapes, they must be dried, either outside, on the vine or laid out on mats in the hot sun, or inside, likewise laid out on mats, or under plastic, protected from the elements. During the drying process it is possible to intensify the smells of Moscato grapes. The ideal situation is to leave the grapes unpicked on the vine but protected from the elements by plastic tarps, netting, and other permeable coverings. This encourages enzymatic action in the skin that creates smell complexity. Unfortunately the skins of Moscato grapes are delicate and easily subject to degradation when left outdoors. Drying the grapes indoors under cool and dry conditions also encourages enzymatic activity. The technology of indoor grape drying is highly developed. The traditional method was to let the grapes dry in the hot sun. But high temperatures and direct sunlight stifle enzymatic activity and damage the typical smells of fresh Moscato grapes. Excessive sun also oxidizes compounds, leading to darker wine and the production of more acetaldehyde.

Another historic white wine in the Syracuse area was made using the Albanello variety. During the nineteenth century Albanello was grown throughout the Syracuse, Noto, and Ragusa areas. At the end of the century the wines Albanello di Siracusa and Albanello di Floridia (from a town about eight kilometers [five miles] west of the city of Syracuse) were the most esteemed. Dry versions were made from fully ripe grapes and resembled a lower-alcohol Marsala. Sweet versions were made from grapes left to dry on the vines.[12] The *Guida Gastronomica d'Italia* of 1931 says that Albanello was grown on the plain of Syracuse. It made two white wines. The dry type was similar to Marsala but lighter in style. The sweet type was yellow-gold and described as *liquoroso*. Each wine's alcoholic degree ranged from 14 to 18 percent.[13] Today Albanello is nearly extinct in this area.

Cantine Gulino.   Sebastiano Gulino, the owner of Cantine Gulino, is the rising star of Syracuse. The winery's official name is Enofanusa. Gulino's family has been producing wine since 1690, and his winery showroom is his family's seventeenth-century palmento. Gulino makes wines that attract attention. For example, he is the only producer of a 100 percent Albanello white wine, called Pretiosa. Gulino planted his two hectares (five acres) of Albanello in 1998 in low-nutrient calcareous soil. If the grapes were harvested at the point of ripening suitable for 12 or 13 percent alcohol wine, the resulting wine would lack aroma and have very high acidity. Instead Gulino, guided by the consulting enologist Antonino Di Marco, late-harvests them, to bring down the acidity and boost the aroma and the potential alcohol, to 14 percent. He cold-macerates to get more aroma and texture from the skin. The result is an elegant white wine with modest fruity aromas, above-age body, and high acidity. Di Marco also makes one of the most successful wines employing Fiano. His Fania is 50 percent Fiano, 50 percent Inzolia. It is less alcoholic but spicier in the nose than the Pretiosa. His Don Nuzzo Moscato di Siracusa is a fresh, sweet wine loaded with peach and Muscat smells. Heavier, thicker, and sweeter is his passito wine, Jaraya, also made with Moscato Bianco. His Drus Nero d'Avola is ripe but has plenty of acidity thanks to the calcareous soil.

Pupillo. The wine producer Pupillo is named after the family of Antonino "Nino" Pupillo. After Pupillo gained his degree in agriculture from the University of Pisa, the artist and Malvasia di Lipari producer Carlo Hauner convinced him to grow vines and make wine at Pupillo's large family farm, Targia, on the coastal plains of Syracuse. It is on the site of the castle named Solacium that Frederick II of Swabia built in 1200 A.D. In 1989 Pupillo replanted twenty hectares (forty-nine acres) of vineyards there For his Pollio Moscato di Siracusa, he harvests overripe grapes in early August. He gently presses them, cleans the juice through cold sedimentation, ferments the must for seven days at 14°C (57°F), and stops the fermentation by chilling. After resting three to four months in vat, the wine is lightly clarified and bottled. Solacium, another Moscato di Siracusa, is more concentrated and sweeter than Pollio. Pupillo harvests the grapes for it later in August, after they have desiccated on the vine. Processing continues as with the Pollio. Pupillo also produces Vigna di Mela, a Moscato di Siracusa that has the same concentration as Solacium but matures in barrique.

Savino. Vittorio Savino, with the help of the consulting enologist Salvo Foti, has revitalized a thirty-year old vineyard of Nero d'Avola on the banks of the Pantano Sichilli, a lagoon along the Ionian coastline. The vineyard is in a natural wildlife preserve, Riserva Naturale di Vendicari. Savino's Nero d'Avola wine, Nero Sichilli, has a pure and intense Nero d'Avola flavor. For those interested in going to where Nero d'Avola was born in name, this is the wine to sample. Only one thousand bottles are produced.

13

VAL DEMONE

Val Demone comprises the northeastern corner of Sicily. It includes the island's second- and third-largest cities, Catania and Messina; Europe's largest active volcano, Mount Etna; and the archipelago of seven volcanic islands known as the Aeolian Islands. In Roman mythology a giant convulsion that tore Sicily from the Italian mainland created the Strait of Messina, which separates Messina from Calabria. From the plains of Catania to the slopes of Etna and the northern coast west of Milazzo, Val Demone has been celebrated for its fertility throughout history. Of the Tre Valli, Val Demone was influenced by the island's Greek and Byzantine rulers to the greatest extent. The three principal wines zones in Val Demone are Etna, the Northeast Coast (including the Faro, Mamertino, and Cefalù subzones), and the Aeolian Islands.

ETNA

The belt of vineyards that girds the slopes of Etna has a climate resembling that of northern Italy. On Etna's slopes the principal grape variety, Nerello Mascalese, can be transformed into unique wines that are site sensitive. This delicate relationship between vine variety and place recalls that between Nebbiolo and the Langhe Hills of Piedmont, where Barolo is produced, and Pinot Noir and the Côte d'Or ("Golden Slope"), the home of red Burgundy. The wine world is discovering Etna before time and neglect have dismantled its stone terraces and uprooted all its old alberello vines. There is now the interest and the will to embrace Etna's remarkable terroir.

MAP 5.
Val Demone

In the middle of the nineteenth century the Etna wine industry shifted gears from producing vino da pasto to vino da taglio. According to the Bourbon land register (cadastre) of 1844, there were 25,600 hectares (63,259 acres) of vines planted there. This amounted to more than 50 percent of the extant farmland.[1] Around 1880, Etna became the area most planted to vine in Sicily, with about fifty thousand hectares (123,553 acres), and the most productive in terms of volume. That prosperity is visible today in the well-built stone houses from that era that line the streets and the Circumetnea railroad circling Etna, in operation since 1895. The dissolution of the vibrant export market to France, the diminution of the agricultural workforce due to emigration, and the decimation of vineyards by phylloxera, followed by the political and economic strife of the first half of the twentieth century, erased the advancements of the early quality wine producers on Etna, such as Spitaleri, Tuccari, and Biondi & Lanzafame, which worked in the late 1800s and early 1900s.

Most of Etna's vineyards are on its northern, northeastern, eastern, southeastern, and southwestern flanks. The preferred historic locations were the fertile plains elevated above the sea and the lower slopes that could be farmed without terracing and were in close proximity to the port of Riposto, the exit point for the area's wine until the early twentieth century. During the nineteenth century, elevations on the eastern slopes tended to be less than four hundred meters (1,312 feet). Here it was warm enough to always ripen grapes. But phylloxera was more devastating here due to the higher proportion of sedimentary soils. Because of both its arrival at the start of the nineteenth century and a worsening market for wines, citrus fruits replaced vines on the plains and the lower slopes. New vineyards were planted at higher elevations, where the greater proportions of lava rock and volcanic sand in the soil were inhospitable to phylloxera and where land was less expensive, though still costly to farm. These vineyards joined existing ones that belted the northern slopes of Etna between Solicchiata and Randazzo. Along the northeastern, eastern, and southeastern flanks vineyards moved up to between four and eight hundred meters (1,312 and 2,625 feet).

During the 1950s, antiphylloxera rootstocks came into use on Etna, decades after they had arrived in other areas of Sicily. Many stone terraces were bulldozed in favor of larger, gently sloping terraces that did not need rock walls. Systems that trained vines on wires, such as single Guyot or cordon-spur, replaced alberello. A continued worsening of the market for wine doomed the new vineyards on Etna's north face. Many vineyards on the eastern and southeastern slopes were sacrificed for buildings.

The wine production that continued served local needs. Families that owned small vineyards and shared small palmentos with other families largely supported the remaining wine culture. They had excellent viticultural skills, some maintaining terraced vineyards trained in alberello. Without sophisticated markets for their wine, though, its quality did not keep pace with that of the rest of Sicily. Until the mid-1990s Etna producers made wine using the pestimbotta method in palmentos. Hygiene was lacking. The wines were flawed. Meanwhile, winegrowers in other areas in Sicily were embracing innovations inspired by the Istituto Regionale della Vite e del Vino (IRVV, "Regional Institute of Vine and Wine").

Giuseppe Benanti, guided by the enologist Salvo Foti, had tried in the 1990s to bring Etna and his estate, Benanti, to the attention of greater Italy and the world. But this was not enough. As is the case so often in history, and particularly the history of Sicily, it took outsiders to bring attention and value to local realities. During the 1990s central and northern Italian wine producers had experienced remarkable growth and profitability. Beginning in the late 1990s they invested in Italy's south, looking for sources of lower-cost yet dependable quality wine. For example, the Piedmont producer Angelo Gaja's 1996 purchase of vineyards on the Tuscan coast, for what would become Ca' Marcanda, created a stampede of investment. Etna, due perhaps to its reputation for defective wines, remained unnoticed. It was an uncut diamond that needed appraisal, recutting, polishing, and marketing to the rest of the world.

In 2000 Etna's wine industry awakened suddenly. Foreign attention and capital arrived. The newcomers Frank Cornelissen from Belgium, Marc de Grazia from Florence, and Andrea Franchetti from Rome bought vineyards on Etna and became evangelists of its potential. From 2003 to 2004, financial help from the regional government of Sicily helped Sicilians plant vineyards on Etna. A planting boom followed in 2005, 2006, and 2007. By 2007 de Grazia had ignited the excitement and enthusiasm of mainland Italian investor-producers through the power of his words and the flavors of his wine, convincing people that there was some truth to his contention that Etna was the Burgundy of the Mediterranean. In 2008 Franchetti created and sponsored the wine fair Le Contrade dell'Etna, Etna's coming-out-to-the-world party. It has been a great success. Every year since then, it has brought nearly all of the region's producers and many journalists from around the world under a single roof.

Mount Etna is an amazing phenomenon and terroir. It is the highest mountain in Italy south of the Alps. At the highest elevations for viticulture, its climate is like that of northern Italy. As one goes down the slopes, the climate becomes gradually more Sicilian. On the slopes, vineyards have different growing environments due to exposure, elevation, and weather conditions that become increasingly local, particularly during the growing season. Underneath this in-the-round vineyard stairway to the sky is an active volcano. The volcano makes the Etna vineyards an evolving terroir. Eruptions change it by ejecting lava, pumice, ash, and steam. To understand the raw material of Etna wine production, Etna grapes, we must recognize how four dynamic forces determine their growing environment: altitude, exposure, wind, and the earth-creating force of volcanic eruption.

At higher altitudes not only is average temperature lower, but there is more day-to-night temperature variation, which preserves grape aroma and resulting wine acidity. These conditions are particularly helpful for white wines. For varieties used for white wine or rosato production, vineyards reach as high as eleven hundred meters (3,609 feet) and in rare circumstances up to thirteen hundred meters (4,265 feet). At such elevations there is more rain, and the combination of winter cold and humidity can result in snowfall. Most fungi can live within only a narrow temperature range, usually between 60°F and 80°F. High-elevation climatic conditions not only reduce the types of mold that can grow but can kill molds that develop during the summer months. The cold also signals the vine to rest and harbor carbohydrates in its roots. The first warm temperatures of the spring induce it to come back to vegetative life. The buds turn from brown to green, and the sap moves up the vine, bringing carbohydrates to the top of the plant until the top of the vine can produce its own carbohydrates through photosynthesis. As a result, vines come out of dormancy, grow, and produce a single harvest simultaneously. This marginal growing environment yields light crops of grapes per vine. Provided that they are not damaged by mold and have achieved full ripeness, these grapes are quality raw material for winemaking. Since they are harvested at low temperatures, the resulting wine acidity is higher, giving the wine stability, longevity, and length. At elevations below nine hundred meters (2,953 feet), the warmer temperatures are helpful for red wines, fully maturing the grape skins so that they can release more pigment and developing the tannins in both the skins and the seeds as much as possible. Red wines wear high alcohol better than whites do. They are more than 13 percent alcohol, while whites from the higher elevations are usually several percentage points lower. The expression of elevation is easiest to understand between Linguaglossa and Randazzo on the north face of Etna. Two roads link the towns. Quota 600 runs at a lower elevation, approximately six hundred meters (1,969 feet). The higher road, Quota Mille, is at one thousand meters (3,281 feet). It used to be commonly believed that the best vineyards for red varieties were below Quota 600. Now, because of either the warming of the climate or the higher-ripening aspirations of modern-day producers, the sweet spot for great Nerello Mascalese wine lies between these two roads. Due to the fame of Etna red wines, risk taking to make great ones is a feature of the competition among producers. Many are willing to take the risks of greater vintage variation to achieve longer hang time and more maturation of the grape skins to try to make more concentrated yet more elegant wines. Above Quota Mille, exceptional red wines can be made only with very low yields harvested very late (mid-November) in propitious (dry and sunny) conditions. Otherwise these thousand-meter-plus vineyards are best suited to white varieties, such as the traditional favorite, Carricante, or the earlier-ripening Chardonnay.

Exposure—the interaction between wind, sun, and slope—has important consequences that create a kaleidoscope of growing environments. As winds move up hillsides, they cool the ambient temperature, and the moisture they bear condenses as rain. The amount of precipitation increases up to the summit. The Nebrodi Mountains only partially protect Etna's northern flank from the rain the maestrale brings during the autumn and winter months. During the entire year this wind vaults over the Nebrodi Mountains and delivers moisture to Etna's summit. Because it moves between the towns of Solicchiata and Randazzo, the subsoil between them benefits from the water that drains from the summit. Unlike the eastern slope of Etna, where rainfall quickly collects and drains into the Ionian Sea, here drainage is more gradual and hence more diffuse. The lava underneath the soil absorbs the water. During the growing season, this humidity rises up through the soil to the roots. This rich, deep store of water stabilizes growth during the warm, dry summers.

For a given elevation, however, the average yearly rainfall is highest on the southeast flank of Etna, roughly between the towns of Sant'Alfio and Nicolosi. From the northwest the maestrale blows the steam from erupting vents to the southeast. This creates some shadow, reducing evaporation. Principally during the autumn and winter, the easterly (grecale) and southeasterly wind (scirocco) blowing off the Ionian Sea bring rain to the eastern and southeastern flanks, which have no mountain or hill protection whatsoever. While the southeastern and eastern exposures are wetter than the other flanks of Etna, they benefit from the rays of the morning sun, which cause an early onset of photosynthesis and reduce fungus growth. This makes this area extremely interesting for quality wine production. These conditions also tip this stretch more toward white wine production, which is more compatible with humid conditions than red wine grape production. The driest area of the mountain is the western exposure, followed by the southwestern and northwestern ones. One lesson to be learned from any discussion of exposures and elevations is that vintage quality varies enormously on Etna. Even if the vintage gets rained on in one part of Etna, harvests in other sectors are likely to be rain-free.

Western exposures are generally the worst for quality wine grape maturation. They get direct sunlight after the ground has had time to heat up all day. In the middle of the afternoon, the ambient temperature just above the soil is at its highest. This increases the likelihood of grape skin sunburn. Photosynthesis also gets off to a late start in the morning, because the sun warms up western exposures last.

Throughout its history Etna has unleashed lava flows that have wiped out vineyards and towns. The tonguelike shapes of lava flows are visible to the eye only when the flows are geologically recent. As they grow older by thousands of years, the flows become invisible. Nonetheless, they create a patchwork of terroirs that is relevant to any discussion of Etna's contradas. In 1981 a lava flow buried the famous vineyards of the Allegracori contrada. Young flows are barren rock pasteurized by heat. The surface of cooled flows takes hundreds of years to erode into soil and develop humus, therefore becoming suitable for vines. This occurs more slowly at higher altitudes because, among other reasons, there is less microbial activity there. The lava eventually erodes to sand rich in potassium and other minerals. As organic matter created by the growth of micro-organisms and later by plants and animals enriches the land, the soil becomes very fertile. Many swaths of the western and northwestern slopes of Etna are barren rockscapes without enough topsoil for extensive vineyard development. These areas have been the farthest from commercial centers and the least agriculturally developed. Over the centuries, the lack of human intervention combined with below-average precipitation for the Etna region helped retard the erosion of lava and therefore the development of topsoils here.

Etna has many active vents that are erupting constantly. They shoot out ash, pumice, and glassy black fragments that vulcanists call lapilli (the plural of *lapillus*) and Etnaens call *ripiddu*. The ripiddu, which rain down like hail, can be blown surprisingly far. According to Francesco Gambino of the Gambino wine estate in Piedimonte, one or two centimeters (0.4 or 0.8 inches) of ripiddu are deposited every one or two years at his property at eight hundred meters (2,625 feet) on the northeast flank. At the vents, deposits of ripiddu build up into cones. On a drive around the mountain, one can see many of these cones, some as small as little hills, others as large as small mountains. Their soil is deep and porous, with numerous tiny air pockets. It is perfect for vines, because their roots can go deep for water and oxygen. Biondi's M.I. Etna Rosso comes from the grapes of an east-facing vineyard on Monte Ilice, a classic conical volcanic hill. Benanti's Serra della Contessa Etna Rosso comes from a vineyard on an old conical hill.

In 2008, when Salvo Foti first showed ripiddu in the palm of his hand to Fran and me, he described how it contained an electric charge that rapidly unlocks the fertility of the soil. Foti was not talking about hundreds of years of waiting. He was telling us that the nutritional benefits were instantly available to vine roots. This attribution of his to ripiddu remained mysterious to me until I met Marco Perciabosco in April 2012. Perciabosco is one of Sicily's leading pedologists. He is the director of the Department of Agricultural Infrastructure Interventions for Sicily's Regional Department of Agriculture and has overseen research on the viticultural capacity of Etna soils. His research team had discovered that pyroclastic deposits of lapilli, cinders, and scoriae were pervasive in Etna soils. Perciabosco described how these deposits were sandy, well aerated, and ideal for the development of vine root structure. They created an environment conducive to chemical reactions. At this point in his explanation he held up his hand, pointing the index finger to the sky. As if he were Ali Baba opening my cave of consternation, he uttered the word *allophane*. This constituent, he told me, is an amorphous clay mineral derived from volcanic cinders. It has cation exchange properties that are essential for plant growth. Volcanic ash containing allophane can transform volcanic soils into fertile soils much more rapidly than the many centuries required for the breakdown of other types of volcanic deposits. High percentages of loam are common to allophane-rich soils. Depending on where and to what degree the flows were pyroclastic, Etna has varying amounts of allophane throughout its volcanic soils. For example, in the vicinity of the village of Nicolosi at seven hundred meters (2,297 feet) on the southeastern slope, the soils are mature and fertile. This area was subject to pyroclastic flow from an eruption in 1669. In adjacent areas, which were subject during the same period to lava flows that did not include pyroclastic ashes, the lava remains hard and there is little soil formation.[2] Four years before I learned of it, Foti had been referring to allophane!

Wind too plays a role in Etna's soil fertility. Volcanic ash is as fine as dust. Ejected from vents at the top of Etna, it becomes airborne. The maestrale and ponente winds blow it onto the volcano's southeast and eastern flanks. During the winter the black ash is easy to see, since it coats the snow. It can cause flight cancellations at Fontanarossa Airport, which is south of Catania along the coast. The soil between Viagrande and Trecastagni contains much ash. Because the ash is so fine and loose, it contributes to fertility within a shorter time period than either pumice or lava would. Older vines can send their roots deep into the ash to find water.

Though it hardly rains on Etna during the summer, irrigation is not needed there. Soil depth varies from site to site. The lava underneath acts like a sponge, absorbing water during the winter months. As a result, the vines rarely lack water. Where lava flows are oldest, the soil depth tends to be greater. Deep volcanic soils allow vine roots to go deep, ensuring they'll find water. The deeper the soil, the more stable vine growth becomes. Due to the rapid-draining nature of volcanic soil, winegrowers can enter their vineyards within three or four hours after the cessation of rain. The high vigor of mature volcanic soils can be restrained by leaving ground cover until July and then disking it into the soil. Organic material, particularly material containing nitrogen, is added periodically to balance the naturally high levels of potassium in the soil. This is particularly important for immature volcanic soils. When planted in alberello, vines have a density between eight and ten thousand per hectare (19,768 and 24,711 per acre). The freestanding nature of alberello helps them withstand the high winds to which the mountain can be subjected. At high elevations where ripening is difficult, low training becomes an asset. In cool conditions, alberello's 360 degree exposure to light aids ripening. In the sun, Etna's black soil absorbs the radiation readily and becomes warm. The vines can bask in a layer of heat that builds up above the soil during the day.

More and more Etna producers are printing contrada names on their wine labels. Beginning with the 2011 Le Contrade dell'Etna, Franchetti arranged the participating producers by contrada location. The fundamental force on Etna that determines the confines of contradas is lava flows. The lava flows (in Sicilian dialect *sciare,* the plural of *sciara*) have distinctive tonguelike shapes and bear descriptive names such as Sciara Nuova ("New Lava Flow"). Former ownership, usage, or particular notoriety can determine how the contradas are named. *Feudo di Mezzo* means "half the fief." *Guardiola* means "guardhouse." *Malpasso* means "difficult or unpleasant to pass." The contrada concept arrives organically from the geological and social history of Etna. It is a powerful concept.

Lava flows radiate down from Etna's summit, more or less, like the spokes of a wheel from a hub. I say "more or less" because Etna is a complex of summits and depressions. All Etna soil rests on or directly derives from lava that has flowed and hardened for thousands of years, along with ejected pumice, lapilli, and windblown volcanic ash. There are lava flows upon lava flows upon lava flows. The hardened flows on the surface each have a different age and different soil constituents.

Certain Etna producers support contrada labeling because it connects Etna to the concept of terroir and, from a marketing standpoint, models Etna on Burgundy, the wine zone with which the concept of terroir is most associated. De Grazia was the first to publically promote the connection between Burgundy crus and Etna contradas and between contradas and lava flows. He maintains that each contrada is different and results in different wines because each lava flow has different mineral constituents. According to Salvatore Giuffrida—the consulting agronomist for Valenti, Gambino, and the IRVV—exposure, soil depth, and elevation have a far greater impact on vines and wine flavor than mineral differences between lava flows.

Tenuta delle Terre Nere, de Grazia's winery, has for several years put contrada names on its labels. With the 2008 vintage, Passopisciaro, Franchetti's winery, also began naming its wines by contrada origin. Printing contrada names on front labels only became legal on wines of the 2011 vintage, but de Grazia and Franchetti were not challenged before then. There is a saying in Italy: "Sometimes what is not allowed is only in advance of the law." For example, the Super-Tuscans were tolerated as extralegal vini da tavola until Law 164/92 absorbed them into the legal system for labeling Italian wines. In effect, de Grazia and Franchetti were agents who pushed wine regulations to evolve in a positive direction. A few producers used contrada names as brand names prior to the new disciplinare. For example, Benanti makes an Etna Bianco Superiore called Pietramarina, which he has registered as a trademark. Pietra Marina is the name of a contrada in the comune of Castiglione di Sicilia. Benanti sources the grapes for this wine from the comune of Milo, which is twenty kilometers (twelve miles) due south of the contrada. The new law will allow producers with vineyards in Pietra Marina to use its name on labels for all types of Etna wines. Despite several historic inconsistencies, contrada labeling is a powerful idea. For consumers of Etna wine and for everyone involved in the industry, it begins the process of connecting place to wine flavor.

Red varieties accounted for 94 percent of the vines planted in the province of Catania as of 2009. The Etna viticultural area is by far the principal one of that province. The fact that international varieties account for less than 5 percent of the hectares planted demonstrates the strong traditions of the province, particularly Etna. Nerello Mascalese is the principal red variety on the volcano. Local farmers working on the Piana di San Leonardello ("Plain of San Leonardello") near the town of Mascali are said to have made the selection centuries ago. In older vineyards, Nerello Mascalese is interplanted with small amounts of Nerello Cappuccio and a smattering of other varieties, red and white, such as Grenache, Merlot, Sangiovese, Carricante, Catarratto, and Minnella. In newer plantings where the intention is to make a varietal wine, varieties are usually in separate blocks or rows. As of 2009 in the province of Catania, Nerello Mascalese accounted for 79 percent of the vines planted. Nerello Cappuccio accounted for only 0.72 percent. Nerello Mascalese has trouble ripening above 950 meters (3,117 feet). As its site-sensitive nature has become more evident and the quality of Nerello wines has improved, interest in this grape has accelerated rapidly. Nerello Cappuccio remains in the background and is unlikely to move out of it. It adds violet color and some texture to Nerello Mascalese wine. On its own it makes less complex and ageworthy wines than Nerello Mascalese.

Carricante is the principal white variety of Etna. Above 950 meters (3,117 feet), it takes over as the dominant variety until it meets its ripening limit at about twelve hundred meters (3,937 feet). As of 2009, it accounted for only 4 percent of the vines planted in the province of Catania. Interest in Carricante, Etna's principal white variety, has increased recently, but there need to be more examples before we can determine whether Carricante varietal wines can be complex, concentrated, and site specific and whether they function best as still or sparkling wines or can be successful as both. Catarratto is allowed to supplement Carricante in Etna Bianco and Etna Bianco Superiore. As of 2009, Comune and Lucido together account for 0.7 percent of Catania vines. From an organoleptic point of view, I am not able to tell the difference between a pure Carricante and a Carricante-dominated Carricante-Catarratto blend.

There are rare local varieties interplanted with both red and white grapevines, principal among them Minnella (0.1 percent of vines planted in Catania), a white variety with elliptical berries. In red wines, Minnella may have been used to add sugar to musts, as Viognier has traditionally been added to Syrah must in the Côte Rôtie blend. Benanti makes a varietal Minnella wine. It is nothing more than a good light white wine. Some Grenache Noir, which Italians commonly call Alicante, is planted in the vicinity of the town of Randazzo. French merchants during the nineteenth century may have encouraged the use of certain varieties to improve the wines that they purchased. Miscellaneous unknown grapes both red and white, some of which may be French in origin, are referred to as *francisi*. During the 1990s and early 2000s some Etna producers, such as Cottanera, planted international varieties.

The historic process of vinification on Etna, pestimbotta in palmento, involved fermenting the juice in vats without skin contact after the initial pressing of grapes underfoot. This process produced white and rosato wines. Red wine was made using skin contact in the vats for several days. The juice was drained from the vats into large chestnut barrels, where it completed the fermentation. Etna's traditional rosato wines were mostly for home consumption, though little is produced today. Nerello Mascalese, because of its light pigmentation and high acidity, is excellent *materia prima* for rosato.

No one in Sicily vinifies in a palmento today. Italian laws for food production forbid the use of surfaces such as volcanic rock for vinification because associated sanitary conditions do not meet official standards. For red wine production, French-derived modern fermentation and maturation techniques prevail. Etna producers most commonly use barriques for maturing red wines. Consumers who would like to experience a well-made Nerello Mascalese that is the result of traditional Italian wine production technology should seek out the wines of Calabretta. Calabretta matures its red wines in fifty to seventy-five hectoliter (1,321 to 1,981 gallon) Slavonian oak casks for thirty-six to forty-two months. Traditional Barolo and Brunello di Montalcino wines mature in much the same way. Franchetti and Graci are pursuing the same pure, classic Italian style. This maturation technique emphasizes the length of the wine, particularly the length of its finish, over depth of pigmentation and fatness in the middle of the mouth.

Wine critics and U.S. consumers, however, tend to prefer red wines that have matured in new 225 liter (fifty-nine gallon) French barrique. Wine producers have to balance the relative importance of their personal preferences, those of wine critics, and those of their consumers. Even so indigenous an enologist as Foti tends to use large French barriques for many of his clients' red wines. Acting as a consultant, he has to interpret their tastes and needs. However, the wines from his own estate, I Vigneri, demonstrate that his personal approach to winemaking defies what is standard. Federico Curtaz at Tenuta di Fessina steers a middle course by maturing in a blend of containers varying in size and material from thirty-six hectoliter (951 gallon) oak casks to tonneaux to small stainless steel tanks.

Carricante is easily overwhelmed by fermentation and maturation in new-oak barrique. It has little varietal smell, and although it has plenty of invigorating acidity, it lacks body. Many tasters claim to smell and taste minerals in it. I sympathize with their efforts to identify the ineffable. Traditionally the white grapes of Etna were trod, and even if skins were added to the fermenting must, the contact time was brief, perhaps one day. Today the white wines of Etna featuring Carricante typically have no skin contact, are cold-fermented with the aid of selected yeasts, usually in stainless steel tanks, and are bottled within a year of harvest. Carricante is rarely fermented or matured in barrique. Barone di Villagrande and Benanti have expertise with the variety. Both have experimented with barrel fermentation of Carricante and maturation on the lees and have integrated what they have learned into their current wines.

The Italian government officially recognized the Etna DOC in 1968, making it Sicily's first. The legislation recognized four basic typologies: Bianco, Bianco Superiore, Rosso, and Rosato. Bianco requires at least 60 percent Carricante, with up to 40 percent Catarratto. Other white varieties, such as Trebbiano, Minnella, and other nonaromatics from Sicily, can amount to up to 15 percent. The Bianco Superiore typology requires that Carricante be at least 80 percent of the blend and that all the wine's grapes originate in Milo, a township high on the eastern slopes of Etna. The remaining 20 percent, consistent with the permissible varieties for the Etna Bianco typology, must be sourced from Sicily. Etna Rosso and Rosato must contain at least 80 percent Nerello Mascalese and a maximum of 20 percent Nerello Cappuccio. Nonaromatic white grapes can constitute up to 10 percent of the Rosso and Rosato blends.

A ministerial decree signed on September 27, 2011, modified the original Etna DOC regulations. The new disciplinare lists 133 contradas with defined borders within the DOC. This will allow for the use of their names on the labels of wines, beginning with the 2011 vintage, made from grapes sourced from the named contrada. The decree also recognizes a Riserva category for Etna Rosso and a Spumante category for Etna. The Etna Spumante regulations allow for rosato and sparkling white typologies. The varietal blend for Etna Spumante must be at least 60 percent Nerello Mascalese, with the balance being varieties allowed for cultivation in the region of Sicily. The Spumante regulations require refermentation in bottle, conformity with the *metodo classico* process, and no less than eighteen months on the lees in bottle before disgorgement. The new decree left maximum yields for Etna Bianco, Rosso, and Rosato at nine metric tons per hectare (8,030 pounds per acre), the limit set by the 1968 law, but did not specify one for Etna Spumante. The maximum yield for Rosso Riserva is set at eight metric tons per hectare (7,137 pounds per acre). The aging period before market release for Rosso Riserva is four years, at least twelve months of which must be in wooden containers. This has to occur within the Etna DOC. There are no such requirements for Etna Rosso, Rosato, Bianco, or Bianco Superiore. In June 2012, the consortium of Etna producers (Consorzio per la Tutela dei Vini Etna) agreed to reduce the yields of Etna Rosso vineyards to eight metric tons per hectare beginning with the 2012 harvest. It will ask the Ministry of Agriculture in Rome to amend the 2011 disciplinare to officially lower the maximum yield of Etna Rosso. The new disciplinare and this proposed amendment demonstrate that Etna producers are aware that the world is watching them. They know that opportunity is knocking at their door, and they want to take advantage of the moment.

Barone di Villagrande. The Nicolosi family's presence at the Barone di Villagrande estate in Milo, at 650 meters (2,133 feet) on the eastern flank of Etna, reaches back to the eighteenth century. The family has a reputation for being model winegrowers. Paolo Nicolosi, in 1869, was the first producer on Etna to process white grapes separately and differently from red. Carmelo Nicolosi Asmundo was quick to raise his family from the ashes of World War II by bottling its production in 1948. The 1968 Etna DOC disciplinare, drafted largely by his son Carlo Nicolosi Asmundo, a professor at the University of Catania's school of enology, made special provision for the Bianco Superiore typology. Since Barone di Villagrande has been the only noteworthy producer of this wine, the appellation could be seen as a monument to its leading and exemplary role. Carmelo was also the first producer on Etna to install refrigeration equipment in the 1950s. Although Marco De Bartoli, in his capacity as the president of the IRVV, selected Carlo in 1993 to be an administrative councilor of the IRVV, Barone di Villagrande did not reach the 2000s with the recognition that it deserved, despite the continuing excellence of its wines. With Carlo sidelined by a stroke in recent years, his wife, Maria Valeria, with a degree in microbiology and a technical degree in wine production, provides a strong foundation for the growing leadership of Marco, their son, a trained enologist. The best wine of the estate is the Etna Bianco Superiore, 100 percent Carricante. Its pale silver color implies its lightness and elegance in the mouth. The oak flavors of the wood-matured Legno di Conzo, an Etna Bianco Superiore, overwhelm its Carricante. Maybe the wine will grow out of the oak with more bottle age. Though white wine is its calling card, Barone di Villagrande produces just as much red wine. Its Etna Rosso is one of the best wines for cost on Etna. Sciara is its more concentrated brother, finished in small instead of large barrel.

Benanti.   In 1988 the Catania businessman Giuseppe Benanti decided that he could make better wine than the local wineries. Given the abysmal average quality of Etna wine of his day, this was not a great challenge. He has done much more. In the 1990s he was the most visible example of what Etna could be. Starting off with family vineyards as his base, he made his most important white wine, Pietramarina, an Etna Bianco Superiore, with grapes from the comune of Milo grown at more than 920 meters (3,018 feet). For several years after 2002 the wine Pietramarina went through a phase that included fermentation and maturation in large wooden cask with lees stirring. Now it is made without oak contact and is better this way. It is a wine that can improve with age in bottle. Benanti's Biancodicaselle, a mix of Carricante from the Caselle contrada in Milo and from the Cavaliere contrada on the south slope, is released closer to the vintage and is likely to be fruitier in taste. His Etna Rosso is also consistently fine. His two contrada red wines from the north face of Etna are Rossodiverzella (Verzella is a contrada), accessible and soft in flavor, and Rovittello (named for a town), which is more complex and astringent and a bit wild. The Etna Rosso Serra della Contessa comes from grapes from an old vineyard at Benanti's estate at Viagrande. The vineyard is on the slope of an ancient spent volcanic cone. The 2000 vintage, which I tasted in 2011, and the 2003 vintage, tasted in 2008, had lots of spice, earthiness, and rich textures. The excellent condition of the 2000 Etna Rosso Serra della Contessa demonstrates that this wine merits long cellaring after release. One surprise from Benanti is the metodo classico Noblesse, which shows that Carricante can make excellent, well-balanced sparkling wine. Benanti has also invested in land in the Pachino area, where he makes two wines, Il Drappo and Majora, and buys grapes and wines from the Mueggen area of Pantelleria to make a Moscato Passito di Pantelleria, Coste di Mueggen. Foti, Benanti's enological consultant until 2011, played a pivotal role in the success of the estate.

Binoche. Piero Portale's wine estate, Binoche, near Biancavilla at 600 to 730 meters (1,969 to 2,395 feet), proves that on the southwest flank of Etna, clean, focused Nerello Mascalese, loaded with wood spices and cherry, can be made. Unfortunately, he makes only eight thousand bottles of it. The label bears the words *Masseria Setteporte,* which means "Farm in [the contrada] Setteporte." Given Portale's sixteen and a half hectares (forty-one acres) of vineyards, he has the potential to make a lot more wine.

Biondi. Ciro Biondi brought his family winery, famous during the early twentieth century, back to life in 1999. It is a spectacular site in the town of Trecastagni. His jewel is an east-facing two hectare (five acre) vineyard clinging to the side of a tall black cinder cone, Mount Ilice. The elevation is between seven and nine hundred meters (2,297 and 2,953 feet). The slope is so steep, at fifty degrees, that winches with cables are needed to transport material up and down it. From Nerello Mascalese and Nerello Cappuccio harvested from this slope, Biondi makes an Etna Rosso named M.I., the initials of the mountain. From Monte Ilice and four other vineyards nearby, he makes Outis Etna Rosso and Outis Etna Bianco. Odysseus identified himself as Outis ("Nobody") to the voracious Cyclops Polyphemus as he escaped from the one-eyed giant's cave on Etna in Homer's *Odyssey.* The Biondi red wines are pale. At first taste they seem light, but they gradually unfold with time in the air or in the bottle.

Bonaccorsi. Alice Bonaccorsi says she "follows the fruit" to find her wines, which are branded as ValCerasa even though her winery name is officially Bonaccorsi. At our first visit to the estate in 2008, the first wine that caught my attention was an IGT Sicilia rosato, Rosso Relativo. To make this wine, Bonaccorsi allows the harvested bunches of Nerello Mascalese to rest in a cool area for twelve to twenty hours. This is a passive way to cold-macerate the grapes. She relies on ambient temperature and yeast for fermentation. The result is an amber-tinted rosato that has a handmade, artisanal character. Her Etna Bianco remains on the lees for twelve months, giving it more body than most. She makes a wine called Noir, which is an Etna Bianco fermented on its skins as if it were a red wine. It is surprisingly dark for a white wine. The taste is rounder and nuttier than that of other whites. She makes a cru Etna Rosso wine, CruciMonaci, which is concentrated and elegant. Never far from Bonaccorsi is her husband, Rosario Pappalardo, who works alongside his wife in the winery and focuses on administration and marketing.

Cavaliere.   Like Binoche, Cavaliere is a notable member of the small enclave of producers on the southwest flank of Etna. Proprietor Margherita Platania has twenty hectares (forty-nine acres) of vineyards from eight hundred to one thousand meters (2,625 to 3,281 feet). They surround a nineteenth-century palmento and farm structure. The site looks every bit like a Burgundy clos except for the patchwork created by the outlines of black basalt walls separating small alberello vineyards. Though the Platania d'Antoni family founded the estate in 1880, Margherita has only recently taken on the challenge of making it a player in the twenty-first century. The Millemetri (named for the elevation of the vines, one thousand meters [3,281 feet]) Etna Bianco is clean and focused. The Millemetri Etna Rosato is fruity and fresh. Older vines provide the Nerello grapes for Don Blasco Etna Rosso, while younger ones supply Millemetri Etna Rosso. The Don Blasco has more depth of flavor, but the Millemetri Rosso has more fruit. Cavaliere's production is fewer than ten thousand bottles per year, but this could be much greater.

Cornelissen.   During his initial visit, in 2000, Cornelissen made his first Etna wine. Three years later he moved to the comune of Solicchiata to pursue his dream on a full-time basis. He had no technical training in winemaking. Not one to take small bites of the apple, he took on the challenge of making Etna white and red wines using indigenous yeast, skin contact for whites, and amphorae. He also does not add sulfites. After making a mix of unusual, faulty, and spectacular wines, he recognizes that he is constantly learning. Nature leads, and he learns from nature. He is not against scientific inquiry and reasoning. He increasingly consults scientific literature for answers. For his white wines, his current preference is Grecanico. He believes that Carricante is "the worst variety" because it is "all acidity." On the other hand, he declares Nerello Mascalese to be "a great variety." Some of his vineyards are outside the Etna DOC borders. For this reason he does not bottle his wines under the Etna DOC. His basic wines, white and red, are called Contadino Bianco and Rosso. Instead of referring to vintages, he identifies his wines by edition number. For example, Contadino 7 is the seventh time of making, or edition of, the wine. The grapes all come from the 2009 harvest, but the vintage is not printed on the label. The white Contadino 7 was dark gold, slightly fizzy in the glass, nutty in the nose, and dry in the mouth, with a hopslike smell in the finish. The red Contadino 7, made from a blend of grapes, had light red fruit and was pale, high in acidity, and very astringent. Using the best lots of Contadino Rosso, Cornelissen makes MunJebel Rosso. The MunJebel 6, a blend of 2008 and 2009 wines (it is traditional to blend vintages here, according to Cornelissen), had moderate red color, strong cherry fruit, high acidity, and fine astringency. He also produces a MunJebel Bianco, a blend of 50 percent Grecanico and 15 percent Coda di Volpe (a Campania variety) with Catarratto and Carricante. Magma is made with fruit sourced from Cornelissen's highest vineyards. In some issues of Magma he makes several different single-vineyard versions. In 2010 the (2008) Magma 7 was pale red and very spicy in the nose, with a palate dominated by astringency. "From 2005 on," Cornelissen explained, "the grapes for this wine have developed a production memory. They now know what to do." While he began with more traditional clay amphorae for fermentation, he now ferments the wine in food-grade plastic tubs and then matures it in epoxy-lined clay amphorae buried in his new cantina. Cornelissen challenges us to assess conventional preconceptions of good, bad, and great wine.

Fessina. Silvia Maestrelli, who owns the wine estate Villa Petriolo in Tuscany, and her husband, Roberto Silva, have teamed up with the Piedmont consulting agronomist and winemaker Federico Curtaz. In 2007 they purchased a seven hectare (seventeen acre) vineyard in Rovittello at 650 meters (2,133 feet), giving it the name Tenuta di Fessina. The vines grow in a thin layer of soil over the basalt stretching between two lava flows. The farm manager, Nino Farfaglia, who personally maintains the vineyard year-round, was born in the home overlooking it and has tended these vines since boyhood. The important wine here is Il Musmeci Etna Rosso DOC, named in honor of the old owner-grower who sold the property to Tenuta di Fessina. The first vintage of Musmeci, the 2007, had too much new oak. The 2008, paler and expressing cherry and mint in the nose, with fine astringency, had a better balance between oak and fruit, a more elegant texture, and a longer finish. Curtaz describes his Nerello Mascalese as a vertical wine, bridging the structure of Nebbiolo and the silk and spice of Pinot Noir. It is, he says, a modern-style wine with backbone (*nerbo* in Italian). A new initiative as of the 2009 vintage is an Etna Bianco, A' Puddara, sourced from a thousand-meter-high (3,281-foot-high) vineyard on the southwest flank of Etna in the vicinity of Santa Maria di Licodia. Curtaz put its Carricante juice in a new thirty-four hectoliter (898 gallon) oak barrel, allowing native yeasts to carry the fermentation. The big barrel exerts less of an influence on the finished wine, letting the pear and straw aromas emerge. In the mouth, astringency follows the initial acidity, giving the wine length and the structure to potentially age well in bottle. Curtaz calls himself and Maestrelli "students of Etna." He communicates a genuine attachment to this unique vinicultural zone. For Curtaz, the challenge for Sicilian winegrowers is to find and express their own identity, "to rediscover the pureness of their raw material and place."

Graci. Alberto Graci is sparing no expense to make Etna wines at the level of quality of his paradigm, Giacomo Conterno Monfortino Barolo. He has taken the risk of planting a vineyard on its own roots. In the winery, all containers are made of wood. He uses no barriques, only oak vats and casks. He bottles Quota 600 Etna Rosso, made with grapes from his vineyards at six hundred meters (1,969 feet), and Quota 1000, made with grapes from a hundred-year-old vineyard between one thousand and eleven hundred meters (3,281 and 3,609 feet). When we visited Graci's highest vineyard in the fall of 2010, there were cows wandering in it, munching on his crop. As we explored the vineyard, he chased the cows into the woods. A negotiation with the cowherd, hatchet at the ready, ensued. This experience gave new meaning to the term *heroic viticulture*.

Passopisciaro. Alessio Planeta has likened Andrea Franchetti, the owner of the Passopisciaro winery, to the German actor Klaus Kinski in his portrayal of Fitzcarraldo in Werner Herzog's movie of that name. In the movie, Fitzcarraldo has a plan to haul a steamboat out of one river at a point in the Peruvian Amazon where two rivers nearly meet and to carry it over a mountain to reach his destination on the other river. The plan is crazy, but Fitzcarraldo's vision, energy, and self-belief nearly make the impossible possible. Franchetti's journey to Passopisciaro is as difficult to dream up as Fitzcarraldo's plan. He comes from a famous, wealthy Roman family with ties to France's Rothschilds. One of his ancestors, Leopoldo Franchetti, wrote a seminal post–Italian unification analysis of conditions in Sicily. How Leopoldo understood Sicily influenced the Italian government's subsequent policies concerning the island. During the 1990s, in the spirit of Fitzcarraldo, Franchetti nearly succeeded in transforming a farm, Tenuta di Trinoro, in Tuscany's Val d'Orcia, an area unknown for quality wine, into a second coming of Tenuta San Guido, the producer who made Sassicaia in an area known for mosquitoes and Tuscan cowboys, called *butteri*. His problem has been one of timing, not effort—but that is another story altogether. Tenuta di Trinoro continues its Fitzcarraldian efforts. Franchetti, at the turn of the twenty-first century in search of a high-elevation vineyard where maturation would take place not in the heat of summer but in the cool of autumn, came upon Passopisciaro, a village on the north face of Etna. In 2000 he bought land there at one thousand meters (3,281 feet). Confusingly, he gave his estate the same name as that of the village. First he planted two varieties, Petit Verdot and Cesanese d'Affile, which he had planted at Trinoro. As if staking his claim, he called the wine they made Franchetti. In addition to being his surname, *Franchetti* evokes the French-influenced flavors of the wine. The pitch-black wine had an inscrutable aroma and was so thick and concentrated in the mouth that I ate it as well as drank it. It is red Bordeaux multiplied by four. But after several years of Franchetti making wine on Etna, it was as if the mountain finally had its way. A dialogue between him and Nerello Mascalese developed. He began making Nerello Mascalese in a way that emphasized the purity of the variety and the place. His Etna Rossos are elegant, slender, and refined. He matures them in large cask. In his Etna wines the mountain speaks to me. My favorite Franchetti contrada wine is Rampante. It comes from his highest source, at more than one thousand meters (3,281 feet). The wine is pale red, with cherry, mint, and flowers in the nose, a high acidity, and a delicately astringent palate. The structure is based more on acidity than on astringency. A contrast is Porcaria, a wine whose acidity is high but hidden in the smells and textures of the midpalate. Its source is between seven and eight hundred meters (2,297 and 2,625 feet). Astringency dominates the palate. Chiappemacine and Sciaranuova each have their personalities, too subtle to express in words. Franchetti also makes a no-oak Chardonnay, coming from a vineyard between nine hundred and one thousand meters (2,953 and 3,281 feet). Franchetti, a man with Bordeaux-classified château wine in his veins, finds it amusing that Etna Chardonnay is his most-sold wine, at fifteen thousand bottles per year.

Russo. From the pianist and Passopisciaro native Giuseppe Russo come not only the sounds of classical music but also the flavors of Etna. After the death of his father, Girolamo, in 2003, he took over the management of the family estate. It now bears his name, but the labels still bear Girolamo's. Initially Russo made his wines with the aid of Marc de Grazia, but now he has flown off on his own. His wines have become richer and more structured with each succeeding release. There is San Lorenzo, from a contrada of the same name at 750 meters (2,461 feet) in altitude with hundred-year-old vines, and Feudo, from contrada Feudo at 650 meters (2,133 feet) with sixty-year-old vines. San Lorenzo has a little more meat on its flavor skeleton than Feudo does. Another Etna Rosso, À Rina, which means "from sand" in dialect, is a blend of grapes from different contradas, matured in older casks. (No affiliation with Cantine Russo.)

Terre Nere. Marc de Grazia, a wine agent from Florence, got off the ground right at the critical time at Etna. His winery cellar opened for the 2007 harvest. With strong ties to the international wine trade, experience working with some of the most talented winemakers in Italy, and a new facility with enough room to house the production of his estate, Tenuta delle Terre Nere, he was able to get his wines immediately into the hands of journalists and out into the market. At the same time, he hosted a handful of fledgling Etna producers who had vineyards and grapes but nowhere to vinify them. He was a stepping stone in the evolution of Russo, Cavaliere, and Terre di Trente, which have since gone on to rely on other enological help, whether in new facilities of their own or other rented space. De Grazia, with the help of the young Sicilian enologist Calogero Statella, continues to house and make the wines of Binoche, Moganazzi, and Vulkaanreizen, among others. Vinifying so many lots of grapes from different locations has given him a lot of experience quickly. With some twenty-one hectares (fifty-two acres) of his own vineyards, he produces at least eight different wines. When he speaks, he equates the term *contrada* with cru. The word *cru*, which is used in many differ-ent contexts in Italy, is strongly associated with Burgundy, where it means a historic, high-performing vineyard. Just as there are many parcel owners within a Burgundy cru, the same is true in a contrada. Not all contradas, however, are crus, since many contradas have no reputation for wine production, let alone famous wine. De Grazia, astute marketer that he is, wants to imprint the association between contrada and cru on the wine world. In his view the one other area in the world that is most like the Côte de Nuits is between Solicchiata and Randazzo on Etna. That is where he owns prop-erty. He has more than eleven hectares (twenty-seven acres) at over 650 meters (2,133 feet) in Calderara Sottana. One hectare (two and a half acres) of this contains vines planted on their own roots. He bottles wine from these grapes separately, as La Vigna di Don Peppino ("Peppino's Vineyard"). He also has vineyards in Guardiola, Feudo di Mezzo, and Santo Spirito. In a blind tasting of 2008 vintage wines in the summer of 2010, I found all the contrada wines powerful, even the mix-of-vineyards wine simply labeled Tenuta delle Terre Nere. I preferred the estate wine, the Santo Spirito, and the Feudo di Mezzo because of the minimal impact of new-toasted-oak contact on their flavor. La Vigna di Don Peppino, though it had more substance and body, also had the most oak flavor. As a group, the wines mimic the prevailing Burgundian phenomenon; simply explained: the more important the cru, the more important the oak. The wines that I tasted were freshly bottled. Oak needs time to integrate, several years at least.

Vigneri. Salvo Foti, like de Grazia, has guided new winegrowers who went on to become their own masters, specifically Ciro Biondi and Alice Bonaccorsi. Edomé, Romeo del Castello, and Il Cantante are a few of the growers for whom he now serves as an agronomist, enologist, and counselor. A new association within his I Vigneri consortium is Quincunx, which acts as the communications vehicle for its portfolio of member growers. The members are a handful of fledgling wine producers (including Mario and Manuela Paoluzi's Custodi delle Vigne dell'Etna and Federico Graziani's Profumo del Vulcano), alongside Foti's more established client Gulfi and his own winery, also named I Vigneri. The message of Quincunx is built on Foti's core mission: the protection of the land, the preservation of alberello viticulture, the cultivation of indigenous vine varieties, the humanity of the grower, and the conservation of Sicilian culture. The workers who tend the vines of Quincunx's producers are also members of the Consorzio I Vigneri, a modern-day guild of winegrowers under the leadership of Foti's right-hand man in the vineyards, Maurizio Pagano. Foti himself only owns about three hectares (seven acres) of vineyards and a clutch of small buildings on Etna. He produces four wines under the I Vigneri label. One is dedicated to the members of the Consorzio I Vigneri. It is simply called I Vigneri Etna Rosso DOC. Some of the bottles are divided among Vigneri members and others are available for purchase. The wine is fermented in cement vat before bottling. It is pure, direct, and powerful. Vinupetra is from half a hectare (one acre) of vines in Feudo di Mezzo. These vines' average age is one hundred years. More than one thousand bottles are produced per year of this sturdy, fiery, oaky, textured, mentholated-cherry-cough-drop-flavored wine. A very special wine is Vinudilice ("Wine of the Ilex Holly Tree"). This is a *clairette,* a red wine so pale and delicate it appears to be a rosato but is not (the term is French). The vineyard its grapes come from is near Bronte at thirteen hundred meters (4,265 feet). It is called Bosco ("Woods"). Some of the vines are 120 years old. Foti harvests Grenache Noir and some Grecanico and Minnella here. Only a mule and human hands cultivate the soil. It is very cool and rainy here. The vines barely ripen their grapes. The wine, not usually sulfited, is about 12.5 percent alcohol. Vinujancu is a white wine that derives from another vineyard, Nave, at Bronte, this one at twelve hundred meters (3,937 feet). The 0.4 hectare (one acre) vineyard was replanted in 2005 with Carricante, Riesling Renano, Grecanico, and Minnella. Uncharacteristically for a white wine, it ferments in five hundred liter (132 gallon) open-top barrels. Foti doesn't sulfite this wine. His approach to making Vinudilice is gentle and sensitive: no fining, no filtration, and racking by the phases of the moon. Only one thousand bottles are produced. When many were rushing to buy vineyard land on Etna in the years immediately following 2000, he bought little. The territory that matters most to him is in the world of ideas, tradition, culture, ethics, and the spirit of Etna. You can't buy that.

Other recommended producers and their wines:

Al Cantarà *O'Scuru O'Scuru* Etna Rosso
Antichi Vinai *Petralava* Etna Rosso
Calabretta Etna Rosso
Calgano *Arcuria* Etna Rosso
Cantine Edomé *Aitna* Etna Rosso
Cantine Nicosia *Fondo Filara* Etna Bianco
Cottanera Etna Bianco
Cottanera Etna Rosso
Cottanera *Grammonte*
Cottanera *Nume*
Destro *Aspide* Etna Rosso
Destro *Isolanuda* Etna Bianco
Destro *Sciarakè* Etna Rosso
Don Saro *Diòniso* Etna Rosso
Duca di Salaparuta *Vajasindi Làvico*
Feudo Vagliasindi Etna Rosso
Firriato *Cavanera Ripa di Scorciavacca* Etna Bianco
Firriato *Cavanera Rovo delle Coturnie* Etna Rosso
Firriato Etna Rosso
Gambino *Tifeo* Etna Bianco
Giovi *Pirao*
Giuliemi *Quantico* Etna Bianco
Giuliemi *Quantico* Etna Rosso
Gulfi *Reseca* Nerello Mascalese
I Custodi delle Vigne dell'Etna *Ante* Etna Bianco
Il Cantante Etna Rosso
La Gelsomina Pinot Nero
Mannino *Donna Letizia* Etna Rosso

Moganazzi *Don Michele* Etna Rosso
Murgo Brut Rosé Spumante Metodo Classico
Murgo Brut Spumante Metodo Classico
Murgo Extra Brut Spumante Metodo Classico
Pietradolce *Archineri* Etna Rosso
Scilio Etna Bianco
Tasca d'Almerita *Tascante* Etna Rosso
Terre di Trente Nerello Mascalese
Valenti *Poesia Rosato* Nerello Mascalese
Valenti *Puritani* Nerello Mascalese
Vivera *Salisire* Etna Bianco

NORTHEAST COAST

Beyond Etna, the viticulture of the Val Demone extends along narrow coastal areas. These stretch north from Taormina, around Cape Peloro, and then west to the port of Termini Imerese. In ancient times the northeast coastal areas skirting the Peloritani Mountains were important sites for wine. Taormina, now a modern-day resort town, on the eastern coast between Messina (to the north) and Catania (to the south), produced a wine, Tauromenitan, famous in Roman times. Tomaso Fazello in his sixteenth-century history of Sicily praises the wines of Savoca, a hilltop town between Taormina and Messina facing the Ionian Sea, as "excellent and held in great esteem."[3] From vineyards near Milazzo came Mamertino, one of the greatest crus of the Roman Empire, ranked fourth in quality by the Roman historian and naturalist Pliny the Elder.[4] While the narrow coastal plain that continues west along the northern coast from Patti to Termini Imerese has never been acclaimed for its wines, in the mid-twelfth century al-Idrisi, the Muslim geographer of King Roger II, recorded the intensive cultivation of vines at the present-day town of Caronia.[5] Fazello also observed an abundance of vines in the vicinity of Caronia.[6] According to *Notizie e Studi Intorno Ai Vini ed Alle Uve d'Italia*, published by Italy's Ministry of Agriculture, Industry and Commerce in 1896, the wines of Patti, just west of Milazzo, along with those of Alì, south of Messina, were exported to Constantinople in the fifteenth century but subsequently lost their renown.[7]

Domenico Sestini, writing in 1812 about his visit to Sicily from 1774 to 1777, mentions "Sabboca" (almost certainly modern-day Savoca), Taormina, Milazzo, and Faro as sites of wine production.[8] In a letter to a victualler supplying his fleet with wine, Admiral Horatio Nelson, writing from HMS *Victory* in 1804, praised the wines of Faro as "excellent."[9] Eight years later, J. Pater provided an in-depth overview of Sicily's northeast coast in a letter to the editor of *The Tradesman*, a British commercial magazine.[10] Milazzo and Messina were important ports for British warships, which had to be supplied with wine.

Moreover, from these ports, wine was shipped to Malta for further exportation. Pater mentions that though a great deal of wine was produced in the vicinity of Milazzo—naming "Barcelona Pozzo di Gotto, Santa Lucia and Vinetico" (the modern-day Barcellona Pozzo di Gotto, Santa Lucia del Mela, and Venetico Superiore)—it was rarely exported, because of duties levied by Milazzo. He describes the wines of Milazzo as "strong bodied, and dry; but the general defect is that of having too deep a colour, and a sweetish taste." The red wines of Faro, he continues, have a "deep or still deeper tinge than that of Melazzo [Milazzo]." He notes that the wines from areas south of Messina on the Ionian coast—in particular the towns of "Contessa, Galate, St. Steffano"—are as good as or better than those from north of Messina. St. Steffano corresponds to the present vicinity of Santo Stefano di Briga, where the modern-day Palari winery is located. Galati Superiore is just to the north. Pater mentions that the coastline south to Taormina "abounds in wine." He estimated that the eastern coastline from Faro to "Scaletto," modern-day Scaletta Superiore, about thirty kilometers (nineteen miles) to the south, produced as much wine as the area around Milazzo.

In contrast with our current epoch, the late nineteenth century was a boom period in viticulture for the northern coastline areas in the vicinities of Milazzo and Messina. French traders, responding to the phylloxera devastation of European vineyards in the 1870s, sought vini da taglio, dark, alcoholic, and tannic wines to add to and enrich their own wines or ones bought from other locations. They particularly prized the wine that they called Milazzo, after the port of origin. Another name traders gave this wine was Capo Rosso, meaning "red wine from the Cape of Milazzo." It was sourced from palmentos in the towns of Milazzo, Santa Lucia, San Filippo del Mela, and Pace. Messina and surrounding areas produced Faro. By the end of the nineteenth century, this wine was less concentrated and alcoholic than Milazzo. Like Milazzo, Faro had low levels of residual sugar. Sometimes it was fortified with 3 percent spirit to stabilize it for travel. Renowned locally and particularly in the city of Messina were Faro wines from several villages near Cape Peloro, notably Faro Superiore and Ganzirri.[11]

Nocera was the most important variety for both Milazzo and Faro wines of the nineteenth century. Ripe Nocera grapes produce deep red, alcoholic, and tannic wines. The combination of water, sun, warmth, nutrient-rich soil, alberello training, and Nocera created ideal conditions for producing high volumes of concentrated red wine. The French bought Milazzo as soon as fermentation was over or almost over and shipped it to the ports of Bordeaux or Sète, where they finished the wine in their own cellars.

The trade with France stopped suddenly, however, in the late 1880s. Milazzo turned to other markets, such as South America, Switzerland, Germany, the Austro-Hungarian Empire, and central and northern Italy. But the overall market was never as vigorous or profitable again. By the end of the century, phylloxera had arrived in Sicily. The northeast coast was in the vanguard in finding a solution to the infestation. In 1893 Giuseppe Zirilli Lucifero, a member of an important winemaking family from Milazzo, started the first private nursery of American vines in Sicily and became an important provider of rootstocks. In 1897 Antonio Ruggeri, the director of the government nursery for the province of Messina, created 140 Ru, which would become the most used phylloxera-resistant rootstock in Sicily in the next century.

Though there was some replanting during the Fascist period of the 1920s and 1930s and some activity in bulk wine sales to Genoa from the port of Milazzo in the 1950s, the decline in viticultural and enological activity continued in northeast Sicily. Since the end of World War II, the construction trade has dominated its economic sector. Also during the twentieth century, Nero d'Avola became more prevalent than Nocera in vineyards in the vicinity of Milazzo, and Nerello Mascalese became more prevalent than Nocera near the city of Messina. As of 2009, Nerello Mascalese and Nero d'Avola together accounted for about 48 percent of the vines planted in the province of Messina. Alberello was the training system for 54 percent of the vines there. Messina ranks fourth-to-last in volume of wine production per province in Sicily, followed by Ragusa, Siracusa, and Enna.

Because these narrow coastal plains face the Tyrrhenian Sea on the north side of Sicily and the Ionian Sea on the eastern side, they are exposed to humid air. Moreover, they back up to mountain ranges where precipitation is high. From west to east, these are the Madonie, the Nebrodi, and the Peloritani. The impacts of the maestrale on the northern coast and the grecale and scirocco on the eastern coast make the coastal plains of the Val Demone some of the wettest locations on the island. Rain falls principally in winter. June, July, and August are dry and sunny. The rain's erosion of the mountain slopes has made the soils of the foothills and plains deep. The coastline area has two DOCs, Faro and Mamertino. There are a handful of producers making wines for each. The volumes of Faro DOC and Mamertino DOC are both minuscule.

FARO

The Faro DOC, created in 1976, wraps around Cape Peloro. At the cape is an imposing lighthouse, Torre Faro, which translates into English as "Tower Lighthouse." There is sand along the coastline here and to the south, and the soils tend to be more acidic. Clay dominates much of the soil in the northern part of the Faro DOC. Below Messina the coastal plain is very narrow. Its climate is rainy and humid, because of the scirocco winds. They blow most often in the months of April, May, and September. The scirocco can be powerful where there are no hills to face off against it. Claudio Barbera has to tie down the furniture on the patio of his estate, which looks down over the Strait of Messina, to keep it from blowing away. Hills protect Bonavita's vineyards in Faro Superiore from the scirocco. It has little impact there. Moving from the shoreline, the land quickly rises into the Peloritani Mountains, which are Sicily's lone stand of metamorphic rock. The Faro DOC allows only a red wine, which calls for 45 to 60 percent Nerello Mascalese, 15 to 30 percent Nerello Cappuccio, 5 to 10 percent Nocera, and up to 15 percent Nero d'Avola, Gaglioppo, Sangiovese, or any blend of these three. The phylloxera infestation of the late nineteenth century sent Faro into a decline. It hit a low point in the mid-1980s, when Giacomo Currò was the only significant producer of Faro, with only two hectares (five acres) in production. The appellation was in danger of extinction until the early 1990s, when Salvatore Geraci of Palari began to produce wine.

Bonavita.   In the epicenter of the nineteenth-century Faro area is Bonavita. This winery's 2006 Faro was its first commercial vintage. Bonavita is the work of the Scarfone family, Emanuela, Carmelo, and their sons Giovanni and Francesco. They are true winegrowers because they participate in all the work on the farm, from taking care of their six hectares (fifteen acres) of vines to making and commercializing the wine. Their vineyards are between the villages of Faro Superiore and Curcuraci. Bonavita is at 250 meters (820 feet), halfway between the Ionian and Tyrrhenian Seas, and protected from the scirocco by the Peloritani Mountains. Its 2008 Faro fused cherry with eucalyptus aromas. The wine had leather nuances in the nose, indicative of artisanal production. Production averages only four thousand bottles per year.

Enza La Fauci.   Another producer of Faro is Enza La Fauci, whose Oblì Faro DOC blends ripe red berry fruits and fine-textured astringency. It is 60 percent Nerello Mascalese, with 15 percent each of Nerello Cappuccio and Nocera, and Nero d'Avola making up the remaining 10 percent. La Fauci also makes Terra di Vento, a more basic Nerello Mascalese–Nero d'Avola blend. It is less round in the mouth and lacks the fine astringent finish of the Oblì. These are handmade, low-production wines. La Fauci's three hectares (seven and a half acres) along the Tyrrhenian Sea face northeast.

Fondo dei Barbera.   Barbera's estate officially bears his name. The branding on the only wine that he produces is *Fondo dei Barbera*, which translates to "Barbera Family Estate." He is an engineer with a love of plants. In his kitchen he has a pneumatic hookup for various contraptions that he uses when he cooks and cleans. His home sits atop a ridge in Faro Superiore that overlooks the Strait of Messina. His is the only significant vineyard in a residential area. He watches the vines grow as he looks down from his patio. He does all his own grafting in the vineyard. Each of the three vineyards around his house bears the names of one of his daughters: Teresa, Valeria, and Claudia. He has planted three varieties, which he vinifies together, for his wine, a Faro DOC. Nerello Mascalese dominates the blend, varying from 40 to 60 percent each year. Its yield is inconsistent, and its quality and character change from year to year. Nocera accounts for 30 percent of the blend. Nero d'Avola makes up the balance. Barbera would like to increase the Nocera at the expense of the Nero d'Avola. He says that Nero d'Avola gives his wine color, Nocera its fruity smell, and Nerello Mascalese its body, structure, and acidity. When the millipedes come out, he knows that the maestrale will bring rain.

When the grecale blows, he knows it's time to fly a kite in its steady, strong wind with nine-year-old Claudia at his side. His winery is the size of a closet in a modern American home. Of course, it is filled to the ceiling with stainless steel tanks. He made 1,243 bottles of the 2008 vintage, his first commercial bottling. It won an award at a wine competition in Asti. It was dark and meaty, earthy with a bit of leather in the nose. In the mouth the wine was soft, with a long astringent finish. Barbera made 1,642 bottles of the 2009. Though it is paler and has less body, I prefer its cleaner fruit and more acidic zip in the mouth. In the same league as an elite Burgundy producer, Barbera makes one bottle of wine per plant. We need more producers like him, to remind us how wine connects us to place and family.

Palari.   The entry of Palari in the market not only helped rescue Faro from oblivion but also brought back its fame. In 1990 the famous gastronomic journalist Luigi Veronelli asked his friend Salvatore Geraci, an architect and gastronomist, to produce Faro commercially. Geraci's family owns six hectares (fifteen acres) of vineyard property south of Messina in Santo Stefano Briga, with which he helped to restore the viability of the Faro DOC. Veronelli put him in contact with the enologist Donato Lanati, who had just started a research laboratory, Enosis, in Piedmont. Lanati told Geraci that he would help only if the goal was to make great wine. Geraci took on the challenge and was soon sending Lanati samples that were of the same quality as the best Barolo and Barbaresco. Geraci gave most of the first vintages of his wine to friends. Veronelli reviewed his 1992 vintage, the first to be labeled, in the January 1995 edition of the prestigious *Catalogo Veronelli dei Vini da Favola*. This set the stage for the commercialization of the wine, which began that year. According to the then-cocurator of the Italian wine guide *Gambero Rosso*, Daniele Cernilli, Geraci was not serious about entering his wine in the guide until the 1996 vintage. Since then Palari has won numerous awards.

Behind the scenes, Geraci's brother Giampiero helps to manage the vineyard and winery. The site of the vineyard is spectacular. A windy dirt road leads up to a precipitous vineyard (with an average slope of seventy-five percent) that looks eastward over the Strait of Messina. The elevation is four hundred meters (1,312 feet). Alberello is trained on sandy soils held on the slope by stone terraces. The stones are jagged and schistose, unlike any others that I have seen in Sicily. The winery is the eighteenth-century Geraci villa. It makes three wines, Palari, Rosso del Soprano, and Santa.Nè. The estate takes its name from the contrada of origin. It is about 50 percent Nerello Mascalese, with the balance being a blend of Nerello Cappuccio, Nocera, Nero d'Avola, and obscure local grapes such as Acitana and Galatena. Rosso del Soprano has the same blend as Palari. *Soprano* is the name in dialect for Santo Stefano Briga, Palari's hamlet. Santa. Nè is a single-vineyard wine. The vines are a mix of varieties of unknown origin, called *francisi* in dialect, suggesting a French origin. The Rosso del Soprano and the Santa. Nè are Sicilia IGT wines. In the summer of 2010 I tasted the 1998, 2000, 2006, 2007, and 2008 Palari, the 2005, 2006, 2007, and 2008 Rosso del Soprano, and the 2005

Santa.Nè. The older vintages had modest depth of color, smelled of ripe and in some cases late-harvested fruit, had some smokiness from toasted barrique, and were very soft and round in the mouth. They made me think of the descriptions of the best late-nineteenth-century Faro. They were Burgundian in style rather than Bordeaux. The Santa.Nè, however, had a vegetal nose and was midweight in the mouth. It had the freshness, elegance, and delicacy of fine red Bordeaux.

MAMERTINO

The Mamertino DOC encompasses a wide area that includes the coastline and the foothills of the Peloritani and Nebrodi Mountains that look northward to the Aeolian Islands in the Tyrrhenian Sea. Because it has greater protection from the grecale and the scirocco, there is less rainfall here than in the Faro DOC, on the other side of the Peloritani Mountains. Due to the presence of iron, the soils have a brown tint. Those west of Milazzo tend to be more clayey and calcareous. At Milazzo they are deep and fertile. As the vineyards back up to the Peloritani Mountains their soils can be slightly acidic.

Modern wine producers have reached back to the fame of a Roman wine made in this area called Mamertino. There are no accurate descriptions of it. A wine by this name was not seen again until the nineteenth century, when at least one Mamertino was bottled. The producer Zirilli Giuseppe and Son of Milazzo entered a Mamertino wine in the Dublin International Exhibition of 1865. In the 1960s the government-supported Cantina Sperimentale at Milazzo made tiny quantities of sweet amber wines bottled as Mamertino. It also planted vine varieties with the goal of developing a Mamertino blend. At the same time, there was a handful of producers in the vicinity of Milazzo making wines labeled *Mamertino*. In 1985 Ruggero Vasari, a wine producer at Santa Lucia del Mela just outside Milazzo, registered the name as a trademark and made a Mamertino only to discover that a producer in Emilia-Romagna had already done the same. Finally, after almost twenty years of wrestling with how to protect the name, he drew up an application for Mamertino to become a DOC. The Italian Ministry of Agriculture accepted Mamertino di Milazzo, or simply Mamertino, as a DOC in 2004. The production regulation prescribes four typologies: white, red, Nero d'Avola, and Grillo-Inzolia. The first three can have riserva status after twenty-four months of aging and meeting other technical requirements. This category, however, is rarely made. Grillo and Inzolia are the two most important varieties in the white Mamertino blend. For the red, the law specifies a minimum of 60 percent Nero d'Avola and 10 to 40 percent Nocera. Other recommended or allowed red varieties can make up the balance. Ironically, the DOC does not specify a sweet white typology, as would approximate a Roman-period Mamertino. Given that Nocera is the dominant historic variety of the Milazzo area, it is fitting that it have a central role in the red Mamertino DOC. Vasari saw Nero d'Avola as the variety that would drive the Mamertino DOC. From a flavor point of view, the selection of Nero d'Avola helps distinguish Mamertino Rosso from Faro. Faro's principal variety is Nerello Mascalese.

Cambria. At Vinitaly 2011 I tasted the 2009 Nocera varietal wine Mastronicola, made by Cambria from Furnari, also in the Milazzo area. The wine was a deep purple red with a ruby rim and had a soft, slightly sweet, overripe taste. Though it was not as dark, tart, or astringent as Milazzo of the nineteenth century was reputed to be, it was very reminiscent of what I have read about the taste of nineteenth-century Faro. It shared with the Vasari Nocera a jammy, juicy character. The 2010 Mastronicola that I tasted at Vinitaly 2012 was more astringent.

Gaglio. Gaglio is a lot easier to say than the official name of this winery: La Flora di Gaglio Maria Teresa e Mondello Flora. Mother Marisa and daughter Flora, both architects by education, run this estate with five hectares (twelve acres) of vines that overlook the Tyrrhenian Sea, dotted with Stromboli and several other Aeolian islands. The location is in the township of Patti, known for its wine for centuries. Not too far away is Tindari, on a high promontory with a fourth century B.C. Greek amphitheater and a sanctuary where busloads of pilgrims arrive to pray to an icon of the Black Madonna. Mother and daughter oversee the growing and harvesting of the grapes. Though the estate has an old palmento that Flora can remember being used when she was a child, they bring the grapes to the Cambria Winery in nearby Furnari for vinification, which the consulting enologist Salvatore Martinico oversees. Grillo is now being planted all over Sicily. I tasted a Gaglio Grillo 2010, which had a mild fruity nose and a mouth with a pleasant sour-salt balance. Their leading wine is Leda, a 70 percent Nero d'Avola, 30 percent Cabernet Sauvignon. The 2008 had a moderate depth of red-brown, with purple at the meniscus. Beyond its mild blackberry nose, the wine had bright sourness and evident astringency. The 2010 Esdra Mamertino, which is a 100 percent Nero d'Avola, raises the ante with its high astringency, but in June 2012, at the time of tasting, it was a baby too young for my glass. Speaking of babies, the daughter of Flora, Giulia, born in 2004, may continue this legacy of women.

Gatti. At Vinitaly 2012 I discovered the Gatti estate, a recent entrant in the Mamertino DOC. In 2005 the owner, Nicolas Gatti Russo, replanted family vineyards dating from 1825 from three to five hundred meters (984 to 1,640 feet) in the Cuprani contrada on the northwest-facing slopes of the Nebrodi Mountains. The estate's 2010 100 percent Nocera wine, Sicè, had fresh sour cherry fruit and an astringent finish. It is a refreshing contrast to the ripe style of Nocera produced by Cambria.

Planeta. Planeta has entered the Mamertino DOC. It has a twenty-five-year lease to manage and use the fruit of nine hectares (twenty-two acres) of vineyards on Capo

Milazzo, a promontory dangling out into the Tyrrhenian Sea. It replanted these vine-yards in 2011. Alessio Planeta foresees a 60 percent Nero d'Avola, 40 percent Nocera blend. He believes that Nocera has potential and hopes that it will play a bigger role in the Mamertino DOC. He would have preferred planting the vineyards 100 percent to Nocera, but the DOC regulations do not allow this. He would even like to officially change the name of the Nocera variety to Mamertino.

Vasari.   Ruggero Vasari is the only producer with a wide range of Mamertino DOC wines. He is the only producer to make Mamertino Bianco DOC (he blends Catarratto, Inzolia, and Grillo) and Mamertino Bianco Riserva. He also makes Mamertino Rosso, the most common Mamertino DOC typology, and Mamertino Rosso Riserva. One of his Mamertino Rosso wines and his Mamertino Rosso Riserva are 100 percent Nero d'Avola. His wines are well made right down the line, except for a Nocera IGT that was jammy, very sour, and too pungent. Vasari doesn't believe that Nocera by itself or as a signifi-cant part of a blend makes a wine with a profile that the modern wine market would appreciate. Planeta's presence in the Mamertino DOC may challenge this perspective.

CEFALÙ

There are two other outposts of fine wine farther west along the coastline, in the vicinity of Cefalù. The vineyards are on hillsides that back up to the Madonie Mountains. They face north toward the Tyrrhenian Sea. Soils are clay-based calcareous. Rainfall is less than in locations to the east but still above average for Sicily. The northern exposure combined with adequate rainfall and the cool, humid clay soils has the potential to produce fresh, fruity wines with acidity and structure. I asked Sicilian wine produc-ers several times why wine production was so marginal in this area. Though they all believed it had potential, they suggested that the lack of a tradition of wine production was the major cause.

Abbazia Santa Anastasia.   Southeast of Cefalù facing the Tyrrhenian at Castelbuono is Abbazia Santa Anastasia. Francesco Lena, a Palermo builder, bought the site in 1980 and poured money into the three hundred hectare (741 acre) farm. His son, Gianfranco, was the business manager, and his daughter, Stefania, the enologist. Riccardo Cotarella followed Giacomo Tachis as the consulting enologist. Leonello Anello, Tuscany's well-known biodynamic consultant, helped to make the estate one of Sicily's leaders in this philosophically based agricultural system. The 2011 Zurrica Inzolia-Chardonnay and 2011 Sinestesia Sauvignon Blanc lacked varietal aromas and were thick in the mouth. The 2010 Passomaggio, a Nero d'Avola–Merlot blend, was aromatic, big, and tactile. Both the 2008 Montenero, a Bordeaux blend, and the 2008 Litra, a 100 percent Cabernet Sauvignon, were similarly rich extracted wines, with the Litra showing more elegance. These are wines to age. Sens(i)nverso, a biodynamic wine, is produced as both a varietal

Nero d'Avola and a varietal Cabernet Sauvignon. The 2007 and 2009 Cabernets were concentrated wines with fine astringency. The 2007 had some leather in the nose and was less tart. The clay soils and northerly exposure of Santa Anastasia's 420 to 450 meter (1,377 to 1,476 feet) elevations are well suited for red wines. At Vinitaly 2012 the red wines showed great character. The whites, in comparison, were heavy and clumsy. If the whites' varieties were planted at higher elevations and on rocky soils, they would be more elegant. As of 2012, Gianfranco Cordero is the new consulting enologist.

Simsider. Just south of Cefalù is Simsider, owned by Gabriele and Giulia Rappa. The vineyards are at six hundred meters (1,969 feet) on calcareous clay soil. Under the Museum label, they produce five different varietal wines: Chardonnay, Merlot, Nero d'Avola, Cabernet Sauvignon, and Sauvignon Blanc. Their Cantina di Suro brand comprises Ribot, a Nero d'Avola–Syrah blend, and Santa Barbara, a red Bordeaux blend. The wines are all well made and clean.

THE AEOLIAN ISLANDS

Malvasia delle Lipari is a sweet white wine that has had an excellent reputation for centuries. It is produced in the Aeolian Archipelago, about twenty-five miles northwest of Milazzo in the Tyrrhenian Sea. In 1883, Egidio Pollacci pronounced, in his respected text on the theory and practice of viticulture and enology, "The Malvasia variety produces excellent wine in several of our regions, but none are as exquisite as those of Stromboli and Sardinia, and above all as those of the Aeolian Islands, which have no equal in Italy."[12] The archipelago contains seven principal islands: Lipari, Salina, Vulcano, Filicudi, Panarea, Stromboli, and Alicudi. Volcanic action formed them, though today only the volcanoes on Stromboli and Vulcano are active. The Aeolian Archipelago is also called the Lipari Islands after its largest, most populous, and best-known island. Salina, smaller, less populous, and less well known, has been more famous than the other islands in the archipelago for the production of Malvasia delle Lipari, olive oil, and capers.

The name *Salina* derives from the saltern on the island's south side, a shallow inlet where salt was produced. The island is mountainous. Monte Fossa delle Felci is its highest peak, at 962 meters (3,156 feet). Monte dei Porri reaches 860 meters (2,822 feet). Both are extinct volcanoes. The town of Leni is on the south side of the island. Malfa is in the north. An inland valley, Valdichiesa, links the two. The most important area for vineyards and wine production is around and between Malfa and Leni.

Remains of obsidian implements that date back to 3000 B.C. have been found on Monte Fossa delle Felci. Obsidian is a black volcanic glass ideal for creating sharp-edged tools and weapons. Though the Lipari Islands have been civilized for thousands of years, the vine variety Malvasia may be a relative newcomer, perhaps taken from Greece by Venetians at the end of the 1500s. In the early 1800s English soldiers who were stationed at Messina to thwart a possible advance from Naples by Napoleon became avid consumers of Malvasia di Lipari. They spread the wine's fame to Britain and the rest of Europe. In the late nineteenth century Neapolitan merchants bought *vino di Salina,* a dark, tannic, and alcoholic red vino da taglio. This wine was also exported to England, South America, and northern Italy. From 1870 to 1890, steamship transport to Palermo routed away much of the sailing ship traffic that had formerly moved through Messina and the Aeolian Archipelago. Then, in 1890 an army of phylloxera devastated Salina's vineyards. Destitution arrived. At the end of the nineteenth century and the beginning of the twentieth, a mass emigration to America depopulated the island. After 1910, islanders left for Australia. Wine production devolved into a purely family affair rather than a commercial one. As Italy rose from the ashes of World War II, wealthy northern Italians discovered the islands as a summer holiday retreat. Carlo Hauner, a designer and artist from Brescia, visited Lipari during the 1960s. In the early 1970s he bought a summer home with vineyards on Salina. He purchased a total of twenty hectares (forty-nine acres) of vineyards, which eventually made him the largest producer on the island. A decade later he was selling his wines to foreign markets. He researched how the wine was traditionally made. He introduced drying on the vine and experimented with cooling techniques in his winery. The industry on the island has not developed much since that time. Only about six or seven producers are currently commercially active on a scale that is more than just local.

Salina's climate is warm, averaging 17.5°C (63.5°F), with little day-to-night temperature variation. Rainfall is low, less than on the Val Demone coastline or in the vicinity of Etna but more than in the rest of Sicily. Volcanic activity began at the site one million to nine hundred thousand years ago and ended thirteen thousand years ago, making Salina one of the oldest islands in the archipelago. Thousands of years of farmers working the soil and breaking it down has created topsoils whose nutrients are available to absorption by plant rootlets. The soil is ash gray, slightly acidic, and composed of sand and pumice. It is fast draining. The island, though, is rich in underground water. At Malfa and Leni the soil is very fertile. Malfa is the best area for growing Malvasia destined for passito wines. Valdichiesa is very sandy and, therefore, less fertile. The day-to-night temperature variation is greater in this upland valley due to its elevation of nearly four hundred meters (1,312 feet). Its location in the center of the island and its protection by mountains on either side enhance this temperature difference. Valdichiesa is the best place for growing grapes for dry red and white wine production.

There are some vineyards on other Aeolian Islands. Volcanic eruptions destroyed vineyards on Vulcano in the late 1880s. In 2000 Carlo Hauner Jr. planted vineyards there at four hundred meters (1,312 feet) where there is tuff and sand. Sulfur abounds in Vulcano's soil, and sulfurous fumes can be smelled in its air. On the plain of Castellaro on the island of Lipari, where Tenuta di Castellaro is, the soil is rich in sand, pumice, and obsidian.

The principal white varieties on the islands are Inzolia, Catarratto, and Malvasia di Lipari. The red ones are Corinto Nero, Nero d'Avola, and Sangiovese. Recent genetic research indicates that Corinto Nero and Sangiovese are the same variety. Wine law does not at present recognize this finding. The traditional method of training was low pergola. Current training systems such as Guyot and cordon-spur position vines lower to the ground and attach them to poles and wires. Vineyards can be found from sea level to four hundred meters (1,312 feet).

While the grape variety is Malvasia di Lipari, the DOC for the islands is named Malvasia delle Lipari. *Delle* is the plural of *di*. *Lipari* is plural in the DOC name because the appellation covers seven islands and not just the namesake one. Malvasia delle Lipari was decreed a DOC in 1974. By law, between 5 and 8 percent of Corinto Nero, which gives it a coppery tint, must be used in a blend that is otherwise Malvasia di Lipari. Malvasia di Lipari provides floral and citrus smells. Corinto Nero may be responsible for some of the cedary smells. Several producers on Salina told me that they do not think Corinto Nero contributes to the quality of the wine and would like to see the DOC regulations changed to make its addition optional rather than obligatory. The law allows three typologies of Malvasia: naturale, sweet but not a product of dried grapes; passito, made with grapes dried in the sun; and liquoroso, made with grapes which have been slightly dried. The naturale is a modern cold-fermented white wine. The passito is the classic version. Few, if any, liquoroso Malvasia delle Lipari DOC wines are made.

The grapes are late harvested, at about the third week of September. To make naturale they are pressed, cold-settled, and cold-fermented, in the same way most white wines are produced. To make passito the bunches are left outside for about seven to fifteen days on cane matting, exposed to the sun to dry. They are turned over at least twice a day so that the drying is even and mold doesn't colonize the side of the bunch not exposed to the sun. At night the bunches are covered to protect against dew. Producers do not want botrytis. They discard bunches that have not dried properly. In some years the drying period is so difficult that producers can't make Malvasia. This happened to Francesco Fenech in 2009, when he had to discard his crop.

Once the drying for passito is complete, the bunches are put into a press so that the juice can be extracted and collected in a tank. The juice cold-settles for a day or so. Selected yeast is added. Fermentation occurs at 20°C (68°F) until it is blocked when the wine reaches 12 to 14 percent alcohol with the desired amount of residual sugar. The wine is racked off the lees and stays in tank for several more months, until the following June at least. Then it is bottled. In the liquoroso version, the addition of spirits blocks fermentation, resulting in a finished wine with high levels of both alcohol and residual sugar. There are four bottlers on Salina: Hauner, Caravaglio, Fenech, and Virgona. There are no regulations prohibiting off-island bottling.

It is useful to compare Malvasia delle Lipari to Pantelleria. The Aeolian Islands are more humid than Pantelleria. The harvest of Zibibbo on Pantelleria begins in early

August, when the climate is sunny and dry. The harvest of Malvasia di Lipari begins in the middle of September, when it is more likely to be rainy. While Zibibbo has a thick skin that resists physical bruising and botrytis, Malvasia di Lipari has a thin one that is susceptible to both. On Pantelleria, Zibibbo bunches raisin under the sun on mats in drier conditions, more quickly, and with fewer mold problems. As a result, their juice is more concentrated. Since the 1980s the wine trade has shown greater interest in and excitement for Pantelleria than Malvasia delle Lipari. While there are 560 hectares (1,384 acres) planted for Pantelleria DOC wines, there are only forty-six (114 acres) planted for Malvasia delle Lipari DOC. The wines of the Aeolian Archipelago had their period of greatest success in the nineteenth century, whereas Pantelleria was most noted for high quality in the late twentieth century. Francesco Intoricia of Casano in Marsala once mentioned, "Salina is more old than young." He could have added that Pantelleria is more young than old. On both islands, however, it is so much easier to make a living through tourism than viticulture and wine production that it is doubtful that either wine culture will expand much in the future.

Fenech. Francesco Fenech comes from a family that produced Malvasia on Salina in the 1800s. He sources grapes from some thirty-five tiny vineyards in Malfa. He produces a highly aromatic but structured Malvasia delle Lipari by cold-macerating the skins of the sun-dried grapes, blending the free-run press juice with the juice from a second hard pressing of the skins, and then combining the two juices for fermentation. From the free-run juice he gets the aroma. From the press juice he gets tannins, which provide the structure. His Malvasia delle Lipari is, along with Tasca d'Almerita's Capofaro, the most aromatic and lively wine on the island. He makes ten thousand half bottles per year. He also buys grapes from off-island to make still dry red wine and white wine, sold under the brand name Perciato.

Hauner. On the death of his father, Carlo Hauner, in 1996, Carlo Hauner Jr. took over responsibility for the family winery. Gianfranco Sabbatino has assisted him. Hauner makes about fifty thousand bottles annually, half of it Malvasia delle Lipari naturale and the other half passito. Of its twenty hectares (forty-nine acres) of vineyards, Hauner owns five on Vulcano, where it makes a red wine called Hierà. While Hauner exports the wine to various countries through different importers, Carlo Pellegrino, the Marsala company, distributes it in the Italian market. Hauner makes a Salina IGT white wine with Malvasia. It is dense, dry, and tangy, with some fig, caramel, apple, and banana smells. The Salina IGT Rosso is a Nero d'Avola–Nerello Mascalese blend that matures some time in barrique before bottling. It is a well-made dry red wine. The estate has another barrique-matured red wine, Rosso Antonello IGT Salina. The wine Carlo Hauner is dedicated to Carlo Jr.'s father. This is a concentrated dry white wine made from a blend of Inzolia, Catarratto, Grecanico, and Grillo. After some cold maceration, it matures in both stainless steel and oak barrel. This wine is thicker and denser than the Salina IGT Bianco.

It has a slight toasty nose. Honey, dried figs, apricots, and a syrupy sweetness dominate the Malvasia delle Lipari passito. Hierà, the Hauner wine made from Vulcano grapes, mixes cedars, spices, and prunes in the nose. In the mouth it is ripe and thick. The grape varieties used are Nero d'Avola, Grenache, and Nocera. Hauner also produces a "riserva" Malvasia delle Lipari. I was unable, however, to find any mention of a "riserva" category in the DOC regulations.

Tasca d'Almerita (Capofaro). Tasca d'Almerita owns five hectares (twelve acres) of vineyards at the site of a lighthouse (*faro*) on the northeast side of Salina. It makes a passito Malvasia delle Lipari–style wine under the name Tenuta Capofaro. The wine is not a Malvasia delle Lipari passito DOC, though the production process is very similar. It is bottled as an IGT Sicilia. Capofaro does not include Corinto Nero with its Malvasia di Lipari. In the vineyard, leaves are left on the vines to shade the berries and to reduce canopy temperature. The resulting wine has more aromas and higher acidity. The grape bunches are dried indoors to preserve fruity aromas. The wine has a lower alcohol level (11 percent) than Malvasia delle Lipari DOC wines. It is pale amber-yellow, with a fruity apricot, crème caramel nose and a sweet but tart, light, and delicate mouth. Tasca d'Almerita also has a luxury boutique resort at this site. From it you can see the white clouds of steam and ash billowing from the volcano on the island of Stromboli at the northeast edge of the Aeolian Archipelago, the most northerly point of the Val Demone and Sicily itself.

Other recommended producers:

Barone di Villagrande
Caravaglio
Colosi
Giona
Lantieri
Salvatore D'Amico
Tenuta di Castellaro
Virgona

14

THE GARDEN-VINEYARD

This mountain side is mine—this living rock
serves as my grottos' roof: there, one need not
endure the dogdays' sun, the winter's cold.
The branches in my orchard bend beneath
the weight of apples; on my trailing vines,
some of my grapes are tawny gold, and some
are purple. . . .
. . . Your own hands will find
tender strawberries in the shaded woods,
and cherries in the autumn, and two sorts
of plums—the purple ones with their dark juice
and plums more prized, as yellow as new wax.
If you would only marry me, you would
not lack chestnuts or fruits of the arbutus—
each tree would serve your pleasure and your use.

Ovid, *Metamorphoses* (translation
by Allen Mandelbaum in *Ovid in Sicily*)

We met Salvo Foti on our first morning on Mount Etna. It was June 2008 and we had come to Sicily to discover the world of Sicilian wine. Salvo was the first winegrower we met on this trip. Crouching in the Benanti vineyard on Monte Serra, he scooped up two handfuls of the loose topsoil. It looked like black rock candy granules. He poured it in our cupped hands so we could feel its surprising lightness. Salvo explained that this ripiddu, as it is called in Sicilian, dusts the vineyard when the prevailing northwest winds carry the volcano's emissions high in the air. Salvo told us how the iron, copper and other minerals in these particles of pumice stone rapidly break down and nourish the vines. It was clear that this wine road on Etna was like no other. Salvo then brought us to see his own vineyard, with individual bush vines (alberello) at more than one thousand meters (3,281 feet) above sea level. Along the way he stopped to show us an ancient gigantic chestnut tree and handed us hazelnuts that were strewn around a smaller cluster of trees nearby. When we parted that afternoon, Salvo brought us a brimming wooden crate of deep red cherries that his vineyard manager, Maurizio, had picked that very morning. Like his Nerello Mascalese and Grenache grapes, these cherries were grown at a high elevation on Etna and were organic. As we drove down from

Mount Etna to the southeast coast of Val di Noto and then west to Val di Mazara, we tasted and relished the fruit of Etna.

During our travels around the island, Sicilian winegrowers would enthusiastically pluck the fruit of a nearby tree or bush for us to taste as we explored their vineyards. There was the Femminello lemon in Syracuse, the *costoluto* cherry tomato in Pachino, the black and white mulberries in Ispica, the Pizzuta d'Avola almonds in Noto, the carob bean in Vittoria, the Fragolina di Ribera strawberries in Menfi, the miniature apples and wild blackberries in Pantelleria, the white plums of Monreale, and the wild caper buds in Salina. Sicily's winegrowers have a deep affection for and attachment to their land—and its *materia prima* ("raw materials"). They are proud of the island's fertility and the quality of its fruit. They also celebrate its diverse agricultural products: the olive oil and honey from the Hyblaean Mountains in Val di Noto, the salt from the saltworks off the coast of Trapani in Val di Mazara, and the manna from the ash trees on the Madonie Mountains in Val Demone.

In contrast with Homer's epic hero Odysseus, we found the Sicilians, from our first encounter with them, to be a people with a deeply rooted sense of place and a profound respect for the fruits of their land. This experience was at its most intense on Etna. The Cyclops of Homer's *Odyssey* was a shepherd who took the fertility of his land for granted. The Cyclops of Ovid's *Metamorphoses*, in contrast, is a lovelorn giant wooing his beloved with the apples, grapes, strawberries, cherries, plums, and chestnuts of his "living rock." Foti was our first guide on Etna. The flavor memory of his mountain cherries still lingers. How could this mountain hardened with ancient and modern lava flows be the garden paradise of Theocritus's bucolic poetry and Ovid's *Metamorphoses*? The Cyclops of Homer's imagination personifies the wildness and ferocity of the volcano. The winegrowers of Etna have always lived with this wildness and ferocity. They cultivate and harvest the renewal that follows from the lava's decay. Their small plots of land are bordered by walls and layered with terraces made of black lava. Their vines are mixed with olive, fruit, and nut trees. Wild greens and herbs carpet the soil beneath the trees. These are the garden-vineyards of Etna.

On the northeast face of Etna is the small town of Linguaglossa. It is a curious name for any speaker of Italian. *Lingua* means "tongue" and *glossa* derives from the Italian word *grossa* (*rossa* in Sicilian), meaning "big or thick." By one account it is the tongue-like shape of the surrounding township, which starts at five hundred meters (1,640 feet) above sea level and rises up the mountain slope to an elevation of eighteen hundred meters (5,906 feet), that has earned it this moniker. Another account attributes the name to the story that the town was originally built on seven ancient lava flows, which also look like tongues. The patron saint of the town is Saint Egidio, who, according to legend, saved it from destruction following an eruption on the northeast flank of Etna in 1566. The five-thousand-plus inhabitants of the town are known as Linguaglossesi. Giovanni Raiti first brought us there in 2008 after a full day of exploring the vineyards and cantinas of Etna. Giovanni is an agronomist from Linguaglossa who has researched autochthonous vine varieties for the Region of Sicily's Department of Agriculture and Forestry for more than a decade. He parked his small, dusty Suzuki 4x4 in a small piazza, and we got out to stretch our legs and catch some of the local color. The only color in sight was black. The roads are made of massive black lava blocks, and so are the surrounding buildings. It was almost dinnertime, so the square was desolate except for a few curious onlookers. Giovanni asked us if we would like to see his own small vineyard, less than a kilometer (0.6 miles) outside the town center, in the Lavina contrada. Giovanni's land is a labor of love. It is a little more than two hectares (5 acres), of which one and a half (3.7 acres) are planted to vines at six hundred meters (1,969 feet) above sea level. Before it was his, all of this land was planted to nut trees. Giovanni explained that by the middle of the nineteenth century, citrus trees (*agrumi*) began to replace vines in the fertile and well-irrigated plains of Mascali, which extend from the Ionian seacoast to the foothills of the eastern flank of Etna. In this period the wine merchants and growers of Mascali increasingly planted their vineyards at higher elevations on the northeastern slopes of Etna. At the beginning of the twentieth century, after the phylloxera epidemic in France had been stemmed and French buyers for Etna's wines had vanished, the mountain vineyards of Etna were in crisis, so the winegrowers in Linguaglossa planted olive trees and groves of hazelnut, pistachio, chestnut, and walnut trees (*nocelletti*) in their place.

Giovanni had planted his Carricante, Catarratto, and Grillo vines only the previous winter. They were baby vines, but we were there to see Giovanni's nascent dream. It was almost dusk as we entered his land through a wire fence. We had to pass through thickets of chestnut and hazelnut trees before the rows of fragile young vines appeared. The centuries-old lava terraces and walls were now overgrown with wild vines, ivy, and prickly pear. The gnarled olive trees stood guard near the walls. In the corner of the vineyard was a menacing tower (*torretta*) of volcanic rock. It looked like an ancient Mayan temple. The peasant farmers (*contadini*) who first cleared the land to plant vines centuries ago built this structure with the blocks of hardened lava that they dug up. This is not the picturesque jewel-like vineyard you might see in Burgundy or Napa. And at first glance it bears no resemblance to the pristine orchard-vineyard of King Laertes (Odysseus's father) in the *Odyssey*, with its well-ordered pear, apple, fig, and olive trees and more than fifty vine rows. Here there was wilderness all around, and the presence of the encroaching forest was imposing. As we walked, Giovanni explained that the lava walls were built to protect the garden's bounty from shepherds and their roaming, hungry flocks. He pointed to different fruit trees scattered around the vineyard, saying that on Etna a small parcel of land was traditionally cultivated by a single family to supply all of its produce throughout the year. His dream from boyhood was to have his own vineyard (*vigneto*), olive grove (*oliveto*), and orchard (*frutteto*)—a garden (*giardino*) that he would tend to provide for his family in every season. Giovanni told us of his plans to use only organic farming methods and to ultimately produce a natural wine of this vigneto-giardino on Etna. The process of decay and renewal was alive—and in the capable hands of an authentic vignaiolo.

There is a gentleness and solidity about Giovanni that is exceptional. One could imagine him in another era as a Capuchin or Benedictine monk tending his monastery's mountain vineyards. As we drove back to town, he regaled us with tales of Linguaglossa and its history. First recorded in 1145 as a commune within the diocese of Messina under the Norman King Roger II, Linguaglossa ultimately bought its freedom from the feudal control of a baronial family in 1630 during the reign of King Phillip IV of Spain. The citizens of Linguaglossa, now a self governing town answerable only to the king of Spain, were free to cultivate their land how they chose. This was the period when the Linguaglossesi first began to plant vines, alongside all of the fruit trees and crops that would nourish their families and commune. For this reason the vineyards in Linguaglossa were among the first on the northeast flank of Etna. We began to wonder to ourselves if Lavina, the contrada where Giovanni's vineyard is located, had taken its name from the Spanish phrase *la viña,* meaning "the vineyard." By the time Giovanni dropped us off at our *agriturismo* (farm holiday house), it was nightfall and we were already planning our road trip south to Val di Noto the next morning.

On a subsequent visit to Etna, in October 2010, we contacted Giovanni to visit his garden-vineyard again. We agreed to meet early one morning at a hotel in the center of Linguaglossa. As we drove on the town's main street, we were reminded of our first visit there with Giovanni two years earlier. Tucked in a narrow alley behind the black and dark gray lava facades of the buildings lining both sides of Via Roma we found Via Marconi, and before us appeared a magnificent pistachio green palace. It was a revelation. Like a venerable pistachio tree flowering on barren volcanic rock, the Shalai Hotel is a verdant oasis in a desert of blackness. It is also a monument to Etna's rich agricultural production of the eighteenth and nineteenth centuries. Inside, cool modernity complements the frescoed palatial architecture. With our cappuccinos we were offered fresh-baked breads and blackberry jam made from fruit picked by the proprietor's mother in a nearby town farther north called Solicchiata. The bowl on our table brimmed with fresh-harvested Red Delicious apples from Etna. Giovanni's garden felt close at hand.

After breakfast we joined Giovanni in his well-worn 4x4 for the drive. He offered to take us around the north flank of Etna first, past Passopisciaro and up to the town of Randazzo. Driving north, he pointed to the pitch-black masses of hardened lava flows (*sciare,* the plural of *sciara*) from the 1981 eruption that had destroyed several vineyards, including those in the Allegracori ("Happy Hearts") contrada in Randazzo. The lava practically reached the street. It looked like the surface of a barren planet, without any sign of the once big-hearted vineyards. It was a vivid and poignant reminder of the volcano's ever-present power. As we drove on, the colors of Etna's vines, olive trees, fruits, and flowers once again filled the scenery. We had reached the road that encircles Etna from 850 to 1,000 meters (2,789 to 3,281 feet), known as the Quota Mille. Traveling around Etna can be disorienting at times, in part because the summit is not always in view. But there was no mistaking that we were at a higher altitude. The forest had become denser. Overgrown oak and chestnut trees, now burned, covered an abandoned set of terraces—the skeleton of a once vibrant vineyard. There were horses grazing in the pasture to our left and gigantic cows that had wandered into the street and were grazing either side of our vehicle. We were in the zone of the forest and the land of the shepherds. Giovanni explained that from the base of Etna to its upper realms is a world of microclimates. In the coastal plains of Mascali, overlooking the Ionian Sea, there is a tropical climate, in which small bananas grow. From there the lemon, orange, mandarin, and other citrus trees flourish at the base of the mountain, where there is plenty of both water and sun. Then the vineyards and olive, fruit, and nut trees climb from four hundred to one thousand meters (1,312 to 3,281 feet). Above one thousand meters the oak, chestnut, and pine trees dominate until eighteen hundred meters (5,906 feet). The tree growing at the highest altitude is the white birch (*betulla*), a species more commonly spotted in the forests of northern Europe.

As we wound our way around the Quota Mille, Giovanni recounted the story of the Benedictine monk Giuseppe Recupero, who in the eighteenth century had walked around Mount Etna twelve times in his quest to discover and chronicle this mountain also known as Mongibello (a name of part Latin and part Arabic origin, both meaning "mountain"). Recupero classified three principal regions of Etna: the Piemontese, defined by its fertility and agricultural production; the Nemorosa, comprising the immense forest that hugs the next-highest band of the mountain; and the Nevosa, from the snow up to the summit cone. As we headed east on the Quota Mille we could see the beginning of the Nemorosa region to our right and the upper reaches of the Piemontese region to our left. We turned left onto the smaller provincial road aptly called the Mareneve ("Sea-snow") to head south, back to Giovanni's land of vineyards, orchards, and olive groves. Along the way he described how the desert of the hardened lava comes back to life on Etna. After about 150 years the first life to emerge are lichens, which begin to break down the lava to create the living soil that will sustain future plant life. The lichens are succeeded by herbs or grasses called *gramineae,* which further colonize the lava. Giovanni told us that driving on the Quota Mille in May is spectacular. It is swept in yellow. The *ginestra,* or broom, covers the old lava flows and signifies the beginning of perennial life. Only after about three hundred years can grapevines and olives begin to sink their roots into the deeper mineral-rich soil. We were at the gate of Giovanni's property and felt like we had traveled through time and space.

We were curious to see how his garden-vineyard had grown in the previous two and a half years. We entered through the same wire gate, but on this day the sun was shining brightly, the birds were trilling, and the walled garden seemed more inviting. Giovanni brought us to a stand of chestnut trees. He had cleared away the trunks of the smaller chestnut trees that cluster around the base of the older trees, to preserve the strength of the bigger ones. We could see the peak of Mongibello in the background.

The summit cone was billowing white smoke, making it look like Etna touched the blue sky. This was one of the clearest views we had seen of the mountaintop. As we walked among the chestnut and hazelnut trees, Giovanni's dedication to his land was clear. He explained that even when the vines were pulled in favor of the nut and olive trees a century ago, the landowner always planted fruit trees for his family's year-round sustenance—cherries, apples, pears, plums, peaches, pomegranates, and figs. This form of intensive cultivation has deep roots on Etna. As a boy Giovanni helped his father tend six or seven small parcels of land throughout the countryside. Giovanni proudly told us how his eighty-three-year-old father still worked side by side with him to clear the ground, tend the vines, prune the fruit trees, and rebuild the igneous walls and terraces.

Giovanni described how the walls restrain the dense forest. If the land is left untended for even two years, the oak trees and the spreading ivy reclaim it. It requires constant cultivation. And yet he leaves the carpet of wild herbs, mushrooms, and greens beneath his hazelnut and olive trees intact, wanting not to simplify his garden but to embrace its *ricchezza* ("richness"). He plucked a handful of the wild herbs and greens, identifying them by their Sicilian names and explaining how they were best prepared at home. He presented us with a bouquet of the *cavulicedda, finochiettu* (fennel), *sparaci* (asparagus), *spinacina*, and *pitrusinu* (wild parsley). Olive oil, garlic, and red pepper are key ingredients in their preparation at Giovanni's home. He bent down to gather several hazelnuts that lay on the ground and with his bare hands cracked them open for us to savor. Then he brought us to see a cluster of olive trees that included the Nocellara di Etna, San Benedetto, and Biancolilla varieties and several other indigenous cultivars. He explained how the Nocellara di Etna olives produce a more bitter and spicier oil than the other two varieties, with its higher level of antioxidants giving it more aging potential. Pointing to the empty parcel up to the wall on our right, Giovanni showed us where he will be planting another vineyard of six thousand square meters (one and a half acres). He has never used chemical fertilizers or pesticides on his land. Instead he plants a leguminous plant (*lupino*) every November and then turns under its thick green vegetation to fix the nitrogen level in the soil. Past the nut and olive trees, pink tiger lilies and a pomegranate tree graced the entrance to the vineyard and fruit orchard. Giovanni told us that the flowers were planted by prior generations of landowners to beautify their vineyards and are found all over Etna, even in abandoned vineyards.

The neat wired rows of Giovanni's then two-and-a-half-year-old vines in the distance stood in stark contrast to the terraces bordering the vineyard that were now home to wild prickly pear plants and wild vines. On one old terrace the vines grew horizontally through small cutouts in the face of the volcanic rock wall. There were small, compact bunches of violet *nerelli* grapes hanging on the old vines, ripe for the picking. Giovanni plucked a handful for us to sample. The whitish bloom (*pruina*) of the native yeast covered the berries. They were crunchy and juicy and sweet. Giovanni explained how these vines were originally planted to grow through the walls in order to expand the growing area of the vineyard and to capture maximum light for the vines. This system is called *sparraturi* in Sicilian. We walked into the vineyard through a passageway between two taller stone walls. There was a lush mound of ivy (*edera*) cascading overhead. The bees were harvesting the pollen from its white flowers. Giovanni said that the flowers' heady honeysuckle aroma always reminds him of the grape harvest (*vendemmia*) in October, when the edera blooms. Up until ten or fifteen years ago the family winegrowers of Linguaglossa would hang a sprig of edera on their front door to signify that they had fresh wine for sale.

Giovanni had harvested his white grapes just two days earlier. After a gentle pressing the berries were left for twenty-four hours to cryomacerate on their skins in the presence of native yeast. The juice would now ferment for the next thirty days in temperature-controlled stainless steel tanks at a modern cantina in Passopisciaro, up the road. Giovanni proudly declared, "*Senza aggiunta di solfiti* [Without the addition of sulfites]!" He showed us several glorious-looking grape bunches that were left on the vines because they had not matured evenly. The vines were tall and lush, harnessed on wires and free of their fruit. Along one side of the vine rows was a row of fruit trees that Giovanni had planted in the past several years. There were the Cola, a small yellow pear-shaped antique apple of Etna, and the Gelato Cola, a cross whose delicate white pulp becomes transparent after a frost. One apple tree had two grafts and grew two different varieties. As we walked at the edge of the vineyard, Giovanni pointed in turn to each passing fruit tree—Tabacchiera peach (shaped like a donut), apricot, Spineddu pear, plum, fig, lemon, and Mastrantona cherry trees. There were also the Sorb apple trees that Giovanni had planted so he could use their wood as stakes in the vineyard. He described the sequence of fruits harvested from May through November. In May the apricots, plums, and cherries ripen, followed by the pears and small wild strawberries from the forest (*fragoline di bosco*) in June. July brings peaches and prickly pears, which ripen through September. In August the almonds, walnuts, and blackberries are ready for harvest. In September the apples ripen alongside the hazelnuts and pistachios. White grapes usually mature by the end of September, and the various red grape varieties ripen in October, at the same time as the pomegranates. By November the chestnuts and olives are ready to be picked, along with the Natalina fig, which earned its name because it is enjoyed through the Christmas season. Giovanni told us that he picks his lemons in every season, as the lemon trees flower five times throughout the year on Etna. How very surprised Homer and his mythological heroes would have been to see the orchard-vineyard of King Laertes thriving right here in the wilds of Etna. The distant voice of Ovid's Cyclops echoed in the cool morning air: "Each tree would serve your pleasure and your use."

We returned to Etna in March 2011 to attend the annual Contrade dell'Etna, at which most of the Etna winegrowers gather for the day in a cavernous stone barn to pour their wines for the public and one another. We saw numerous winegrowers whom we had seen on our previous visits to Etna, including Pietro Di Giovanni. We had met Pietro on our first trip to Etna, in 2008. He is as unique for his diminutive stature as for the intensity of his energy. In 2008 he was undeterred by the cast on his leg as he raced up steep slopes to show us several high-elevation vineyards. At the time he had also been preparing to run the annual Etna Sky Marathon, which he had completed the previous November. In 2011 he greeted us enthusiastically and invited us to come taste a new wine, Quantico. After making our way through the crowd, we arrived at his stand to see Giovanni Raiti exuberantly pouring Quantico. Giovanni and Pietro explained that they are partners in the creation of this natural white wine. Giovanni is the agronomist and uses only organic methods to work the soil and care for the vines. Pietro is the enologist and makes the wine without the addition of any sulfites or other additives. It is a 70 percent–20 percent–10 percent blend of the Carricante, Catarratto, and Grillo that we had first seen in 2008. Giovanni was pouring for us from one of only two thousand bottles produced in 2009. The name *Quantico* was hand-painted in white letters on a block of pine wood propped on Giovanni's small slice of the table. There was a wooden stand with carved-out cups filled with pistachios and hazelnuts to savor with the wine. The wine was fresh and clean, with aromas of candied citrus peel, honey, and white pear—the fruits of Giovanni's garden-vineyard.

In a small museum in Messina, the capital city of Val Demone, northeast of Linguaglossa, hangs a quiet jewel of a painting. It was created in Messina in 1473 and is known as *Madonna with St. Gregory and St. Benedict.* It is the work of a fifteenth-century artist, Antonello da Messina, a native son of the city. The centerpiece of a religious multipanel work, the painting was created for the Monastery of St. Gregory, which stood on a summit overlooking the Strait of Messina and was believed to occupy the site of an ancient temple of Jupiter. In commissioning the polyptych, the monks of St. Gregory agreed to pay Antonello six *salme* (almost twenty hectoliters [528 gallons]) of fresh must from their next grape harvest. Antonello presented the completed painting to the monks by the third week of September, in time for the upcoming vendemmia. In 1908 the monastery was destroyed by an earthquake that laid waste to the city and killed more than sixty thousand people. The painting survived and is a symbol of what once was and could still be realized by Sicily—and its artists, writers, and winegrowers. From an island that was considered an artistic hinterland during the Italian Renaissance, a young Sicilian ventured to Naples on mainland Italy to master the skill of oil painting when it was largely unknown in the artistic centers of Rome, Florence, Milan, and Venice. He is believed to have learned this fine art from Flemish artists schooled in the techniques of Jan van Eyck. Antonello is known to have then spent a formative period in Venice and to have influenced the work of Giovanni Bellini (who later schooled Titian, considered the most accomplished artist of the Venetian School of oil painting in the sixteenth century).

It would be easy to pass by this painting as another Madonna and child set against a gilded two-dimensional background. But the luminous blue eyes of the Christ child, who wears a vinelike piece of red coral at the end of a fine necklace graced with a single bead resembling a red currant, catch our eyes. The delicate fingers of his right hand grasp a yellow apple flushed with a ripe russet. His left hand holds two cherries joined by their lignified stems. The Madonna's right hand clasps the baby on her lap, and her outstretched left hand delicately holds several more cherries for her child. They are ripe ruby globes, translucent on one face and opaque on the other, covered with the whitish yeast fresh from their harvest. It is the pruina, or bloom, that Giovanni showed us on the ripening grape berries on his old wall vines. The vinelike foliage of the wild lily covers the Madonna's burgundy velvet mantle from top to bottom. Even without knowing the religious iconography of these fruits and plants, the viewer understands that Antonello da Messina was intimately familiar with the materia prima of his Val Demone.

There is a more famous painting of a similar scene, known as *Madonna of the Cherries*, created by Titian around 1516 and now hanging in Vienna's Imperial Picture Gallery. While Antonello's earlier work is less recognized than Titian's, it is clear that the Sicilian's exquisite mastery of light and expression of natural detail had a profound impact on the renowned artists of the High Renaissance. In our current enological epoch the wines and winemakers of Piedmont, Tuscany, and the Veneto (much like the art and artists of the Italian Renaissance) are on prominent display. And yet in the garden-vineyards of Sicily, authentic winegrowers like Salvo Foti, Giovanni Raiti, and Pietro Di Giovanni are creating wines that capture the vibrant light and fruit of their island home—and making their own lasting impression on the world of wine.

AFTERWORD

To the parade of enlightened travelers who ventured to Sicily from the classical age through the early twentieth century, the island represented "that miraculous centre upon which so many radii of world history converge."[1] These explorers, writers, and artists set out to discover this ancient "land of gods and heroes," in the words of Alexis de Tocqueville.[2] Their journals provide detailed accounts of Sicily's history, topography, geology, climate, culture, agriculture, food, and wine. In the early seventeenth century the Frenchman Pierre d'Avity declared that Sicily "perhaps surpasses, in fertility, any island in the Mediterranean, yielding every kind of fruit" and "produces the most delicious wine in the world."[3] In 1787 Johann Wolfgang von Goethe, who pioneered ideas at the core of modern botany, described the grapevines on Mount Etna as giving "evidence of meticulous cultivation."[4] Traveling around Mount Etna in the early nineteenth century, Tocqueville was struck by the prosperity in the towns around Etna compared with those in the rest of Sicily. He described an "enchanted country" where in almost every field "corn, vines, and fruit-trees" were "growing and thriving together."[5] These continental explorers also brought with them the rational and scientific principles that would help to illuminate the thinking of Sicily's most enlightened reformers.

The modern-day enologists who have come to Sicily from Piedmont, Tuscany, and other points north since the 1980s have been similarly drawn to the island's history and potential for quality. Along with their continental grape varieties, they brought the knowledge and experience that had earned them respect among international wine journalists and merchants. Sicilian winegrowers welcomed these outsiders to their soil. They knew they had much to learn. Having established themselves in the export market with star international varieties, alone and married with Nero d'Avola, the winegrowers of Sicily are now planting new roots. They are discovering the potential of their indigenous varieties and the diversity of their island's territories. They are rediscovering alberello and even amphorae. They are learning how to integrate the foreign with the native and the modern with the ancient. They are striving to unite for a common purpose and to honor their rich diversity. This is a search for identity.

In this quest there are no better models for the winegrowers of Sicily than the incisive Sicilian authors who have given Sicily its own identity on the global stage. So long denied that identity by the circumstances of history, Sicily has been honored nonetheless by the authentic voices of its brilliant poets, playwrights, and storytellers. Remarkably, the Sicilian language does not have a future tense. It would be easy to conclude that the absence of "*I will*" stems from a lack of free will. The story of Sicily is one of domination. But it is also one of survival. The story of the Sicilian language is as rich and complex as Sicily's history. Sicilian is considered one of the oldest Romance languages to derive from Latin. It is laced with Arabic, Old Provençal, and Spanish words, which evoke images of those now-distant conquerors and their diverse cultures. The Sicilian word *taibbu*, for example, derives from the Arabic *tayyib* (meaning "good") and was used to refer to a "perfect wine that has a fine taste."[6] The only surviving poem of the woman whom some scholars believe was the first female poet of Italy, La Nina Siciliana, was written in thirteenth-century Sicily in a proto-Italian influenced by the refined style of the Provençal troubadours. However, it was the Tuscan dialect of the late-thirteenth and early-fourteenth-century Florentine poets Dante, Boccaccio, and Petrarch that became the official language of Italy, with Sicilian (and all other regional languages) being relegated to the status of dialect. And while the Sicilian School that flowered in the court of Frederick II is credited with writing the first lyric poetry in Italianate vernacular, it would be several more centuries before literary works in Sicilian or by Sicilian authors were recognized beyond the island.

Antonio Veneziano was a sixteenth-century Sicilian poet who was a contemporary of Miguel de Cervantes. He wrote his love songs in Sicilian. He was strident about its use at a time when the Tuscan dialect was becoming widely accepted as the purest form of Italian. Veneziano also drew on popular Sicilian folktales and fables for his themes, making his poetry autochthonous in both form and substance. In his time he was recognized outside Sicily for his poetic greatness, and in the intervening centuries Sicilians have embraced him as a heroic literary figure. He argued that it was only right and natural that he should express himself in his mother tongue: "Perhaps the world expects different fruits from my wit, but in what language could I begin if not with the language that I learned first and suckled with my milk? . . . It would certainly be odd if Homer who was Greek and wrote in Greek, Horace who lived where Latin was spoken and wrote in Latin, Petrarch who was Tuscan and wrote in Tuscan, if I who am Sicilian did not find it more appropriate to write in Sicilian."[7]

Like Veneziano, Giovanni Meli wrote his moral fables and other poems in Sicilian. Early in his career Meli trained as a physician, ministering to the peasants and the dispossessed in a rural town outside Palermo, and he later became a professor of chemistry. While honoring his authentic Sicilian voice, Meli was influenced by the Enlightenment's embrace of both culture and science. He became one of the most respected Italian poets of the late eighteenth century. The following stanza is from a drinking song that he wrote in the form of a dithyramb, an ancient Greek hymn to the wine god Dionysus.

> If you want to live in joy
> drink red wine throughout your life,
> the red wine that's made in Mascali
> which when sold out of a stein
> will be looked on with disdain,
> but when it's bottled,
> well tarred
> and sealed
> by a clever foreigner
> who comes barking in the square:
> "Drink, my friends, this wine's from France!"
> then it's bought as an elixir.[8]

While celebrating wines from various Sicilian towns, Meli's drinking song provides us with an ironic image of Sicilian wine being bottled and sold as a prized French wine by "a clever foreigner."

In the line of Sicilian authors who championed the Sicilian language, Nino Martoglio has a place of prominence. Martoglio lived in Catania at the end of the nineteenth and beginning of the twentieth century. He is credited with founding modern Sicilian theater and was an early mentor to Sicily's most renowned playwright and first Nobel laureate, Luigi Pirandello. Martoglio was also a poet who wrote solely in Sicilian. In the preface to a posthumous collection of poems by Martoglio, Pirandello honored his teacher's native Sicilian voice and authentic expression of the "flavor and color that cannot exist anywhere else."[9] In one of his poems, Martoglio celebrates his ability to capture these flavors and colors:

> Because the way I talk, they like to swear,
> brings smells of home: pistachio nuts, a hint
> of shelled, dry almonds, rows of prickly pears,
> of orange blossoms and of calamint.[10]

Like Veneziano, Meli, and Martoglio, the authentic winegrowers of Sicily who are finding expression in their native grape varieties and distinct growing areas are capturing the "flavor and color that cannot exist anywhere else." In their heroic efforts to express the essence of this magnificent place to the world, they need look no further than their own poets. For a young Marsala winegrower named Marco De Bartoli, the Sicilian poet Salvatore Quasimodo was such a guiding star. Quasimodo won the Nobel Prize for Literature in 1959. His lyrical poetry evokes both the ancient and the ephemeral sensations of his island home. Like his ideal of the modern poet, the modern Sicilian winegrower is called to express his own land and time.[11]

> Look! on the trunk
> buds break:
> a newer green than the grass,
> balm to the heart:
> the trunk seemed already dead,
> leaning over the gully.
>
> And everything seems to me like a miracle;
> . . . .
> this green, bursting the bark,
> that even last night was not there.[12]

As the bud "bursting the bark" of an ancient, gnarled vine, the culture of wine in Sicily is reborn.

NOTES

Epigraph. Ovid, "My Eyes," in *Ovid in Sicily: A New Verse Translation of Selections from the "Metamorphoses,"* translated by Allen Mandelbaum (New York: Sheep Meadow Press, 1986), 13. Reproduced with permission from the Allen Mandelbaum Estate.

CHAPTER 1. THE ORIGINS OF SICILIAN WINE AND CULTURE

1. Homer, *The Odyssey of Homer: A New Verse Translation,* translated by Allen Mandelbaum (Berkeley: University of California Press, 1990), 176.
2. Ibid., 178.
3. William Younger, *Gods, Men, and Wine* (Cleveland: Wine and Food Society, 1966), 91–92.
4. Homer, *The Odyssey,* 185.
5. Ibid., 492.
6. Michael Gagarin, ed., *The Oxford Encyclopedia of Ancient Greece and Rome* (Oxford: Oxford University Press, 2010), 1:235.
7. We use the English name *Syracuse* throughout the text, except when referring to the province of Siracusa (where the city of Syracuse is located) or to the wine appellation Moscato di Siracusa.
8. Richard Cumberland, "Fragments of Epicharmus," no. 136 in *The Observer,* vol. 40 of *The British Essayists* (London: Wright, 1807), 192.
9. Theocritus, *The Idylls of Theocritus,* translated by James Henry Hallard (London: Rivingtons, 1901), 58.

10. Ibid., 42.

11. Archestratus, quoted in Athenaeus, *The Learned Banqueters: Books I–III.106e,* edited and translated by S. Douglas Olson (Cambridge: Harvard University Press, 2006), 165.

12. Ibid., 167.

13. Strabo, *The Geography of Strabo,* translated by H. C. Hamilton (London: Henry G. Bohn, 1854), 1:405.

14. Ibid., 406.

15. Columella, *De Re Rustica,* vol. 1, translated by H. B. Ash (Cambridge: Harvard University Press, 1977), 31.

16. Pliny, *Natural History: A Selection,* translated by John F. Healy (New York: Penguin Putnam, 1991), 153.

17. Younger, *Gods, Men, and Wine,* 157.

18. Pliny, *Natural History: Books 12–16,* translated by H. Rackham (Cambridge: Harvard University Press, 2005), 203.

19. Andrew Dalby, *Food in the Ancient World from A to Z* (London: Routledge, 2003), 8.

20. Virgil, *The Aeneid,* translated by Allen Mandelbaum (Berkeley: University of California Press, 2007), 8.

21. Ibid.

22. Jeremy Johns, *Arabic Administration in Norman Sicily: The Royal Diwan* (Cambridge: Cambridge University Press, 2002), 26.

23. Ibid., 146–147.

24. Karla Mallette, *The Kingdom of Sicily, 1100–1250: A Literary History* (Philadelphia: University of Pennsylvania Press, 2005), 133.

25. Gianni Pirrone, "Sicilian Gardens," translated by Lucinda Byatt, in *The Italian Garden: Art, Design and Culture,* edited by John Dixon Hunt (Cambridge: Cambridge University Press, 2006), 258.

26. David Abulafia, *Frederick II: A Medieval Emperor* (Oxford: Oxford University Press, 1988), 47.

27. Ibn Jubayr, *The Travels of Ibn Jubayr,* translated by R. J. C. Broadhurst (New Delhi: Goodword Books, 2008), 350.

28. Hugo Falcandus, *The History of the Tyrants of Sicily, 1154–69,* translated by Graham A. Loud and Thomas Wiedemann (Manchester: Manchester University Press, 1998), 261–62.

29. Falcandus, quoted in Mallette, *The Kingdom of Sicily,* 160.

30. My term *wine-dark ages* is a play on Homer's stock epithet *wine-dark* for the color of the sea in the *Odyssey.*

31. M. I. Finley, Denis Mack Smith, and Christopher Duggan, *A History of Sicily* (New York: Elisabeth Sifton Books / Viking, 1987), 139.

32. Denis Mack Smith, *Medieval Sicily: 800–1713* (New York: Dorset Press, 1968), 157.

33. For a historical account of the social excesses of the Sicilian nobility, we recommend Denis Mack Smith's "The Baronage," in ibid. We also recommend Federico De Roberto's novel *The Viceroys* (*I Viceré*), which was first published in 1894 but has languished in the shadow of Giuseppe di Lampedusa's *The Leopard. The Viceroys* provides a less nostalgic and more penetrating literary portrait of the Sicilian nobility than Lampe-

dusa's novel. De Roberto, *The Viceroys,* translated by Archibald Colquhoun (New York: Harcourt, Brace and World, 1962).

34. Denis Mack Smith, *Medieval Sicily,* 132.

35. Ibid., 149.

36. Ibid., 119.

37. Denis Mack Smith, *Modern Sicily: After 1713* (New York: Dorset Press, 1968), 380.

38. Giuseppe di Lampedusa, *The Leopard,* first revised paperback edition, translated by Archibald Colquhoun (New York: Pantheon Books, 1960), 177.

39. Ibid., 10.

40. Ibid., 73–74.

41. Ibid., 88.

42. Antonino Venuto, *De Agricultura Opusculum* (Naples: Sigismondo Mayer Alemanno, 1516).

43. Tomaso Fazello, *Dell'Historia Di Sicilia,* translated by P. M. Remigio (Venice: Domenico and Gio. Battista Guerra, Fratelli, 1573), 1:26.

44. Ibid.

45. Stephan R. Epstein, *An Island for Itself: Economic Development and Social Change in Late Medieval Sicily* (Cambridge: Cambridge University Press, 1992), 179.

46. Paolo Balsamo, *A View of the Present State of Sicily: Its Rural Economy, Population, and Produce,* translated by Thomas Wright Vaughan (London: Gale and Curtis, 1811), appendix, xii.

47. Ibid., 16.

48. Ibid., 63.

49. Ibid., 66.

CHAPTER 2. THE LOST OPPORTUNITY

1. Domenico Sestini, *Memorie sui vini siciliani,* edited by Alfio Signorelli (Palermo: Sellerio Editore, 1991), 31–54.

2. Ibid., 55.

3. M. I. Finley, Denis Mack Smith, and Christopher Duggan, *A History of Sicily* (New York: Elizabeth Sifton Books / Viking, 1987), 162.

4. G. A. Arnolfini, *Giornale di Viaggio e Quesiti Sull'Economia Siciliana (1768),* edited by C. Trasselli (Rome: Salvatore Sciascia, 1962), 117.

5. Ibid., 118–19.

6. John R. Hailman, *Thomas Jefferson on Wine* (Jackson: Univ. Press of Mississippi, 2006), 305.

7. Salvatore Lanza, *Guida del Viaggiatore in Sicilia* (Palermo: Fratelli Pedone Lauriel, 1859), xix. The wine from the higher eastern slopes of Etna was called "vino del bosco" (wine of the forest) and was lower in alcohol and higher in acidity than the "terre forti" wine.

8. William Stigand, *Report for the Year 1887 on the Trade of Palermo,* Diplomatic and Consular Reports on Trade and Finance, no. 395, Foreign Office, Great Britain (London: Harrison and Sons, 1888), 3.

9. William Stigand, *Report on the Wine Produce of Sicily,* consular report, no. 143, Foreign Office, Great Britain (London: Harrison and Sons, 1889), 36.

10. Ibid., 40.

11. William Stigand, *Report on the Sicilian Vintage of 1889*, consular report, no. 155, Foreign Office, Great Britain (London: Harrison and Sons, 1890), 18.

12. Stigand, *Report on the Wine Produce of Sicily*, 36.

13. Ibid., 3–4.

14. Ibid., 28.

15. Ibid., 17.

16. Ibid., 15.

17. Laura Stassi, "La Fattoria dello Zucco," accessed July 9, 2012, www.regione.sicilia.it/beniculturali/museodaumale/museo_PianoZucco.htm.

18. Stigand, *Report on the Wine Produce of Sicily*, 17.

19. Stigand, *Report on the Sicilian Vintage of 1889*, 14.

20. Ibid., 15.

21. Stigand, *Report on the Wine Produce of Sicily*, 28.

22. Stigand, *Report on the Sicilian Vintage of 1889*, 23.

23. Stigand, *Report on the Wine Produce of Sicily*, 39.

24. Jessie White Mario, "Prodotti del Suolo e Viticoltura in Sicilia, Parte Seconda e Ultima," in *Nuova Antologia Di Scienze, Lettere Ed Arti* (Rome: Direzione Della Nuova Antologia, 1894), 52:712.

25. Stigand, *Report on the Sicilian Vintage of 1889*, 13.

26. Mario, "Prodotti del Suolo e Viticoltura in Sicilia, Parte Prima," 51:654.

27. Mario, "Prodotti del Suolo e Viticoltura in Sicilia, Parte Seconda e Ultima," 52:719–41.

28. Stigand, *Report on the Sicilian Vintage of 1889*, 14.

29. *Report on the Sicilian Vintage of 1889*, 15, 21.

30. Ibid., 21.

CHAPTER 3. THE MODERN SICILIAN WINE INDUSTRY

1. The countries that signed the treaty on March 25, 1957, were Belgium, France, Italy, Luxembourg, the Netherlands, and West Germany.

2. "Grapes of Wrath," *Time*, April 14, 1975.

CHAPTER 6. VINE VARIETIES

1. Francisco Cupani, *Hortus Catholicus* (Naples: Apud Franciscum Benzi, 1696), 234.

2. Domenico Sestini, *Memorie sui vini siciliani*, edited by Alfio Signorelli (Palermo: Sellerio Editore, 1991), 46, 60.

3. Egidio Pollacci, *La Teoria e la Pratica della Viticultura e della Enologia*, fourth edition (Milan: Fratelli Dumolard Editori, 1883), 260.

4. Cupani, *Hortus Catholicus*, 232.

5. Sestini, *Memorie sui vini siciliani*, 37.

6. M. Crespan, A. Calò, S. Giannetto, A. Sparacio, P. Storchi, and A. Costacurta, "'Sangiovese' and 'Garganega' Are Two Key Varieties of the Italian Grapevine Assortment Evolution," *Vitis* 47, no. 2 (2008): 97–104.

7. Cupani, *Hortus Catholicus*, 233; Sestini, *Memorie sui vini siciliani*, 38.

8. Cupani, *Hortus Catholicus*, 231.

9. Sestini, *Memorie sui vini siciliani*, 46.

10. See, e.g., Antonio Calò, Attilio Scienza, and Angelo Costacurta, *Vitigni d'Italia* (Bologna: Calderini Edagricole, 2001), 448, which cites G. Bambara and G. Nicosia, "Il Malvasia di Lipari," in *Vini d'Italia* (1959), 119–25; Daniela Bica, *Vitigni di Sicilia* (Palermo: Regione siciliana, Assessorato agricoltura e foreste, Servizi allo sviluppo, 2007), 50; Jancis Robinson, *Oxford Companion to Wine*, third edition (Oxford: Oxford University Press, 2006), 423.

11. Giovacchino Geremia, "Continuazione del Vertunno Etneo, ovvero Stafulegrafia," *Atti dell'accademia gioenia di scienze naturali di Catania* 13 (Catania: Agatino La Magna, 1839): 63.

12. Cupani, *Hortus Catholicus*, 234.

13. Sestini, *Memorie sui vini siciliani*, 40, 60.

14. Baron Antonio Mendola, "Estratto del catalogo generale della collezione di viti italiane e straniere radunate in Favara" (1868), referenced in Salvatore D'Agostino, *Annuario della filiera vitivinicola siciliana* (Palermo: Istituto Regionale della Vite e del Vino—Regione Siciliana, 2009), 3:42.

15. William Stigand, *Report on the Wine Produce of Sicily*, consular report, no. 143, Foreign Office, Great Britain (London: Harrison and Sons, 1889), 13.

16. Laura Stassi, "La Fattoria dello Zucco," accessed July 9, 2012, www.regione.sicilia.it/beniculturali/museodaumale/museo_PianoZucco.htm.

17. Sestini, *Memorie sui vini siciliani*, 45.

18. Geremia, "Continuazione del Vertunno Etneo," 13, 53.

19. Bica, *Vitigni di Sicilia*, 59.

20. Clemente Grimaldi, "La fiera—esposizione enologica di Catania," *Giornale Vinicolo Italiano Commerciale, Industriale e Scientifico* 16 (1890), 326.

21. Sestini, *Memorie sui vini siciliani*, 60.

22. D'Agostino, *Annuario della filiera vitivinicola siciliana*, 47.

23. Paolo Balsamo, *A View of the Present State of Sicily: Its Rural Economy, Population, and Produce*, translated by Thomas Wright Vaughn (London: Gale and Curtis, 1811), 92.

24. Girolamo Molon, *Ampelografia: Descrizione delle Migliori Varietà di Viti per Uve da Vino, Uve da Tavola, Porta-Innesti e Produttori Diretti* (Milan: Ulrico Hoepli, 1906), 2:587.

25. Ibid., 589.

26. Ministero d'Agricoltura, Industria e Commercio, *Bollettino Ampelografico*, anno 1875 (Rome: Eredi Botta, 1876), no. 1, 890.

27. Pollacci, *La Teoria e la Pratica della Viticultura e della Enologia*, 260.

28. Stigand, *Report on the Wine Produce of Sicily*, 8.

29. William Stigand, *Report on the Sicilian Vintage of 1889*, consular report, no. 155, Foreign Office, Great Britain (London: Harrison and Sons, 1890), 15.

30. Ministero di Agricoltura, Industria e Commercio, *Notizie e Studi intorno Ai Vini ed Alle Uve d'Italia* (Rome: G. Bertero, 1896), clxxx.

31. Ibid., clxxxii.

32. D'Agostino, *Annuario della filiera vitivinicola siciliana*, 51.

33. Cupani, *Hortus Catholicus*, 235; Sestini, *Memorie sui vini siciliani*, 60.

34. Ministero di Agricoltura, Industria e Commercio, *Bollettino Ampelografico*, anno 1883 (Rome: Regia tipograhia D. Ripamonti, 1883), fasc. 16, 260.

35. Stigand, *Report on the Sicilian Vintage of 1889*, 11.

CHAPTER 8. ENOLOGY IN SICILY

1. Johann Wolfgang von Goethe, *Italian Journey, 1786–1788*, translated by W. H. Auden and Elizabeth Mayer (London: Penguin Books, 1970), 247.

2. Giovanni Meli, "Sulla Maniera Di Far Fermentare e Conservare I Vini ne' Tini a Muro," in *Opere di Giovanni Meli* (Palermo: Roberti Editore, 1838), 758–64.

3. Saverio Landolina Nava, *Il Vino Pollio Siracusano*, edited by Carlo Morrone and Dario Scarfi, translated by Nello Amato (Syracuse: Maura Morrone, 2000) 82–84.

4. Ministero di Agricoltura, Industria e Commercio, *Notizie e Studi intorno Ai Vini ed Alle Uve d'Italia* (Rome: G. Bertero, 1896), clxxx.

5. Enrico Iachello, "Il Vino: Realtà e Mito Della Sicilia Ottocentesca," in *La Sicilia del Vino* (Catania: Giuseppe Maimone, 2005), 44.

6. William Stigand, *Report on the Sicilian Vintage of 1889*, consular report, no. 155, Foreign Office, Great Britain (London: Harrison and Sons, 1890), 12.

7. Felice Lioy, *Memoria per la manipolazione dei vini* (Palermo: Reale Stamperia, 1800). Available online at http://casarrubea.wordpress.com/2008/11/05/felice-lioy-come-si-fa-il-vino/.

8. Domenico Sestini, *Memorie sui vini siciliani*, edited by Alfio Signorelli (Palermo: Sellerio Editore, 1991), 49.

9. Jessie White Mario, "Prodotti del Suolo e Viticoltura in Sicilia, Parte Seconda e Ultima," in *Nuova Antologia Di Scienze, Lettere Ed Arti* (Rome: Direzione Della Nuova Antologia, 1894), 52:717.

CHAPTER 9. AT THE HEART OF SICILY

1. Andrea Bacci, *De Naturali Vinorum Historia* (Rome: Niccolò Muzi, 1596), 5:236, 237.

CHAPTER 11. VAL DI MAZARA

1. Nicola Trapani, *Marsala: Il Vino e La Citta dell'Unita d'Italia* (Marsala: Enovitis, 2011), 240.

2. Ibid., 247.

3. Giovanni Meli, "Sulla Maniera Di Far Fermentare e Conservare I Vini ne' Tini a Muro," in *Opere di Giovanni Meli* (Palermo: Roberti Editore, 1838), 758–64.

CHAPTER 12. VAL DI NOTO

1. Domenico Sestini, *Memorie sui vini siciliani*, edited by Alfio Signorelli (Palermo: Sellerio Editore, 1991), 56.

2. Paolo Balsamo, *A View of the Present State of Sicily: Its Rural Economy, Population, and Produce*, translated by Thomas Wright Vaughan (London: Gale and Curtis, 1811), 91.

3. Touring Club Italiano, *Guida Gastronomica d'Italia* (Milan: Pol. G. Colombi, 1931), 465.

4. Domenico Sestini, *Memorie sui vini siciliani*, 56.

5. Balsamo, *A View of the Present State of Sicily*, 159.

6. Saverio Landolina Nava, *Il Vino Pollio Siracusano*, edited by Carlo Morrone and Dario Scarfi, translated by Nello Amato (Syracuse: Maura Morrone, 2000), 21, 22.

7. John R. Hailman, *Thomas Jefferson on Wine* (Jackson: University Press of Mississippi, 2006), 48, 49.

8. Cyrus Redding, *A History and Description of Modern Wines* (London: Henry G. Bohn, 1860; reprint, Bedford, MA: Applewood Books, 2008), 281.

9. Landolina Nava, *Il Vino Pollio Siracusano*, 81.

10. Ministero di Agricoltura, Industria e Commercio, *Notizie e Studi intorno Ai Vini ed Alle Uve d'Italia* (Rome: G. Bertero, 1896), cxc.

11. Touring Club Italiano, *Guida Gastronomica d'Italia*, 462.

12. Ministero di Agricoltura, Industria e Commercio, *Notizie e Studi intorno Ai Vini ed Alle Uve d'Italia*, clxxxix.

13. Touring Club Italiano, *Guida Gastronomica d'Italia*, 464.

CHAPTER 13. VAL DEMONE

1. A. Sparacio et al., *Nuovi Vini Per il Territorio Etneo* (Palermo: Istituto Regionale della Vite e del Vino, 2010), 1.

2. David K. Chester, Angus M. Duncan, and Peter A. James, "Mount Etna, Sicily: Landscape Evolution and Hazard Response in the Pre-Industrial Era," in *Landscapes and Societies: Selected Cases*, edited by I. Peter Martini and Ward Chesworth (Guelph, Ontario: Springer, 2011), 249.

3. Tomaso Fazello, *Dell'Historia di Sicilia*, translated by P. M. Remigio (Venice: Domenico and Gio. Battista Guerra, Fratelli, 1573), 75.

4. Pliny, *Natural History: Books 12–16*, translated by H. Rackham (Cambridge: Harvard University Press, 1945), 231.

5. Al-Idrisi, *La Sicilia di al-Idrisi ne "Il Libro di Ruggero,"* edited by Luigi Santagati, translated by Michele Amari (Caltanissetta: Salvatore Sciascia, 2010), 42.

6. Fazello, *Dell'Historia di Sicilia*, 285.

7. Ministero di Agricoltura, Industria e Commercio, *Notizie e Studi intorno Ai Vini ed Alle Uve d'Italia* (Rome: G. Bertero, 1896), clxxxii.

8. Domenico Sestini, *Memorie sui vini siciliani*, edited by Alfio Signorelli (Palermo: Sellerio Editore, 1991), 35.

9. Horatio Nelson, *The Dispatches and Letters of Vice Admiral Lord Viscount Nelson*, vol. 6 (London: Henry Colburn, 1846), 118.

10. J. Pater, "A Memorandum Concerning the Wines of Sicily," *The Tradesman: Or, Commercial Magazine*, July 1, 1812: 8–10.

11. Ministero di Agricoltura, Industria e Commercio, *Notizie e Studi intorno Ai Vini ed Alle Uve d'Italia*, clxxxii.

12. Egidio Pollacci, *La Teoria e la Pratica della Viticultura e della Enologia,* fourth edition (Milan: Fratelli Dumolard Editori, 1883), 260.

CHAPTER 14. THE GARDEN-VINEYARD

Epigraph. Ovid, *Ovid in Sicily: A New Verse Translation of Selections from the "Metamorphoses,"* translated by Allen Mandelbaum (New York: Sheep Meadow Press, 1986), 70. Reproduced with permission from the Allen Mandelbaum Estate.

AFTERWORD

1. Johann Wolfgang von Goethe, *Italian Journey, 1786–1788,* translated by W. H. Auden and Elizabeth Mayer (London: Penguin Books, 1970), 220.
2. Alexis de Tocqueville, "Extracts from the Tour in Sicily," in *Memoir, Letters, and Remains of Alexis de Tocqueville,* translated by the Translator of Napoleon's Correspondence with King Joseph, vol. 1 (Boston: Ticknor and Fields, 1862), 120.
3. Pierre d'Avity, *An Accurate Description of the Island and Kingdom of Sicily,* translated by D. Macnab (London: The Booksellers, 1786), 8–9.
4. Goethe, *Italian Journey,* 279.
5. Tocqueville, "Extracts from the Tour in Sicily," 115.
6. Alexander Metcalfe, *Muslims and Christians in Norman Sicily* (New York: Routledge-Curzon, 2003), 236.
7. Antonio Veneziano, *Ninety Love Octaves,* edited and translated by Gaetano Cipolla (Mineola: Legas, 2006), 11.
8. Giovanni Meli, "Dithyramb: Sarudda," in *Moral Fables and Other Poems: A Bilingual Anthology,* edited and translated by Gaetano Cipolla (Mineola: Legas, 1995), 182.
9. Luigi Pirandello, quoted in Nino Martoglio, *The Poetry of Nino Martoglio: Selections from "Centona,"* translated by Gaetano Cipolla (Mineola: Legas, 1993), xvi.
10. Martoglio, "Dialogue between the Author and His Book as a Way of Preface," in ibid., 35.
11. Salvatore Quasimodo, "Discourse on Poetry," in *The Selected Writings of Salvatore Quasimodo,* edited and translated by Allen Mandelbaum (New York: Farrar, Straus and Cudahy, 1960), 7–14.
12. Salvatore Quasimodo, "Mirror," in *Complete Poems,* translated by Jack Bevan (London: Anvil Press Poetry, 1983), 39. Reproduced with permission from Anvil Press Poetry.

SELECTED BIBLIOGRAPHY

Abulafia, David. *Frederick II: A Medieval Emperor*. Oxford: Oxford University Press, 1988.

Anderson, Burton. *The Wine Atlas of Italy*. New York: Simon and Schuster, 1990.

Archestratus. *Gastronomia*. Translated by Da Domenico Scina. Venice: Giuseppe Antonelli Editore, 1842.

Arnolfini, G.A. *Giornale di Viaggio e Quesiti Sull'Economia Siciliana (1768)*. Edited by C. Trasselli. Rome: Salvatore Sciascia, 1962.

Athenaeus. *The Learned Banqueters: Books I–III.106e*. Edited and translated by S. Douglas Olson. Cambridge: Harvard University Press, 2006.

Bacarella, Antonino. "Economia e Marketing Vitivinicolo Nella Storia Recente Della Sicilia." Accessed July 25, 2012. www.coreras.it/Upload/allegatipubblicazioni/Economia_e_marketing_vitivinicolo_nella_storia_recente_del%E2%80%A6.pdf.

Bacci, Andrea. *De Naturali Vinorum Historia*. Vol. 5. Rome: Niccolò Muzi, 1596.

Backman, Clifford R. *The Decline and Fall of Medieval Sicily*. Cambridge: Cambridge University Press, 1995.

Balsamo, Paolo. *A View of the Present State of Sicily: Its Rural Economy, Population, and Produce*. Translated by Thomas Wright Vaughan. London: Gale and Curtis, 1811.

Belfrage, Nicholas. *Brunello to Zibibbo: The Wines of Tuscany, Central and Southern Italy*. London: Mitchell Beazley, 2003.

Bica, Daniela. *Vitigni di Sicilia*. Palermo: Regione siciliana, Assessorato agricoltura e foreste, Servizi allo sviluppo, 2007.

Bussagli, Marco. *Antonello da Messina*. Vol. 221. Milan: Giunti Editore, 2006.

Buttitta, Antonino. "Coppe di stelle nel cerchio del sole." In *Sicilia: L'isola del vino*, 21–54. Palermo: Kalos, 2005.

Calò, Antonio, Attilio Scienza, and Angelo Costacurta. *Vitigni d'Italia*. Bologna: Calderini Edagricole, 2001.

Chester, D. K., A. M. Duncan, J. E. Guest, and C. R. J. Kilburn. *Mount Etna: The Anatomy of a Volcano*. Stanford, CA: Stanford University Press, 1985.

Chester, David K., Angus M. Duncan, and Peter A. James. "Mount Etna, Sicily: Landscape Evolution and Hazard Response in the Pre-Industrial Era." In *Landscapes and Societies: Selected Cases*, 235–53. Edited by I. Peter Martini and Ward Chesworth. Guelph, Ontario: Springer, 2011.

Columella. *De Re Rustica*, vol. 1. Translated by H. B. Ash. Cambridge: Harvard University Press, 1977.

Consolo, Vincenzo. *Reading and Writing the Mediterranean: Essays by Vincenzo Consolo*. Edited by Norma Bouchard and Massimo Lollini. Toronto: University of Toronto Press, 2006.

Coria, Giuseppe. *Il Libro d'Oro dei Vini d'Italia*. Milan: U. Mursia, 1981.

Cumberland, Richard. "Fragments of Epicharmus." No. 136 in *The Observer*. Vol. 40 of *The British Essayists*. London: Wright, 1807.

Cupani, Francisco. *Hortus Catholicus*. Naples: Apud Franciscum Benzi, 1696.

Cusimano, Girolamo. "I grappoli del futuro." In *Sicilia: L'isola del vino*, 55–112. Palermo: Kalos, 2005.

D'Agostino, Salvatore. *Annuario della filiera vitivinicola siciliana*. Vol. 3. Palermo: Istituto Regionale della Vite e del Vino—Regione Siciliana, 2009.

Dalby, Andrew. *Food in the Ancient World from A to Z*. London: Routledge, 2003.

———. *Siren Feasts: A History of Food and Gastronomy in Greece*. London: Routledge, 1996.

D'Ancona, Caterina. *Il Passito di Pantelleria*. Pisa: Pacini, 2009.

d'Avity, Pierre. *An Accurate Description of the Island and Kingdom of Sicily*. Translated by D. Macnab. London: The Booksellers, 1786.

De Roberto, Federico. *The Viceroys*. Translated by Archibald Colquhoun. New York: Harcourt, Brace and World, 1962.

Diodorus Siculus. *The Historical Library of Diodorus the Sicilian in 15 Books*. Translated by G. Booth. Vol. 1. London: W. McDowall, 1814.

Donati, Bruno. *Giacomo Tachis: Enologo Corsaro*. Vicenza: Terra Firma, 2005.

Epstein, Stephan R. *An Island for Itself: Economic Development and Social Change in Late Medieval Sicily*. Cambridge: Cambridge University Press, 1992.

Falcandus, Hugo. *The History of the Tyrants of Sicily, 1154–69*. Translated by Graham A. Loud and Thomas Wiedemann. Manchester: Manchester University Press, 1998.

Fazello, Tomaso. *Dell'Historia di Sicilia*. Translated by P. M. Remigio. Venice: Domenico and Gio. Battista Guerra, Fratelli, 1573.

Finley, M. I. *Ancient Sicily to the Arab Conquest*. New York: Viking, 1968.

Finley, M. I., Denis Mack Smith, and Christopher Duggan. *A History of Sicily*. New York: Elisabeth Sifton Books / Viking, 1987.

Forte, Alberto, and Antonino Bacarella. *Analisi strutturale e congiunturale della filiera vitivinicola siciliana*. Coreras—Consorzio Regionale per la Ricerca Applicata e la Sperimentazione—Regione Sicilia, n.d.

Foti, Salvo. *Etna: I Vini del Vulcano*. Catania: Giuseppe Maimone, 2005.

————. "Sicilia vitivinicola." In *La Sicilia del Vino*, 213–272. Catania: Giuseppe Maimone, 2005.

Gabbrielli, Andrea. "I protagonisti del vino siciliano." In *La Sicilia del Vino*, 189–212. Catania: Giuseppe Maimone, 2005.

Gagarin, Michael, ed. *The Oxford Encyclopedia of Ancient Greece and Rome*, vol 1. Oxford: Oxford University Press, 2010.

Gilmour, David. *The Last Leopard*. London: Eland, 1988.

Goethe, Johann Wolfgang von. *Italian Journey, 1786–1788*. Translated by W. H. Auden and Elizabeth Mayer. London: Penguin Books, 1970.

Hailman, John R. *Thomas Jefferson on Wine*. Jackson: University Press of Mississippi, 2006.

Homer. *The Odyssey of Homer: A New Verse Translation*. Translated by Allen Mandelbaum. Berkeley: University of California Press, 1990.

Hunt, John Dixon, ed. *The Italian Garden: Art, Design and Culture*. Cambridge: Cambridge University Press, 2006.

Iachello, Enrico. "Il Vino: Realtà e Mito Della Sicilia Ottocentesca." In *La Sicilia del Vino*, 37–66. Catania: Giuseppe Maimone, 2005.

————. *Il vino e il mare: "Trafficanti" siciliani tra '700 e '800 nella Contea di Mascali*. Catania: Giuseppe Maimone Editore, 1991.

Ibn Jubayr. *The Travels of Ibn Jubayr*. Translated by R. J. C. Broadhurst. New Delhi: Goodword Books, 2008.

al-Idrisi. *La Sicilia di al-Idrisi ne "Il Libro di Ruggero."* Edited by Luigi Santagati. Caltanissetta: Salvatore Sciascia, 2010.

Jenster, Per V., David E. Smith, Darryl J. Mitry, and Lars V. Jenster. *The Business of Wine: A Global Perspective*. First edition. Copenhagen: Copenhagen Business School Press, 2008.

Johns, Jeremy. *Arabic Administration in Norman Sicily: The Royal Diwan*. Cambridge: Cambridge University Press, 2002.

Lampedusa, Giuseppe di. *The Leopard*. First revised paperback edition. Translated by Archibald Colquhoun. New York: Pantheon Books, 1960.

Landolina Nava, Saverio. *Il Vino Pollio Siracusano*. Edited by Carlo Morrone and Dario Scarfi. Translated by Nello Amato. Syracuse: Maura Morrone, 2000.

Lanza, Salvatore. *Guida del Viaggiatore in Sicilia*. Palermo: Fratelli Pedone Lauriel, 1859.

Lewis, Norman. *The Honoured Society*. London: Eland, 2003.

Lioy, Felice. *Memoria per la manipolazione dei vini*. Palermo: Reale Stamperia, 1800.

Malaterra, Geoffrey. *The Deeds of Count Roger of Calabria and Sicily and of His Brother Duke Robert Guiscard*. Translated by Kenneth Baxter Wolf. Ann Arbor: The University of Michigan Press, 2005.

Mallette, Karla. *The Kingdom of Sicily, 1100–1250: A Literary History*. Philadelphia: University of Pennsylvania Press, 2005.

Mario, Jessie White. "Prodotti del Suolo e Viticoltura in Sicilia." Vol. 51: "Parte Prima," 639–65; vol. 52: "Parte Seconda e Ultima," 708–41. In *Nuova Antologia Di Scienze, Lettere Ed Arti*. Rome: Direzione Della Nuova Antologia, 1894.

Martoglio, Nino. *The Poetry of Nino Martoglio: Selections from "Centona."* Edited, introduced, and translated by Gaetano Cipolla. Mineola: Legas, 1993.

Mathew, Donald. *The Norman Kingdom of Sicily*. Cambridge: Cambridge University Press, 1992.

Meli, Giovanni. *Moral Fables and Other Poems: A Bilingual Anthology*. Edited, introduced, and translated by Gaetano Cipolla. Mineola: Legas, 1995.

———. "Sulla Maniera Di Far Fermentare e Conservare I Vini ne' Tini a Muro." In *Opere Di Giovanni Meli*. Palermo: Roberti Editore, 1838, 758–64.

Metcalfe, Alexander. *Muslims and Christians in Norman Sicily*. New York: RoutledgeCurzon, 2003.

Ministero di Agricoltura, Industria e Commercio. *Notizie e Studi intorno Ai Vini ed Alle Uve d'Italia*. Rome: G. Bertero, 1896.

Molon, Girolamo. *Ampelografia: Descrizione delle Migliori Varietà di Viti per Uve da Vino, Uve da Tavola, Porta-Innesti e Produttori Diretti*. Vol. 2. Milan: Ulrico Hoepli, 1906.

Nelson, Horatio. *The Dispatches and Letters of Vice Admiral Lord Viscount Nelson*. Vol. 6. London: Henry Colburn, 1846.

Ovid. *Ovid in Sicily: A New Verse Translation of Selections from the "Metamorphoses."* Translated by Allen Mandelbaum. New York: Sheep Meadow Press, 1986.

Papo, Luigi, and Anna Pesenti. *Il Marsala*. Milan: Fabbri, 1991.

Pastena, Bruno. *La Civilta della Vite in Sicilia*. Palermo: Istituto Regionale Della Vite e del Vino, 1989.

Pirrone, Gianni. "Sicilian Gardens." Translated by Lucinda Byatt. In *The Italian Garden: Art, Design and Culture*, 250–73. Edited by John Dixon Hunt. Cambridge: Cambridge University Press, 2006.

Pliny. *Natural History: Books 12–16*. Translated by H. Rackham. Cambridge: Harvard University Press, 2005.

———. *Natural History: A Selection*. Translated by John F. Healy. New York: Penguin Putnam, 1991.

Pollacci, Egidio. *La Teoria e la Pratica della Viticultura e della Enologia*. Fourth edition. Milan: Fratelli Dumolard Editori, 1883.

Quasimodo, Salvatore. *Complete Poems*. Translated by Jack Bevan. London: Anvil Press Poetry, 1983.

———. *The Selected Writings of Salvatore Quasimodo*. Edited and translated by Allen Mandelbaum. New York: Farrar, Straus and Cudahy, 1960.

Recupero, Giuseppe. *Storia Naturale e Generale dell'Etna*. Edited by Agatino Recupero. Vol. 1. Catania: Universita Degli Studi, 1815.

Redding, Cyrus. *A History and Description of Modern Wines*. London: Henry G. Bohn, 1860. Reprint, Bedford, MA: Applewood Books, 2008.

Robinson, Jancis. *Oxford Companion to Wine*. Third edition. Oxford: Oxford University Press, 2006.

Sestini, Domenico. *Memorie sui vini siciliani*. Edited by Alfio Signorelli. Palermo: Sellerio Editore, 1991.

Smith, Christopher, and Serrati, John, eds. *Sicily from Aeneas to Augustus: New Approaches in Archaeology and History*. Edinburgh: Edunburgh University Press, 2000.

Smith, Denis Mack. *Medieval Sicily: 800–1713*. New York: Dorset Press, 1968.

———. *Modern Sicily: After 1713*. New York: Dorset Press, 1968.

Sparacio, A., S. Sparla, G. Genna, L. Prinzivalli, F. Capraro, and V. Melia. *Nuovi Vini Per il Territorio Etneo.* Palermo: Istituto Regionale della Vite e del Vino, 2010.

Spera, Roberto. *I Vini dell'Agrigentino: Vigneti e luoghi incantati della Valle dei Templi.* Perugia: ali&no, 2008.

Stassi, Laura. "La Fattoria dello Zucco." Accessed July 9, 2012. www.regione.sicilia.it/beni-culturali/museodaumale/museo_PianoZucco.htm.

Stigand, William. *Report for the Year 1886 on the Trade and Commerce of Sicily.* Diplomatic and Consular Reports on Trade and Finance, no. 239. Foreign Office, Great Britain. London: Harrison and Sons, 1887.

———. *Report for the Year 1887 on the Trade of Palermo.* Diplomatic and Consular Reports on Trade and Finance, no. 395. Foreign Office, Great Britain. London: Harrison and Sons, 1888.

———. *Report on the Sicilian Vintage of 1889.* Consular report, no. 155. Foreign Office, Great Britain. London: Harrison and Sons, 1890.

———. *Report on the Wine Produce of Sicily.* Consular report, no. 143. Foreign Office, Great Britain. London: Harrison and Sons, 1889.

Strabo. *The Geography of Strabo.* Translated by H.C. Hamilton. Vol. 1. London: Henry G. Bohn, 1854.

Theocritus. *The Idylls of Theocritus.* Translated by James Henry Hallard. London: Rivingtons, 1901.

Tocqueville, Alexis de. "Extracts from the Tour in Sicily." In *Memoir, Letters, and Remains of Alexis de Tocqueville.* Translated by the Translator of Napoleon's Correspondence with King Joseph. Vol. 1. Boston: Ticknor and Fields, 1862.

Touring Club Italiano. *Guida Gastronomica d'Italia.* Milan: Pol. G. Colombi, 1931.

Trapani, Nicola. *Marsala: Il Vino e La Citta dell'Unita d'Italia.* Marsala: Enovitis, 2011.

Veneziano, Antonio. *Ninety Love Octaves.* Edited, introduced, and translated by Gaetano Cipolla. Mineola: Legas, 2006.

Venuto, Antonino. *De Agricultura Opusculum.* Naples: Sigismondo Mayer Alemanno, 1516.

Vinci, Attilio L. *Carlo Nicolosi Asmundo.* Veronelli, n.d.

———. *Marco De Bartoli.* Veronelli, n.d.

Virgil. *The Aeneid.* Translated by Allen Mandelbaum. Berkeley: University of California Press, 2007.

Younger, William. *Gods, Men, and Wine.* Cleveland: Wine and Food Society, 1966.

Zanfi, Andrea. *Journey among the Great Wines of Sicily.* Translated by An.se SAS. Poggibonsi, Siena: Carlo Gambi, 2003.

INDEX

Abbazia Santa Anastasia, 80, 123, 135, 187, 256–57

Abraxas, 91, 111, 137, 166–67

Acate, 105

acid adjustments, 74, 85, 128–29, 132

acidic soils, 73, 183, 254, 258

acidity, 48, 49, 120, 191; climate/exposure and, 76, 77, 233; soils and, 222; training methods and, 118

Adragna, Giuseppe Agostino, 179

adulteration, illegal, 41, 52

Aeneid (Virgil), 8

Aeolian Islands, 115, 155, 230, 257–61; geography, soils, and climate, 75, 113, 257–58; map, 231; overview, 257–60; recommended producers, 260–61. *See also* Malvasia delle Lipari; *specific islands*

aging. *See* maturation and aging; *specific wines, producers, and varieties*

agriculture, 26, 72; ancient Sicily, 5, 6, 8; declines after Norman rule, 12, 13–14; diversity and quality of Sicilian foods, 5, 7, 263; impact of emigration, 31, 32, 115, 231, 258; labor availability, 32, 113, 115, 118, 158; later agricultural treatises, 18, 19, 20; Muslim and Norman Sicily, 9–10, 11; Sicily as a garden, 10, 11, 17, 262–69; sixteenth through nineteenth centuries, 16, 18–20, 30–31; traditional polyculture, 112, 113, 122, 262–63, 267, 268. *See also* European Union policies and programs; land ownership; viticulture; *specific crops*

Agrigento, 115, 150, 198; ancient, 6, 8; red varieties, 95, 97, 100–101, 105, 109, 110, 111; sulfur mining, 74; white varieties, 83–86, 89, 91, 92, 95

Agrigento-Caltanissetta Highlands, 154, 198–201; geography, soils, and climate, 198–99; grape varieties, 198; maps, 153, 181

Agueci, Leonardo, 61

Albanello, 209, 228

Alba School of Enology, 43

alberello training, 35, 115–18; Grillo, 70, 87, 88; Nero d'Avola, 96–97; Val Demone, 136, 237, 251, 253; Val di Mazara, 117, 163, 171, 172, 176, 191, 196; Val di Noto, 211, 220, 223, 224, 225

Alcamo, 154, 176, 183, 186; alberello training, 117–18; DOC, 176, 184; map, 181; varieties, 84, 175, 183, 184; wines before the 1980s, 22, 24, 183

Al Cantarà, 248

alcohol content, 131, 132; EU regulations, 219; high-alcohol wines, 35, 65, 90, 127; prices based on, 217. *See also* fortified wines; sugar content; *specific wines*

Aleatico, 96

Alessandro, Antonino, 185

Alessandro di Camporeale, 45, 94, 183, 185; recommended wines, 95, 100, 185

Alessandro, Natale, 185

Alessandro, Rosolino, 185

Alfonso V, 19

Algerian wines, 35
Alì, 249
Alia, Francesco, 212
Alicante, 111. *See also* Grenache Noir
Alicante Bouschet, 111, 175
Allegracori, 235, 265
Alliata, Edoardo, 27, 29, 30, 33, 43, 182
Alliata, Enrico, 30
Alliata, Fabrizio, 27
Alliata, Giuseppe, 24, 126
Alliata, Topazia, 43
allophane, 236
Alto Belice, 183
Amarone, 197
ambra and *ambrato* wines, 106, 127, 158; Ambrato
    di Comiso, 209, 212; Marsala, 168, 169
American grapes: Jacquez hybrid, 217; phylloxera-
    resistant rootstocks, 59, 66, 113, 114, 115,
    250–51
Aminnia, 7, 8
amphorae, 4, 7; for vinification, 138, 139–40, 211,
    243, 244
Anca, Gabriella, 45, 54–55, 159
ancient Sicily, 4–8; Phoenicians, 3, 4, 61, 65–66,
    156, 176; ruins and archaeological sites,
    65–66, 176, 200, 202, 206, 255; viticulture
    and winemaking, 4, 7–8, 116, 125, 139. *See also*
    Greek Sicily; Roman Sicily; Roman viticulture
    and winemaking
Anello, Leonello, 256
Annuario della filiera vitivinicola siciliana, 104
Ansaldi, Giacomo, 64, 65–71, 177, 180. *See also*
    Divina
Ansonica, 85. *See also* Inzolia
Antichi Vinai, 102, 248
Antonello da Messina, 269, 270
appellation law, 61, 119, 150–53. *See also* DOCs;
    IGTs; *specific locations and appellations*
Arancio, 121, 123, 190, 193–94
Archestratus, 5–6
Archimedes vineyard, 223
Arfò, 98, 226
Argentina, as export market, 32
Armani, Giorgio, 159
Arnolfini, Giovanni Attilio, 22
Asian export markets, 63
Assovini, 60
astringency, 48, 49, 77, 132, 138, 145
Athenaeus, 7
Aumale, Henri d'Orleans, Duc d',' 28, 83–84, 101,
    103, 128. *See also* Zucco
Australia, 27, 43, 115, 258
Australian wines, 100; enological consultants, 126,
    134–35, 178
Austria and Austria-Hungary, 32, 122
Avide, 210
Avity, Pierre d',' 271
Avola, 217, 220
award-winning wines: modern, 253; nineteenth
    century, 27, 28, 29, 30, 182

Bacci, Andrea, 143
Bagheria, 24, 126, 180
Baglio dei Florio, 64, 68–69
Baglio di Pianetto, 55, 91, 101, 185, 218;
    recommended wines, 91, 101, 109, 185, 226
Baglio Donna Franca, 64, 68–69
Baglio Musciuleo, 68
baglios, 65, 67
Baglio Woodhouse, 67, 68
balata, 220
Balata di Baida, 174
Balestrate, 24
Balsamo, Paolo, 19–20, 104, 206, 221
Bambina, Vincenzo, 51, 94, 136–37, 185, 213
banditry, 15, 24
Barba, Marina, 59
Barbera, Cantine, 53, 86, 104, 190, 192
Barbera, Claudio, 251–53
Barbera, Fondo dei, 252–53
Barbera, Marilena, 192
Barbera, Pietro, 190
Barbera (variety), 98
Barilla, 48
Barolo, 230, 239
Barone di Villagrande, 58, 240–41, 261;
    recommended wines, 93, 94, 226, 241
Barone Sergio, 92, 98, 221, 226
Baroni, 219, 222, 223
Barraco, Nino, 138, 176–77
barrel aging, 49; red varieties, 102, 105, 107, 109,
    220–21; white varieties, 51. *See also* barriques;
    specific producers and wines
barrel-fermented wines: Carricante, 240, 244;
    Chardonnay, 49, 51, 54, 56, 88, 134–35; Fiano,
    95, 194; Grillo, 51, 87, 177; *pistammuta* process,
    129
barrels: chestnut cooperage, 24, 26, 134, 239.
    See also barrel aging; barriques;
    containers; oak
barriques, 223; early users, 44, 45; Val Demone
    wines, 239, 254, 260; Val di Mazara wines,
    165, 186, 188, 197; Val di Noto wines, 210, 214,
    216, 220–21, 223, 225
Basile, Fabrizio, 166
Bastonaca, 210, 211
Baucina, Prince, 27, 80, 128, 131. *See also*
    Contessa
B&C Enologists, 136–37. *See also* Bambina,
    Vincenzo; Centonze, Nicola
Beaujolais, 217
Belice earthquake, 182, 188
Belice River and Valley, 154, 175, 189, 191. *See also*
    Terre Sicane
Bellini, Giovanni, 269
Benanti, 58, 93, 136; contrada labeling, 237–38;
    Etna wines, 232, 238, 240, 241–42, 262; Noto
    wines, 218, 226; recommended wines, 93,
    102, 103, 106 *(see also specific zones);* vineyard
    expansions, 61, 218
Benanti, Giuseppe, 58, 218, 232, 241

Carricante, 51, 92–93, 239; Etna, 58, 92–93, 213, 238–44, 248; recommended producers, 93 *(see also specific zones)*; Vittoria, 213

Cartabellotta, Dario, 59–60, 61–62

Carthaginians, 65

Caruso & Minini, 107, 177; recommended wines, 85, 86, 88, 100, 108, 177

Caruso, Stefano, 107, 177

Casano, 172

Casanova, Giacomo, 156

Casavecchia, Carlo, 51, 86, 187

Case di Pietra, 167

Caselle, 241

casks. *See* containers

Cassa per il Mezzogiorno, 38–39

Castel Calattubo, 28

Casteldaccia, 107, 128, 182, 187

Castel di Mezzoiuso, 29, 33

Castellammare del Golfo, 22, 24, 174

Castellare, 211, 212

Castellaro, 258, 261

Castello Maniace, 29–30, 128. *See also* Hood, Alexander Nelson

Castellucci Miano, 85, 107, 108, 137, 196–97

Castelvetrano, 22, 24

Castiglione di Sicilia, 50, 110

Catania, 18, 102, 110, 134, 150, 238

Catania, Vito, 55, 212–13, 218. *See also* Gulfi

Catarratto, 56, 82, 83–85, 175; Aeolian Islands, 259, 260; Agrigento-Caltanissetta Highlands, 198, 200; blending partners, 84, 86, 91, 107, 127; Catarratto Comune, 84, 175, 196; Catarratto Extralucido, 84, 175, 188; Catarratto Lucido, 84, 175, 188, 238; Etna, 238, 240, 243; Mamertino, 256; Marsala/Western Sicily, 84, 168, 175, 176; nineteenth-century wines, 28; Palermo Highlands, 183–86, 188; Pantelleria, 163; recommended producers, 85 *(see also specific zones)*; related varieties, 86; Sicily-Center, 143, 196–97; skin-contact wines, 138–39; Terre Sicane, 191, 192, 194; Val di Noto, 212, 221

Catarratto Mantellato, 221

Catarratto Rosso. *See* Perricone

Catholic Church, 7

Catholic University of the Sacred Heart, Milan, 123

Cattedrale del Lavoro Pachinese, 218

Cattolica, Prince of, 126, 180

Cavaliere, 93, 103, 241, 243, 246

Cefalù, 80, 155, 256–57; maps, 153, 231

Cellai, Alessandro, 212

Cellaro, 190, 193

cement vats, 126, 134, 165, 224

Centonze, Nicola, 136–37, 185, 213

Centonze, Silvio, 188. *See also* Rapitalà

Centro Innovazione Filiera Vitivinicola di Marsala, 83

Cerasuolo di Vittoria, 105, 202–3, 207–9, 211; Classico wines, 208, 212, 214, 215–16; notable/recommended wines, 210–16

Cernilli, Daniele, 253

Cesanese d'Affile, 245

Ceuso, 98, 184, 186

Chardonnay, 56, 88–89, 91, 138, 177; Agrigento-Caltanissetta Highlands, 200; barrel-fermented wines, 49, 51, 54, 56, 88, 134–35; in Burgundy, 49; Cefalù, 256, 257; Etna, 246; Palermo Highlands, 188–89; recommended producers, 89 *(see also specific zones)*; Sicily-Center, 196; skin-contact wines, 138; Terre Sicane, 76, 88, 121, 191–95; Val di Noto, 205, 216, 223, 224; Western Sicily, 175, 177, 179. *See also* international varieties

chemical use, 119, 122, 123. *See also* biodynamic viticulture; organic viticulture

Chenin Blanc, 47, 195

chestnut cooperage, 24, 26, 134, 239

Chianti, 93

Chiaramonte Gulfi, 207, 214, 222

Chioccioli, Stefano, 179

chlorosis, 114, 121

Cilia, Giambattista, 45, 140, 210. *See also* COS

Ciliegiolo, 196

Cinzano, 32

Circolo Enofilio Siciliano, 27

clairette wines, 137, 179, 247

clay soils, 73, 74, 75, 80, 143; Northeast Coast, 254, 256, 257; Val di Mazara, 174, 175, 196, 199; Val di Noto, 209, 213–14, 222

clay vessels: amphorae for vinification, 138, 139–40, 211, 243, 244; ancient trade in, 4, 7, 65–66

climate, 49, 75–80; appellation system and, 151; vine training and microclimates, 116. *See also* specific locations

climate change, 80, 124

Coda di Volpe, 243

Colli Ericini IGT, 175

Colomba Bianca, 176

colombo soils, 219

Colosi, 261

Columella, 7

comuni, 150

Conca d'Oro, 181

concrete vats, 126, 134, 165, 224

Consorzio Tutela Vino Cerasuolo di Vittoria, 209

Constance (daughter of Roger II), 12

consumer preferences, 49, 50, 51, 127, 239; selected yeasts and, 138; Sicilian tastes, 127; sulfites and, 137; varietal selection and, 81–82, 83

containers: acacia cooperage, 185; amphorae for vinification, 138, 139–40, 211, 243, 244; ancient wine vessels, 4, 7, 65–66; chestnut cooperage, 24, 26, 134; cleaning and disinfection methods, 131–32, 140; concrete vats, 126, 134, 165, 224; for Marsala maturation, 169–70; for Pantelleria wines, 165; polyethylene, 138; stainless steel, 134, 165; traditional vats and

geography, 72–80; appellation law and, 151; climate and water availability, 49, 75–80, 116; provinces of Sicily, 150; topography, 72–73; the Tre Valli, 153–55. *See also* soils; *specific locations*

Georgian viticulture and winemaking, 139

Georgofili Academy, 21, 83, 206

Geraci, Giampiero, 253

Geraci, Salvatore, 135–36, 252, 253. *See also* Palari

Geremia, Giovacchino, 94, 101

Germany: as export market, 32, 35, 122; German-Italian relations, 25–26

gesso, 128–29

Gewürztraminer, 212

Giacosa, Franco, 74, 96, 204, 205; at Duca di Salaparuta, 44, 97, 111, 175, 187, 203–4; at Principi di Butera, 204–06. *See also* Duca di Salaparuta; Principi di Butera

Giakè (Jacquez), 217

giardini arabi, 157

Giarre, 16, 102

Gibellina, 174, 175

Gilbee, Lisa, 134

Gill, Joseph, 68

Giona, 261

Giornale del Viaggio Fatto in Sicilia (Balsamo), 19–20, 104, 206, 221

Giornale Vinicolo Italiano, 103

Giovi, 248

Giovinco, Vito, 137

Girelli, Stefano, 215

Giuffrida, Salvatore, 237

Giuliemi, 137, 138, 248, 264–69. *See also* Raiti, Giovanni

GIV (Gruppo Italiano Vini), 55, 188

Global Impact, 124

global warming, 80, 124

Goethe, Johann Wolfgang von, 125, 271

The Golden Ass, 69

Gorghi Tondi, 88, 91, 137, 179

Gorgone, Salvino, 166

Goths, 9

Graci, 103, 136, 244–45

grafting, 119, 145–48

grain, 6–7, 8, 9, 13, 14, 19, 195

Grand Sicilian Fair and Enological Exposition, 27, 28, 29

grape varieties. *See* varieties; *specific varieties*

Gravner, Josko, 139

grecale, 234, 251, 253, 254

Grecanico, 56, 89–90; Aeolian Islands, 260; amphorae-fermented wines, 140; Etna, 243, 247, 248; Noto region, 224; recommended producers, 90 *(see also specific zones)*; Sicily-Center, 196; Terre Sicane, 90, 192, 194, 195; Vittoria, 211; Western Sicily, 175

Grecanico Dorato, 89

Greek literature, 5, 7; *Odyssey*, 1–2, 3, 4, 242, 263, 264

Greek Sicily, 4–8, 156, 230; sites, 200, 202, 255

Greek viticulture and winemaking, 4, 8, 116, 125, 139

Greek wine culture, 1, 4–5

green harvest subsidies, 41–42, 63

Grenache, 82, 238

Grenache Noir, 29–30, 111, 211; Aeolian Islands, 261; Etna, 238–39, 247; Pantelleria, 163; recommended producer, 111 *(see also specific zones)*; Vittoria, 211

Grillo, 56, 82, 86–88, 91, 255; Aeolian Islands, 260; Agrigento-Caltanissetta Highlands, 200; botrytis wines, 137, 179; characteristics, 84, 87–88, 174; Mamertino, 254, 255; for Marsala, 69, 84, 168, 170, 171, 172; origins, 86; Palermo Highlands, 183, 186–89; recommended producers, 51, 61, 88 *(see also specific zones)*; Sicily-Center, 143, 197; for *vino perpetuo*, 65, 66, 70–71; Vittoria, 215, 216; Western Sicily, 174–77, 179, 180

Grimaldi, Clemente, 103

Grossonero, 207

Gruppo Italiano Vini (GIV), 55, 188

Guardiola, 58, 247

Guarnaccia, 111

Guarrasi family, 188. *See also* Rapitalà

Guarrasi, Gigi, 45, 184, 188

Guccione, 138, 189

Gulfi, 55, 61, 136, 212–13, 218, 222–23; recommended wines, 93, 99, 103, 213, 248

Gulino, 228–29

Gulino, Sebastiano, 228

Gurra vineyard, 194

Guyot pruning, 105, 118, 120

Guzzo, Tonino, 137, 196, 197, 199–200

gypsum, 74

"The Harvest Home" (Theocritus), 5

harvesting, 76, 79, 120–21, 128

harvest moths, 122

Hauner, 258, 260–61

Hauner, Carlo, Jr., 258, 260

Hauner, Carlo, Sr., 229, 258, 260

Henri d'Orléans, 28, 83–84, 101, 103, 128. *See also* Zucco

Henry VI, 12

herbicides, 119, 122

Hermitage, 86

Hiero II, 6

high-elevation vineyards, 76, 77, 79; Aeolian Islands, 258; Northeast Coast, 253, 257; for sparkling wines, 140–41; Val di Mazara, 27, 142–49, 191, 193–97; Val di Noto, 204, 206, 211. *See also* Etna

A History and Description of Modern Wines (Redding), 227

Homer, *Odyssey*, 1–2, 3, 4, 242, 263, 264

Hood, Alexander Nelson, 29–30, 101, 103, 111, 128, 131. *See also* Castello Maniace

Hopps, John, 22, 68

Nero d'Avola, 44, 50, 56, 95–99, 217; Aeolian Islands, 259, 260, 261; Agrigento-Caltanissetta Highlands, 198, 199, 200–201; blending partners, 50, 86, 97, 98, 100, 104–5, 107, 108; characteristics, 76, 96–98; IGT wines, 57, 207, 224, 226; Northeast Coast, 251, 252, 254–55, 256–57; Noto region, 82, 97, 217, 218, 220–26; Palermo Highlands, 183–89; recommended producers, 98–99 *(see also specific zones);* Riesi-Piazza Armerina, 82, 97, 202, 203–4, 205–6; rosatos, 98, 179, 223; Sicilia Qualità certification, 98; Sicily-Center, 142, 144–45, 196, 197; soils for, 74–75, 179, 196, 204, 205; Syracuse, 229; Terre Sicane, 191, 193, 194, 195; Vittoria, 97, 206, 207, 209–16; Western Sicily, 175–80. *See also* Cerasuolo di Vittoria; *specific locations and producers*

Nero Pachino, 96, 217
Nicolosi, 236; map, 231
Nicolosi Asmundo, Carlo, 46, 241
Nicolosi Asmundo, Carmelo, 45, 241
Nicolosi Asmundo, Marco, 241
Nicolosi, Paolo, 241
Nicosia, 248
Nicosia, Filippo, 20
night harvesting, 120–21, 191
Nigrello, 101
Nocera, 108–9; Northeast Coast, 250–52, 254–56, 261; recommended wines, 109, 255, 261
Norman Sicily, 10–12, 143, 156, 184, 265
Northeast Coast, 249–61; Cefalù, 80, 155, 256–57; Faro, 108, 249, 250, 251–54, 255; grape varieties, 250, 251–52, 254; Mamertino, 7, 60, 108, 249, 254–56; maps, 153, 231; overview, 249–51. *See also* Aeolian Islands
Notarbartolo, Ginevra, 185. *See also* Baglio di Pianetto
Notizie e Studi intorno Ai Vini ed Alle Uve d'Italia, 108, 127, 227, 249
Noto (city), 134, 216, 219, 220, 221; map, 203
Noto DOC, 153, 155, 220; recommended producers, 221, 223, 224
Noto wine zone, 55, 155, 216–26; appellations, 220; geography, soils, and climate, 74, 219–20, 222–23, 224, 225; grape varieties overviews, 209, 220–22; history, 216–19; Inzolia, 86; landowners, 218–19; maps, 153, 203; Moscato di Noto, 92, 220, 221–22, 224; Nero d'Avola, 82, 95–96, 97, 98, 203, 217–21; recommended producers, 222–26
Novara Di Gaetano, Salvatore and Vinzia. *See* Firriato

oak: for fermentation vats, 126, 239; taste for, 56, 135. *See also* barriques; containers; *specific producers and wines*
Occhipinti, Arianna, 106, 209–10
Occhipinti, Giusto, 45, 209, 210. *See also* COS
Odyssey (Homer), 1–2, 3, 4, 242, 263, 264
Oenotria, 4

oidium (powdery mildew), 74, 85, 95, 106, 121, 168
olives, 6, 19, 263, 267
On Agriculture (Columella), 7
organic viticulture, 119, 122, 123, 191; permitted fungicides, 121; producers practicing, 122, 211, 213, 262, 264–65, 267, 269
Oudart, Louis, 27
Ovid, 262, 263, 268
oxidation, 76, 137, 138, 228; oxygen exposure in traditional vinification, 65, 126, 131, 139; vinification techniques and, 126, 131, 132–33, 138–39
oxidized wines: Marsala, 127, 168, 169; pre-twentieth century, 125, 126, 127, 129

Pachino, 31, 74, 216–18, 219, 220–21; Eloro Pachino, 220, 223; map, 203; recommended producers, 222; traditional vinification, 130, 131, 217. *See also* Noto wine zone
Padova, Marianta, 224
Padova, Massimo, 224, 225
Pagano, Maurizio, 247
Palari, 75, 80, 136, 250, 252, 253–54
Palermo, 150, 156; red varieties in, 100–101, 106–7, 109; under Norman rule, 10–11, 14; white varieties in, 83, 84, 85, 91
Palermo Highlands, 154, 180–89; appellations, 184–85; geography, soils and climate, 182, 183; grape varieties, 183–84, 185; history, 180–83; maps, 153, 181; notable/recommended producers, 182–83, 185–89
Palermo Royal Nursery of American Vines, 114
palmentos, 128, 130, 132, 239; Etna, 232, 243; Val di Noto, 206, 217, 218, 226
palomina soils, 219
Panerai, Paolo, 211–12
Pantano Sichilli, 229
Pantelleria, 143, 156–67, 210; appellations, 160–62; challenges and conflict, 161–62; dry wines, 165, 166–67; fortified wines, 161, 162; geography, climate, and soils, 75, 79, 113, 157–58, 162–64, 167; grape varieties, 90–91, 111, 163, 167; history, 156–57, 158, 159; maps, 153, 157; modern viticulture and winemaking, 158–61, 163–65; off-island bottling, 161–62; recommended producers, 165–67; traditional viticulture and winemaking, 114, 117, 158–60, 164, 165; water availability, 79, 159, 163. *See also* Moscato di Pantelleria; Passito di Pantelleria; *specific producers*
Pantelleria DOC, 161
Papé di Valdina, Pietro, 28
Pappalardo, Rosario, 129, 242
Partanna, 174
Partinico, 24, 111
passa Malaga grapes, 164
Passito di Pantelleria, 90–91, 152, 210, 259–60; history and traditional methods, 158, 159–60, 164, 165; modern versions, 46, 159, 160, 162;

prices: cooperative wineries and, 39, 40, 42; EU pricing policies, 37

Principi di Butera, 55, 96, 204, 205–6; recommended wines, 89, 99, 100, 101, 104, 205–6

"Prodotti del Suolo e Viticoltura in Sicilia" (Mario), 31, 133

Profumo del Vulcano, 247

promotion. *See* marketing

propaggine, 114

provinces of Sicily, 150

pruning techniques, 105; Guyot, 105, 118, 120; tendone, 118, 119, 120, 200. *See also* alberello training

Pupillo, Antonino, 227, 229; recommended wine, 92

Pythagoras, 5

quality: appellation standards, 151, 152; Assovini's improvement efforts, 60; British merchants' influence, 23, 68; consumer pressure for, 82; cooperative wineries and, 39; eco-friendly protocols and, 122; Ferdinand III's improvement efforts, 127–28, 180–81; French and Piedmontese enological expertise and, 44–45; IRVV efforts under Planeta, 46–48; nineteenth- and early twentieth-century improvements, 23, 26–27, 30. *See also* award-winning wines

quality problems, 82, 125; insufficient hygiene, 49, 125, 132, 133, 143, 232. *See also* stability and spoilage

Quasimodo, Salvatore, 274

Quincunx, 247

Quota Mille (Etna), 265–66

racking, 131, 132–33, 139, 180

Ragusa, 74, 92, 105, 150, 202, 226, 251; map, 203

rainfall, 78–79, 116. *See also specific locations*

raisins, 90, 158. *See also* drying grapes

Raiti, Giovanni, 101–2, 137, 263–68, 269. *See also* Giuliemi

Rallo, Antonio, 55, 60, 193

Rallo (Cantine), 167, 174, 180

Rallo (Diego) e Figli, 45

Rallo, Gabriella, 193

Rallo, Giacomo, 45, 54–55, 60, 159, 193

Rallo, Josè, 55, 193

Rampante, 245

Randazzo, 239, 246, 265; map, 231

Rapitalà, 45, 182, 188–89; recommended wines, 85, 88, 89, 99, 100, 188, 189

Rappa, Gabriele, 257

Rappa, Giulia, 257

Real Cantina Borbonica, 180, 181

"Recollections of Sicilian Wines" (Sestini), 21. *See also* Sestini, Domenico

Recupero, Giuseppe, 266

Redding, Cyrus, 227

red varieties and wines, 95–111; climate and exposure for, 76–77; notable nineteenth-

century wines, 29; red and white grapes vinified together, 127–28, 129; *ribollito* wines, 133; soils for, 74, 80, 143; tendone training and, 118; traditional vinification, 129–30, 217. *See also specific varieties, locations, and producers*

refrigeration, 134

Regaleali, 43, 182, 196, 197; founding, 143; grape varieties, 44, 88, 89, 97, 104, 107, 110; growing conditions, 77, 197; history, 44, 54, 182; land redistribution at, 38, 148; marketing and exports, 44, 54; notable/recommended wines, 89, 104, 110, 197

regulations: EU policies, 34–37, 40–42, 217, 219; IGT and DOC designations, 56–58; IGT labeling, 56–57; Sicilia DOC regulations, 57–58

Renda, 29

Rheingau varieties, 27, 28, 178. *See also specific varieties*

Rhone wines, 100

Ribera, 86

ribollito wines, 133

Riesi DOC, 154, 202, 204, 206

Riesi-Piazza Armerina, 26, 82, 110, 202–6, 208; maps, 153, 203; Nero d'Avola in, 82, 97–98, 202, 203–4; overview, 202–4; recommended producers, 204–6

Riesling, 80, 93

Riesling Renano, 248

Riofavara, 99, 224, 225

ripening of grapes, 76–77, 78, 79, 116, 120. *See also specific varieties*

ripiddu, 235–36, 241, 262

Riposto, 16, 23, 24, 26, 206, 232; map, 231

Riserva Naturale di Vendicari, 229

Risignolo, 87, 175, 187

ritornato wines, 133

Riunite, 42

Rivella, Ezio, 45, 134, 187

rivers, 72, 74, 79. *See also specific rivers*

Rizzo, Giovanni, 94, 137, 205, 210

roads and infrastructure, 11, 15, 16, 18

Rocca di Frassinello, 211

Roccazzo, 214

rock salt, 74

Roger, Count of Sicily, 10

Roger II, 10, 11, 12, 249, 265

Roman agriculture, 7

Roman literature, 7, 8, 262, 263

Romano, Giuseppe, 105, 137, 215, 216

Roman Sicily, 6–8, 143, 156, 206, 213

Roman viticulture and winemaking, 4, 7–8, 19, 90, 125, 139; Mamertino, 60, 249, 254; Vittoria, 206, 213

rootstocks: grafting, 119, 145–48; own-root vines, 113; phylloxera-resistant, 59, 66, 113, 114, 115, 250–51

rosatos (rosé wines), 126, 128, 129; Etna, 103, 129, 239, 240, 242; Frappato for, 105; Nerello Mascalese for, 102, 239, 242; Nero d'Avola for, 98, 179, 223; Perricone for, 106, 107, 188; *pistammutta* wines, 129, 217; recommended producers, 103, 179 *(see also specific zones)*; Val di Mazara, 179, 184, 188, 196; Val di Noto, 214, 217, 223

varieties, 175; overview, 174–76; recommended producers, 176–80. *See also* Marsala *entries*

wheat, 9, 13, 14, 195

Whitaker Foundation, 70, 176

Whitaker, Joseph, 32, 87, 176

white varieties and wines, 30, 49, 83–95; barrel-fermented wines, 49, 54, 56, 134–35; climate and exposure for, 76, 77; fermentation temperatures, 77; notable nineteenth-century wines, 27, 28, 29, 30; pressing, 128; red and white grapes vinified together, 127–28, 129; skin contact for, 138–39; soils for, 74, 143; Tachis and, 49, 51; tendone training and, 118 200; traditional vinification, 126, 128, 129; wild yeasts for, 138. *See also specific varieties, locations, and producers*

wild yeasts, 138, 243

William II, 11, 12

winds, 77–78, 112, 117–18, 121, 142. *See also specific winds and locations*

Winebow, 54

wine competitions: modern, 253; nineteenth century, 27, 28, 29, 30, 182

wine consumption, 35–36, 63, 126

wine industry, before 1775: ancient Sicily, 4, 6, 7–8; during "wine-dark ages," 13, 16, 19; Muslim Sicily, 10; Sestini's study, 21. *See also* Roman viticulture and winemaking

wine industry, 1775 to 1950, 21–33; after liberation, 24–25; British influence, 22–23, 24–25, 68, 249–50; eighteenth and nineteenth centuries, 16, 22–25, 82, 126–27; export merchants and markets, 22–23, 25–28, 30, 32, 217; fine wine producers, 24, 26–30, 128, 131–33, 180–83; French expertise in, 44–45, 118, 126; phylloxera and, 25, 26, 30, 32, 250; Sicilian entrepreneurialism, 23–25; taxation and, 25, 32, 69; twentieth-century declines, 31–33, 134. *See also specific locations, wines, and producers*

wine industry, post-1950, 34–64; Assovini's quality efforts, 60; cooperative wineries and, 38–40, 42–43, 55, 134; current market situation, 62–63; early quality producers, 43–46; enological consultants, 44–45; off-island

bottling, 57–58; outside investment, 55–56, 232–33, 271–72; overproduction problems, 35–37, 41–42, 63; Planeta at IRVV, 46–48, 52; production statistics, 35, 36, 37; rise of family wineries, 52–55; rise of IGT wines, 56–57; Sicilia DOC, 57–58; Tachis's impact, 48–52. *See also* European Union policies and programs; IRVV; *specific locations, wines, and producers*

wine law, 56, 61, 119, 150–53, 162, 164, 170–71

winemaking methods. *See* enology

wood. *See* barrels; containers; *specific woods*

Woodhouse, John, 22–24, 32, 66, 68, 168, 171; baglio of, 67, 68, 69

World War I, 32, 69

World War II, 32, 115, 157, 158

yeasts, 138, 140; ambient/wild, 133, 138; NDA21, 224; as preservative, 127; as spoiling agents, 137; sulfiting of casks and, 131–32; yeast selections, 50, 138

yields, 35, 36, 37, 119; tendone training and, 118; vine age and, 121; viticultural practices and, 118, 122; yield limits, 35, 52, 56

young vines, 121–22

Zenner, Dó, 123, 225. *See also* Tridente Pantalica

Zenner, Hans, 123, 225

Zenner, Nina, 225

Zibibbo (Muscat of Alexandria), 82, 86, 90–91, 221; amphorae-fermented wines, 140; Palermo Highlands, 187; Pantelleria, 90, 158, 163, 165–66, 167, 259–60; recommended producers, 90, 91 *(see also specific zones)*; skin-contact wines, 138; Terre Sicane, 194; Val di Noto, 209, 221; Western Sicily, 175, 177, 179, 180

Zirilli Lucifero, Giuseppe, 250–51, 254

Zisola (contrada), 225

Zisola (producer), 55, 99, 135, 218, 225–26

Zonin, 55, 204

Zonin, Giovanni, 55

Zucco, 28, 29, 101, 111, 127, 182, 183. *See also* Aumale, Henri d'Orleans, Duc d'